Earth's Insights

Earth's Insights

A Survey of Ecological Ethics
from the Mediterranean Basin
to the Australian Outback

J. BAIRD CALLICOTT

University of California Press

BERKELEY   LOS ANGELES   LONDON

University of California Press
Berkeley and Los Angeles, California

University of California Press
London, England

First Paperback Printing 1997

Library of Congress Cataloging-in-Publication Data
Callicott, J. Baird.
    Earth's insights : a survey of ecological ethics from the
Mediterranean basin to the Australian outback /
J. Baird Callicott.
        p.   cm.
    Includes bibliographical references and index.
    ISBN 978-0-520-08560-2
    1. Environmental ethics. I. Title.
GE42.C35   1994
179'.1—dc20   94-13636
                                                     CIP

Printed in the United States of America

11 10 09
10   9   8

The paper used in this publication meets the minimum requirements of
ANSI/ NISO Z39.48-1992 (R 1997) (*Permanence of Paper*). ∞

For Burton—
my father, my son

The ontological shift for an ecologically sustainable future has much to gain from the worldviews of ancient civilizations and diverse cultures which survived sustainably over the centuries.

—Vandana Shiva
Staying Alive: Women, Ecology, and Development

Contents

Preface

I vividly remember standing beside my father in the driveway of our house in Memphis, Tennessee, one summer evening in 1955. As we gazed at the stars, Dad began to talk of the technological achievements he had witnessed in his own lifetime. In 1915, he said, he had ridden to school in a horse-drawn wagon and would run out of his house to see an automobile go by. He pointed to an airplane passing overhead and marveled at how far we had progressed in less than half a century. The peaceful development of nuclear energy was just then getting under way, and he boldly predicted that when I got to be his age I might own a car that would run for years on a single pellet of uranium the size of a dime. As a mosquito fogger cruised through the neighborhood, he told me how as a boy he had labored in his parents' vegetable patch, picking weevils off the leaves of potato plants by hand. DDT had forever freed boys like me from such drudgery, he said, and he envisioned the eventual eradication of all harmful insects. He concluded his celebratory monologue—without a hint of concern—by informing me that the global human population had just passed the two-billion mark, having doubled since he was born. He was confident that in my lifetime I would witness equally wonderful technological innovations, piling up even more profusely, attended by a no less rapid and pleasant expansion of the human race.

My father is an artist, a critical thinker, and not at all an insensitive or unintelligent man. That was just the way things looked to practically everyone at midcentury. In 1955 I, too, had not the slightest doubt that the future Dad imagined would, at least in general outline, come to pass.

A decade later, the Cultural Revolution wracked China. It is evident in retrospect that a cultural revolution of a different sort was also overtaking the West. The civil rights movement, the peace movement, and the women's movement—not to mention television, recreational drugs, casual sex, and rock 'n' roll—thoroughly transformed Western society. In the 1960s the West discovered as well that its technology had limits and that its industrial civilization had not been achieved without an environmental price. Many of the great rivers of the world had become virtual open sewers—including the Mississippi, whose banks I had roamed and in whose waters I had swum as a boy. The atmosphere over many large cities was choked with noxious gases. Open space and wildlife habitat had given way to highways, strip development, shopping malls, and suburbs. Fertile soil was being eroded many times faster than it was being created. Industrial and agricultural toxins were showing up everywhere—including, of all places, in mother's milk and birds' eggs.

In her sobering book *Silent Spring*, Rachel Carson disabused us of the hope of reaching the promised land through pesticides. Barry Commoner's *Closing Circle* clearly detailed the incompatibility of modern industrial civilization and ecological processes. Paul and Anne Ehrlich's *Population Bomb* called attention to the frightening consequences of unstinted exponential population growth. By the end of the decade, the public had been awakened to a wholesale "environmental crisis," as it was characterized in Stewart Udall's book *The Quiet Crisis*. The very "advances" that my father had extolled fifteen years before—the internal combustion engine, nuclear power, D.D.T., and exponential population growth—had ceased to seem modern miracles and seemed instead to be modern debacles.

Some styled the 1970s the Environmental Decade. The United States Congress, at the behest of Senator Gaylord Nelson (D.-Wis.), proclaimed the first Earth Day, in the spring of 1970, and there followed a spate of palliative environmental legislation in the Western industrial countries. In the United States, for example, Clean Air and Water, Endangered Species, Marine Mammals Protection, and many similar Acts were passed, and a whole new federal bureaucracy—the Environmental Protection Agency—was created.

During most of the 1980s, under the Reagan Administration, the environmental regulations enacted in the 1970s were relaxed and eroded. People seemed to tire of the environmental "issue," and a mood of dreamy indifference and economic self-absorption prevailed.

Then, in the late 1980s, the second wave of the twentieth century's environmental crisis began to crest. Word reached the public that a "hole" in the planet's protective membrane of ozone had been discovered over the Antarctic, caused by the migration of volatile, long-lived synthetic chemicals—chlorofluorocarbons—into the upper atmosphere. Each spring the hole has grown larger. Because of the continuing increase in carbon dioxide and other "greenhouse" gases in the earth's atmosphere, most scientists now agree that the planet will warm up, with potentially disastrous environmental consequences. The assault on Earth's girdle of moist tropical forests, home to half the planet's complement of species, has intensified. Our generation may preside over a rare episode of abrupt, mass species extinction. Mass extinctions have occurred in the past, but *Homo petroleumus* may be the first biological agent of a mass extinction event in the 3.5-billion-year tenure of life on the third planet from the sun. Ocean species fare little better than those in the rain forests. As I write, whales continue to be hunted to extinction, and myriads of other marine organisms and whole marine ecosystems are globally threatened as the seas are being strip-mined by drift-net fishing.

The environmental crisis—discovered in the industrial West in the 1960s, plastered over with regulative legislation in the 1970s, then forgotten only to return with a vengeance in the 1980s—is now global in scope and focus. South and East Asian countries have become full-fledged members of the club of industrial nations, widening the scope of the crisis. In the 1960s, with the world's rain forests still largely intact and the atmosphere largely unmonitored, the focus of the nascent environmental concern was local—primarily on point-source pollution, such as raw municipal and industrial wastes, which were fouling urban air and surface waters; broadcast pesticides, which were poisoning soils and groundwater; and oil spills, which were blackening beaches and killing resident wildlife. Now the focus of environmental concern is holistic and systemic—centering on the integrity of the planetary ecosystem and the earth's living atmosphere and hydrosphere. The ongoing environmental crisis, hardly mitigated by the Band-Aid legislation of the 1970s, is so pervasive that it cannot be ignored.

So, what can we do about it?

Everyone can pitch in. Those of us living in affluent industrial societies can change our habits and life-styles—what we eat, how we travel, and so forth. We can recycle. Above all, we can consume less. Those living in less-developed areas of the world can learn from the mistakes of the ill-developed countries and resolve not to repeat them. Those countries that have become monetarily rich and environmentally poor can help those that are monetarily poor to conserve their environmental wealth by financing nature reserves and ecologically sound economies.

What each of us can do as individuals, and what our organizations can do, is often limited by subtle but enormously powerful social forces. Therefore, we also need to have a clear critique of the political and economic structures that profoundly influence individual actions. What are the environmental consequences of the emergence of multinational corporations and a global marketplace? How are the choices made by investors, bankers, developers, small businesspersons, farmers, and so on influenced by prices, interest rates, taxes, government subsidies? How do the policies of entrenched bureaucracies, oligarchies, and plutocracies drive the engines of environmental destruction? These and similar questions are being explored by a new breed of environmental economists, political scientists, and sociologists. Such questions must be raised and clearly answered, so that we can understand the structural underpinnings of the environmental crisis and move strategically to reform them.

But to me, a philosopher, it seems that to effect change in both individual behavior and social, political, and economic institutions we have to do more than preach and browbeat, analyze and reform. Considered both as individual persons and as complex societies, we operate within distinct intellectual and moral atmospheres. How can we make ourselves and our institutions more environmentally responsible in the absence of an ecological outlook and deeply felt environmental values? Undergirding individual resolve and the incisive criticism and reform of our social structures, I think we must deliberately explore the contours of an ecological consciousness and conscience. We must, in other words, also work at articulating an environmental ethic. I have applied myself to this task for the past twenty years.

A persuasive environmental ethic, however, cannot be constructed *de novo*. It must be located in a more general cognitive context, and it must retain continuity with the moral ideas and ideals of the past. Accordingly, the handful of Western philosophers working in the field of environmental ethics have begun with various strains of Western moral philosophy and sought to extend or apply them to the new environmental question. After two decades of work, this enterprise has borne modest fruits. A scholarly literature has been created, and several distinct approaches to environmental ethics have been outlined and continue to be explored and refined. And environmental ethics has begun palpably to influence American conservation policy, at last—in both the public and the private spheres.

The twentieth-century environmental crisis, however—as I have been at pains to point out here—albeit Western in provenance is now a worldwide menace. While the Western world needs an environmental ethic evolved in concert with its intellectual traditions, an environmental ethic is needed just as badly in Egypt, Iran, India, China, Japan, Brazil, and everywhere else in the so-called developing world. But it is as arrogant as it is hopeless to suppose that environmental ethics can be exported without attunement to resonant elements in the rich intellectual traditions of non-

Western cultures. Just as Western philosophers have begun to explore environmental ethics dialectically developed out of the Western intellectual tradition, so might non-Western and comparative philosophers begin to explore the possibility of developing indigenous environmental ethics working in, and out from, non-Western intellectual traditions.

This study began in 1983, when Abdul Ghafoor-Ghaznawi, the director general of UNESCO, commissioned me to write a paper on international environmental ethics for a "nonformal environmental education" initiative sponsored by his agency. Pursuant to the research for the UNESCO work, I became a fellow of the Institute for Comparative Philosophy at the University of Hawaii, in the summer of 1984. There I interested the comparativists Roger T. Ames, Eliot Deutsch, and others in the global dimension of environmental philosophy and ethics. Together, we convened panels on the general topic "Conceptual Resources for Environmental Ethics, East and West" at several scholarly meetings in 1985 and 1986, and from them we selected papers, which were published in special issues of *Philosophy East and West* and *Environmental Ethics* (in the 1986 and 1987 volumes, respectively). Ames and I went on to collect, reedit, and introduce some of these papers and other scattered essays touching on the general topic of environmental attitudes and values latent in non-Western, and more especially in Asian, worldviews in an anthology titled *Nature in Asian Traditions of Thought: Essays in Environmental Philosophy*, which the State University of New York Press published in 1989. With some previous research in American Indian thought—"Far Western Philosophy," as Ames characterized it—under my belt, and having become acquainted with Polynesian cosmology during my visits at the University of Hawaii, I decided that I was uniquely situated to attempt to extend comparative environmental philosophy beyond the East-West axis.

I thank Norton Ginsburg, the director of the Environment and Policy Institute of the East-West Center in Honolulu, for arranging additional support for my stint as visiting professor of philosophy and geography at the University of Hawaii during the fall semester of 1988, and for encouraging me to commit my thoughts on comparative environmental ethics to writing. I thank Jean Jackson and Terrence Turner for advice on indigenous South American worldviews. I thank Martha Borchart for assisting my research for the final chapter of this book. I thank Roger T. Ames, Arthur L. Herman, David Edward Shaner, Steve Odin, Thomas W. Overholt, Warwick Fox, and Dusty Gruver for reading draft chapters of this monograph, each in his areas of expertise, and for correcting a number of my errors. Blame for errors that escaped the critical notice of these scholars is, of course, entirely mine to bear. I thank Frances Moore Lappé for carefully reading the first draft of this book and for her sympathetic but uncompromising criticism of its organization, style, and substance. I thank Karen J. Warren and David Abram for reading the second draft and for their positive suggestions for final revisions and additions. I thank Edward Dimendberg and Rebecca Frazier of the University of California Press for substantive advice and criticism and for guidance through the labyrinthine process of converting a manuscript to a book. And finally, I thank Sara Lippincott for expert and thorough editing.

For intellectual stimulation and inspiration as I prepared this monograph, I am deeply indebted to my associates at the East-West Center and to my students, friends, and colleagues in the Departments of Philosophy and Geography at the University of Hawaii. And I gratefully acknowledge that I have been largely informed by the work of the contributors to *Nature in Asian Traditions of Thought,* as the frequent citations herein to their essays will attest. In fact, the Asian chapters of the present study are a critical redaction, synthesis, and extension of the many ideas presented (necessarily in a less systematic and concordant way) in that multiauthored volume.

Let the reader be forewarned that I am principally an environmental philosopher, thoroughly steeped in Western ideas and patterns of thought, not a comparative philosopher, nor for that matter an environmental activist or social scientist. I offer this monograph as a continuation of the effort to build a wider and deeper environmental consciousness and conscience; as an invitation to others more expert than I to join the effort to create an intellectually diverse global network of indigenous environmental ethics, each adapted to its cultural and ecological bioregion; and, ultimately, as one person's contribution to the conservation of biodiversity and ecological integrity.

Healing the biosphere will head the agenda of global problems that we, the people of Planet Earth, will face in the twenty-first century. To augment personal commitment and structural reform, developing a network of indigenous environmental ethics will help set us on our way toward that goal. But we shall need some common environmental attitudes and values on which to base a common vision of a whole and healthy world; we shall want, in other words, a genuine network, not a patchwork. The most challenging aspect of this study has been to resolve the tension between a plurality of environmental attitudes and values drawn from a multiplicity of independent intellectual traditions, on the one hand, and a common ecological conscience drawn from the contemporary international scientific worldview, on the other. I hope I have been able to show that these perspectives—the one and the many—are mutually reinforcing, not contradictory and divisive.

Foreword

by Tom Hayden

As the environmental movement has arisen these past two decades, the environmental crisis itself has deepened. Paradoxically, a majority of Americans describe themselves as strongly committed to the environment, yet our soils, water, air, and countless species of plants and animals degrade and disappear at catastrophic rates. Globally, population has doubled and natural resources have been cut in half in only fifty years.

The crisis cannot be resolved simply by making present arrangements more efficient, although that would help. Our political and economic systems are based on obsolete notions that the environment is an infinite storehouse of raw materials for industry, as well as a bottomless container for waste. These assumptions are about as accurate as the long-held belief that the world is flat, yet they endure as the source of everyday behavior.

Examples of this blind denial come before me everyday as a state senator in Sacramento. Environmental law has made a difference for advocates, but less so for living ecosystems. California forestry law, for example, mandates "maximum timber productivity" as the official policy goal. If you are an ancient redwood tree on our North coast, "maximum productivity" means a death sentence. A 700-year-old redwood has no intrinsic value apart from the price it will command as the deck of a condominium.

Our California telephone books, as well as the edition of the *New York Times* I read every morning, come from cutting the ancient forests of Clayoquot Sound on Vancouver Island. The economic benefit of such forests was stated long ago by President Theodore Roosevelt, a conservationist in his time, who pronounced in 1901, "Forest protection is not an end in itself; it is a means to increase and sustain the resources of our country and the industries that depend on them."

Even closer to our immediate self-interest, our national health care debate fails to address the environmental dimension of disease. As predatory governments countenance the destruction of their rain forests, malaria and infectious diseases explode out of the swamps that "development" creates. "A dozen new diseases have shown up in humans since the 1960s," *Newsweek* reports, "nearly all of them the result of once-exotic parasites." Five hundred million people already suffer from tropical diseases. At home, one in three Americans will contract cancer, an increase of 20 percent since 1960.

Our bodies and nervous systems continue to be testing grounds for the thousands of chemicals invented and proliferated by the pharmaceutical industry. Disease prevention and public health are low priorities compared to the latest "miracle cures" spawned by the scientific model of medicine. Our leaders cannot seem to understand that we cannot both pollute ourselves and prevent disease. This unconscious dualism assumes that the environment "environs" us on the outside while disease develops on the inside, and that medical practice is a quasi-military attack on an enemy agent, not a matter of promoting organic health.

Our urban crisis also involves the ecosystem, not simply racial and economic considerations. The inner cities are the burial grounds of nature. The most polluted zip code in Los Angeles is that of South Central, where the greatest urban violence of the century occurred in 1992. Because of polluted workplaces, toxic dumps, and poisoned air and drinking water, urban residents are saturated with threats to their lungs, immune systems, and general health. The death rate from asthma alone has increased 31 percent since 1980, especially among urban minorities and children.

There is also a spiritual impact associated with our cities becoming such suffocating sepulchres. Life itself is out of balance. Burying the urban earth under asphalt, garbage, congestion, and smog promotes the alienation and rising violence that make so many cities unlivable. We need the green space, running streams, blue skies, and open vistas that are being obliterated to accommodate cars and commercial development.

Young people in particular need to be raised with a sense of meaning and ritual that requires roots not only in human family but in the family of the natural world. The fastest-growing holiday in America, for example, is *Kwanzaa* in the African-American community, a period between December 26 and January 1 for family and community sharing that harks back to African harvest festivals. Not only is *Kwanzaa* important for black cultural identity amidst the consumer frenzy of "white Christmas," but it reminds us of the need to preserve our green ecological identity as well. Christmas itself was originally a time of "pagan" celebration of the winter solstice, and Christmas trees came from sacred groves dedicated to the goddess. Today "holy day" has become "holiday," and consumption is worshiped as much as God.

The problem of the environment is one of perception, cultural mores, ethics, and spirituality. On one side of the cultural divide are those like U.S. Interior Secretary James Watt, who testified in the 1980s against the protection of national forests for future generations, saying "my responsibility is to follow the Scriptures. . . . I don't know how many generations we can count on before the Lord returns." The philosophy of endless growth is the secular equivalent, as expressed by *Forbes* magazine in 1992:

> [a] ceaseless aspiration . . . to break the bonds of humankind . . .
> [for] in the end, of course, catastrophe awaits us anyway, whether
> from the eccentricities of a passive asteroid or the dying of the sun,
> but that doesn't challenge the desirability of postponing the day of
> reckoning as long as possible.

On the other side is the emerging ethic of the ecological age. Just as the great African-American W. E. B. DuBois predicted in 1903 when he said that "the problem of the twentieth century will be the problem of the color line," we can make a parallel prediction that the crisis of the twenty-first century will be the crisis of the ecology line. As African slaves once were treated as subhuman cogs in the machinery of agricultural economies, so is the whole natural world ground up in the machinery of industrialism today. Just as facing the racial crisis required a moral and perceptual reorientation to the humanity of the slaves, so facing the environmental crisis demands a reorientation toward nature as a valued living process not apart from ourselves.

J. Baird Callicott sensed the need for this transformation before nearly all the rest of us. For two decades, he has pondered, researched, and written extensively on the need to develop an environmental ethic to guide our personal lives as well as our institutional behavior. Now, with *Earth's Insights*, Callicott offers a panorama of earth-based spiritual and ethical traditions which, considered together, offer a new planetary vision for the next century.

Baird Callicott lives and teaches in my "second" native state of Wisconsin (which was my parents' home state, although I was raised mostly in Michigan). It is a place where traditions of the land, the waters, and the native people have a living presence. It is also the home of Aldo Leopold, the great conservationist and educator whose 1940s *Sand County Almanac*, especially the chapter titled "The Land Ethic," is an environmental gospel. Baird Callicott not only lives in Leopold Country, he is very much an intellectual descendent of that great Midwestern writer. Callicott's *In De-*

fense of the Land Ethic (1989) is the best overview of Leopold's work that I have read.

Baird Callicott is very much a globalist as well. He is also the editor, with Roger Ames, of the fine collection *Nature in Asian Traditions of Thought* (1989). I first met him in 1992 at the Earth Summit held by the United Nations in Rio de Janeiro, where 100 national governments finally responded collectively to the environmental crisis. Unfortunately, traditional values dominated the proceedings, as exemplified by the summit organizers' own declaration of "the sovereign right (of each nation) to exploit their own resources pursuant to their own environmental and developmental policies." That placed Baird Callicott, like myself, outside the formal conference proceedings with thousands of environmentalists who came to raise the deeper questions of values.

At present, the myopic momentum of industrial "growth" continues on a collision course with the environmental underpinnings of life. It is assumed that environmental destruction along the way can be "mitigated" without eliminating the addiction to this "growth." As a result, otherwise sensible, even eminent people continue to embrace frontier expansion and technical fixes. Humanity as a whole indeed may go the way of particular empires that ignored what Robert Louis Stevenson called "the great Law of Compensation," leading to a condition of impossible overextension and final collapse.

There is another and better possibility. As our growth machine sputters, as human health deteriorates, as resource shortages occur, and as the whole living environment decays and withers, a new consciousness is arising from a desperate human effort to adapt and survive in a new evolutionary condition. This is the course of action in which I believe: the possibility of choosing life in harmony with the earth instead of death in futile competition for diminishing resources. For this awareness to grow, it needs the nurturing education that is provided in Callicott's *Earth's Insights*.

Callicott's thesis is that a new empirical worldview, based on ecology, is beginning to shatter our established ways of thinking and undermine our institutions based on material growth. Briefly stated, the new worldview is *organic* as opposed to *mechanistic*. The emerging paradigm, he notes, has "conceptual affinities with preindustrial natural attitudes and values." Obedient to the law of diversity, Callicott explores the earth-based traditions of the world's many cultures, from our own Western Judeo-Christian tradition to the aboriginal creation stories of Australia. Some of those traditions lie buried and neglected, like those of the Christian nature mystics. Others, like the ancient Taoist concept of *wu-wei*, seem ready-made for a generation that wishes to harmonize with natural forces instead of seeking to selfishly dominate or degrade them.

As Callicott proceeds with his inventory of these traditions, we are given hope that there is an ancient tie to nature in our human consciousness that simply needs to be rediscovered, reawakened, and restored. Moreover, although what I call this *eco-soul* manifests itself in diverse forms of culture, worship, and tradition, it carries a universality that teaches us what it means to be a human community within a larger earth community and universe.

The inventive brilliance of Callicott's work is that he seeks the universal without diminishing our diversity. Whereas many global thinkers, strategists, and institutions implicitly seek a *homogenous* "new world order" organized around a single Great Power, a single currency, a single market, a single cultural/religious standard that all should emulate, Callicott suggests exactly the reverse. Not a babble of balkanized cultures, but a genuine diversity and interdependence true to the principles of ecology.

Callicott has developed a creative interpretation of the biblical Genesis stories which is sure to provoke healthy debate. There still are leading voices in our Christian and Jewish establishments who claim a moral superiority for humans over all of nature, based on the Genesis mandate of "dominion." There are many others, myself included, who question whether monotheistic religions based on covenants with a God above can embrace a serious covenant with Earth below. The latter camp draws sustenance from Christian mystics like Francis of Assisi but most of all from ancient earth-based spiritualities. This was the sensibility of my druid ancestors when the Irish were the Indians of Europe, and I believe it provides both spiritual and ecological integrity. It may make sense as well for those millions of people who are dissatisfied with the emptiness of secularism but cannot swear allegiance to what they consider to be worn-out religious dogmas.

Callicott chooses a third way toward a greener Genesis, that of a "stewardship" ethic in which humankind is given a moral obligation to protect and care for the larger garden of life. Here Callicott the conservationist is also motivated by environmental pragmatism. Stewardship is easier to promote than deep ecology or Native American shamanism. It is much simpler to convince people that environmentalism is consistent with their existing religious beliefs than to ask them to denounce their respected religious institutions in order to save the earth.

The concept of stewardship, as used here by Callicott and Vice-President Albert Gore, is a powerful and plausible argument to Christian, Jewish, and

Islamic communities to take responsibility for the earth. That it is based on scant empirical evidence and a debatable reading of scripture may be irrelevant, for it reconciles the yearning of many people to hold both to their faith tradition and to a new reverence for all creation.

Let me now turn to the broader importance of Callicott's work, which is very much a reflection of our times. All over the world, a deep reappraisal of the human condition is occurring in response to the environmental crisis. At the aging bookends of the established order there is emerging a change in perception of reality itself and the values considered necessary to our successful survival.

Simply stated, the shift is from viewing the earth as a vast resource of raw materials for our utilitarian exploitation, to viewing it as a vast community of life with a moral or sacred value of its own. The shift goes much further, into every cranny of human experience:

> From a conception of God as a transcendent Being *outside* nature, to a belief in a God or sacred dimension *within* creation.
>
> From a mechanistic view of the universe as composed of inert physical matter to an organic view of the universe, the earth, and ourselves as a living whole, containing energy, spirit, and creativity.
>
> From an ethic that values the earth only for its benefits to industrial growth to an ethic respecting its independent grandeur and value.
>
> From a psychology that has attempted to split the ego from nature, to a psychology that tries to heal the alienation of the self from nature.
>
> From acceptance of patriarchal dominance—whether in our conception of God or the distribution of power—to one of gender balance in all things.
>
> From homogenous culture to an embrace of diversity in both culture and environment.
>
> From an economics based on maximizing the gross national product to one based on sustainability from generation to generation.
>
> From a politics based on a Leviathan machine allocating resources to powerful interests, to one based on participatory democracy, community-based governance, and representation of the interests of nature in making decisions.

Some will object that envisioning such a broad "paradigm shift" is simplistic. I agree. But no less dramatic was the shift from accepting the "divine right of kings" to the belief in representative democracy, or the shift from seeing slaves as beasts of burden to seeing them as human beings.

Debates over such issues were complex, and indeed took centuries to re-solve, but finally a new consensus emerged and became simplified into an accepted worldview. The same awakening process is happening once again, this time in our cosmology and our dawning understanding of the human community as being derived from the community of nature.

Of course, the great transition of which I write is only in its infancy. It may not survive its birth trauma. But it clearly has been born. A change of heart, habits, and consciousness always precedes political and economic change. In 1987, for example, representatives of Christianity, Judaism, Is-lam, Buddhism, and Hinduism met in Assisi, Italy—the birthplace of St. Francis—to declare their religious commitment to preserving the planet. It was the first such declaration in the history of religion. A similar gathering of spiritual leaders took place at the Earth Summit in 1992.

In 1993, American religious leaders of all denominations formed the National Partnership for the Environment to begin incorporating an en-vironmental ethic into the preaching and practice of 55,000 congregations.

In the same two years, Albert Gore became vice-president of the United States after writing the best-selling *Earth in the Balance.* That he has not always been able to implement his book in the White House does not de-tract from its importance, but only indicates the special-interest resistance that even a vice-president must face. And finally, the environmental move-ment continues to grow, despite a lessening of media coverage and a back-lash from threatened industries. In California, an isolated and beautiful valley in the Mohave Desert, now called Ward Valley but long a juncture of native cultures, is being defended by environmentalists against the nu-clear industry. There is hope that the site will not become a nuclear waste dump. Further north, environmentalists have won an order that provides fresh water for the dying salmon population against the wishes of urban developers and valley agribusinesses.

And as I write, for example, 800 Canadians are being persecuted for blocking roads in the remote temperate rain forest of Clayoquot Sound in British Columbia, possibly the largest act of civil disobedience in that coun-try's history. What possible self-interest do these Canadians have in going to jail and paying steep fines? Are they not living evidence of a wider expression of human self-interest, an emerging eco-self which feels a *per-sonal* loss when a forest is decimated?

Of course, the obstacles to a sustainable ethic are extremely formidable. And yet, as Thomas Berry and Theodore Roszak might say, the environ-mental movement is nothing less than an emerging dream, or voice, of the earth that cannot be suppressed. As the pain and destruction deepen, as the loss of balance accelerates, an environmental consciousness evolves in response, racing against the ruin. I have faith that humanity will adapt and creatively evolve. The work of Baird Callicott helps consciousness find its many moving voices, assembling on these pages a living orchestra that sings and tells a healing vision for the earth and ourselves.

Winter Solstice
December 21, 1993

1 Introduction

The Notion of and Need for
Environmental Ethics

ETHICS AND ENVIRONMENTAL ETHICS

Since the 1960s, those Western scholars who responded professionally to industrial civilization's environmental crisis have argued that an implicit environmental ethic has existed in many indigenous and traditional cultures.[1] And in the body of this study I shall sketch a variety of representative indigenous and traditional examples. Nevertheless, the term "environmental ethics" is a relatively new addition to our vocabulary, and the concept it denotes is not familiar. Here at the outset, an informal comparison of environmental ethics with the more commonplace social sort of ethics—and with the more pedestrian concept of environmental law—may help locate the coming discussion on a cognitive map and obviate misjudgment of both the enterprise and its efficacy.

In his essay "The Land Ethic," the seminal classic of contemporary Western environmental ethics, the American conservationist Aldo Leopold understood ethics to impose "limitations on freedom of action in the struggle for existence."[2] Though typically terse, Leopold's characterization is sound and gets at something fundamental. Our familiar social ethics would impose limitations on interpersonal freedom of action and on personal freedom in relation to society as a whole. Lying to a friend and falsifying scientific data are examples, respectively. Both are regarded as equally unethical or immoral, though in the former case the victim is an individual and in the latter a community—the scientific community, or society itself (at least, among those societies that venerate science), or, more abstractly still, the institution of science per se. Similarly, *an environmental ethic would impose limitations on human freedom of action in relationship to nonhuman natural entities and to nature as a whole.*

The philosophical lexicon, incidentally, does not finely discriminate be-

1

tween "ethics" and "morals," as ordinary English does. In this discussion, I will follow philosophical convention and use the two terms more or less interchangeably. "Ethics," further, in conjunction with a singular verb, may refer to a subdiscipline of philosophy—to wit, moral philosophy. In conjunction with a plural verb, it may refer to several moral systems—that is, it may simply be the plural of "ethic," which in every case refers to a more or less coherent set of moral ideas and ideals.

Ethical or moral limitations, especially in Western cultural traditions, are formulated as behavioral rules or, more generally, as precepts and principles. In non-Western traditions, such limits may be articulated as behavioral expectations, customs, taboos, and rites, or implicitly exemplified in myth, story, and legend. In political cultures, the most vital moral limitations on human freedom—those on which the very existence of society rests—are encoded into statutes or laws.

We may conceive of a prohibitive law as a moral injunction so broadly agreed on and perceived as so vital that it has been formally adopted and specifically sanctioned by society. Personal ethics, by contrast, may be conceived of as those restraints, rules, or principles not formally encoded but nevertheless recommended and sanctioned by social approbation. Ethics, in short, at once lie at the basis of laws and supplement laws.

Environmental ethics—however novel and exotic the ideal may seem, and however incipient and inchoate our environmental moral sensibilities may be—undergird, I therefore suggest, the body of current national and international environmental law and regulation.

But in whatever way institutionalized, ethics exist by convention, not by nature. They are culturally (and sometimes personally) generated and sanctioned. One cannot disobey a law of nature, but of course one can disobey a statute, ignore a custom, transgress a taboo, disregard an ethical principle, or violate a moral rule.

This difference between natural and moral limitations on human behavior entails a fundamental consequence important to bear in mind: Compliance with an ethic, even one hardened into law, is to some extent voluntary. Those laws that enshrine the most fundamental social limitations on human behavior are enforced by the most severe punishment society can impose. Still, they are continually violated. An ethic is never perfectly realized on a collective social scale and very rarely on an individual scale. An ethic constitutes, rather, an ideal of human behavior.

In the more familiar context of human social intercourse, if society is to flourish, even strict obedience to the letter of the law must be complemented and supplemented by moral sensibility and conscience. Similarly, in the environmental arena, if a mutually enhancing relationship between human civilization and the natural environment is to evolve, environmental law and regulation must be complemented and supplemented by environmental moral sensibility and what Aldo Leopold calls an "ecological conscience."[3]

For example, in many countries laws have recently been enacted setting aside game parks, wilderness reserves, or other kinds of natural sanctuaries. Such enactments reflect a new collective moral sensitivity to the environment. Other lands, privately owned, remain open to laissez-faire economic development and hence remain vulnerable to the most violent exploitation. An explicit and broadly endorsed environmental ethic, however, might discourage the most egregious abuse. Were an environmental ethic to become a cultural commonplace—and were economic, social, and political conditions congenial—lands in private hands might be used with even greater care and sensitivity than required by statutory environmental restrictions on the economic disposition of private property. If forested, they might be selectively harvested and gradually converted to multispecies permacultures, rather than clear-cut, burned off, and converted to pasture. If farmed, they might be husbanded to assure soil stability, the maintenance of pure surface and ground waters, and the integrity of neighboring biotic communities, rather than row-cropped and doused with synthetic fertilizers and chemical herbicides and pesticides.

THE PRACTICALITY OF ETHICS

Social ethics—ideals of mutual forbearance, justice, compassion, and so on—are immemorial in human experience. But there does not exist today, nor has there ever existed, a perfectly benign, just, and compassionate human being and certainly not such a society. Why then bother to envision ideals—either shining cities on hills à la Ronald Reagan or pristine emerald forests à la the World Wide Fund?

Although an ethic, whether environmental or social, is never perfectly realized in practice, it nonetheless exerts a very real force on practice. Ideals do measurably influence behavior. In envisioning, inculcating, and striving to attain moral ideals, we make some progress both individually and collectively, and gain some ground. We are just as unlikely ever to attain a complete and perfect harmony with nature as we are to realize a utopian society, but the existence of an environmental ethic—partly encoded in laws, partly a matter of ethical sensibility and conscience—may draw human behavior in the direction of that goal.

A moral ideal also functions in another practical way. It provides a standard, a benchmark, in reference to which policies and actions may be applauded or criticized. An ethic thus is said to bear a normative rather than a descriptive relationship to human behavior. How people actually treat one another and the natural environment is the subject of the behavioral sciences—of history, psychology, sociology, anthropology, geography. How people ought to treat one another and the natural environment is the subject of philosophy—of social ethics and environmental ethics, respectively.

Because it attempts to distill and articulate ideals from culturally ambient but inchoate moral sensibilities rather than truck and trade in the "real world" of politics and policy, and because it assumes a normative rather than a descriptive posture, environmental ethics—as an exercise in speculative moral philosophy—may appear hopelessly quixotic. But broad cultural change—*pace* Marx and other materialistic interpreters of cultural dynamics—is drawn along by a cognitive dialectic no less than pushed about by a dialectic of economic forces and evolving technologies. Historically, speculative moral philosophy has not been in the business of inventing new ethics from scratch. Rather, it has more typically served to define, systematize, and defend emergent collective conscience. Speculative moral philosophy assists the birth of new ethics (to adapt a Socratic metaphor), or (to shift metaphors) it heralds their arrival. Hence moral philosophy in general, and environmental ethics more especially, can be of the greatest practicality, albeit indirectly.

Finally, it is important to note that an ethic—despite the professionally decreed divorce between fact and value, *is* and *ought*—does not exist in a cognitive vacuum, hermetically sealed off from larger systems of ideas (or, for that matter, from the rough-and-tumble of the real world). Ethos and worldview are married by common law, even if their union has not been celebrated by the high priests of modern moral philosophy.[4]

At the farthest limits of practicality, changing worldviews open up and shut down possibilities, either implicitly or explicitly. European discovery that the earth is round opened up the possibility of getting to the Far East by sailing west. The more recent discovery that the speed of light is finite and a "limiting velocity"—a velocity faster than which nothing can travel—shuts down the possibility of timely communication with alien worlds. To take a more down-to-earth (and germane) example, the contemporary realization that our environing world consists of hierarchically ordered ecological systems closes off the possibility—envisioned by Mill, Marx, and other nineteenth-century utopians—of a wholly industrialized planet.

Further, changing philosophical anthropologies—reflections on human nature and the perennial question of "man's place in nature"—periodically recast the human self-image, the archetypal human being that, consciously or unconsciously, we strive to realize in our own lives. At the beginning of the now obsolescing modern period, Descartes, Locke, and Hobbes variously articulated a modern image of human nature as essentially individual, rational, and autonomous—a free-moving social atom complementing the more general picture of nature that was simultaneously taking shape in Western natural philosophy. A new, more organic image of human nature is currently assuming definite outline—one in which people are essentially connected to the environment through ecological dependencies and to one another through social relationships. The twenty-first-century Western archetype of human nature, while still providing for individual uniqueness, will hardly countenance the classically modern Western concept of the rugged individualist. Rather, individuals will be seen as knots in a net of dynamic social and ecological relations, or as intersections of an ever-changing four-dimensional ecosocial web of life.

In sum, ethics are embedded in larger conceptual complexes—comprehensive worldviews—that more largely limit and inspire human behavior. And although idealistic, ethics exert a palpable influence on behavior. They provide models to emulate, goals to strive for, norms by which to evaluate actual behavior.

Though the people of Earth are all members of one species and share one ecologically integrated planet, we nevertheless live in many and diverse worlds. Each person at once lives in a planetary culture united by economic interdependency, jet transport, and satellite communications systems, and in a separate reality shaped by his or her formerly isolated cognitive cultural heritage. The revival and deliberate construction of environmental ethics from the raw materials of indigenous, traditional, and contemporary cognitive cultures represents an important step in the future movement of human material cultures toward a more symbiotic relationship—however incomplete and imperfect—with the natural environment.

Criticism and strategies for reform of the economic and political impediments to the expression of the world's many peoples' rediscovered environmental values is also of the utmost importance, if we are really to change our human relations with the natural environment. For example, in the United States the destruction of the last stands of old-growth forest in the Pacific Northwest grinds on, despite the recent emergence of an ecological conscience so widespread that environmental issues head the national political agenda. The implementation of this nascent grass-roots sentiment for environmental salvation is thwarted by a complex web of economic and bureaucratic exigencies: leveraged acquisition of forests by multinational corporations, for whom thousand-year-old trees, like a large inventory of widgets, are only a liquidable asset; an attractive foreign market for high-quality unmilled logs; a Forest Service bureaucracy bedded with the timber industry; and elected officials who are politically indebted to the few who stand to gain by cutting the trees. Such factors as these conspire against the realization of the popular will to protect the endangered northern spotted owl and, more generally, to preserve the region's natural beauty and ecological integrity. In Brazil, forest destruction is encouraged by, among other forces, the World Bank and the sort of capital-intensive development projects it funds; government subsidies for cattle ranching; the need to export forest products to earn hard currency to repay a staggering foreign debt; and, in order to avoid genuine land reform, a policy inducing landless homesteaders to clear virgin forests and plant their crops. In Southeast Asia, ecologically benign traditional agricultural practices are being driven to virtual extinction by the economies of scale associated with the agro-industrial Green Revolution. Just as a few philosophers have begun to respond to the environmental crisis by criticizing the prevailing environmental attitudes and values and exploring alternatives, a few agronomists, economists, political scientists, and sociologists are beginning to respond by outlining alternatives to the social, political, and economic regimes that are wreaking environmental destruction.[5]

Ecofeminist critics have also made a compelling case for thinking that "patriarchy," the institutionalized dominance of men over women, is intimately associated with the bid by "man" to dominate nature. The "logic of domination" is the mind-set common to both situations.[6] At its heart is a dualism—white against black, male against female, culture against nature—and the assertion that the first term of each pair is superior to the second, thus justifying the subjugation of the one by the other. The subjugation of women by men, sanctioned by the logic of domination, is distressingly familiar all over the world. The link between the domination of women by men and the domination of nature by man has, however, been reinforced in the West by the ideological identification of woman and nature.[7] In the West, going back to ancient Greek mythic and philosophical thought, women belong to the natural realm and men to the transcendental, and material nature is feminine while the abstract and rational principles or laws of nature are masculine. In the so-called developing societies, environmentally destructive industrial development often disproportionately benefits men—when it benefits local people at all—and harms women.[8] Women's work in those societies typically involves such subsistence activities as gardening, tending animals, and fetching water, firewood, and fodder. Thus Green Revolution agriculture, industrial forestry, mines and factories, massive irrigation works, and similar development projects disproportionately disrupt or displace the female sector of the traditional subsistence economy. In such cases, man's domination of nature is materially as well as formally equivalent to men's domination of women.[9]

Comparative environmental ethics, environmental social science, and ecofeminist analysis are mutually supporting. Human social, economic, and political organization are embedded in and arise out of human values and intellectual constructs. Both domains—the cognitive and structural— are dialectically intertwined and interactive. The United States Forest Service, the World Bank, the Green Revolution, and capitalism are all, one way or another, expressions of the pre-ecological modern worldview. The emerging postmodern ecological paradigm will, we can be confident, gradually transform today's social, economic, and political institutions just as surely as the modern paradigm gradually but thoroughly transformed medieval social, economic, and political institutions. Meanwhile, just as the lingering social, economic, and political institutions of the Middle Ages delayed the full flowering of modern industrial attitudes and values, today's social, economic, and political realities—to say nothing of the insidious and ubiquitous patriarchy—thwart the expression of incipient postmodern ecological attitudes and values.

The body of this monograph is devoted to exploring the intellectual potential for environmental ethics in a variety of representative cultural worlds. The penultimate chapter attempts to articulate a cognitive motif— the postmodern ecological worldview—concordant with them all. And it attempts to orchestrate the diverse environmental ethics distilled from a plurality of intellectual traditions in order to achieve a global chorus of voices singing of a human harmony with nature. The final chapter describes how several of the traditional environmental ethics explored here are being put into practice by people on the ground in various parts of the real world.

TRADITIONAL, MODERN, AND POSTMODERN ENVIRONMENTAL ETHICS

Until recently, it may seem, human material culture—human technology—was powerless to affect seriously the natural environment for better or worse. Preindustrial *Homo sapiens* is not thought to have posed a significant threat to the natural environment. It has therefore been argued that the indigenous and traditional environmental ethics here alleged to exist probably did not, because they would have been unnecessary.[10]

However, a reexamination of human history and prehistory from an ecological perspective reveals a long-standing pattern of anthropogenic environmental degradation. Paleolithic hunter-gatherers armed with stone-tipped spears and arrows, snares and traps, and (not least) fire may have caused local extirpation—and may even have played a key role in the global extinction—of other animal species, and in any case probably profoundly altered the character of biotic communities.[11] Neolithic, ancient, medieval, and modern agriculturalists caused soil erosion, siltation of surface waters, deforestation, salinization of arable lands and fresh waters, and desertification.[12]

A reexamination of human history and prehistory also reveals the existence of culturally evolved and integrated environmental ethics that served to limit the environmental impact of preindustrial human technologies. A more systematic discussion of representative indigenous and traditional environmental ethics is the central subject of this monograph. Suffice it to say for now that in many indigenous cultures nature was represented as inspirited or divine, and was therefore the direct object of respect or of reverence; that in some traditional cultures nature was the creation of God, and thus was to be used with care and passed on intact; that in still others human beings were thought to be part of nature, and a good human life was therefore understood to be one in harmony with it. Consistent with the limits to the practical efficacy of ethics discussed earlier in this chapter, such environmental ethics evidently did not prevent environmental degradation from occurring in the pre-Columbian Americas, the ancient Levant, or medieval China, but it may have considerably tempered such degradation.

Industrial civilization, of course, has not only intensified the kinds of environmental mischief already afoot in the activities of preindustrial people but has polluted the environment with synthetic toxic chemicals and radioactive elements. With the emergence of an industrial human culture of global reach, the human impact on nature has so increased in force, intensity, and ubiquity that in the worst possible scenario imaginable—thermonuclear holocaust—people may well destroy the biosphere itself.[13] Short of this cataclysm, the global ecosystem may gradually be degraded to the extent that many higher forms of life (including *Homo sapiens*) will no longer be adapted to it.

The emergence of global industrial culture was accompanied by a loss of the sorts of preindustrial environmental ethics just mentioned. The secularism, humanism, and materialism characteristic of the modern worldview demystified and undermined earlier environmental ethics, aggravating the destructive impact of industrial technology. Here thus is an irony: Just when we needed an environmental ethic more than ever, global industrial civilization, with its infinitely greater power for environmental destruction, eclipsed the environmental ethics (along with many other traditional cultural values) that had prevailed in the past and had served to restrain traditional human patterns of resource exploitation.

The secularism, humanism, and materialism characteristic of contemporary industrial culture has, on the other hand, evolved a protean social ethic peculiar to itself. The moral concept reposing at its core is the intrinsic value, autonomy, and dignity of the individual, as glossed by Descartes, Hobbes, Locke, and other early modern Western philosophers. Two streams of moral philosophy have flowed from this central source: utilitarianism (first set out by Jeremy Bentham), which emphasizes aggregate human welfare as a goal of individual action and public policy, and deontology (first set out by Immanuel Kant), which emphasizes human dignity as a basis for human rights.

A latter-day modern secular environmental ethic may be developed as an addendum to the moral implications devolving from consideration of human welfare and human rights. With the emergence of the science of ecology and related sciences, it is now painfully clear that human actions which have direct deleterious effects on the environment often also have indirect deleterious effects on human beings. For example, cutting and burning a tropical rain forest in order to create pasture not only destroys an ecosystem and its nonhuman native denizens, it also adversely affects aggregate human welfare, because of the now well-understood ecological effects of deforestation.

From a classical utilitarian point of view, massive tropical deforestation would appear to be unethical because it benefits a few people (lumber and cattle barons) in the short run at the expense of many people (indigenous forest dwellers, the local landless population, and, less directly, people everywhere in the world) now and in perpetuity. From a classical human-rights point of view, however, the immorality of deforestation is less clear, because of the historical conflation of human rights generally with human property rights more particularly and with "free enterprise." But again, the exercise of one person's rights, in theory, is limited by the rights of others. And increasingly these days, "human rights" are construed more broadly to include, in addition to the right to political liberties and unfettered economic activity, the right to certain amenities—subsistence with dignity, access to rudimentary education and basic health care, and a viable natural environment.[14]

One might thus develop a modern secular environmental ethic erected on the twin pillars of human welfare and human rights.[15] Environmental ethics would consist of a thorough integration of environmental science and technical expertise with the conventional values of contemporary industrial civilization. A contribution to a mature environmental ethics, so conceived, would attempt to predict the effects on human welfare and human rights (broadly construed) of human behaviors that have environmental impact. State-of-the-art utilitarian and rights theory is only a little less complicated and sophisticated than state-of-the-art environmental-impact assessment. By combining the two—no small task—human environmental behavior could be ethically evaluated.[16]

More profoundly, however, the science of ecology and related sciences, in tandem with relativity and quantum theory (together sometimes called the "new physics"), are creating a postmodern scientific worldview. There is another, stronger, more direct approach to environmental ethics which is more resonant with this emerging scientific worldview—and with most of the traditional and indigenous environmental ethics of preindustrial cultures. This approach would make the effects of human actions on individual nonhuman natural entities and on nature as a whole directly accountable, regardless of their indirect effects on other people. Such an environmental ethic would be stronger as well, since it could ethically evaluate environmentally destructive human action that had little or no negative effect on human beings.

The conservation biologist David Ehrenfeld, in a justly celebrated classic appeal for a nonanthropocentric approach to environmental ethics, cites the case of the endangered endemic Houston toad (*Bufo houstonensis*) as an example. "This animal has no demonstrated or conjectural resource value to man; other races of toad will replace it; and its passing is not expected to make an impression on the *Umwelt* of the city of Houston or its suburbs."[17]

Thousands of species could be cited as similar cases of threatened environmental entities whose destruction would not appreciably diminish human welfare or significantly abridge human rights. Yet many people, Ehrenfeld prominently among them, feel morally uneasy about willy-nilly anthropogenic extinction of natural nonresources. Traditional anthropocentric ethical theory is unable persuasively to articulate and underwrite such environmental ethical intuitions as those of Ehrenfeld and kindred spirits. Yet those intuitions clearly lie behind the U.S. Endangered Species Act, which, despite a strictly anthropocentric preamble, "operationally" extends rights to the endangered species listed in its provisions.[18]

An environmental ethic that takes into account the direct impact of human actions on nonhuman natural entities and nature as a whole is called an ecocentric environmental ethic. An ecocentric environmental ethic conforms not only to the evolutionary, ecological, physical, and cosmological foundations of the evolving postmodern scientific worldview, as more fully explained in the penultimate chapter of this book, but also to most indigenous and traditional environmental ethics, as the historical and cultural sketches in the next several chapters will indicate.

COMPARATIVE ENVIRONMENTAL ETHICS AND THE ONE-MANY PROBLEM

Indeed, Western philosophers initially turned to traditional Eastern wisdom for help in their search, begun in earnest in the late 1960s, for an environmental ethic located in a deep ecological consciousness. And in fact Eastern philosophy has historically shaped the gradually emerging environmental consciousness in the West. The transcendentalism of Ralph Waldo Emerson and Henry David Thoreau—who were among the first American thinkers to look on nature as something more than an obstacle to progress and a pool of natural resources—was inspired by Hindu thought. In the mid–twentieth century, the emerging contemporary environmental movement was profoundly influenced by Japanese Zen Buddhism.

Zen had been powerfully and persuasively represented in the West by the philosopher D. T. Suzuki in the early twentieth century, and Alan Watts, an American devotee of Zen, popularized Suzuki's somewhat more academic representation. Inspired by Watts, the nature poet Gary Snyder studied Zen Buddhism in Japan, and in his work a raw and uncultivated American love of and sensitivity to nature is integrated with the advanced natural aesthetic cultivated for centuries among the Japanese. Snyder was a charter member of the beat generation—the midcentury American counterculture romanticized by the enormously popular novelist Jack Kerouac. Thus when Americans awoke to the environmental crisis in the late 1960s, they turned for philosophical guidance to the cultural alternatives then popular, and Zen Buddhism was by far the most visible.

More recently, the attention of Western environmental philosophers has gravitated toward Taoism. The concept of living in accordance with the *tao* of nature complements the evolutionary and ecological axiom that human beings are part of nature and must conform human ways of living to natural processes and cycles. Especially in the Taoist concept of *wu-wei*, Western environmental ethicists have found a traditional Eastern analogue of what they call "appropriate technology"—technology that blends with and harnesses natural forces, as opposed to technology that resists and attempts to dominate and reorganize nature.

With the current and more ominous second wave of the twentieth century's environmental crisis now washing over us, we have both a mandate and an opportunity to facilitate the emergence of a global environmental consciousness that spans national and cultural boundaries. In part, this requires a more sophisticated cross-cultural comparison of traditional and contemporary concepts of the nature of nature, human nature, and the relationship between people and nature than has so far characterized discussion. The intellectual foundations of the industrial epoch, far from being absolute, are now actually obsolete. A new scientific paradigm is emerging which will sooner or later replace the waning mechanical worldview and its associated values and technological esprit. The coming twenty-first-century paradigm has many conceptual affinities with preindustrial attitudes toward nature, especially those of the East. Thus, detailed cross-cultural comparison of traditional concepts of the nature of nature, human nature, and the relationship between people and nature with the ideas emerging in ecology and the new physics should be mutually reinforcing. Traditional environmental ethics can be revived and, just as important, validated by their affinity with the most exciting new ideas in contemporary science, while the abstract and arcane concepts of nature, human nature, and the relationship between people and nature implied in ecology and the new physics can be expressed in the rich vocabulary of metaphor, simile, and analogy developed in the traditional sacred and philosophical literature of the world's diverse cultures.

One might therefore envision a single cross-cultural environmental ethic based on ecology and the new physics and expressed in the cognitive lingua franca of contemporary science. One might also envision the revival of a multiplicity of traditional cultural environmental ethics, resonant with such an international, scientifically grounded environmental ethic and helping to articulate it. Thus we may have one worldview and one associated environmental ethic corresponding to the contemporary reality that we inhabit one planet, that we are one species, and that our deepening environmental crisis is worldwide and common. And we may also have a plurality of revived traditional worldviews and associated environmental ethics corresponding to the historical reality that we are many peoples inhabiting many diverse bioregions apprehended through many and diverse cultural lenses. But this one and these many are not at odds. Each of the many worldviews and associated environmental ethics can be a facet of an emerging global environmental consciousness, expressed in the vernacular of a particular and local cultural tradition.

Cultural diversity is a reflection of biological diversity and depends on it. The homogenization of the landscape leads to the homogenization of culture, and vice versa. As traditional societies "develop," in the modern Western paradigm, industrial methods of farming and forestry, mechanical modes of transportation and distribution, the "international style" of architecture and urban configuration all replace their vernacular counter-parts. Such "maldevelopment" leads by a wearily familiar dialectic to an erosion of indigenous beliefs and values, as well as to the extirpation and extinction of indigenous species. Conversely, the persistence of local biotic communities often attends the successful resistance of traditional societies to external pressures to develop.

Biological diversity is complemented by ecosystemic integration, how-ever. Each species is distinct from all others, but by no means does each exist in splendid isolation from the rest; all are integrated into ecosystems, and each distinct local ecosystem is integrated into the global biosphere. Cultural fragmentation—inwardness, isolation, mutual hostility, intoler-ance—is no less destructive of human and biotic communities than is cul-tural homogenization. An analogue to ecosystemic integration is needed to complement cultural diversity. A tie that may bind the many cultural worlds into one systemic whole is the postmodern scientific worldview and its associated environmental ethic, envisioned in chapter 9.

2   The Historical Roots
of Western European
Environmental Attitudes
and Values

THE JUDEO-CHRISTIAN TRADITION

During the past two decades of heightened environmental awareness, intense controversy was swirled around the environmental attitudes and values of the Judeo-Christian tradition. Throughout the discussion of this controversy, the word "man" will be used deliberately, with apologies, to refer generically to the sexually dimorphous species *Homo sapiens.* Using a gender-neutral term would sacrifice the rich historical connotations of "man"—among them its decidedly sexist connotation. The Judeo-Christian tradition has, after all, been a bastion of the Western patriarchy—a fact that cannot be obscured by a verbal smoke screen. With similar intent and deliberation, the masculine personal pronouns "He," "Him," and "His" will here stand in for "God" and "God's." Another terminological caveat: The term "Judeo-Christian" may suggest a historically and doctrinally insensitive conflation of Judaism with Christianity. Judaism is a communal and profoundly this-worldly religion, while Christianity is an individualistic and profoundly otherworldly religion. However that may be, and however future Judaic and Christian environmental ethics may differently evolve, contemporary discussion has focused on texts (the first few chapters of Genesis) and ideas (the God-man-nature relationship) common to the two religions. Therefore, for present purposes, carefully distinguishing between Judaism and Christianity is not germane. Indeed, the vortex of the controversy about the environmental attitudes and values common to Judaism and Christianity has centered even more narrowly on the appropriate interpretation of the relationship between God, man, and nature set out in Genesis 1:26–28:

> 26 And God said, Let us make man in our image, after our likeness: and let them have dominion over the fish of the sea, and over

the fowl of the air, and over the cattle, and over all the earth, and over every creeping thing that creepeth upon the earth.

27 So God created man in His own image, in the image of God created He him; male and female created He them.

28 And God blessed them, and God said unto them, Be fruitful, and multiply, and replenish the earth, and subdue it: and have dominion over the fish of the sea, and over the fowl of the air, and over every living thing that moveth upon the earth.[1]

The Despotic Interpretation

Environmentally oriented critics have claimed that since, according to Genesis, man is created in the image of God and given dominion over and commanded to subdue the earth and all its other creatures, Genesis clearly awards man a God-given right to exploit nature without moral restraint (except insofar as environmental exploitation may adversely affect man himself).[2] Man's unique status among creatures, constituted by his creation in the image of God, confers on man unique rights and privileges. Further, God seems to have intended man to be His viceroy on earth. Man is to the rest of creation as God is to man. Indeed, according to the British biblical scholar James Barr,

> the dominant tendency has been to identify the image [of God in man] as being [just] man's dominion over nature—which after all occurs in the same passage. . . . For instance, [the authors of] *God in Nature and History* [write]: "When Genesis 1:27 says that God created man in His own image, the whole passage, 1:26–28, makes it clear that what is mainly thought of is man's dominion over nature. As God is the lord over His whole creation, so He elects man as His representative to exercise this lordship in God's name over the lower creation."[3]

Thus, if God is the self-described jealous and wrathful lord and master of man, man is, by implication, the jealous and wrathful lord and master of nature.

This reading is called the "mastery" or "despotic" interpretation of Genesis. It seems clearly the intent of God that man be master and nature slave, since not only is man given dominion over the earth, he is expressly enjoined to subdue (Hebrew: *kabas*, "stamp down") the earth—as if nature were created unruly and were in need of breaking to become complete.

Genesis sets the stage for the rest of the biblical drama. If this is the correct interpretation of Genesis, then it would seem that the only environmental ethic consistent with the Judeo-Christian worldview is a weak, indirect, anthropocentric environmental ethic—one that would prohibit only those abuses of the environment which adversely affect human welfare or infringe on human rights. Under such a moral regime, certainly the northern spotted owl, the Furbish lousewort, and all the other small, rare, endemic nonresources would stand little chance of survival in competition with the whims and fancies of "lord man" (as the American wilderness advocate John Muir frequently characterized the human self-image associated with the despotic interpretation of Genesis).

The Stewardship Interpretation

Not surprisingly, Judeo-Christian apologists have contested both this interpretation of Genesis and the untoward (and unflattering) environmental implications drawn from it by its critics.[4] Being created in the image of God confers, it might be argued, not only special rights and privileges on human beings but also special duties and responsibilities. Paramount among these responsibilities, it might be supposed, is man's duty wisely and benignly to rule his dominion, the earth. To abuse, degrade, or destroy the earth is to violate the trust that the regent (God) placed in His viceroy (man). Far from being warranted by God's injunction to have dominion over the earth and subdue it, environmental degradation and destruction in pursuit of putative human interests is a direct violation, or more precisely a perversion, of that unnumbered "first commandment"—a perversion stemming from the subsequent Fall of man.[5]

This reading is known as the stewardship interpretation. It is reinforced by passages preceding and following the environmentally inflammatory verses of Genesis 1:26–28. In those preceding, God declares each successive part of His creation to be "good," thereby conferring intrinsic value—or, at least, more than mere utilitarian value—on nonhuman natural entities and nature as a whole, fresh from creation. And in those verses following (which in fact have no original narrative connection with verses 26–28, as it shall be immediately explained), man (represented by Adam) is placed by God in the Garden of Eden to "dress and keep it." To "dress and keep the garden" is a horticultural analogue of the pastoral "stewardship" metaphor ("steward" comes from the Old English *stī-weard*—that is, "sty ward").

Actually, Genesis contains not one but two separate creation myths. "P" and "J" (as biblical scholars label them)—the six-day account of creation and the Garden of Eden story, respectively—are not usually distinguished by either the environmental critics of or the apologists for Genesis, thus adding to the confusion.[6] The J, or Yahwist, narrative begins with the creation of *a* man in a single day, and goes on to the creation of plants (the Garden of Eden), animals, and, finally, a woman. Composed in the ninth century B.C.E., J is nearly half a millennium older than P, the Priestly narrative, which begins with the creation of light and the division of the waters on the first day and ends with the simultaneous creation of sexually dimorphous "man" on the sixth. This older, even more richly ambiguous myth is also the subject of conflicting interpretations about the proper role of man, as represented by Adam, in relation to nature.

In J, which begins at Genesis 2:4, one finds the pivotal passage supporting stewardship: that the role God assigned to man is to dress the Garden of Eden (the geography of which—from the Nile on the west to the Tigris and Euphrates on the east—suggests that it is coextensive with the whole known world) and keep it. On the other hand, Adam is created first and the garden later, as if the garden (nature) were designed for his comfort and convenience. Further, in this older myth the man names the animals and thus establishes, according to primitive logomancy, a magical power over them and prerogatives respecting them. Thus J, too, contains passages that might be cited to support the despotic interpretation. Taken together, however, these elements of the Garden of Eden creation myth might be understood to corroborate the responsible but utilitarian, benign but authoritarian vice-regency of man over nature developed by the stewardship interpretation of the environmentally controversial elements (the *imago dei*, dominion, and subduction) of the foregoing but more recent myth.

The Citizenship Interpretation

However, a more radical interpretation seems required by other elements of the older text.[7] First of all, the Hebrew name Adam derives from *adamah*, meaning "earth." The first man's very name thus associates him with the most material element—with the soil, with nature, and not, as the later *imago dei* suggests, with the heavens, the ethereal, and the divine.

Notice next that the animals—which, to be sure, the man names—are created by God from the same stuff. And they are created as potential companions for Adam. As the text plainly says,

> 18 And the Lord God said, It is not good that the man should be alone; I will make an help meet for him.
> 19 And out of the ground, the Lord God formed every beast of the field, and every fowl of the air.

This passage suggests that man is neither essentially different from the other creatures nor separated from them by a metaphysical gulf, as the

Priestly creation myth, in which man alone is created in the image of God, implies. Yet it is true that among these earth-creatures the earth-man finds no proper help meet. So God created woman to fill that niche.

In the midst of the beautiful and delectable permaculture in the agro-forest that God planted for Adam are two mysterious species—the tree of life and the tree of the knowledge of good and evil (2:9), the fruit of the latter of which the man is expressly forbidden to eat, on pain of death (2:17). The most tantalizing interpretive problem of this venerable biblical text concerns the exact nature of this forbidden knowledge.

So as not to distract attention from the environmental theme of this discussion, the notoriously misogynistic episode—in which the woman, heeding the counsel of the serpent, eats the fruit of the tree of the knowledge of good and evil and gives it to her husband to eat—may be passed over without further comment. Rather, keeping the ethico-epistemic problem of the nature of the knowledge of good and evil clearly in view, it may be said, first, that this knowledge cannot be the same as simple awareness of the difference between good and evil. Were it so, God would be slandered by implication. For until they ate the fruit of the tree of the knowledge of good and evil the woman and the man could not have known that it was good not to eat the fruit of the tree and evil to eat it. And so the tree would have been a trap, a standing "Catch 22," and God would have been unjust to punish them for eating its forbidden fruit.

What then does "knowledge" of good and evil mean, if not simply knowing how to follow rules or having the ability to obey? The whole story is erotically charged—a naked, perpetually youthful adult couple who innocently idle away their days in a lush garden full of delicious (and mysterious) fruits, a phallic serpent who beguiles the woman, and so on. Thus the knowledge of good and evil has been inevitably confused with knowledge of sexual congress. But neither can that be the correct understanding of the knowledge at issue, since, before eating the fruit of the tree of the knowledge of good and evil, Adam and his wife had, according to the text, become "one flesh"—which could hardly mean anything other than that they were already sexually active.

Two elements of the myth point to the conclusion that the knowledge of good and evil must mean the power to judge for oneself what is good and what is evil rather than either (simply) to hear and obey or (narrowly) to be acquainted with sexual pleasure. The first is that the knowledge of good and evil is twice said (3:5, 3:22) to be a divine knowledge (a further argument against the conventional sexual interpretation). The second is that after eating the forbidden fruit the first (and the only mentioned) discovery or knowledge that the woman and the man acquire is the knowledge that they are naked. They had been naked all along, as the text explicitly points out (2:25), but until they ate the fruit of the tree of the knowledge of good and evil they were not aware that they were naked. Upon eating the forbidden fruit, they became self-conscious, self-aware—and it seems that that is all that happened. A small thing, perhaps, but a most momentous thing. For having become self-aware, they then could decide what is good and what evil, in relation to themselves. And this is where they went astray. For the right to decide, and to declare, what is good and what is evil is properly God's alone. Man's proper lot is to accept God's judgment about good and evil and to obey.

In this interpretation—which may be called the citizenship interpretation—of the oldest biblical creation myth, anthropocentrism itself is man's original sin and is responsible for the famous Fall. God presumably cared for the whole of His creation and for each of its parts equally. When man—originally just one part of creation—acquired the divine knowledge of good and evil, he began to size up the rest of the creation as it pertained to himself. The animals, plants, soils, and waters that were useful to him he called "good," and those that made his life less comfortable, more burdensome, or more dangerous he called "evil." Man nurtured and cultivated the anthropocentrically "good" parts of nature, domesticating the tractable animals and edible plants, and attempted to destroy the anthropocentrically "evil" parts—the "pests," "vermin," "varmints," and "weeds." This, we may suppose, upset the balance and order of nature as a whole—as God had created it and as, surely, He wished it to remain. God, we may suppose, intended man to live harmoniously within the whole creation as a member, not to transcend it as its master—or, for that matter, as its steward.

That God did indeed have a different vision of nature than man, after man had illegitimately appropriated the knowledge of good and evil, is confirmed in the story of the flood. The key passages, from the sixth chapter of Genesis, read:

> 6 And it repented the Lord that he had made man on earth, and it grieved Him at His heart. . . .
> 11 The earth also was corrupt before God, and the earth was filled with violence. . . .
> 13 And God said unto Noah, The end of all flesh is come before me; for the earth is filled with violence through them; and behold I will destroy them with the earth.

The wickedness and corruption emphasized here appears to be specifically willful violence on the part of all creatures, not licentious sexual indulgence. We may speculate that such universal violence was supposed to have been set in motion by man's pushiness and spread through to all flesh.

In any case, God set curses upon the man and the woman. If the part would elevate itself above the whole by illegitimately judging good and evil, then the part must be removed from the whole and isolated. God thus drove Adam and Eve out of Eden (the vast extent of which, as noted, suggests that the Garden of Eden represents the whole of nature). And their most natural and vital organic functions—nutrition and reproduction—became labored. These curses may serve as marks and reminders to Adam and Eve and their progeny of their alienated and unnatural condition.

In this reading, the environmental moral of the story of Adam and Eve, the Garden of Eden, and the fruit of the tree of the knowledge of good and evil is essentially atavistic. Man's acquisition of self-consciousness—and perforce self-centeredness—was the original sin. If myth may be read as the ethno-history of oral cultures, this myth, so interpreted, laments the emergence—which occurred in this very vicinity—of Neolithic and eventually civilized man from the Paleolithic state of nature. More radically still, it seems even to lament the emergence of man from a more universal simian condition, since clothing, carnivorousness, and self-awareness are implicitly decried. It represents man—and more especially the new managerial man, who looks on nature as a pool of "natural resources"—as living in a cursed, alienated condition. Man's salvation would thus seem to lie in a return to innocence, nakedness, and reimmersion in nature. In effect, to be redeemed would entail abandoning industry, certainly, and agriculture, and perhaps even all tool use by means of which man bends nature to his will. At the very least, it would mean reverting to savagery, a condition in which man lived as an integral part of the natural world and took what it freely offered; or, even more radically, devolving to an arboreal, fruit-eating primate existence—more or less the carefree, gorillalike life-style of the first couple glimpsed in Genesis before the terrible trespass.

Thus there are, to sum up, three possible environmental ethics consonant with three interpretations of the Judeo-Christian worldview based on biblical texts: (1) an indirect, human interest/human rights environmental ethic associated with the "despotic" reading; (2) a more direct, ecocentric environmental ethic associated with "stewardship"; and (3) an uncompromising ecocentric environmental ethic associated with "citizenship"—a radical biblical biotic communitarianism.

While the environmental ethics associated with both stewardship and citizenship are direct and ecocentric, they differ markedly in their practical implications. The former would permit benign management of the earth and all its creatures for the mutual benefit of man and nature, while the latter would imply a much more passive way of life—one incompatible with the present civilized, and perhaps even humanized, condition of mankind. The ecocentric environmental ethic associated with stewardship is thus the most effective, practical, and acceptable environmental ethic consistent with the Judeo-Christian worldview. Further, since it is a possible interpretation of the role intended for man by God in both of the creation myths of Genesis, stewardship seems the most plausible interpretation of the overall gist of the text as it has come down to us in its present composite form.

The Stewardship Environmental Ethic

As a philosopher who has struggled for most of two decades to develop a theoretically well-formed, adequate, practicable, and persuasive nonanthropocentric environmental ethic, I would like to intrude on the impersonal voice of this discussion to say that the Judeo-Christian stewardship environmental ethic is especially commendable.

Theoretically, it provides a simple and direct solution to the most vexing problem of contemporary secular nonanthropocentric environmental ethics—of which Aldo Leopold's land ethic (to be elaborated in chapter 9) is a familiar example. And that problem is the problem of providing intrinsic value (or, as it is sometimes called, "inherent worth") for nonhuman natural entities and nature as a whole. In most of the familiar Western social ethics, human beings are supposed to be intrinsically valuable ends in themselves, and all other things are supposed to be means—possessing, at best, "instrumental value." A strong, direct nonanthropocentric environmental ethic would promote some nonhuman natural entities and nature as a whole from the instrumentally to the intrinsically valuable class. However, in the absence of God—who serves the Judeo-Christian stewardship environmental ethic as, so to speak, an independent axiological point of reference—one is hard-pressed to find a source of value outside finite (human) consciousness. And finite consciousness always has a point of view. It is a truism of modern science that nature is value-free. From a "scientific" point of view, all value is in exactly the same boat as one of its types, beauty—viz., in the eye of the beholder. Value is a relationship between conscious, never entirely disinterested subjects and neutral objects. How, then, can ardent environmentalists certify (to take a case in point) the value of David Ehrenfeld's Houston toad, the plight of which was noted in chapter 1? In the absence of some disinterested valuer beyond human consciousness, and in the absence of any resource value to us (of which the Houston toad has little or none, even when "resource value" is extended to the furthest limits of the term, as in aesthetic and scientific utility), the

Houston toad is worthless. And so, in competition with a proposal to convert its habitat to satisfy any human interest, however trivial—imagine that developers petition the city of Houston to build a dog track on the site of its last refuge—the Houston toad would lose out.

In the Judeo-Christian stewardship environmental ethic, God steps in to fill the axiological void. The Houston toad, and all the other small, insignificant, inconsequential rodents, reptiles, molluscs, beetles, plants, and so on are literally God's creatures, and according to Genesis He pronounced each of them, and the replete creation as a whole, "good." They possess independent intrinsic value by the most redoubtable of all arguments—divine fiat.

Another problem for secular environmental ethics is the problem of moral reciprocity. If people are but "plain members and citizens of the biotic community," as in the Aldo Leopold land ethic, and this membership and citizenship generates ethical obligations on our part to the other members and citizens of the biotic community and to the community as such, then we must explain why the similar membership and citizenship of other forms of life generates no corresponding ethical obligations on their part to us and to one another. Surely tigers and other predators are not immoral beasts. And it is patently absurd to think that human parasites and disease-causing organisms ought (in the ethical sense) not to afflict mankind; or that natural calamities—like tsunamis and earthquakes—are moral evils. Happily, in the Judeo-Christian stewardship environmental ethic, man's uniqueness among all the other creatures—his creation in the image of God—results in a moral asymmetry that cuts through this conundrum. We are uniquely privileged, and uniquely responsible. We do not exist as resources for other creatures, as they do for us; but we are burdened with duties to them, from which they are correspondingly exempted.

The Judeo-Christian stewardship environmental ethic is also eminently practicable. We can have our cake—intrinsic value for nonhuman natural entities and nature as a whole, which we alone among creatures must acknowledge—and eat it (literally as well as figuratively) too. For it is clear in Genesis that when God is creating the various living creatures He is establishing species, not specimens severally. Accordingly species, not specimens, are intrinsically valuable—the sperm whale, not Moby Dick; the redwood, not the specimen named for Louis Agassiz in Big Trees State Park, Calaveras County, California; and so on. Hence people may freely use individual living beings as natural resources—sentient and nonsentient alike—without the least moral compunction, as long as the earth's complement of species and inorganic natural appointments are not destroyed or degraded. Central to the stewardship idea is that each human generation holds God's creation in sacred trust, lives on the surplus, and passes on to the next generation a renewed edition, complete and intact.

As to the persuasiveness of the Judeo-Christian stewardship environmental ethic, that depends, from a strictly logical point of view, on whether or not one can accept its premises and the cognitive complex in which it is embedded. Rationally to espouse the Judeo-Christian stewardship environmental ethic, one must, in other words, believe that a transcendent, personal God exists in fact as well as story; that the natural environment was created pretty much as described in the Bible, and so on. Taken literally, these larger propositions are, to say the least, dubious.

But logic and reason are not the only means of persuasion. The stewardship environmental ethic may also appeal to those who, as it were, "come from" the Judeo-Christian tradition and who remain less intellectually than culturally and emotionally rooted in it. Purged of its literal elements, the Judeo-Christian stewardship environmental ethic powerfully speaks to the present condition of the relationship of human beings to nature. We are in fact the dominant species on the planet; we do in fact hold the fate of the earth in our hands; and we are indeed moral beings in a largely amoral world. Without taking the Bible literally, one may feel, further, that somehow there is more to heaven and earth than science can know and tell and that humanity is somehow a uniquely privileged but uniquely responsible creature among creatures.

Furthermore, interpreted liberally, the creation accounts in Genesis are more or less consistent with what we think we know about the world through science. Current cosmology posits a beginning of the universe in time. Beyond the Big Bang science cannot see, and scientific Christians are free to believe that God directly created the enormous energy that coalesced into the spatio-temporal-material universe that is the object of scientific investigation.

Further, the scientific scenario of the development of the universe roughly corresponds to the successive stages of creation in the Priestly narrative, which begins with the creation of light. That first act of divine creation correlates rather well with the latest thinking about the first micromoments of the Big Bang, before any matter had precipitated—during which creation was, so to speak, all flash and no substance. Genesis moves on, in the same order as our current scientific myth, to the creation of the celestial bodies. As in our contemporary Darwinian epic of terrestrial evolution, the geomorphological features of the earth are formed first, the plants come into being before the animals, and the other animals before

Homo sapiens. Thus, if we read the six "days" of creation in the first chapter of Genesis as eons, we can find a remarkable, albeit only rough-and-ready, correspondence with the current scientific origin story.

The older and very different Yahwist creation myth is out of phase with contemporary scientific beliefs about cosmic and terrestrial evolution, but it is remarkably consistent with what science tells us about human evolution. It accurately suggests that *Homo sapiens'* earliest ancestors dwelt in a tropical forest and fed on fruit. It marks the dawn of the Neolithic as the moment when people ceased to be merely a part of nature and began to enslave other species and to undertake other forms of deliberate mastery over nature. Indeed, it is more than merely consistent with current anthropological thinking: it supplements science with a moral insight about the price we have paid for our species' transcendence of the arboreal primate condition in which we once lived innocently and blissfully. The J account in Genesis regards an agricultural way of life as cursed. It fairly yearns for a return to a simian livelihood of unself-conscious ease and absorption in the eternal present.

However all that may be, the principal conclusion reached here is that the stewardship environmental ethic is the most consistent interpretation of the man-nature relationship set out in the Bible overall, and that it is, theoretically speaking, elegant and, pragmatically speaking, both powerful and practicable. Whether or not one subscribes to it and determines to live one's life by its lights depends on whether or not one can, either literally or liberally, credit its associated claims, or can at least remain culturally sympathetic with the general contours of the Judeo-Christian worldview.

It is fitting to begin this global survey of the environmental attitudes and values implicit in some of the world's most enduring intellectual traditions with the Judeo-Christian conceptual complex, because its implications for environmental policy and behavior have been the subject of extensive and intensive discussion—as both the cause and cure of our contemporary global environmental malaise. Hence it may serve as a model, and a familiar model as well, of how a traditional cultural worldview may support one or another environmental ethic.

GRECO-ROMAN HISTORICAL ROOTS

The other primary source of Western culture and civilization is Greek mythology and, afterward, philosophy, which were disseminated throughout the Mediterranean Basin by the Alexandrian conquest and later by the Roman Empire. It seems to be generally assumed that Greco-Roman religious mythology nicely epitomizes a belief system that would naturally support a bio- or ecocentric environmental ethic, because the ancient Greeks and

Romans were nominally pagans, and paganism by definition deifies natural entities and forces. Yet much less attention has been paid to the environmental ethical implications of the Greco-Roman belief and value systems than to those of the Judeo-Christian.

The Greco-Roman contribution to Western culture and civilization is more complicated, historically, than that of the Judeo-Christian. Genesis, and the Bible more generally, represent a living mythology that has directly and continuously informed Western civilization right down to the present. Homer's *Iliad* and *Odyssey* and Hesiod's *Theogony* and *Works and Days*—all of which served the ancient Greeks as a sacred literature somewhat as the Torah served the ancient Hebrews—are, by contrast, a fossil record of a religion long dead. The comic poet Aristophanes suggests in *The Clouds* that Greek philosophy fatally undermined Greek religion—an opinion that contemporary scholars might seriously consider. But whatever led to the extinction of their religion, the more influential and lasting contribution of the ancient Greeks to modern Western cognitive culture and civilization is Greek philosophy.

Mythology

However, before turning to an assessment of the environmental attitudes and values implicit in Greek philosophy, a brief synopsis of the environmental attitudes and values implicit in Greek mythology may be of perspectival interest. Homer's *Iliad* and *Odyssey* are concerned with the foreground of human events and the doings of the highly anthropomorphic deities. Like Genesis, Hesiod's *Theogony*, as its name suggests, is more concerned with the Big Picture. In both creation myths of Genesis, the world is represented as an artifact, created by God, who plays the role of a divine craftsman, dividing, arranging, and molding a preexisting plastic material. In sharp contrast, the *Theogony* represents the world not as having been created but as having been procreated. In the ordinary course of events, we observe things to come into being in either of two ways. Some of them are made, but others—and by far the most—spring from seeds, eggs, or wombs. The ancient Hebrew and Greek mythographers seem to have extrapolated from their observations of how everyday things come into being in order to paint a picture of how the whole world came into being. That the world as we know it was created rather than procreated may seem the more reasonable hypothesis only because it is more familiar. Both hypotheses—the world's creation, on the one hand, and procreation, on the other—are, in any case, equally mundane and pedestrian.

Things made—artifacts—are inert or lifeless, while things born are alive and inspirited. In the *Theogony*, the masculine Heaven and feminine

Earth join in sexual union and Earth gives birth to the first generation of gods. Among these divine beings are massive features of the natural environment—the sun and moon, the sea, time, mountains, and so on. Hence the sky and the earth, the oceans and atmosphere are all major and the most venerable of divinities. They are sacred in and of themselves. Moreover, since all living things—plants, animals, and human beings—are descended ultimately from Heaven and Earth, all living things are members of one family. In the *Theogony*, there is no metaphysical gulf separating people from the rest of nature, as there is in the Priestly narrative of Genesis. In sum then, pagan Greek mythology represents nature as having come into being by an essentially organic process, and as sacred; and it represents human beings as an integrated part of nature. On the other hand, the tendency toward anthropomorphism—the portrayal of the gods in human form and with human foibles—evident in the epics of Homer and Hesiod but especially conspicuous in the former, contributed to a corresponding anthropocentrism.

Philosophy

Early in the sixth century B.C.E., a few Ionian Greeks living in polyglot centers of commerce—centers of commerce in ideas, we may suppose, as well as in goods—hazarded a more rational account of the world. Olympian Greek religion continued to hold sway thereafter, but—as we know well from our own, in many ways parallel, modern experience—a mythopoeic worldview existing alongside a more empirical alternative must be held by "faith" in the face of an unremitting current of skepticism and cynicism. In any event, the Greco-Roman tradition's living legacy to contemporary Western cognitive culture is a rational tradition of thought about the world. After a period of intellectual decline, followed by a period during which a Greco-Hebraic hybrid religious worldview—Christianity—dominated European thought, ancient Greek natural philosophy was revived during the European Renaissance. The Renaissance was followed directly by the rapid development of Western science. Hence, it would be no exaggeration to say that the contemporary scientific worldview is essentially Greek, in both origin and fundamental character.

Environmentalists seeking a foundation for environmental ethics in ancient Greek philosophy have cited the philosophies of Heraclitus and Pythagoras as models.[8] Heraclitus was regarded even by his contemporaries as obscure and elusive; hence, it is hard to know for certain just what his views were—especially as only fragments of his work are extant. The authentic philosophy of Pythagoras is equally uncertain, but for a different reason: His philosophy was kept a secret and revealed only to initiates.

About Heraclitus this much seems clear. The *archê*, or fundamental substance, is fire: all is motion and process, and things continually change into other things. For Heraclitus, fire is not so much the stuff of nature—as water and air are for Thales and Anaximenes, respectively—as its cachet. This dynamic world, however, is orderly, regulated by something Heraclitus called the "Logos." Heraclitus's very general description of the world thus roughly corresponds to natural ecological cycles, in which organic things come into being only to be metabolized and transformed into other things—just as the materials that compose plants are eaten and transformed into animal tissue. Plant detritus and animal feces and cadavers are decomposed by fungi and bacteria, which retransform organic matter into its elemental constituents. Ecological processes, though admittedly less rigorously lawful than physical processes, are by no means random or chaotic. The oxygen, carbon, and nitrogen cycles, the hydrologic cycle, plant succession, and the like have remained regular, though not entirely predictable. An order—a Logos—prevails, as Heraclitus intimated. And, as he also suggested, the global ecosystem is kept alive and dynamic by a constant flow of energy from the sun. Heraclitus may thus fairly be said to have proposed an ecological worldview—a dynamic but ordered system through which there flows a current of energy—or fire, as he somewhat crudely characterized it.

Some scholars have seen an incipient environmental ethic in Pythagoras's belief in the transmigration of souls from dying human beings to newborn animals and from dying animals to newborn human beings, and in his related prohibition on the eating of animal flesh.[9] Thus, they argue, Pythagoras's ethic clearly extended beyond the sphere of human relationships to nonhuman natural beings. Certainly, his ethic was not anthropocentric, but one would be mistaken to conclude that it was therefore bio- or ecocentric. It has closer affinities to the contemporary animal-welfare ethic than to ecologically informed environmental ethics.

Indeed, Pythagoras's concept of the soul—in which his animal-welfare ethic was grounded—was distinctly otherworldly, and therefore antienvironmental in the last analysis. According to Pythagorean doctrine—as represented in Plato and other sympathetic sources—the soul is a fallen divinity, incarcerated or entombed in the body. The goal of Pythagorean religious practice and intellectual discipline was to free the soul from the cycle of reincarnation, thus enabling it to rejoin the company of the gods, to which it properly belonged. Celibacy, vegetarianism, and abstract mathematical exercises were undertaken: to avoid contamination of the soul by its earthly prison or tomb, in the case of the first two practices; and to cultivate and strengthen the soul's essential nature, in the case of the third.

Such a philosophy of the soul is fundamentally and profoundly anti-thetical to an environmental ethic. In the Pythagorean view, the soul—the essential self—is thoroughly alien to the natural environment. The natural physical world was loathed and contemned by the Pythagoreans and their sympathizers as the source of all evil and sin: "a joyless place where murder and vengeance dwell, and swarms of other fates—wasting diseases, putrefactions, and fluxes—roam in darkness over the meadow of doom."[10] According to Pythagorean doctrine, in short, one's aim in life should be to live as purely as possible in order to transcend earthly existence. The soul's reincarnation in an animal or human body was not an optimistic prospect; rather, Pythagorean ascetic practices and intellectual disciplines were undertaken precisely to avoid it. Only thus could the soul attain final liberation from the body. But since the body is part and parcel of the physical world, to seek final liberation from the body is to seek final liberation from the natural environment. Pythagoras's philosophy of soul and body is, indeed, the very epitome of an alienated, otherworldly outlook.

Pythagoras's essentially dualistic concept of human nature—a divine soul in an alien mortal body—became a cornerstone of the philosophy of Plato. And because of Plato's enormous influence it became virtually institutionalized in Western cognitive culture, both religious and secular. Meanwhile, Greek natural philosophy was proceeding apace. For two-and-a-half centuries, indeed, Greek natural philosophy was continuously occupied with the problems of substance, order, and movement in the physical world—the same problems, generally described, that occupy physics today.

During the sixth and fifth centuries B.C.E., various candidates for the basic material of which nature is made were proffered: water, air, fire, a combination of these "elements" plus earth, the *apeiron* (or indefinite), and others of the sort. Leucippus and Democritus brought this line of thought to a satisfactory culmination with the atomic theory of matter. According to their theory, all manifest objects are divisible into component atoms. The atoms themselves are indivisible solid particles. (*Atom*, in Greek, means "indivisible.") They possess substance or "mass," shape, and size, and move in the void, or infinite space. All other perceived qualities of things are secondary—the effects of these primary characteristics on our senses. The primary characteristics of atoms are very amenable to quantitative expression. All natural processes, therefore, according to this theory could be described mathematically.

In the portrait of the physical world drawn by the atomists, nature is inert, material, quantitative, mechanical, and reducible to its parts, which are externally related to one another. After the Renaissance, the atomic theory became institutionalized in Western cognitive culture by the intellectual triumph of Newtonian mechanics. As the Harvard philosopher of science Thomas Kuhn succinctly comments, "Early in the seventeenth century, atomism experienced an immense revival. . . . Atomism was finally merged with Copernicanism as a fundamental tenet of the 'new philosophy' which directed the scientific imagination."[11]

The worldview bequeathed to Western cognitive culture by Greek philosophy is therefore one in which nature is essentially profane, while man, because of his soul, is essentially divine and metaphysically distinct from nature. The profane, reductive, material, and mechanical picture of nature suggests that the environment can be radically rearranged and violently transformed without destroying its organic integrity—since it has none. And man's separateness from and superiority over nature suggest that he has a right to radically rearrange and to violently transform the natural environment and that he is disassociated from the harmful consequences of doing so, if any there be.

The eventual dominant Greek philosophical tradition—Pythagorean-Platonic dualism and Democritean atomism—lies at the roots of our present false environmental attitudes and values more than it represents a conceptual resource for an environmental ethic. Aristotle, whose philosophical system dominated the medieval European worldview, was neither a dualist nor a mechanist, but his taxonomical, teleological, and hierarchical picture of the world order nevertheless represented the environment as both discontinuous with and at the service of man. The environmentally positive aspects of Aristotle's philosophy—his organicism and holism—were vanquished by the Renaissance victory of the Pythagorean-Democritean-Platonic cognitive complex in the struggle for the modern European mind. Unfortunately, among all the ideas involved in Aristotle's rich philosophy of nature, his system of taxa (in which living things are ordered by logical categories rather than functional relationships) and his concept of a teleological hierarchy in nature (wherein plants exist for the sake of animals and animals for the sake of people) seem to be the ones that have endured the longest. Like Plato's theory of ideas, the former orders the living landscape somewhat like an automobile-parts warehouse is ordered, and the latter is preserved today in our habit of referring to our senior fellow voyagers in the odyssey of evolution as "lower" forms of life.

To sum up, ancient Greek philosophy, not ancient Greek religion, has exerted an enduring influence on Western concepts of nature. From a contemporary environmental point of view, Greek philosophy is a part of the problem—indeed, a very big part—not the solution. To be sure, a few minority traditions of ancient Greek thought, like those of Heraclitus or Xenophanes, might be of some use for the development of an environmental ethic, but on the whole they are submerged by the more dominant Greek legacy of dualism, mechanism, and hierarchy.

ISLAM

Islam, arising in the seventh century C.E. and built on the mytho-history of Judaism and Christianity, can be considered a Western worldview. Muhammad, the Prophet of Islam, regarded himself as a prophet of the same God, and in the same prophetic tradition, as Jesus, Moses, and Abraham. Furthermore, during the European Dark Age, Islamic scholars were the principal custodians of Greek science and mathematics. Certainly, Greek science and mathematics were further developed during their Islamic sojourn, but, reciprocally, they also informed the evolving Islamic worldview. While Christianity and, after the Renaissance, Greek natural philosophy eventually colonized the allied Western European and Euro-American thought world, Islam spread to the south and east.

The Quran, like the books of the Bible, is not without its ambiguities.[12] However, it seems to be less ambiguous than Genesis—which was compiled from several mutually inconsistent sources—about the relationship of human beings to nature. The Quran makes explicit certain themes that are only implicit, or for which two contradictory accounts exist side by side, in the more ancient text. One might plausibly find either despotism or stewardship implied by the Quran, but it would be quite impossible to develop a citizenship interpretation of Muhammad's sacred verses.

According to the Quran, Allah created the first man, Adam, from a clot of blood, as some verses say, or from potter's clay, as others say, and breathed into His creation the breath of life.[13] From Adam's body, He created woman. All other things are explicitly created by Allah for the sake of, the use of, and the benefit of man.[14] Adam and his seed are explicitly created to be the viceroys of God on earth.[15] As one interpreter of the Quran, Fazlur Raman, has succinctly put it, "Nature exists for man to exploit for his own ends, while the end of man himself is nothing else but to serve God, to be grateful to Him, and to worship Him alone. The utility, serviceability, and exploitability of nature are spoken of in many verses."[16]

A consortium of Saudi Arabian scholars confirm Raman's judgment: "The relation between man and the universe, as defined and clarified in the 'Glorious Quran,' is as follows: A relationship of utilization, development, and subjugation for man's benefit and for the fulfillment of his interests."[17]

According to Islam, then, man is at the moral center of creation and is, indeed, the very *telos* of creation. As in the Priestly narrative of Genesis, so also in the Quran: it is man's right to have dominion over and to subdue the earth and all its nonhuman denizens. Indeed, in the Quran not only are animals and plants subjected to and subservient to man, but the rivers, the sea, even the sun and moon are also subjected to and subservient to man. Man's dominion over the earth and the subordination of the creation to man is consistently spelled out in the Quran in no uncertain terms.

Man's role as viceroy or regent does not warrant his ruthless tyranny over an enslaved natural world—at least, not necessarily. Man's dominion over the earth might be benign, rather than wantonly destructive. The Pakistani geographer Iqtidar H. Zaidi, the first contemporary Islamic scholar to assess the environmental values and attitudes embedded in the Quran, insists that the doctrines of Islam explicitly and emphatically require that man's relation to nature should be one of stewardship rather than mastery:

> There are a number of verses in the Quran which make it abundantly clear that God has created the earth for the service of man, but at the same time man is also constantly reminded that the earth, whatsoever is on its surface, in its interior, and in its atmosphere, belongs to Almighty Allah, so that He gives all the individual human beings (as His Vice-regents), without any distinction or discrimination, the right of ownership of the natural resources for the purpose of their utilization and development. For example, "Unto Allah (belongeth) whatsoever is in the heavens and whatsoever is in the earth; and whether ye make known what is in your minds or hide it, Allah will bring you to account for it. He will forgive whom He will and He will punish whom He will. Allah is able to do all things."[18]

The Saudi scholars agree. Man, they declare, is "a mere manager of the earth and not a proprietor; a beneficiary, not a disposer or ordainer."[19]

The Saudi environmental philosopher Mawil Y. Izzi Deen reinforces the stewardship interpretation of the Quran's environmental message by pointing out that Allah had offered other creatures dominion over the earth but that "the duty of vice-regency [is] so onerous and burdensome that no other creature would accept it: 'Lo! We offered the trust unto the heavens and the earth and the hills, but they shrank from bearing it and were afraid of it. And man assumed it' (Surah 33:72)."[20] He has also found some quranic basis for the belief that other forms of life may have some role in the creation besides that of serving man: "The component parts of nature are entities in praise of their Creator."[21] And he points out that in one verse of the Quran, 6:38, other forms of life seem to have an existence comparable with that of human beings: "There is not an animal in the earth, nor a flying creature flying on two wings, but they are peoples like unto you." According to Deen, this verse shows that "while humans may have the upper hand over other 'peoples,' these other creatures are beings and, like us, are worthy of respect and protection.''[22] Similar passages, incidentally, may be found in the Old Testament. For example, Ecclesiastes 3:19 reads in part, ''a man hath no preeminence above a beast, for all is vanity.''

Moreover, Allah's creation is, as it were, a divine work of art. The whole world and all its parts are understood in Islam as ''signs'' to man, indicative of the greatness, the goodness, the subtlety, the richness, and so on, of the Creator.[23] To deface, defile, or destroy nature would be an impious or even blasphemous act. Although man is accorded the usufruct of the earth, he is not given the right to abuse it with impunity.

In Western thought there runs a strong strain of otherworldliness which has direct bearing on Western environmental attitudes and values. If we are not of this world but of another, better, more enduring world, then why should we be concerned about the fate of this world? It is not our world, and besides it is both corruptible (in Aristotle's sense of changeable and degradable) and corrupting (in the Pythagorean-Platonic sense of morally debasing). What stand does Islam take on this issue?

The Judeo-Christian tradition, it might be worth repeating, is not unequivocally otherworldly. In its older, Hebrew roots there is hardly any concept of life after death. This may be so, in part, because the effective religious and behavioral unit in the Old Testament is the people as a whole—Israel as a nation—but not the individual. An individual person may have a *nefesh*, or soul—an older version of the hylozoistic breath of life—but a people as a whole do not. And while individuals are born, live, and die, the nation enjoys, if not an eternal life on earth, at least an indefinite life on earth—a life that may endure, as have the Jews themselves, for millennia.

Christianity seems to have borrowed the notion of a pure, individual, immortal soul from its Greek intellectual ancestry. The New Testament, let us remember, is written in Greek, not Hebrew, and is decidedly Greek in its metaphysics and eschatology. We might think of Christianity—oversimply but not untruly—as the response of the Hebrew historico-religious tradition to the powerful intellectual advances of Greek philosophical thought, which had become, by the end of the Hellenistic period, thoroughly disseminated throughout the eastern Mediterranean.

As David Ehrenfeld and Philip J. Bently point out, the fact that Judaism is this-worldly and Christianity is otherworldly has important environmental ethical implications. ''The problem of the chasm between humanity and the rest of nature exists more for Christians than for Jews. Christianity has a stronger emphasis on the Other World than on this world, and classical [Greek] thought has a much stronger hold on Christianity than on Judaism."[24] Is Islam, in this respect, more like Judaism or Christianity?

Islam here seems to have been influenced by the Greco-Christian, not the older, earthier Hebrew alternative. Like Christianity, Islam is definitely an otherworldly religion. The earth is a temporary abode for man. After death, individuals will be judged. Those who have believed in Allah and in the Quran as His Word, and who have kept His laws and done good deeds, will be sent to Paradise—equated with the Garden(s) of Eden. Those who have not submitted (*Islam* means "submission")—that is, believed in the truth of the Quran, which constantly declares itself to be the true Word of God and insists that it must be believed—and those who have not lived according to quranic dictates and behaved justly and generously will be consigned to Hell.

The picture of Paradise in the Quran is quite detailed. It is a lush green garden, with flowing streams of water, honey, and milk, and shade trees laden with fruit. After death, the faithful and righteous will dwell there eternally, finely attired, ornamented with bracelets and jewels, lounging on brocade pillows and fine carpets, served by good-looking boys, and serviced by beautiful dark-eyed virgins. Hell, by contrast, is full of fire and brimstone, and the damned are tormented incessantly by devils and demons. Lost in the millennium between the sixth century B.C.E. and the seventh century C.E. is the Pythagorean-Platonic-Christian idea that it is an unphysical *psyche* that lives on after death and enjoys an afterlife of spiritual and/or intellectual bliss. In the Quran, life after death is consistently portrayed in a physical, sensual fashion.

The Islamic prohibition of environmental abuse (direct abuse of the natural environment, setting aside for a moment the indirect threat to people) is therefore quite clear. Those who blaspheme against God by defiling or destroying His creation will be corporally punished by Satan's minions with Hell's fires in the afterlife.

Even though the earth is only a temporary abode for man, and all things are created for man's sake and subjected to man, man is very much a creature of Allah and therefore shares the lot of other creatures—at least, while living on earth. Man is made of an earthly substance, and he is, albeit exalted above all others, a creature among creatures. There should thus be a kind of fellowship between man and the other creatures, according to Islam.

The problematic relationship in Islam between man and other creatures—in this case, other animals, from mites to mighty lions and elephants—was explored in a remarkable tenth-century fable, *The Case of the Animals versus Man Before the King of the Jinn*. A *jinni* is a spirit—made of the fiery element, according to the Quran—commonplace in the world of the Muslim believer. In this fable, the animals protest the arrogance of man in assuming that they are his God-given slaves. The human apologist opens his case as follows:

> Praise be to God who formed man . . . saying, "Cattle He cre-
> ated for you, whence you have warmth and many benefits. You eat
> of them." . . . He also said, "You are carried upon them and upon
> ships," and "horses, mules, and asses for riding and for splendor."
> He also said, "so that you may be mounted upon their backs. . . ."
> And there are many other verses in the Qur'an and in the Torah
> and Gospels which show that they were created for us, for our sake,
> and are our slaves and we their masters.[25]

This is as plain a statement of the Muslim mastery or despotic inter-pretation of the biblical-quranic message regarding the correct relationship between man and nature as one could hope to find anywhere. In the reply of a mule, speaking on behalf of his fellow animals, we find an equally clear statement of the Muslim stewardship interpretation:

> There is nothing in the verses this human has cited to substanti-
> ate his claims that they are masters and we slaves. These verses
> point only to the kindness and blessings which God vouchsafed to
> mankind, for God said that He made them your servants, just as
> He made the sun, the moon, wind, and clouds your servants. Are
> we to think . . . that these too are their slaves and chattels and that
> men are their masters? No! God created all his creatures on heaven
> and earth. He let some serve others either to do them some good or
> to prevent some evil. God's subordination of animals to men is
> solely to help men and keep them from harm . . . not, as they de-
> ludedly suppose and calumniously claim, in order that they should
> be our masters and we their slaves.[26]

The debate goes on for days, fills thirty chapters, and would be impos-sible to summarize here. Suffice it to say, first, that human abuse of and cruelty to animals is graphically portrayed as the animals state their case; second, that the alleged superiority of humans—their upright posture, beauty of form, skills, sagacity, intellect, and so on—is matched in one way or another by one or another of the animals or is counterbalanced by hu-man deficiencies (for example, some humans may have mastered medical lore, but only because the sloth and gluttony of humans creates a need for it); and third, that the fabric of the creation is a tightly woven web of mu-tual services and benefits. This third point made by the animals on their own behalf draws a remarkably ecological picture of nature—though quite without benefit of a theory of evolution by natural selection. Each animal has its place in nature, serving some and being served by others; and all is orchestrated to form a complex and replete whole, of which man is a part, not the pinnacle.

However, when the argument shifts from physical, intellectual, and technological attributes to distinctly spiritual—or, perhaps it would be better to say, distinctly religious—attributes, the humans win the debate. The authors, the Ikhwan al-Safa, do not gloss over the fact that many humans wallow in adultery, idolatry, and faithlessness. But the fact that man alone among all the creatures possesses an immortal soul and therefore, as a reward for obedience, can enjoy the pleasures of Paradise makes man, in truth, master and the animal slaves.

More than any other religious worldview, Islam insists on the literal truth of its Prophet's revelation. Islam is not hostile to scientific knowledge of nature, however. The doctrine of signs is, as it were, the epistemological interface between revealed and empirical knowledge. As we learn more about the natural world through the geological and biological sciences, it has become abundantly clear that the natural environment is a systematically integrated, seamless whole. Though uniquely endowed with an immortal soul, man is made of the stuff of the earth, a creature dependent on other creatures no less than they are dependent on one another. A price thus must be paid for environmental destruction—a this-worldly price as well as an otherworldly one.

Despite the disappointing conclusion of the Ikhwan al-Safa in *The Case of the Animals versus Man*, the Islamic tradition might very well support (as Iqtidar Zaidi argued a millennium later), no more ambiguously than the Judeo-Christian tradition, a direct, biocentric, stewardship environmental ethic. The environment, though given over to man's rule and subservient to man, might nevertheless be the direct object of respect and care because it is the handiwork of God and a sign of His power and majesty. The bulk of *The Case of the Animals versus Man*, in fact, humbles human pretensions in respect to the rest of animate nature; and although man finally wins the argument, the point of the authors seems less to establish the legitimacy of man's mastery of the animals than to insist on the need for obedience, good character, and good works as the only way to earn a reward in the afterlife.

In any event, the Islamic tradition also quite unambiguously supports an indirect anthropocentric environmental ethic. According to Islam, all human beings are descended from Adam. Hence all human beings—irrespective of race, color, or national origin—are equally members of one extended human family. While Muslims certainly regard Islam as God's chosen religion, no particular people are privileged or chosen. Anyone may become a Muslim. And no one is inherently better than anyone else.[27] In Islam there is, further, a strong emphasis on justice. Since environmental abuse and destruction are more often than not harmful to people, they are a form of injustice. To ruin or destroy the environment is tantamount to inflicting bodily injury on someone else, or depriving others of their property, or both.[28]

GAIA REDUX

The mainstream Western traditions of thought so far reviewed and assayed for their environmental attitudes and values go back to the dawn of history. Indeed, history as presently understood—a linear sequence of events in time—is an artifact of both Judeo-Christian and Greco-Roman thought. A historical consciousness lies at the very foundations of Judaism and Christianity, so much so that history may be the abstract sense of the Judeo-Christian thought world—a world with a temporal beginning and end, between which an eventful and portentous cosmic drama is played out. And the world's first historians were fifth-century Greek writers—Herodotus (from whose book, titled *History*, comes the common noun) and Thucydides.

An indigenous conceptual complex, however, antedated these historical worldviews in the West. At its core was the belief that the earth was a great Goddess. She was known by many names—Hekate, Eurynome, Demeter, Rhea. Her most familiar current moniker is Gaia—a transliteration of the Greek name for Her most ancient and venerable manifestation as Mother of all beings.

Mesolithic and Neolithic images of a female figure with pendulous breasts and rotund hips, dug up all over the eastern Mediterranean Basin, mutely testify to the antiquity and ubiquity of the Goddess throughout the region. From these and other contemporaneous material remains, archaeologists have speculated on the ancient Gaian worldview. Scholarly reconstruction of Her identity, powers, and cultus has also been based on the work of the ancient Greek mythographers, who provide the earliest accounts of the Goddess and Her devotions to have been preserved in decipherable writing. This unfortunate state of affairs puts us in a position similar to trying to understand American Indian religious beliefs only on the basis of pottery shards and the reports of early Euro-American Christian missionaries and Puritan preachers. The Greek mythographers had their own, very different story to tell. Knowing their bias, however, we can correct, at least partly, for the spin they put on Mother Earth.

As mentioned earlier in this chapter, Gaia plays a starring role in Hesiod's *Theogony*. Among its many functions, myth preserves an oral culture's past in the form of a cosmic legend. Hesiod's story of the triumph of thundering Zeus, the Greek name for the supreme weather-god of the Indo-European invaders of the Mediterranean Basin, mythically recapitulates the struggle of the invaders to dominate the region's Earth-worshiping indigenes.

The poet and scholar Robert Graves speculates that the Goddess religion developed during a time in which the male role in procreation was unknown. For the people then living in that part of the world, motherhood was the "prime mystery."[29] When subsequent generations began to understand fatherhood, perhaps in the process of domesticating animals, the male principle was epitomized by a bull and represented graphically by bovine horns.

Whether or not the indisputably matrifocal religion of the old Old World correlated with matriarchal social regimes is a matter of dispute, obfuscated by contemporary gender politics. Graves claims that it did:

> The tribal Nymph, or Queen, chose an annual lover from her entourage of young men, for sacrifice at midwinter when the year ended; making him a symbol of fertility, rather than the object of her erotic pleasure. His sprinkled blood served to fructify trees, crops, and flocks, and his flesh was, it seems, eaten raw by the Queen's fellow-nymphs.[30]

The feminist writer and peace activist Riane Eisler argues that typical Goddess-worshiping societies were not upside-down images of later patriarchal societies, with the roles of dominator and dominated inverted; they were, rather, egalitarian "partnership" communities.[31] Gaia, by whatever name, enjoyed a long tenure in the region; hence, both representations may be true, but of different societies at different times. It is possible to suppose that the early Neolithic horticultural villages portrayed by Eisler were partnership communities, and also to credit the evidence Graves amasses documenting his assumption that more recent and more centralized agricultural societies—such as that of pre-Hellenic Crete, "the apogee of Goddess culture"—may have been matriarchal and may also have involved (male) human as well as animal sacrifice.[32]

That the participants in the Neolithic revolution—the transition from a gathering-hunting to a farming economy—might deify the earth, from which their sustenance directly and palpably flowed, should not be surprising. People who plant, tend, and harvest crops must of necessity be attuned to the annual vegetal cycle of germination, growth, fruiting, wilting, and decay. Therefore, they might soon learn to count lunations and perhaps would see in lunar phases an image both of plant growth and of the larger sidereal cycle, as the moon grows, becomes ripe and full, then wanes and dies. The waxing and waning of the moon also resembles the conception, gestation, birth-giving, and shrinking of a fertile woman, and also a woman's life cycle from pubescence to fecundity to menopause. The exact correlation of the lunar cycle and the menstrual cycle—both twenty-eight days—might well constitute proof, for the primal human mind, that the mystery of the moon and the mystery of womanhood were intimately related, if not essentially the same. So much may be inferred from Neolithic pottery, which is frequently decorated with crescent moons and crescent-shaped bull horns.[33]

Successive waves of Indo-European pastoralists, hailing from the steppes to the north and east, overran these Gaian agrarian peoples and eventually established hegemony over the eastern Mediterranean Basin. In their own mytho-history, the Indo-European Greeks represented this conquest as the ultimate triumph of their male sky-god over a previously supreme female earth-goddess. According to Graves, Greek myth—and, later, Greek drama and philosophy—explicitly celebrated men and the male principle and denigrated women and the female principle. (Against the background of male sacrifice in the erstwhile matriarchy—if true—religio-gender struggle is perfectly understandable, however regrettable it may be.) Thus, in the twilight zone between Western history and prehistory, the complex of ideas and institutions which feminists today call patriarchy seems to have been deliberately and self-consciously constructed and asserted. If so, the mainstream of subsequent Western thought flows from sources that are not merely incidentally or collaterally patriarchal; they are, rather, essentially and fundamentally so.

Goddess Spirituality

One contemporary ecofeminist approach to environmental ethics is "Goddess spirituality." At the core of contemporary ecofeminism is the claim that patriarchy is responsible not only for the subjugation and exploitation of women by men but for the subjugation and exploitation of terrestrial nature by man.[34] The Indo-European conquest of the eastern Mediterranean, with its decided geo-gender ideology, historically supports this claim, since at the fountainhead of Western civilization women and the earth were mythopoeically linked. Corollary to this historical claim is the prognostication that a thoroughgoing overthrow of patriarchy would not only liberate women from subordination and domination by men but would also liberate terrestrial nature from subordination and domination by man.

Elinor Gadon is so far the most ambitious and visionary exponent of Goddess spirituality. She suggests that Gaia redux might not only inspire and encourage people to overcome the social inequities and insults of patriarchy in all its manifestations but also direct the groundswell change—the "paradigm shift"—that many thinkers believe to be currently taking place in global civilization:

> In reclaiming the Goddess, in recovering our full human history as men and women, we can learn other patterns of behavior. We can redress the imbalance between the human species and our natural environment, exploring the possibility of living in harmony and justice with all things. This [effort] is not about the idealization of women, but about life, connection, and responsibility.[35]

Reclaiming the Goddess—recovering the indigenous prehistorical (and prepatriarchal) Western worldview—is one of the most fascinating fields of contemporary inquiry. However, since we lack both a Wellsian time machine and Minoan scriptures comparable to the *Enuma Elish*, the *Theogony*, or the Torah, doing so necessarily involves a substantial element of speculation and creativity. As the ecofeminist thinker Charlene Spretnak frankly admits,

> the contemporary expressions of Goddess spirituality . . . are not merely attempts to replicate the extremely ancient religion that long preceded "the lost weekend" of patriarchal culture. Rather they are creative spiritual practice, which is embedded in profound historical tradition and, more fundamentally, in the female dimension of being.[36]

The Gaia Hypothesis

The Goddess is simultaneously reappearing on another intellectual front and in another vocabulary. James Lovelock has introduced and popularized the "Gaia hypothesis"—the suggestion that the "biosphere may be more than just the complete range of all living things within their natural habitat of soil, sea, and air." In other words, Lovelock claims that Earth is an organic whole, greater than the sum of its parts. Earth is "a single organism."[37]

Lovelock bases this scientifically radical way of comprehending the biosphere on two general observations.

First, living things produced, and continue to maintain, the far-from-equilibrium chemical composition of Earth's lithosphere, hydrosphere, and atmosphere. To take the most obvious case, oxygen, which is continuously generated as a waste product of photosynthesis by green plants, composes

21 percent of Earth's atmosphere. On a lifeless (or, more precisely, plantless) planet, very reactive elements such as oxygen are bound to other elements, such as carbon and sulfur, in various compounds, such as carbon dioxide and sulfuric acid. Indeed, without the ongoing activity of living things, neither would nitrogen, the preponderate component of Earth's atmosphere, exist in an elemental gaseous form.

Second, living things maintain critical optima in the absence of which life on Earth (at least, as we know it) would not be possible. To take the most obvious example, in order for life to exist, Earth's surface temperature must remain well within a range of between 0° and 100°C—respectively, the freezing and boiling points of water. For thousands of millions of years, Earth's average surface temperature has been remarkably constant—between 10° and 20°C—despite a whopping 30 percent overall increase in solar energy output since life evolved.[38] Lovelock argues that the earth's temperature is regulated by its organismic components. Other cases in point are the degree of salinity of the ocean, the proportion of atmospheric oxygen (much more, and fires would burn unchecked; much less, and aerobic organisms would suffocate), and the pH of the atmosphere and ocean—all maintained within tolerable ranges, and often at the optimum set point, by living things working in concert.

Lovelock is an "independent" scientist, a maverick thinker permanently employed by no academic, industrial, or governmental institution. His initial, somewhat casual expression of the Gaia hypothesis quite naturally and appropriately attracted criticism from more conventional members of the scientific community.[39] For one thing, it has been summarily dismissed as untestable. That may be true, but Lovelock's thesis is less a scientific hypothesis in the strict and technical sense of the term than an organizing idea. Lovelock himself refers to it more accurately as a "model" for thinking about the organization and processes of the biosphere—a model that might well generate testable scientific hypotheses. Moreover, the Gaia model might suggest new and fruitful lines of scientific inquiry.

The Gaia model has also been criticized for being infected, through and through, with teleology—the scientific anathema of explaining things in terms of final, rather than efficient, causes. Teleological language, however, is often used in evolutionary contexts as a kind of shorthand to characterize the end result of adaptive trial and error, because a more exact account often requires awkward circumlocution. Physiologists, for example, often speak of the "purpose" of animal organs such as the spleen or the kidney, knowing full well that they came about through natural selection rather than design; nor do such scientists intend to suggest otherwise. The Gaia model is further liable to the charge that it flirts with vitalism on a grand scale, as it may suggest that some immanent Intelligence anticipated problems and contrived a complex of intricate self-regulating systems in order to maintain an optimal environment for Herself—for organismic and supraorganismic life on Earth. Gaia may have a consciousness of sorts. But if so, Hers may be no less epiphenomenal than ours—the result, rather than the cause, of organic integration.

Elaborating the Gaia model in reply to his critics, Lovelock has attempted to identify the "mechanisms" that restore optimal temperature, salinity, pH, and so on in the face of perturbations.[40] Pointing out the automatic responses made by many and diverse organisms to such things as slight changes in the earth's orbit, periodic fluctuations and gradual increase in solar energy, periodic volcanic activity, and the like dispels the scientifically malodorous air of teleology and vitalism. For example, as solar radiation gradually increased, the amount of atmospheric carbon dioxide, a "greenhouse" gas, decreased. Why? Because plants, in what was for them a nutrient-rich atmosphere, flourished and over time competitively evolved greater biomass and deeper root structures. Tall long-lived trees store CO_2 in wood, and their roots bury it. As plants gradually soaked up and removed more carbon from the atmosphere, more heat could escape the earth's surface, thus maintaining a near optimal average temperature in the face of increased levels of solar radiation.

Though one ought not to be complacent in respect to our present experiment with the living planet's carbon cycle, Gaian negative-feedback mechanisms may kick in to save us from runaway global warming. As we burn fossil fuels, we increase the level of carbon dioxide in the atmosphere. But that may stimulate plant growth, as well as warm the planet up. More luxuriant plant growth would remove from the atmosphere some of the carbon dioxide coming from fossil-fuel combustion, and could thus restore homeostasis, perhaps at a somewhat higher level of both atmospheric CO_2 and average temperature. The transition period—during which sea level rises and ecotones and agrozones shift in response to increased warmth and changed weather patterns—will likely be abrupt and ecologically as well as economically unpleasant. But Gaia's thermostat may prevent an upwardly spiraling positive-feedback relationship between increasing atmospheric carbon dioxide and temperature, with deadly Venuslike conditions as an end point.

The Earth Ethic

What would a comprehensive Gaian environmental ethic look like? It would somehow unite contemporary ecofeminist Goddess spirituality with the Gaia hypothesis (or model) in contemporary science. So far, though mutually acquainted, the two have not been mutually informing. In his land ethic, Aldo Leopold, the great synthesizer of the life sciences and ethics in the twentieth century, drew out the moral implications of midcentury community ecology. A quarter-century before that, he sketched a very different ethic—an "earth ethic" (as one might dub it), based on distinctly Gaian reflections.

In a paper innocuously titled "Some Fundamentals of Conservation in the Southwest," which remained unpublished for more than thirty years after his death in 1948, Leopold noted the presence of the stewardship environmental ethic in the Old Testament. Then, in the distinctly religious context he evokes, he takes up the more radical, and un–Judeo-Christian, suggestion that the earth may be a living being. It is "not impossible," he writes,

> to regard the earth's parts—soil, mountains, rivers, atmosphere, etc.—as organs or parts of organs, of a coordinated whole, each part with a definite function. And if we could see this whole as a whole, through a great period of time, we might perceive not only organs with coordinated functions, but possibly also that process of consumption and replacement which in biology we call metabolism and growth. In such a case we would have all the visible attributes of a living thing, which we do not now realize to be such because it is too big and its life processes too slow.[41]

Like Lovelock, who believes that pictures of the earth taken from the moon have precipitated a popular, intuitive Gaian consciousness, Leopold stresses the importance of scale and perspective. In the next sentence, Leopold forges the link between Gaian science and spirituality. He seems less reluctant than others who have reached Gaia through science to embrace the religious and moral corollaries of the conception of Earth as a single living being, composed, as we ourselves are composed, of a multitude of smaller, subordinate beings: "And there would also follow that invisible attribute—a soul, or consciousness—which . . . many philosophers of all ages ascribe to all living things and aggregates thereof, including the 'dead' earth."

Leopold suggests in effect that we are as cells in the body of Mother Earth. There is a moral dimension to this vision, as well as a spiritual one. "Perhaps in our intuitive perceptions," he goes on,

> we realize the indivisibility of the earth—its soil, mountains, rivers, forests, climate, plants, and animals, *and respect it* collectively not only as a useful servant but as a living being, vastly less alive than ourselves in degree, but vastly greater than ourselves in time

and space—a being that was old when the morning stars sang together, and, when the last of us has been gathered unto his fathers,
will still be young.[42]

Note the patriarchal language ("his fathers") in Leopold's last sentence,
but also note that, like the ancient Greek mythographers, Leopold acknowledges a much older—and perennially younger—abiding Being, for
whom we and our fathers are but a fleeting dream.

3 Environmental Attitudes and Values in South Asian Intellectual Traditions

HINDUISM

Elinor Gadon undertook her monumental study of "the female image—what it means in traditional cultures and in the work of contemporary women artists" after a visit to India. There "the feminine was celebrated everywhere in sensuous images of great power." Nevertheless, Gadon sadly reports, while "the worship of the Goddess never died out among the common people and was reabsorbed into evolving Hinduism in the first millennium, the culture [of India] continues to be patriarchal and the status of women inferior to that of men."[1]

In sharp contrast to Islam—which is of relatively recent origin, as global religions go—the origins of Hinduism reach into that dim twilight zone between prehistory and history. Also in sharp contrast to Islam—which is self-contained and doctrinally well defined—Hinduism is so varied, both classically and in its eventual modern forms, that it resists facile doctrinal definition. Further, unlike Islam—an aggressive, colonizing religion (similar in this respect to Christianity) which has converted much of Africa and Central, South, and Southeast Asia to its creed—Hinduism remains largely an indigenous religious tradition. Nonetheless, its subtle and seductive metaphysical ideas have found their way into many of the world's most sophisticated philosophical systems, among them post-Kantian German voluntarism and American transcendentalism.[2]

Roughly contemporary with the Greek epics of Homer and Hesiod is the period of Vedic literature in India. (The word *veda* means "sacred knowledge.") The four collections of Vedas—the *Rig-Veda, Sama-Veda, Yajur-Veda*, and *Atharva-Veda*—were composed by the Aryan invaders of India. The polytheism we find in them has clear affinities with the polytheism of the Greeks, who were from the same Indo-European linguistic, cultural,

44

and racial stock. The gods manifested—and were identified with—features, forces, and processes of nature: sky, wind, thunder, and so on. They were propitiated with animal sacrifices, entreated with prayer, and commanded by magical incantations. Among the Greeks, such religious functions remained in secular hands. Agamemnon (notoriously) and the other political and military leaders commemorated by Homer performed their own sacrifices and otherwise interacted personally with the gods. In the first book of Plato's *Republic*, Cephalus, a wealthy citizen of the Piraeus, exits with the remark that he must go and attend to the family sacrifices, a casual indication that a similar entrepreneurial religious climate prevailed down to the Greek high classical period. In India, by contrast, a Brahmin caste of priests gradually arose who alone could perform public religious functions (although, to be sure, private sacrifices and prayers remained the prerogative of heads of households). In any case, the Brahmins grew powerful and eventually became India's highest caste.[3]

Another distinctive feature of early Hindu religious practice was the use of *soma*, a narcotic beverage that induced hallucinations and religious ecstasy. A Greek analogue to this practice may be found in the Dionysian orgies and in the other "mysteries," of which the Eleusinian are the most renowned.[4]

As the role of the Brahmins increased in importance, a secondary literature, the Brahmanas, became attached to each of the Vedas. The Brahmanas are, in effect, handbooks of priestcraft. They supply detailed instructions for the conduct of sacrifices, and they explain the meaning and "logic" of the efficacious rites accompanying the Vedic hymns and prayers. From the Brahmanas it is clear that the rites and associated verbal incantations were thought to have a compulsory power over the gods and therefore, by association, over nature. The Brahmins thus acquired enormous prestige and assumed an ever higher social status in an increasingly stratified society.[5]

Roughly contemporary with the emergence and development of Greek philosophy is the emergence in the Hindu tradition of a more speculative and intellectual system of belief, expressed in the Upanishads—commonly called the Vedanta, or concluding portions of the Vedas. Perhaps because of the earlier belief in the coercive power of the ritual word spoken by Brahmins—an unseen, but active, animate force—Hindu thought during this period gravitated toward speculation about an inner invisible abstract reality underlying the manifest world. Significantly, this reality was called *brahman*, which originally meant prayer, as the Brahmins were the prayer sayers.[6]

Simultaneously, religious practice was changing. The public sacrifices and prayers conducted by the Brahmins continued to be offered, but a religious discipline of withdrawal, asceticism, and contemplation was also growing in popularity. Asceticism might be understood as external sacrifice internalized, and meditation correspondingly understood as the uttered sacred word turned inward. To accommodate this evolution of religious expression, a vigorous distinction between inner and outer forms of reality emerged. *Atman* was a person's inner self. The spiritual realm was of a superior order of reality in comparison to the external world of nature (*prakriti*). A better and holier life could thus be attained by abandoning the body and freeing the soul.[7]

If the soul and body are distinct, then it is possible to imagine the existence of one independent of the other. During this period, unanticipated in the earlier Vedic literature, the allied doctrines of reincarnation and *karma* arose: The soul survives the death of the body, not to be judged by a personal God and thence to enter either Heaven/Paradise or Hell and remain there for eternity, as in the Christian-Islamic complex, but to be reborn again and again. The soul's present and future incarnations are determined by the law of *karma*. The moral quality of one's actions—indeed, the moral quality of one's words and very thoughts—during one's past lives have determined one's station and fate in the present life; and how one lives, speaks, and intends during one's present life will fix one's lot in the next cycle of birth and death. There is no all-seeing, all-powerful, all-just Arbiter of these fates; the "law" of *karma* is as impersonal and implacable as Newton's later law of gravity.

Parallels between these Indian ideas and the doctrines of Pythagoras and his intellectual fellow traveler Plato are too obvious to ignore. They have given rise to speculations about the influence of Indian mysticism on Pythagoras which can be neither definitively confirmed nor refuted.[8]

Also *brahman* and *atman* came to be identified with each other, just as Pythagoras and Plato associated—though they did not, strictly speaking, identify—the soul with the hyperreal Forms or Numbers. For the Greeks, underlying the nature manifest to the senses was an unseen, abstract reality, which was not exactly its soul but was apprehensible only through the innate powers of mind. There is an affinity of the *psyche* for the Numbers or Forms, according to Plato. For the Indian sages, the inner self, or *atman*, was the core reality, or *brahman*, of the human being. Generalizing the human case, *brahman*, the unseen reality of all phenomena, was correspondingly *atman*, or pure consciousness—as one experienced it in one's reflective and contemplative exercises. Objective knowledge and subjective knowledge thus coalesce. To know one's self—not one's personality or empirical self but one's transcendental self—is to know the absolute substance of all things.

More important, to reach one's transcendental self, through meditative consciousness, is to reach the reality underlying all things. If one's true self is none other than *brahman*, or absolute reality, the palpable realization of that fact might free one from the cycle of birth and the law of *karma*: If, through discipline, one could reach one's true self, *atman*, then one might merge with the undifferentiated oneness of reality, *brahman*, and thus attain liberation from a fragmented and particular mode of existence—an existence fraught with suffering because it is premised on appearance, not reality.[9]

Comparison of the philosophy of the Upanishads with a major current in Greek philosophy requires entry of an important caveat. The Pythagorean-Platonic philosophy remained essentially dualistic, as noted above, while Indian thought has a strong propensity toward a strict monism. (The Pythagorean-Platonic philosophy may thus more closely resemble the Samkhya system, a minor key in the Hindu intellectual fugue, than it resembles Vedanta, and Jainism more than Hinduism.) If, as Vedanta posits, there is but one changeless and formless reality, we may wonder how there can appear to be a fragmented, differentiated, ever-changing plenum. This was a conundrum to which the Greeks were led by Parmenides, and for which he offered no satisfactory resolution.

In the Upanishads, less bound by the either/or logic fettering Greek thought, the undifferentiated and unmanifest *atman-brahman* is the source and ground of all manifest and differentiated things. Such things, though relatively existent, are not ultimately real. They are *maya*—illusion, or (perhaps better) appearance. That *maya* is the play or sport of *brahman* is one answer to why such a quasi reality as the world disclosed to ordinary consciousness should exist at all.[10]

The Hindu tradition of monism and mysticism, no less than the theism and human supremicism of the Judeo-Christian and Islamic traditions, has ambivalent implications for environmental ethics. Philosophical Hinduism, as it was finally systematized by Sankara in the eighth century C.E., tends to be world-denying. The world, as it is manifested to the senses, is but a beguiling appearance, or an outright illusion. It cannot be fully real as experienced, since it is experienced as an articulate manifold, whereas true reality is one and undifferentiated. Much advanced religious practice aims at the unity of the self with the Self, of *atman* with *brahman*. Through ascetic rigors, physical regimens, and disciplined meditation, the practitioner hopes to achieve a state of consciousness in which all distinctions and differences are merged with the unity of the One-and-Only-True-Being. Upon attaining this goal, one achieves freedom from the wheel of births—final liberation from the world.

Many Westerners are drawn to the Indian and Pythagorean doctrines of reincarnation on first hearing, because reincarnation offers them hope—hope for future lives on earth, rich in fresh experience. Today in the West, growing old is resented, because with age one's appetites become dull and one's energy in the pursuit of happiness flags. Death is regarded as the ultimate evil, because it means an end to the pleasure-filled life of materialistic consumption. "You only go around once," a beer ad used to say, "so grab all the gusto you can"—while you can. Au contraire, Pierre, you can go around again and again, promises the doctrine of reincarnation. But for the ancient Greeks and Indians, the same prospect was profoundly discomfiting. Clearly, for them, this world is a vale of tears. And this life, if not a continual parade of misfortunes—hunger, poverty, slavery, disease, violence—is a continuous state of ennui and lack of satisfaction. (Even the most worldly of wealthy and famous contemporary Western hedonists discovered a truth known to Hindu sages, as he lamented in song, "I can't get no satisfaction.") Add to this disaffection the law of *karma*—which states that the greater the (fleeting and imperfect) satisfactions one does manage to get in this life, the more likely one's next incarnation is to be filled with pain and frustration—and one begins to get a sense of the pessimism at the foundation of the Hindu worldview.

Looked at from the Hindu perspective, therefore, the empirical world is both unimportant, because it is not ultimately real, and contemptible, because it seduces the soul into crediting appearances, pursuing false ends, and thus earning bad *karma*. It distracts the soul from seeking its own true nature and thereby attaining liberation from the empirical world and merging with the essential, transcendental, undifferentiated Being/Consciousness.

However signed, sealed, and delivered the antienvironmentalism of the Hindu tradition may seem, it has been defended as a valuable conceptual resource for a positive and direct environmental ethic. And if the proof of the pudding is in the eating, Hindu thought has in fact grounded and inspired one of the world's most successful environmental uprisings, the Chipko movement in northern India. Chapter 10 provides a detailed account of this movement and its philosophical foundations. Here, the theoretical discussion of Hindu thought as a conceptual resource for environmental ethics is reviewed.

In the early 1970s, the "Environmental Decade," the Hindu apologist

Rajagopal Ryali found an organicism in Hindu thought that may serve as an analogue of the organicism characterizing contemporary ecological thought. According to Ryali, "how an individual as a unit plays a symbolic and a functional role within the context of a wider animate and inanimate world, seems to be the type of question that should interest us presently. The theme of Hinduism viewed on these lines is one of organic solidarity."[11]

Ryali tries to prove his claim that Hinduism posits an organic solidarity between humanity and nature first in terms of the basic Hindu belief in the transmigration of souls—according to which the soul of a human being may once have been, and may once again turn out to be, the soul of an animal. Hence "organic solidarity." Second, in Hindu polytheism the "lesser gods" are manifested in natural forms—the monkey, the snake, the cow, certain trees and grasses. Again, organic solidarity is implied. As Ryali puts it, "through polytheism the Hindu worshipper acknowledged the power of nature and the need for human symbiosis with nature."[12] Third, Ryali finds an organic solidarity in Hinduism's deep-rooted tendency to symbolic mysticism and monistic philosophy. About the latter more will be said in a moment. About symbolic mysticism he writes, "this organic unity is symbolized in Indian art as *mandala* (the wheel). The outer rim of the wheel and its inner hub and the spokes that unite both denote the oneness of *atman-brahman.*"[13] In support of this claim, he quotes Donald Swearer, an American specialist in Theravada Buddhism, who wrote, "The *mandala* is a cosmogram designed basically as a cosmic circle. . . . It epitomizes the Indian view of man in organic relationship with his world—a valorization.'"[14]

The similarities with an ecology-like organic unity provided by the central monistic philosophy of Hinduism was earlier explored by the comparative philosopher Eliot Deutsch. In a 1970 contribution to the infant field of environmental philosophy, before that field even had a name and identity of its own, Deutsch wrote:

> In order for us to work out a proper relationship with nature we must, I think, come to understand and to feel deeply a natural kinship with all life. . . . But what does it mean to affirm continuity between man and the rest of life? Vedanta would maintain that this means the recognition that fundamentally all life is one, that in essence everything is reality, and that this oneness finds its natural expression in a reverence for all things. The term *ahimsa*, of non-injury to all living creatures, is cast in the negative, *a-himsa*, but its import is clearly positive. It calls for a loving care of everything

in nature. It demands that we accept responsibility for being guardians of, as well as participants in, the natural order and balance of things. [15]

Deutsch here clearly and explicitly states an apparent similarity between the core metaphysical ideas of the major current of Indian philosophy, Vedanta, in the Hindu tradition and the metaphysical implications of ecology. On the basis of this similarity, he suggests that an ethical implication of the Vedantic philosophy would be equally an ethical implication of ecology. Philosophical Hinduism and ecology, in other words, portray reality similarly, and thus their environmental ethical implications are equivalent. Hence, those who come from the Hindu tradition, or those who have adopted it, may construct an ecologically resonant environmental ethic from its core concepts. The political scientist O. P. Dwivedi goes so far as to aver that an explicit ecologically grounded environmental ethic existed in Hindu India in the past and was forgotten during the colonial era: "Hindu scriptures revealed a clear conception of the ecosystem. On this basis a discipline of environmental ethics developed which formulated codes of conduct (dharma) and defined humanity's relationship to nature." [16]

In 1973, the distinguished Norwegian philosopher Arne Naess launched the Deep Ecology movement, the environmental philosophy of choice among radical environmentalists. [17] Between then and now, the concept of "Self-realization" has emerged as centrally important to Deep Ecology. [18] As Naess explained, this doctrine was inspired by Hindu metaphysics. Like Eliot Deutsch, Naess finds a similarity between ecology and Vedanta—namely, the oneness of reality:

> As a student and admirer since 1930 of Gandhi's nonviolent direct action, I am inevitably influenced by his metaphysics. . . . Hearing Gandhi's description of his ultimate goal may sound strange to many of us. "What I want to achieve—what I have been striving and pining to achieve these thirty years—is self-realization . . . to attain *moksha* (liberation)." This sounds individualistic to the Western mind, a common misunderstanding. If the self Gandhi is speaking of were the ego or the "narrow" self (*jiva*) of egocentric interest, or narrow ego gratifications, then why work for the poor? For him it is the supreme or universal Self—the *atman*—that is to be realized. . . . Through the wider self, every living being is connected intimately, and from this intimacy follows the capacity for *identification* and its natural consequences, the practice of nonviolence. [19]

Later in the 1970s, the Austrian physicist/philosopher Fritjof Capra found a similarity between the new physics of relativity and quantum theory and an eclectic "Eastern mysticism"—a similarity that he expounded in a best-selling book, *The Tao of Physics*.[20] But there is a significant difference between the oneness of nature posited in ecology and the new physics, on the one hand, and, on the other, the oneness of nature posited in mainstream Hindu philosophy. In both ecology and the new physics, nature is one because of a network of relations. Reciprocal dependencies not only connect but mutually define the parts of nature. In Hindu philosophy, nature is one because all phenomenal things variously manifest a single substantive essence. In ecology, the empirical world is also the actual world; in Hinduism, it is not. In ecology, the various components of nature, although interconnected and mutually defining, remain essentially different from one another; in Hinduism, they are essentially the same. Finally, in ecology, the experience of the oneness of nature is empirical and articulate; in Hinduism, it is homogeneous and oceanic.

To his credit, Naess acknowledges the difference. "The expression 'drops in the stream of life' may be misleading," he writes, "if it implies that the individuality of the drops is lost in the stream. Here is a difficult ridge to walk: To the left we have the ocean of organic and mystic views, to the right the abyss of atomic individualism."[21] Interpreting Naess on this point, the Australian Deep Ecologist Warwick Fox insists that "the realization that we and all other entities are aspects of a single unfolding reality—that 'life is fundamentally one'—does not mean that all multiplicity and diversity is reduced to homogeneous mush."[22]

If the metaphysical equivalence of ecological holism and Hindu monism is superficial at best, will Eliot Deutsch's suggestion that in *ahimsa* we may find an ancient Indian environmental ethic withstand critical scrutiny? We might ask the same question about the Deep Ecological extension of Gandhian nonviolence from our fellow man to our fellow creature. As Deutsch hints, the ethical posture of *ahimsa* is supported by (but may not be dependent on) the central metaphysical concepts of Hindu philosophy. According to Arne Naess, so is Gandhi's philosophy of nonviolence: It is "through the wider self [that] every living being is connected intimately." Since, according to Advaita ("not dualistic") Vedanta, the essential or transcendental self of each person, animal, and plant is the same ("same" in the strongest sense of the word: literally identical with the Self or Being per se in everything else), one is led to empathy and compassion. Other forms of being, particularly other forms of life, are victims of the same deceit, frustration, and suffering as oneself. Unenlightened, they cannot be aware that their suffering is unreal, and should therefore be both pitied and spared. Moreover, one cannot profit at the expense of others—either other human beings or other natural environmental beings—since ultimately there are no "others": all are ephemeral manifestations of one indivisible Being.

This ethical attitude has been fully explored and applied to nature in a modern context by Albert Schweitzer—whose "reverence-for-life ethic" has its roots in Indian soil but is expressed in a vocabulary drawn directly from the eighteenth-century voluntarist philosophy of Arthur Schopenhauer.[23] While Schweitzer's ethic is laudable and certainly preferable to no nature-oriented ethic at all, it is not a perfect fit with an ethic fully informed by ecology. For example, Schweitzer had little sympathy for predators who inflict suffering on their fellow creatures—although Schopenhauer himself, incidentally, saw a complete, if macabre, justice in the Will-to-Live divided against itself.[24] Moreover, an ecologically fitting environmental ethic ideally would make some provision for wholes—species, ecosystems, the global biosphere—while *ahimsa* seems to be confined to individual subjective and protosubjective beings: to other people, animals, and plants, in other words.

Eliot Deutsch has recently provided a more sophisticated and persuasive eco-ethical interpretation of the same core concepts of Hindu metaphysics. He writes,

> the undifferentiated fullness of being—designated as *brahman* or *atman*—is utterly incommensurable with all subject/object, time-bound, spatial multiplicity. . . . Nature then is *maya*. Drawing from Advaita [Vedanta], I argue that rather than undermining the idea of natural reverence, this radical discontinuity provides its surest foundation. Without *maya*, there cannot, I think, be the creative play that is required for a proper man/nature relationship.[25]

Fully realizing the paradoxical cast of his proposition, Deutsch goes on to explain that it is precisely when one becomes detached from nature—in the fullness of the revelation that "*brahman* is real, the world is false, the self is not different from *brahman*"—that one can express "reverence" for it.[26] As one is then no longer caught up in the world—egoistically involved or self-interested in it—one can live disinterestedly in respect to it. One, as it were, consciously participates in the play of *brahman*, and helps to create the world as an artist creates a work of art—not with an eye to one's own advantage but with an eye to the beauty and integrity of the whole wonderful show.

Given the scant cognitive resources in the intertwined strands of the historical Western intellectual tradition for a philosophy and ethic that affirms the unity and solidarity of humanity and nature, Ralph Waldo Emerson and Henry David Thoreau, who were among the first Western thinkers to feel the stirrings of an environmental consciousness and conscience, looked to the wisdom of India for guidance and inspiration. Ever since, it has been assumed that Hindu philosophy offers an attractive, if elusive, alternative to the predominant imperialistic Western concept of the human/nature relationship. On critical examination, however, the protean Hindu intellectual tradition appears as ambiguous about the value of nature and the proper relationship of human beings both to nonhuman natural entities and to nature as a whole as the strands of thought forming the Western intellectual tradition—though, of course, ambiguous in a quite different way.

But if one steps back from the doctrinal details—here assayed for their ecological mettle and environmental purity—one may appreciate a certain grandeur in the Hindu view of life, a grandeur that was not achieved in the West until geology revealed the immense age of our everyday surroundings and Darwin directly united us with the long caravan of extinct biota petrified in the fossil record. Compared with the brassy anthropocentrism of Islam, Christianity, and Judaism, and with the (complementary) geocentrism and humanism of Greek science up to Copernicus, Hinduism affords a distinct and unique perspective on human existence. Each of us has experienced and will experience thousands of personal incarnations, separated by thousands of years and embracing thousands of specific forms of life, before achieving liberation. This belief—and the concept of liberation itself (personal extinction as we unite with undifferentiated Being)—certainly does not encourage people to set themselves up as the measure of truth, goodness, and beauty, or to exaggerate their own importance in relationship to the universe at large, or to feel superior to so-called (in the West) subhuman creatures.

JAINISM

In Jainism, more explicitly than in philosophical Hinduism, one can find the conceptual grounds for and the development of an environmental ethic. However, the Jain environmental ethic, no less than the Vedantic environmental ethic expounded by Deutsch, is not without its special irony.

Historically, Jainism seems to have been founded in the sixth century B.C.E. by Nataputta Vardhamana, who was called Mahavira, or "Great One." He may have developed it from Samkhya thought (eventually written down in the second century C.E.), which itself was based on minor themes of the Upanishads. The Jains believe that Mahavira was only the most recent *jina*, or complete victor over suffering, and was preceded by twenty-three previous victorious ones.

In contrast to the core philosophy of Hinduism, Samkhya is dualistic. Matter is as real as mind; body is as real as soul. Each soul, moreover, maintains its own integrity; it is not a manifestation or a splinter of the universal soul. Every living thing has such a soul, of which there are infinitely many, and each soul is immortal.[27] According to Jain belief, the soul in each living thing is, as it were, crusted over with the grossest of matter, and its consciousness is dimmed and confused with sensory perceptions of various modes and degrees of clarity. Nevertheless, all souls are equally pure and perfect in and of themselves.

In Jainism, the orthodox Hindu doctrines of reincarnation and *karma* are taken for granted. Any taint of desire or passion further clads the soul and causes it to sink deeper into the grosser regions of the cosmos. After each life, the condition of the soul determines its next birth, into either more or less association with the material realm. The purpose of religious practice is to purify the soul and eventually liberate it from karmic bodily matter, however refined and ethereal such matter may be. Obviously, the most direct path to the liberation of the soul from the body is asceticism. Accordingly, the soul must not succumb to appetites of any kind; it must take no account of physical discomforts or privations. In short, it must become utterly indifferent to pleasure and pain—sensations alien to its true, essential nature.

Mahavira exhibited such asceticism and mortification of the flesh in the extreme. He lived outdoors and went about completely naked. Unclothed and unsheltered, he endured heat and cold, rain and wind. He did not wash, nor did he clean his teeth. He eschewed the pleasures of human society, even refusing to salute passersby—for which offense he was often verbally reviled and sometimes physically abused. He slept hardly at all.

Equal in importance to ascetic rigors, and at the moral core of Jainism, is *ahimsa*, the determination not to kill or harm any living being, since each contains a soul as perfect and complete as one's own and each is as capable of suffering as oneself. Given what has been said, this is hard to understand. For if concern with pleasure and pain and various physical fates only mires the soul in matter and adds to its karmic debt, then inflicting pain on or killing other living beings should be a matter of no concern. Their *souls* are not injured thereby; and if their souls are enlightened, injury to their bodies will only provide them with an occasion for ascetic indifference and karmic credit.

But only human souls in the human condition may be so enlightened.

According to Christopher Chapple, a scholar of Indian religions, the state of being human

> is the only state in which the living being (*jiva*) can be freed from the bondage of action (*karma*). For the Jainas, *karma* is a physical entity, a viscous mass that adheres to the *jiva* and causes attachment and suffering. The average person is filled with *karma*, which obstructs one's true nature of infinite knowledge, bliss, and energy. The influx (*samvara*) of new *karma* must cease if a person is to achieve the pinnacle of all life, the state of liberation . . . wherein there is no more attachment to passion and impurity.[28]

Thus the necessity of *ahimsa* might be understood as follows: Other-than-human beings cannot know these truths and thus cannot resolve to achieve victory over pleasure and pain. According to a Jain sutra, "All beings are fond of life; they like pleasure and hate pain, shun destruction and like to live. To all, life is dear."[29] They don't know any better. One ought not to cause an ineducable soul to suffer. We ought to be compassionate. Besides, and most important, if one injures another living being, one accumulates bad *karma* of one's own.

In any case, *ahimsa* is of extreme importance, and Mahavira also practiced it, too, in the extreme. He ate only the leftover food that had been prepared for someone else—which he first examined in order to remove any small creatures it may have attracted while sitting around. He strained his water, for the same reason. He swept his path clear of insects and worms, lest he inadvertently step on something alive. He even refused to swat biting insects—flies, lice, fleas, mosquitoes—thus (to employ a totally inappropriate metaphor) killing two birds with one stone: that is, he practiced ascetic indifference and *ahimsa* at the same time.

In descriptions of Albert Schweitzer's practice of the "reverence-for-life" environmental ethic, we can see the influence of Jain-style *ahimsa*. For example, Schweitzer was accustomed to removing earthworms that were washed onto his walkway by a ground-soaking rain. The focus of *ahimsa*, once more, is on individual living things, not wholes, and such an environmental ethic therefore makes for an imperfect fit with ecological concerns.

But the irony of a Jain-based environmental ethic runs deeper. Of all the religious worldviews to which India has given birth, Jainism seems to be the most uncompromisingly world-denying. The physical world is real, to be sure; indeed, it is all too real. It ensnares and encrusts the soul, robbing it of its purity of consciousness, clarity of mind, and fullness of knowledge. Worse, association with the physical world condemns the soul to the tread-

mill of rebirth governed by the law of *karma*. To free the soul from contamination by the physical and from the wheel of birth, and to endure forever in immaterial purity, clarity, and knowledge, is the goal of the Jain.
The practice of *ahimsa*, thus, is motivated less by a Jain's concern for other
souls for their own sakes—let alone for living beings per se—and more by
a concern for eventual personal liberation. The Jain Acaranga Sutra states
the need for *ahimsa* as follows:

> Injurious activities inspired by self-interest lead to evil and dark-
> ness. This is what is called bondage, delusion, death, and hell. To
> do harm to others is to do harm to oneself. . . . We corrupt our-
> selves as soon as we intend to corrupt others. We kill ourselves as
> soon as we intend to kill others.[30]

As Christopher Chapple puts it, "given its *telos*, this religious tradition
may seem utterly otherworldly and simply incapable of addressing the issue of environmental destruction."[31] But there is a dialectic of irony here.
Whatever the rationale, as Chapple points out, the Jains have been at the
forefront of animal-welfare issues in India and are the foremost advocates
of vegetarianism in a country noted for its moral dietary.[32] Environmental
ethics is not the same as animal-welfare ethics.[33] But vegetarianism is certainly ecologically advisable, because raising domestic animals and then
eating them uses much more land and water than would raising fruit,
grains, legumes, and greens for human consumption. A vegetarian human
population allows more lebensraum for forests, native grasslands, and
wildlife.

Similarly, the otherworldliness of the Jains and their asceticism leads
them to practice a life of low material consumption. The most rigorous and
devoted Jains live without any material possessions whatever, not even
clothing. These Jain *munis*, or holy men, represent an ideal, a model of
right livelihood, for all Jains. Certainly, the practice of Jainism—no matter
that the rationale is purely ego-spiritual—is entirely consonant with an
environmental ethic. When Christopher Chapple "inquired as to whether
the Jaina religion is responding to the current ecological crisis," Acharya
Tulsi, the head of the Terapanthi Svetambara Jain sect,

> spoke not of political or legislative action (though I did ask him
> about such matters) but rather referred to his own life-style. . . .
> In a very direct way he was showing me the most radical form of
> ecological life-style. No automobile. No house. Few clothes. *Apari-
> graha*, one of the five requirements for Jain living, eschews attach-
> ment to anything.[34]

In 1991, at the behest of the Jains, the putative birthday of Mahavira—March 28—was proclaimed the first annual Ahimsa Day in the Indian state of Maharashtra.[35] To supplement the Jain *ahimsa* tradition of feeding sick and old animals and providing hospitals and homes for them, Ahimsa Day launched a campaign for tree planting and environmentally correct living. Concern for the welfare of other living beings plus a contempt for material possessions, comforts, and luxuries lead (in practice, at any rate) to an indisputable Jain environmental ethic.

Jain leaders are currently bidding for an environmental ethical leadership role for their religious worldview, not only in India but throughout the world. L. M. Singhvi, the author of *The Jain Declaration on Nature*, argues that *ahimsa* "is nothing but environmentalism."[36] He also points out that "the ancient Jain scriptural aphorism *Parasparopagraho jivanam* (All life is bound together by mutual support and interdependence) is refreshingly contemporary in its premise and perspective." And he claims that "Jain cosmology recognizes the fundamental natural phenomena of symbiosis or mutual dependence which forms the basis of the modern-day science of ecology."[37]

BUDDHISM

Buddhism is, if anything, more difficult to characterize definitively than Hinduism. Hinduism's beginnings reach beyond the historical horizon of identifiable individual founders, if any there were, and its tenets changed and evolved over many centuries. But it remains a largely indigenous religious belief system. By contrast, while the life and teachings of Buddhism's founder—Siddhartha Gautama, the Buddha, or "Enlightened One"—are discernible with some clarity, over the centuries Buddhism spread and adapted to its several foster cultures, dying out in its mother country, the valley of the Ganges, after seeding itself in lands far from its place of origin. In the new environs in which it took root, Buddhism was nourished by the local intellectual air and flowered into several disparate systems of thought. The purity of the Buddha's original (and very abstract and subtle) philosophy is best preserved in Theravada Buddhism, which found a permanent abode in Sri Lanka. Explored in this chapter are the environmental attitudes of this native Indian worldview in its ancient original, and more southerly eventual, forms; a subsequent chapter treats its northern and eastern siblings.

Siddhartha Gautama, the Buddha-to-be, was born to aristocratic parents in the sixth century B.C.E. But he had a more religious than princely nature, and left the comfort and opulence of his father's demesne to seek his salvation from sorrow and frustration—from the *dukkha*-ridden world, in short—as a mendicant. He sought guidance from practitioners of the two major religious alternatives in his region of India—Hindu Brahmins and Jain ascetics.[38]

Siddhartha tried meditation, only to come to doubt the existence of *atman-brahman*. A major philosophical difference between Theravada Buddhism and the Vedanta legacy remains centered on the issue of ultimate reality. The Buddha professed the doctrine of *anatman*—that there is no substantive immaterial self—first of all. There is no soul-substance. Rather, as in modern phenomenalism, the self is a series of conscious states, one giving rise to the next. And second, there is (analogously) no universal and undifferentiated reality underlying the dynamic manyness of *maya*.[39] At the core of all phenomenal things lies *sunyata*—emptiness.

Next Siddhartha tried the rigors of extreme asceticism—almost killing himself in the process—again with negative results. In opposition to the ascetic excesses to which Jainism is liable, a central teaching of the Buddha is the Middle Path. The vulgar majority, if given the chance, would follow the path at one extreme—the pleasures of sensual self-indulgence. But the opposite extreme is no less destructive of body, mind, and estate—if not of character—and is equally unrewarding in the quest for enlightenment and *nirvana*. The Middle Path, a moderate life no more given to extremes of physical self-denial than to extremes of physical self-indulgence, provides one with the equanimity of body and mind necessary to seriously pursue enlightenment and freedom.

The young Siddhartha's legendary epic quest dramatizes the fact that the tenets of Buddhism are dialectically related to those of mystical-monistic Hinduism and dualistic Jainism. Buddhism may be understood, in part, as a deconstruction of the core concepts of both.[40]

At its point of departure, Buddhism is no less pessimistic, world-denying, and, verily, life-loathing than the other leading philosophies of its time and place. The young man who was destined to become the Buddha left home in search of salvation—but not from death and annihilation, from which it is assumed in the West that one naturally seeks "salvation." Quite the contrary, annihilation—freedom from the wheel of rebirth—was the very thing for which he strove, and with which he was finally rewarded. Ordinary life was the evil from which he sought relief.[41] Indeed, the world denial implicit in Gautama's evaluation of life (as it is given to our experience) seems more profound than anything so far considered. The first of Buddhism's Four Noble Truths is the noble truth of suffering: "Birth is suffering; decay is suffering; illness is suffering; death is suffering; the presence of objects we hate is suffering; the absence of objects we love is suffering; not to obtain what we desire is suffering."[42]

From the point of view of a search for conceptual sources of indigenous environmental ethics, this is not a very promising beginning. The central facts of organic life: birth, growth, age, sickness, and death—with no prospect other than starting the moribund process over again—are simply assumed to be horrifying. In the received biography of the Buddha, we are told that his father tried to hide these facts from him—unsuccessfully, as it turned out—so that he would not go over the top in seeking somehow to escape them.[43] To Siddhartha, no less than to Parmenides and Plato, change itself seemed distressing. Life is, if nothing else, change; and change—becoming and passing away—is only quasi being. In a world infected with change, there is no good thing that one can have and hold.

At the heart of the Enlightened One's enlightenment is the realization that desire itself is the only pole of *dukkha*—suffering—over which one can exercise control. The phenomenal world will roll on, one state giving rise to the next, things coming and things going, no matter what. The reason for his lack of success in finding release from the world, the Buddha discovered, was that he had only shifted his craving from obviously unsatisfying ephemeral *phenomena* to one or another speculative, transcendent *noumena*: self-realization and merger with *brahman*, or freeing the soul from its besmirching *karma*-woven bodily cladding. Setting aside the very real possibility that these might be mere figments of the perfervid religious imagination, desiring even the noumena also led to frustration and dissatisfaction—to *dukkha*.

As an ascetic, Siddhartha had simply exchanged one sort of desire, the desire for the comfort and the pleasure of the body, for another sort— the desire for the freedom, perfection, and wisdom of the soul. But the latter desire, while perhaps less vulgar than the former, was desire nonetheless and led inevitably to its own distinct, and perhaps even more abject, dissatisfaction and suffering. The key to salvation, therefore, is to extinguish all desire—the desire for wisdom, for purity, even for salvation itself, no less than the commonplace desires for comfort and pleasure. This insight was accompanied by a melting away of all desire per se. The condition of *dukkha* was replaced by a condition of rest, peace, radiant joy, loving kindness, and illumination.

The second of Buddhism's Four Noble Truths is the noble truth of the cause of suffering: It is "thirst, that leads to rebirth, accompanied by pleasure and lust, finding its delight here and there . . . . namely thirst for pleasure, thirst for existence, thirst for prosperity."[44] One may achieve liberation only through extinguishing desire itself. The third of the Four Noble Truths is the noble truth of cessation of suffering: "the complete cessation of . . . thirst—a cessation that consists in the absence of every passion—with the abandoning of this thirst, with the doing away with it, with the deliverance from it, with the destruction of desire."[45]

Just as Siddhartha seems simply to have accepted without question the world-denying climate of religious opinion into which he was born, he also seems to have accepted without question the ambient belief in reincarnation and *karma*, thereby creating a sticky metaphysical wicket for himself. For if there is no *atman*, then what accumulates *karma* and reincarnates?

"Nothing!" is the answer. What passes over from one life to the next is, actually, no more difficult a problem for the phenomenalist than the problem of what binds the moments of phenomena that one calls one's present life into a coherent whole—into something that one can call one's "self." There is no soul-substance of which our several experiences are states or modes. Rather, each new phenomenal moment in one's life exists without a substrate; but it arises conditioned (*pratityasamutpada*) nonetheless by its predecessors in the series. Personal experience, after all, is not random; it is orderly and "causally" (though not necessarily in the mechanical sense) integrated. So we may think of personal death and reincarnation as the end of one such series and the beginning of another—which at its beginning certainly, and in its entirety, is conditioned by the character of the foregoing series. Hence one's next life is one's own, not someone else's; nor is it an entirely new life, since it is conditioned by one's present life, no less than one's present life's future is conditioned by one's present life's past. A Buddhist metaphor for understanding what "passes over" from one life to the next is the transference of a flame from one lamp to another: The newly kindled flame arises directly from the other, but it is not substantively the same. And it arises from just this lamp and not from some other.

The difference, of course, is that the phenomena of one's present life are also united by memory. And in the absence of memory "passing over" and linking the several series connected by *pratityasamutpada*, it is difficult to see why one in the midst of *this* series should be concerned with what the nature of a future series might be. It is all too clear that what each of us does affects the lives of others—sometimes profoundly. One's experiences may be serially dependent, arising one from the other, but it is also true that someone else's experiences may be causally conditioned by one's own, and vice versa. If one thinks through the Buddhist interpretation of reincarnation and the law of *karma*, it is possible that one may be as indifferent about the effects of one's present behavior on one's "own" future life as about the effects of one's present behavior on someone else's present life. Thus the retributive justice at the heart of the law of *karma* may be blunted by Buddhism's uncompromising antisubstantialism. The motive for a moral existence, in other words, seems to be sympathy—sympathy for the virtual subject of a future series of phenomena—rather than prudent concern for oneself. But one might just as well regard that motive as a moral asset, in comparison with the egocentric Jain conception of *karma*, Buddhism's metaphysical and moral antithesis.

Classical Buddhism's point of departure may be abjectly world-denying, but its point of arrival is not so at all. True, once one has overcome desire, one's *karma* is shut down, and one is released from the doleful wheel of rebirth. Like the flame of a lamp that does not ignite another, one is extinguished without further issue. But what is the quality and character of life while still living one's last life after enlightenment?

It is *nirvana*.[46] Such a conception of *nirvana*, notice, involves no otherworldliness: no ascension of the soul from the physical plane, as in Jainism; and no merging—during deep meditation and after death—with featureless Reality, as in Vedanta. The world we experience is the real world—or, at least, the only world. One continues to live in it as before. But one is not caught up in its ebb and flow by desire of this and dread of that. One remains disinterested and impassive. But that leaves one in nearly the same state described by Eliot Deutsch, as quoted in an earlier section of this chapter: One's life, then, may have the quality of play and/or a work of art.

A difference may be that in the case of Buddhist enlightenment one's posture is more passive. One is, as it were, the beholder, the appreciator, rather than the cocreator, of the whole wonderful show—as one who is not an interested bit player may now call it.

This difference between the Vedantic disinterested artist and the Buddhist disinterested spectator—experiencing the world as *maya*, and experiencing the world as a series of ultimately real but insubstantial phenomena, respectively—should not be overdrawn. The Buddha, after all, did not keep his wisdom to himself. He shared it with others. He led an active life—in other words, a creative life. Moreover, his teachings were as richly ethical as they were subtly metaphysical. At the center of his ethical principles lay an all-embracing goodwill—flowing perhaps from the pure joy attending the release from desire-created *dukkha*—which extended not only to human beings but to all living beings.[47]

David J. Kalupahana, a contemporary Buddhist philosopher reflecting on Buddhist implications for environmental ethics, remarks that Buddhism does not presuppose the sharp dichotomy between human life and nature used by others to make the latter an absolutely irresistible force which human beings have to contend with, or an external object created for their pleasure or enjoyment. . . . The human being [is n]either a hapless object [n]or the epicenter of the universe. A human being is a part of nature. Like everything else in the teeming and dramatic richness of nature, he is dependently arisen or causally conditioned. He comes into being depending upon various conditions, contributes his share to the drama, and makes his exit.[48]

Buddhism is not only resolutely this-worldly, it is in the last analysis world-affirming rather than world-denying. After attaining enlightenment—by understanding the cause of suffering and then extinguishing the desire that is its cause—one enters *nirvana*. But *nirvana* is not heaven, not some place or state of mind other than the ordinary world and the ordinary consciousness of it—minus craving. Of course, that is a big minus. First, the absence of craving clarifies one's apprehension of reality, because one's perception of things is not distorted by desire and aversion. And second, more obviously, the subtraction of craving reorganizes one's values. Everything becomes of equal value—a most important point, as Kalupahana hints, from the environmental perspective. In the absence of interestedness, economically "valuable" plants, animals, and other "resources" are not necessarily good; "weeds," "pests," "vermin," "varmints," "trash" species, and "marginal" lands are not necessarily bad; and the many "useless" creatures and landscapes "filling out" the rest of nature are not axiologically irrelevant. In calling such a state of disinterested objectivity "*nirvana*," the Buddha implied that it is—though lacking *dukkha*-making passion—a joyous, even ecstatic way to be in and relate to the world.

The comparative philosopher David E. Shaner, specifically addressing the environmental attitudes implicit in Buddhism, is even more emphatic than Kalupahana:

Buddhism is *not* world-denying. . . . Suffering . . . defines the perspective of those whose perception of nature is clouded by desires. . . . The nondiscriminating mind can engage in intersubjective experience with nature. . . . One loves nature more fully by participating in an intimate experience with the phenomenal world itself. In general, when the Buddhists speak of detachment, it must be interpreted not in the context of denying the phenomenal world of nature but in the context of detaching oneself from one's own striving for permanence in a changing world. . . . When one is freed from permanence, one enters fully into the process of becoming within nature's context.[49]

The observations of Ienaga Saburo, a contemporary Japanese historian of ideas, counterbalance Shaner's categorical claims and temper his apologetic verve. In attempting to understand the twelfth-century Japanese poet Saigyo's religious involvement with nature, Ienaga simply assumes that even Japanese Buddhism, let alone the earlier Indian Buddhism, was essentially world-denying. He writes,

> Especially for priests or novices who, through their Buddhist faith, were in the process of bringing to completion their own deliverance from the world's bonds of suffering and illusion now to be drawn into nature's captivating beauty was something that gave rise to a type of very strange contradiction.[50]

Such a monk was Saigyo, who wrote the following telling lines: "Why do I, who broke / So completely with this world, / Find in my body / Still the pulsing of a heart / Once dyed in blossom's hues?"[51] Saigyo, Ienaga continues,

> did not try, on account of his Buddhism, forcibly to dispose of his "flower-and-moon-enchanted" sensibility. On the contrary, it is as though his real peace or tranquility is one which is gained not through Buddhist austerities but by going all the way with his "blossom-dyed" heart.

As one can see, the environmental ethical implications of classical Buddhism are not without ambiguity, although they are perhaps less ambiguous than the other principal cognitive complexes native to South Asia. Of this much one may be confident: The presence, the givenness, of nature characteristic of Buddhism resonates well with the scientific realism of contemporary environmentalism. Nature is not mere appearance or illusion in contradistinction to some other transcendent reality. Further, Buddhism, here mapping well onto ecology, discloses a unity in nature that nevertheless respects genuine diversity and multiplicity. In its stress on process and the affirmation of change (after having extinguished one's initial longing for permanence) Buddhism, moreover, has something of value to teach contemporary environmentalists, who are just beginning to come to terms with the necessity of adding a fourth dimension—evolutionary, climatic, successional, seasonal, and stochastic change—to a working definition of the integrity, stability, and beauty of natural environments.

On the other hand, Buddhism seems to condemn, as the root of all suffering, the very thing that (at least psychologically) drives evolutionary and ecological processes. Heraclitus berated Homer for wishing for the end of war, because in so doing he (Homer) was wishing for the end of the world; in Heraclitus's view, "war is the father and king of all." Similarly, the Buddhist wish for the extinguishment of desire may also be a wish for the end of the world—the organic world, at any rate, if not the cosmos. Desire is what moves animals. Nature implants desire in each living being with good reason. Even plants have unconscious conations, which move them to strive for a place in the sun and a rootage in the soil. Without "thirst," organisms would not strive to survive and reproduce.

But maybe Buddhism could be interpreted, in the spirit of its original dialectical subtlety, so as not to condemn desire per se. Do animals experience *dukkha*, as well as simply suffering? That is, do they *self*-consciously suffer as well as experience simple appetites and pleasure and pain in their satisfactions and frustrations? Do they size up the world in relation to their interests, thus not only evaluating it but misapprehending it?[52] Walt Whitman, for one, did not think so:

I think I could turn and live with animals, they are so placid and self-
    contain'd,
I stand and look at them long and long.
They do not sweat and whine about their condition,
They do not lie awake in the dark and weep for their sins,
They do not make me sick discussing their duty to God,
Not one is dissatisfied, not one is demented with the mania for owning
    things,
Not one kneels to another, nor to his kind that lived thousands of
    years ago,
Not one is respectable or unhappy over the whole earth.[53]

If this portrait of animal consciousness is correct in principle, then desire alone is not sufficient to produce *dukkha*, since animals experience the former without the latter. Upon this consideration, the importance of the realization of nonself in Buddhism is thrust to the fore. For it seems that only desire plus self-consciousness equals egocentrism equals *dukkha*. If this interpretation is defensible—and some of the environmentally sensitive contemporary apologists for Buddhism seem to take this tack—then Buddhism would provide an exact counterpart to the antianthropocentrism of contemporary Western environmental philosophy.

In his study of *ahimsa* in South Asian traditions of thought, Christopher Chapple points out that this moral concept, though original with the Jains, has also long been a cornerstone of Buddhist ethics.[54] And like Jain leaders, some contemporary Buddhists have assumed intellectual and spiritual leadership in the development of global environmental ethics—perhaps most notably the Dalai Lama, who is one of the world's foremost environmentalists. In 1985, the Buddhist environmental activist Nancy Nash launched the Buddhist Perception of Nature Project, a massive scholarly effort to extract and collate the many environmentally relevant passages from Buddhist scriptures and secondary literature and thus demonstrate the relevance of Buddhism to contemporary environmental concerns, and also to raise the level of environmental consciousness and conscience in Buddhist monasteries, schools, colleges, and other institutions.[55] Bhikku Bodhi, a contemporary Buddhist environmental philosopher, provides a succinct summary of what Buddhism might contribute to the development of environmental ethics:

> With its philosophic insight into the interconnectedness and thoroughgoing interdependence of all conditioned things, with its thesis that happiness is to be found through the restraint of desire, with its goal of enlightenment through renunciation and contemplation and its ethic of noninjury and boundless loving-kindness for all beings, Buddhism provides all the essential elements for a relationship to the natural world characterized by respect, care, and compassion.[56]

CONCLUSION

What can be said, in summary, about the potential of South Asian intellectual traditions to fund the development of indigenous environmental ethics and to amplify the tidal wave of an emerging global ecological awareness? There is something to be said, from an environmental point of view, even for the world-denying proclivity universally evident in South Asian thought from the Axial Age. The tendency to regard existence in this world as a problem to be solved not by changing the world but by transcending it would hardly inspire the development of an aggressive technology meant to remodel nature to suit human specifications. Further, the contempt, typical of such an attitude, for worldly possessions encourages an environmentally laudable life-style of low consumption of natural resources and energy.

But beyond this rather negative recommendation, South Asian transcendentalism opens universal horizons for human consciousness. In comparison with the West, there is refreshingly less preoccupation with strictly human affairs and less focus on individual human salvation. From an Indian point of view, we are all in the same predicament—not only all we human beings but all other living beings as well. (And for the Hindus at least, the predicament is literally—not in the sense of "similar" but in the sense of "identical"—the same.) A solidarity between human beings and nature leading to sympathy for other creatures, to compassion—that is, to *ahimsa*—is implied. And while *ahimsa* may not be all that we would want in an environmental ethic, limited as it is to individual sentient beings (or perhaps, if we stretch, to conative ones), certainly it represents an advance beyond egocentrism and anthropocentrism. There is also discernible a transcendence of another kind in the dialectical exfoliation of South Asian assumptions—a transcendence of pessimism, a movement from world denial to world affirmation. The Vedantic notion of *maya* as the play of *brahman* and the Buddhist equation of *nirvana* and *samsara* are distinctly world-affirming, not world-denying, ideas.

4   Traditional East Asian Deep Ecology

67 – 86

Chap. 5 87 – 108

TAOISM

Contemporary Western environmental ethicists scouring Eastern traditions of thought for ecologically resonant ideas and environmentally oriented philosophies of living have been drawn chiefly to Taoism. Deep Ecology's spokesperson, George Sessions, has labeled John Muir—a spiritual progenitor of the American environmental movement—"the Taoist of the West"; and a major new biography of Muir, titled *The Pathless Way*, further evokes the associations between Taoism and Muir.[2]

Environmentalists urge us to cultivate a closer "harmony with nature," and to "follow nature" in pursuing our own ends. Taoism, similarly, draws its inspiration from nature untransformed and untrammeled by the works of man.[3] The Australian environmental philosophers Richard Sylvan and David Bennett have recently drawn a detailed comparison between Taoism and Deep Ecology. In their view, "Taoism is throughout ecologically oriented; a high level of ecological consciousness is built into it, and it provides the practical basis for a way of life whose main tenet is 'Follow Nature.'"[4] Moreover, the classical Taoists, like contemporary environmentalists, were vaguely antiurban, antihumanistic, and antibureaucratic. In the argot of contemporary environmentalism, they were "bioregionalists." Indeed the *Tao te ching* goes even further:

> Reduce the size and population of the state. Ensure that even
> though the people have . . . ships and carts, they will have no use
> for them. Bring it about that the people . . . will find relish in their
> food and beauty in their clothes, will be content in their abode, and
> happy in the way they live. Though adjoining states are within
> sight of one another, and the sound of dogs barking and cocks

crowing in one state can be heard in another, yet the people of one state will grow old and die without having any dealings with those of another.[5]

The idea that one might find a personal reward in so close an identity with a particular habitat and in cultivating a harmony with nature, and that one can accomplish one's own ends with ease and grace only if one attunes oneself to nature are among the cardinal practical principles of Taoist philosophy. Taoism jibes well even with contemporary feminist environmental thought, as will be more fully explained a little farther on.

The concept of "harmony with nature" is a much bruited, but little explored, modern environmental metaphor, and the suggestion that we "follow nature" is, on analysis, ambiguous and paradoxical advice:[6] Everything that one does is natural—in the sense that one cannot violate the laws of nature. On the other hand, everything that one does is unnatural—if "natural" means "that which is not wrought by man." The Taoist world is not dualistic, and Taoism's abnegation of dualism includes the human/nature dualism assumed in the admonition to "follow nature." Still, even within Taoism the paradox can be formulated: Human beings, all too apparently, may live in discord with nature rather than in harmony with it. Distinguishing between the constant *tao* ("the unconditioned . . . the all-pervading, the ineffable") and the natural *tao* ("the underlying principles of natural change"), the comparativist Roger T. Ames at once states the paradox and resolves it:

> The constant *tao* must account for the human maverick which is very capable of living in discord with the natural *tao*. That is to say, the constant *tao*/natural *tao* distinction is necessary in order to accommodate conduct on the part of man which is inconsistent with and an exception to the natural *tao*, but which does not go beyond [since nothing can] the parameters of the constant *tao*.[7]

A comparative study of the contemporary environmental ideal of "harmony with nature" and the advice to "follow nature" with their classical Taoist antecedents could, as this brief discussion hints, be mutually illuminating and enriching.

The Chinese word *tao* means, literally, a "way" or a "road." The metaphorical concept of the Tao, the Way of things—the Way of heaven and earth—is immemorial in Chinese thought. The world in which we find ourselves is evidently orderly and harmonious. The diurnal, monthly, and annual motions of the heavenly bodies; the cycle of the seasons; the rhythm of rainy and fair weather; the growth, reproduction, and death of plants and animals—all these things bespeak a cyclic coherency in diversity. The coherency in the dovetailing diversity of the cosmos is the ("natural") Tao. But the Tao is both *what there is* and *how it is*. The law or governing principle of nature is not separate from nature itself.

The cyclical nature of the Way is of particular interest to contemporary environmentalists, because ecology also discloses cyclical and reciprocal processes in nature. In addition to cyclical global processes—such as the carbon, oxygen, nitrogen, and hydrologic cycles—nutrients cycle within ecosystems, and wildlife populations exhibit tidelike cycles of expansion and contraction, to mention only a couple of examples. As the comparative philosopher D. C. Lau comments, "the movement of the *tao* is described as 'turning back.' This is usually interpreted as meaning that the *tao* causes all things to undergo a process of cyclic change."[8] Thus if the Tao is cyclical and we implement the Tao in our human activities, then human technologies might be designed to take this principle into account. Environmentalists promote "recycling" as much for symbolic as for practical reasons— as a gesture, quite in keeping with the spirit of Taoism, to tune the human microcosm to the ecosystemic macrocosm.

It is important, given the preceding discussion of South Asian mystical monism and the Western tendency to lump Eastern traditions of thought into a monolithic "Oriental wisdom," carefully and decisively to distinguish the Tao from *atman-brahman*. The latter is a static, immaterial, undifferentiated essence or substance. It lies hidden in each thing without exception. And it is the self-same, the identical reality in all. Genuine diversity, plurality, and change are illusory or at best only apparent. The Tao has none of these characteristics. Even the pedestrian starting point is different. Manifest nature to the Chinese experience is less a set of entities undergoing generation and corruption (with a stress on the latter, in the Indian worldview) than a mix of self-grounded processes. Change, thus, is not illusory. On the contrary, it is a fundamental, not to say essential, feature of reality. The Tao is, as it were, the coordinated direction of diverse, multifarious natural processes.

It is equally important, given the preceding discussion of Greco-modern natural philosophy and the human tendency to conflate foreign concepts with familiar ones, carefully and decisively to distinguish the Tao from the Logos of Heraclitus, the Forms of Plato, and from all the other precursors of the concept of the Laws of Nature in modern Western science. In Plato's vivid and archetypal Western metaphysics, matter is a plastic "female" substance on which form or order is imposed. The Platonic Forms and the Newtonian "laws of nature" preexist as abstract, eternal structural principles that discipline a recalcitrant, material flux. David L. Hall and Roger T. Ames, following Alfred North Whitehead, have styled this classically

Western understanding of natural order "logical" and "transcendent."[9] By contrast, the classical Chinese understanding of order tends toward the "aesthetic" or "emergent." Order builds from the bottom up, rather than coming from the top down. And it arises from the mutual adjustment of the many natural forces and processes, among which conflicts and tensions are resolved and accommodations worked out to achieve a synergistic whole.

Imagine cooking a stew. The Western concept of order is like preparing it from a recipe. A certain Stew-universal or Form—let's say Hungarian goulash—calls for such and such ingredients, in measured proportions, cooked at a set temperature, for just so long. One finds the recipe in a cookbook. It exists there in a changeless and abstract state. One draws up a grocery list and goes to the supermarket and buys the ingredients. Finally, one assembles the ingredients according to the specifications of the recipe.

The Chinese concept of order is rather like cooking a stew in the following way. One collects seasonally available vegetables and herbs and perhaps a little fresh local seafood—the catch of the day. One begins not with a recipe but with the particulars that happen to be at hand, considering not only their generic characteristics but the idiosyncrasies of each. Perhaps the carrot is a bit overgrown—tough but tasty; the bok choy, inadvertently left out of yesterday's stir-fry, a bit wilted; the potatoes new and very crisp; and so on. One cuts, boils, and tries; one decides to add a little of this and more of that; one turns up the flame a little and then, finding it too high, turns it down—until the blend is just right. If it is done well, the flavor of each of the components is present in its insistent particularity, but complemented—and complimented—by all the others. Each ingredient is enhanced by virtue of its relationship to the others. The whole is a harmony, not just an aggregate.[10]

Imagine next the combined flow of water down a broad hillside after a rain. There are many rivulets and freshets. Each follows a different path, but all flow—time is the cosmic analogue here—in a single general direction. Currents run together, joining forces. They do not conflict with or cancel one another. There is a gathering force or power, which is inherent in the process itself. There is harmony in the whole, but with no composer and no conductor. Such is the Tao—not the water, nor the rivulets, nor the paths they cut, but the orchestrated and mutually reinforcing tendency of the hydrologic process.

Finally, to go straight at the harmony metaphor, imagine music—harmony per se. Classical Western music, once again, typifies the top-down or typically Western concept of logical and transcendent order. The composer creates a score, which is like a recipe: abstract, rather mathematical, and static. Before the symphony begins, the orchestra sits, each player bowing or blowing into or tapping his or her instrument. The whole effect is one of disorder and chaos. The conductor (the Demiurge) opens the score and commands the orchestra. All the players are disciplined, and harken: the random chaos of the sound materials is transformed into a wonderful order, a harmony.

The Chinese concept of the Tao as the harmony in nature is more like Afro-American jazz. The drummer, after seemingly random tuning and testing, gradually falls into a beat; the bass player picks up on it, and over it lays a pattern of pitch and timbre; the piano player embellishes with a melody; and the horn players fill the available sonic spaces. Music emerges; and then changes, transformed into something ever new and unique as the players respond to one another's additions and innovations. In this concept of "aesthetic" order, Taoism is particularly consonant with the contemporary evolutionary-ecological worldview, in which the incredibly rich and detailed order of terrestrial nature is emergent, not designed. The earth sciences do not conform to the hypothetical-deductive-experimental-predictive model epitomized by classical physics. There is a good deal of history in natural history—in geology, climatology, evolution, and ecology. Taoism could help environmentalists express the emergent order of nature, which is the outcome of a process of mutual adjustment among plants, animals, the earth, and the atmosphere over many millennia. Just as important, the contemporary evolutionary and ecological worldview might be welcomed in modern China—and better appreciated there than in the West—as a scientific expression and confirmation of a classical Chinese insight.

Indigenous Chinese thought about nature is so process-, as opposed to entity-, oriented that Western translators have consistently misrendered the Chinese word *ch'i* as "matter." There must be some term in Chinese, they seem to have reasoned, for matter, the physical stuff from which things are made. But *ch'i* is more accurately translated as "hylozoistic energy" than as material substrate. It might as well refer to the spirit of a being as to its corporeality.[11] If *ch'i* provides natural processes with a kind of internal motive power, the Tao is the choreographic character of their combined exfoliations.

Mention of the conventional mistranslation of *ch'i* thrusts to the fore another difference between Chinese thought, on the one hand, and a certain distinctive feature of South Asian and Western thought on the other. *Ch'i* is as nearly spirit as matter, as nearly soul as body. The Chinese understanding of nature is polar, as distinct from dualistic. In the dualistic Jain and Greco-Christian picture of reality, soul can exist without body, and vice versa. *Devas*/angels, for example, are bodiless souls, and stones are soulless bodies. By contrast, in a polar—as opposed to dualistic—conception of opposites, one opposite helps to define the other; one cannot be conceived without the other, and neither can exist apart from the other.[12] Thus, for example, night may be defined as the negation of day, and vice versa; the one is inconceivable without the other; and day follows night as night follows day. Perhaps even more transparently, male and female are polar rather than dualistic opposites, dependent on one another for their respective natures, meanings, and very existence. The peculiarly Western "war" between the sexes, now prosecuted with some intensity by radical feminists and recalcitrant male chauvinists, may result from reducing a quintessentially polar opposition to a dualistic one. However that may be, the *yin/yang* concept—one cognitive coin with two sides—is a generalization of the polar understanding of opposites: as unitary, not exclusionary; as complementary, not conflicting.

The familiar *yin/yang* symbol pictures the idea perfectly and in an appropriately nondiscursive way. A circle, suggesting unity and wholeness, is divided evenly—but fluidly, organically, embryonically—into white and black fields. In the center of the lobe of each is a small circle of the opposite value. One circle embraces polar opposites; the head of one lies over the tail of the other; and at the center of the maximal extension of each lurks its counterpart—its alter ego, so to speak.

Like the Tao, the *yin/yang* polarity is an aboriginal Chinese concept. The *yang* is active, hard, hot, bright, assertive, masculine. The *yin* is yielding, soft, dark, wet, quiescent, female. The many kinds of things in the world manifest the *yin* and *yang* in different combinations, some having more, some less, of the one or the other. The ebb and flow of meteorological, personal, national, and historical events reflect the alternate influence, the reciprocal waxing and waning, of the *yin* and the *yang*.

Taoism's legendary founder, and the putative author of the *Tao te ching*, Lao Tzu, lived—if he lived at all—during the sixth and fifth centuries B.C.E., a contemporary of the early pre-Socratic philosophers in Greece and the Buddha and Mahavira in India. The *Tao te ching* and the *Chuang Tzu*, both apparently composite texts, probably took their eventual forms three or four centuries later.[13] We must bear in mind throughout this gloss that, as the *Tao te ching* states in its very first verse, the Tao that can be expressed in words is not the true ("constant") Tao.

That caveat having been registered, we may say that the ("natural") Tao is the way of the universe, the orderly and harmonious unfolding of its phenomena, the complementary developmental tendency of things. But one must not separate order from being. The Tao is both the order and the phenomena that express it. Moreover, this "way" that things go, though not conceived of as compassionate or loving or even as benevolent, brings peace and health, which are simply order and harmony in the body politic and in the human body, respectively. If allowed to take its course, the Tao results in natural fulfillment and perfection.

While a great deal of expository attention has been paid to the concept of *tao* in Taoist studies, rather little has been devoted to its complement, *te*. *Te* is an equally subtle idea, equally difficult to define in words. For the limited purposes of this monograph, it may be characterized as the disposition of a particular—dynamic, of course, not static—being.[14] The carrot, the potato, and the oyster of our Chinese stew each has its *te*. In our jazz, the drums and the drummer, the bass and the bass player each has its *te*. The harmony that is the Tao arises as each particular, with its particular *te*, comes into being—in the context of what has gone before—and asserts itself in relation to, and in response to, all the others, near and far. As David L. Hall expresses it, like the *yin* and the *yang*, "the concepts of *tao* and *te* form a single notion, *tao-te*, which is best understood in terms of the relationship of field (*tao*) to focus (*te*)."[15]

Of particular practical interest to environmentalists has been the Taoist ideal of action, *wu-wei*, which literally and paradoxically means not-doing. *Wu-wei* and its correlative notions, *wu-chih* (not-knowing), and *wu-yu* (not-desiring), have been subjected to the most complex and painstaking philological, conceptual, and philosophical analyses—analyses that go far beyond the requirements of this global sampling of cultural environmental ideas.[16] Suffice it to say here, negatively, that practicing *wu-wei* does not entail simply quietism or passivity, whereby the practitioner lets himself go with the flow of the Tao, or floats with the current of the universe. The many Taoist illustrations of *wu-wei*, in juxtaposition with its opposite, *yu-wei*, suggest, rather, a doing that is neither coercive nor assertive—a doing that proceeds from one's own *te* and respects the myriad *te*s of one's surroundings, in order to achieve a creative harmonious and mutually beneficial result.

Here is an illustration. One farms in a hilly region in which rains are plentiful but seasonally concentrated. One must irrigate one's fields during dry spells in order to obtain a crop. A *yu-wei* approach would be laboriously to clear the uplands, which are more extensive, of timber, and plant one's crops there. But since this will result in rapid runoff of rains and cause flooding of the narrow valleys, one also builds dams, at great cost of labor, both to control the floods and to impound the water for irrigation. To deliver the impounded water to one's fields, one must carry or pump it uphill—also at great cost of labor or energy—to the high ground. While this style of agriculture may work for a while, and even yield large short-term profits, it cannot last long, because the soil will eventually wash off the unprotected hillsides, and the silt will settle behind the dams. A *wu-wei* approach, on the other hand, would be to leave the forests on the highlands to hold the soil and plant one's crops in the lowlands, diverting the steadily flowing streams to the planted fields by means of a series of ditches. One thus accomplishes the same general ends without all the back-breaking work and expenditure of energy. One's short-term gains may be less, because one has put less land under cultivation, but they will be sustained indefinitely into the future. Just as important, the *te* of the hills (which is to grow trees), the *te* of the upland trees themselves (which is to seek deep soil-holding rootage), and the *te* of the streams (which is to flow sinuously down to the sea) are all acknowledged, respected, and accommodated. The whole farmer-environment complex is both productive and beautiful, profitable and long-lasting.[17]

In such parables of *wu-wei*, contemporary environmentalists have read ancient homilies of what today we call "appropriate technology" and "sustainable development."[18] Nuclear power—essentially boiling water to generate electricity, using an exotic and risky technology, and expending huge amounts of capital and labor—is *yu-wei*. Wind-generated electricity, solar space-heating, commuting by bicycle, and the like are *wu-wei*. The capital-intensive Green Revolution approach of increasing yields per acre to feed a growing human population is *yu-wei*. Land reform combined with creative improvements in diversified peasant subsistence agriculture and family planning—to achieve a balance between increased productivity and decreased demand—is *wu-wei*. And so on.

Bioregionalists, wilderness activists, soft-path energy theorists, organic agriculturalists, and other advocates of environmental pragmatics have thus understandably claimed an intellectual ancestry in Taoism. Ecofeminists have not; also understandably, because the ancient Chinese Taoists are often pictured as antisocial curmudgeons. According to D. C. Lau, the name "Lao Tzu" means "Old Man"—a designation with which ecofeminists may find little to identify.[19] But ecofeminists argue that the domination of nature by man, as well as the domination of women by men, is rooted historically in patriarchy: Expose and attack the hierarchical, top-down, exploitative social and political organization characteristic of patriarchy and one will expose and attack the exploitative, coercive, destructive relationship of agricultural-industrial civilization to the natural environment.[20] Taoism's historical preference for "low" and "soft" technologies, and especially its historical association with anarchism and egalitarianism, resonate well with ecofeminism's evocation of consensual horticultural village societies prevailing in a golden age prior to the emergence of male-dominated, large-scale, socially stratified urban-agricultural empires.[21] But most directly of interest to ecofeminism is Taoism's ideal of androgyny and compensatory affinity for the *yin*—the female energy pole in nature. Here is a kind of cognitive-evaluative Affirmative Action. The *Tao te ching*, indeed, specifically says, "Know the male, but keep to the role of the female."[22] In a passage that, if quoted without attribution, might be mistaken for something written by a contemporary ecofeminist, the *Tao te ching* comments,

> A man is supple and weak when living, but hard and stiff when dead. Grass and trees are pliant and fragile while living, but dried and shriveled when dead. Thus the hard and the strong are the comrades of death; the supple and weak are the comrades of life.[23]

Perhaps the best metaphor is the power of water, which can level mountains and cut chasms through solid rock, while water itself, the very embodiment of *yin*, is at the same time utterly yielding: "In the world there is nothing more submissive and weak than water. Yet for attacking that which is hard and strong nothing can surpass it."[24]

Taoism certainly warrants the interest and rewards the attention of contemporary environmental ethicists, including ecofeminists as well as Deep Ecologists. Taoism is decidedly this-worldly in its concerns. Its practical advice, especially the ideal of *wu-wei*, can serve as an infinitely adaptable pattern and venerable tradition of wise living for environmentally sound contemporary applications. And the subtle elaboration and interplay of its central concepts—*tao* and *te*, "field" and "focus"—can enrich and illuminate contemporary ecological thought, and vice versa.

CONFUCIANISM

It is fitting that we have much more confidence in the historicity of Confucius—though not, perhaps, in the attribution of the *Analects* to his hand—than we do in the historicity of Lao Tzu. Taoism emphasizes a blending of self with nature, while Confucianism emphasizes personal virtue and greatness of mind, soul, and character. Lao Tzu, according to legend, rode off into the sunset and faded into the mountains of the West, while Confucius, a venerated public servant and teacher, died after a dignified retirement.[25]

Confucius was born in the mid–sixth century B.C.E. and lived well into the fifth. Though roughly contemporary in Chinese intellectual history—

as we might say that the Pythagoreans and the Peripatetics were roughly contemporary in the history of ancient Greek philosophy—Confucianism antedates Taoism.[26]

Taoism has often been construed as an anarchic critique of the conventionalism of Confucian morality. According to Roger T. Ames,

> There is a common ground shared by the teachings of classical Confucianism and Taoism. . . . Both express a "this-worldly" concern for the concrete details of immediate existence rather than exercising their minds in the service of grand abstractions and ideals. Both acknowledge the uniqueness, importance and primacy of particular persons and their contributions to the world, while, at the same time, stressing the ecological interrelatedness and interdependence of this person with his context. . . .
>
> For the Taoists, the Confucian penchant for reading the "constant *tao*" too myopically as the "human *tao*" is to experience the world at a level that generates a dichotomy between the natural and human worlds. The [Taoist] argument . . . seems to be that the Confucians do not take the ecological sensibility far enough. . . . The Taoists do not reject human society and culture as such; rather, they reject the notion that human experience occurs in a vacuum, and that the whole process of existence can be reduced to human values and purposes.[27]

Confucius did not question the existence of the Tao. While Taoists turned to the contemplation of nature and its inherent orderly processes for the secret of how to live well, Confucius focused—myopically, as Ames puts it—on the order of human society. Just as nature, especially *t'ien* (heaven), is an orderly and harmonious whole, so ought human society to be an equally orderly and harmonious microcosm. The social order, however, though ultimately existing within and resting on the order of nature, seems to have been regarded by Confucius as a relatively self-contained order, having its own principles and forms. To bring society into conformity with the Tao, Taoists recommended political *wu-wei*—anarchy and bioregional autonomy.[28] Confucius had other ideas. In any case, Confucius was a humanist, and his teaching almost exclusively concerned moral and political matters.

His was an ethic of noble "virtue"—as opposed to an ethic of rule-following or principle-applying—similar in some respects but very different in others to the ethics of his younger Greek contemporaries Socrates, Plato, and Aristotle. As in Greek aretaic ethics, Confucius posited five cardinal "virtues," but they overlap only slightly—if at all—with the

Hellenic set. The cardinal virtues explored by the ancient Greek moral philosophers (roughly translated) are *dike* (justice), *andreia* (courage), *sophrosyne* (temperance), *sophia* (wisdom), and *hosia* (piety). The cardinal virtues enshrined by Confucius (even more roughly translated) are the all-important, all-encompassing virtue—analogous, in this capacity, to the role that *dike* plays for Plato—*jen* (humanity), *li* (ritual action), *yi* (appropriateness), *hsin* (honoring one's word), and *chih* (wisdom).[29] Confucius's moral ideal was that of an excellent or superior person who had become accomplished in these virtues and who lived unfailingly and impeccably by them.

Here a caveat is necessary: It may be as misleading to label Confucius's moral concepts "virtues" as to translate the Greek word *aretê* with the same term. Nevertheless, we must make do with the English language, with all its limitations. The important point—negatively, and thus more safely, albeit less precisely, stated—is that Confucius and his reflective Greek contemporaries did not, as modern inheritors of the Judeo-Christian intellectual legacy usually do, think of morality as consisting of rules (such as the Ten Commandments) or the principles grounding rules (such as Kant's categorical imperative).

An aristocratic prince or lord should govern his realm in large measure by personal moral example. He should be morally worthy of leadership, and his people should follow him not because they are coerced by force of arms, or constrained by laws and edicts, but because of the trust, loyalty, and affection inspired by his character. Perhaps it would be better to say that such a person reigns rather than governs.[30]

Taoism and Confucianism are commonly portrayed as diametrically opposed. The nature orientation of Taoism, on the one hand, contrasts sharply with the moral, social, and political orientation of Confucianism, on the other. The anarchy and free-spiritedness of Taoism contrasts sharply with the apparent demand of Confucianism that the individual conform to an imposed and artificial order, constituted by social hierarchy and the corresponding *li*, or body of ritual action. But the Confucian image of a noble prince contemplating the order of heaven, re-creating it in his own character, and, essentially by that modus vivendi, bringing order, peace, prosperity, and harmony to his province is not altogether un-Taoist in its vision. The *li*, furthermore, are "rituals . . . [originally] constituted in imitation of perceptible cosmic rhythms as a means of strengthening the coordination of the human being and his natural and spiritual environment."[31] Actually, the more radical difference lies between the contemporaneous Chinese Legalists, who advocated government by edict (truly an imposed, artificial order), on the one hand, and the Taoists and Confucians on the other. Lao Tzu and Confucius, Chuang Tzu and Mencius, simply had different notions of what it meant to align oneself and society with the Tao.

Self-realization is the common project of both the classical Confucians and the Taoists, to put it in terms made current by Deep Ecology's reigning guru, Arne Naess. The important distinction between the two is this: For classical Confucianism, human realization is to be found predominantly in human society and its network of human-to-human relationships. That is why the consummate virtue in Confucianism is *jen*. The Taoist critique of such a concept of self-realization is that it ignores the fact that the human being is also embedded in a larger-than-social natural environment. As each person is a person in a social context, so also is humanity and its social organization embedded in a natural, ecological context.

It is principally because of the eventual institutionalization of Confucianism in China, and its eventual ossification, that Confucianism seems to hold little promise as an intellectual soil in which to cultivate an environmental ethic. Confucius himself was a bureaucrat and a pedant, and his philosophy has come to be associated with the intransigence of self-serving petty officialdom in a highly structured, hidebound hierarchy. Confucianism connotes to most moderns, Asian and Western alike, blind conservatism, slavish adherence to custom and hollow social forms, fulsome filial piety, and resignation to feudal inequality.[32] But, of course, Confucius can no more be blamed for the desiccation of his teachings by subsequent generations of Confucians than Jesus can be blamed for a similar desiccation of his by subsequent generations of Christians.

At the very least, Confucianism could support an indirect anthropocentric environmental ethic. The environmental historian J. Donald Hughes has explored the *Mencius* (putatively the work of Mencius, the most systematic of Confucius's exponents, born some two centuries after the master) in search of an incipient environmental ethic. According to Hughes,

> for Mencius, land management was an important topic which he considered to be one of the primary responsibilities of the state. He advised rulers to make periodic tours of inspection of their territory, and to use the condition of the land as prime evidence of the quality, or lack of it, of the stewardship of his important noblemen. . . . Of course this is resource conservation, not deep ecology, and assumes a purely anthropocentric framework.[33]

But that is to damn by faint praise, since the same can be said of any humanistic moral philosophy. Environmental destruction, degradation, and defilement almost always have harmful effects on people individually and society collectively. Poor environmental management would be unwise and unprincely. It would be an insult to one's ancestors and an injury to one's offspring. So much is obvious. Hughes goes on to point to the Taoist overtones in the *Mencius* and concludes his discussion with the following remark: "Mencius used [the peasant So Shun] as an example to show that any human being can become a sage by living according to nature in which every creature participates. Perhaps Mencius is not so anthropocentric after all."[34]

But I think we can do even better than that on behalf of the potential for environmental ethics represented by Confucianism. In classical Confucianism, as newly interpreted by Hall and Ames (among others), there may repose an insight that could be the source of a much more subtle and powerful indigenous Chinese environmental ethic and a comparative resource for articulating one of the most elusive (to the Western mind) cognitive implications of ecology.

What does it mean to be a human being? More personally and especially, Who am I? In the Western tradition, a human being has been understood, as have many other kinds of things, by means of the concept of an essence. From the Judeo-Christian tradition has come one answer to the question, What is "the essence of man?": "The image of God." And from the Greco-Roman tradition has come another: "The rational animal." During the European Renaissance, these originally independent notions of human nature were synthesized. Reason, in the Enlightenment, came to be understood as the divine spark in human beings. The effect of this synthesis, in any case, was to reinforce the subtext—to wit, that to be human or any other kind of particular is to participate in a universal, to have an essence. An individual human being is thus a token of the type, cast from a die, however defined. One strives to establish one's individuality within the parameters set by one's essence. But the salient point for this discussion is that a defining relationship exists vertically, so to speak, between token and type—not horizontally, between oneself and others. One's relationship to others is "external"—that is, one's relationship to others in no way defines oneself.

When the mind-body dualism endemic in Western thought since Plato is added to this notion of what it means to be human, then a human being's relationship to others and to society—both to human and nonhuman others and to human society and the biotic community—becomes doubly external. *I* am a *psyche*—a soul, a conscious mind, or "thinking thing"—inhabiting a physical body. Here I temporarily reside, somewhere behind the eyes and between the ears of this mechanical vehicle, navigating fearfully through an alien world (which is, moreover, misrepresented to me by the bodily senses). Other insular psyches, I timorously speculate, occupy other bodies similar to my own, but I can know them and communicate with them (if they exist) only indirectly, through the layers of the gross physical medium separating us. Because I am hopelessly isolated, my private inner life is my real life. My outward social life is artificial at best and a sham at worst. One often hears Western persons say, cynically, that they are off to "play" student or professor, doctor, lawyer, stockbroker, or what-have-you. Clearly, such people consider their social "roles" to be inauthentic, and their private lives—especially their inner private lives—to be genuine.

The environmental consequences of this inherited view of self are no less untoward than the social consequences. We human beings are strangers in a strange land. We entertain fantasies of colonizing other planets, bespeaking our alienation from this one.

Confucianism offers a radical alternative to this archetypal Western image of the self. We may style it the "socially constituted" self. Abstractly speaking, it turns on a concept of internal relations. Who or what one is is defined not by reference to an essence, type, or universal but by one's natural and social relationships. Immediately it is essential to remember the emphasis on process which is indigenous to Chinese thinking. Human nature is no more static than given; it has "evolved"—less by Darwinian natural selection than by accumulation. Hence one's humanity is, as it were, an ongoing work of art, inherited from one's forebears, to which one may contribute creatively. And one's social role is not a fixed slot or niche to which one is consigned from birth for life. Confucius, we may note, was born poor and took his "stance"—the posture he struck as a person and his position and rank in society—at the age of thirty.[35]

The socially constituted individual is defined, constituted, by his or her social relationships. One *is* the son or daughter of one's parents, the brother or sister of one's siblings, the father or mother of one's children; one *is* a butcher, baker, candlestick maker, doctor, lawyer, or Indian chief; an Asian, European, or mestizo; a painter, poet, or musician. To say that a person's relationships are internal is to say that in describing them one describes the person himself or herself. They are not roles external to the person; the person, rather, is the sum of his or her relationships. Or, allowing that the whole may be greater than the sum of the parts, we might better say that the person is the sum of his or her relationships plus the uniqueness, the individuality, that emerges from just this particular blend of natural and social interactions.

The *li*—which, especially from a Western point of view, may seem so artificial and self-stultifying—are simply formalized actions that structure interpersonal behavior. They therefore offer a pattern of behavior for establishing relationships. One takes one's stance, but in doing so one is not fitting oneself to a preestablished rank and social niche so much as one is creating oneself—becoming a particular person. The *Analects* portray Confucius as throwing himself so intently and completely into the ritual actions that he becomes transformed.[36]

Just so. But that is only half the story. The other half is *yi*. *Yi* is the raw material one brings to *li*.[37] Anyone who has been a parent knows that an infant comes into the world with certain proclivities. Some children are very active, others more passive; some are self-directed, others are in need of external stimulation and discipline; some are artistic, others less so; and so on, and on. *Yi* is personality in the richest sense of the word. It is connected with *ch'i* and *te*. Thus, to act in accordance with the virtue *yi* is to do what is fitting, what is appropriate—for oneself—in context. It is inappropriate, for example, for a person who lacks comic sense and timing to act the clown, or for one who is full of clownishness to preside over solemn religious ceremonies. It is inappropriate to do now what might be appropriate at another time, and so on.

One might wonder if an inner essential self is being slipped in sub rosa in this interpretation of *yi*. It is not. Hall and Ames write, "the person-in-context understands 'self' as a dynamic and changing focus of existence characteristically expanding or contracting over some aspect of the process of becoming, the interpretation of which is grounded in and involves reference to the environing whole."[38] *Li* and *yi*, like *tao* and *te*, are complementary. The *li* are conventions, artifacts. Each ritual act therefore must have originated with someone as the expression of that person's *yi*. The person who performs a ritual not only taps into the power and personality of a great person of the past, he or she puts his or her *yi* into it—thereby reanimating it and giving it a subtle variation, the imprimatur of his or her personality. One thus constitutes and is constituted by the ritual action. As Hall and Ames comment,

> ritual actions lack any real significance when they consist merely in baldly imitating the actions of others. It is ritual actions personalized so as to disclose oneself which constitute truly meaningful human activity. Ritual actions achieve significance to the extent that the person, stimulated by the import given these actions in the tradition, infuses them with his own commitment.[39]

This Confucian sense of the individual-in-context is important to environmental philosophy in the following ways: If we expand the humanistic Confucian philosophy of the fully realized person from social context

to environmental context, we can manufacture, in effect, a nonanthropocentric Confucian environmental ethic. Moreover, when the Confucian
philosophy of the fully realized person is compared with concepts central
to ecology, we may find that the former illuminate the latter, as well as vice
versa.

An ontological discontinuity between individuals is an assumption per-
meating Western thinking about all ethics, social no less than environmental. Like Newton, who formulated laws of absolute motion for ideal
bodies isolated in a void, Western ethicists have imagined similarly isolat-
able agents and patients and sought to formulate universal principles of behavior that would govern the actions of the one as they affect the other.
Indeed, the task for environmental ethics has been generally characterized
as finding a theoretical justification for admitting nonhuman natural entities and nature as a whole to the status of moral patients.[40] If, by contrast,
we begin with the assumption that one is constituted by one's relationships, then socially untoward or destructive actions redound not only upon
"others" but immediately upon oneself. It is less the case, under such an
assumption, that in ethics, as in physics, "for every action there is an equal
and opposite reaction"—a law of instant retributive *karma*—than that no
sharp distinction can be drawn between oneself and one's social context and
hence between oneself and "others." The upshot is that antisocial behavior
is self-destructive, while socially conducive behavior is self-creative. If one
is nothing other than the distinctive, active, and creative center of a complex of relationships, then one's well-being is tied to other similar centers,
and threaded into the social fabric as a whole.

Now simply expand this analysis from society to environment, *et voilà!*,
we have, *mutatis mutandis*, the metaphysical foundations of an environmental ethic. Confucius may have been inclined to focus less on the atmosphere, oceans, and other living species than we do, and more on spirits
and the Way of heaven. One may speculate that if he had lived in our time
of environmental crisis, he would have pointed out that the dynamic web
of relationships—as an intersection or node of which each of us is—includes our relationships with plants, animals, soils, and waters as well as
with other human beings. The environment thus is an extension of the
self; and the self, the individual person, is, complementarily, the focus of
the environment in a particular space-time nexus. Among Asian traditions
of thought, Confucianism provides a worldview much more consonant
with ecology for grounding Arne Naess's Deep Ecological "Self- [with a
capital 'S'] realization" than is the Vedantic worldview, which (as documented in the previous chapter) actually inspired the idea. The Confucian
self is neither a discrete entity, a social atom, nor a playful manifestation

of *atman-brahman*. Rather, oneself is a unique center in a network of internal social *and natural* relationships. The social *and natural* environment is the wider "Self." Thus, the Confucian philosophy of the self and deep, genuinely ecological Self-realization should be mutually illuminating. For among the general cognitive implications of ecology is holism—a unity and oneness in nature—premised on natural internal relations, not on an underlying metaphysical identity. Here is another interesting parallel between ancient Chinese philosophy and contemporary ecofeminist philosophy. Val Plumwood, among other ecofeminists, has criticized the Deep Ecological project of Self-realization through mystical identification with all of nature, and suggests instead a view of "self-in-relationship" as an alternative:

> This view of self-in-relationship is, I think, a good candidate for the richer account of self deep ecologists have sought for. . . . It is an account that avoids atomism, but that enables a recognition of interdependence and relationship without falling into the problems of indistinguishability; that acknowledges both continuity and difference; and that breaks the culturally imposed false dichotomy of egoism and altruism of interests. It bypasses both masculine "separation" and traditional feminine "merger" accounts of the self. It can also provide an appropriate foundation for an ethic of connectedness and caring for others as argued by [Carol] Gilligan and [Jean] Miller.[41]

But the Western tradition affords few resources for expressing an appropriate and genuinely deep ecology. Indeed, discontinuity and a cognitive stress on discreteness has typified Western thought about nature. On the one hand, the atomic theory of matter (broached by Leucippus and Democritus in the fifth century B.C.E. and institutionalized by Newton and his successors in modern Western natural philosophy in the seventeenth and eighteenth centuries C.E.) represents the physical world to be composed of externally related material particles. And on the other, the theory of types or essences (broached by Plato and Aristotle in the fourth century B.C.E. and institutionalized by Carolus Linnaeus in the eighteenth century C.E.) represents living aggregates of atoms—not only human beings but all other species—as organized by a logical schema into a variety of externally related kinds. As the ecologist and natural philosopher Paul Shepard expressed it, in the West's inherited picture of the natural world, animals and plants are arrayed on the landscape like furniture arranged in a room. As chairs are related to tables, so is the fauna to the flora. There may be order, but it is imposed from without; there may be a relationship, but it is external.[42] Or, as the philosopher Anthony Quinton puts it, in the predominant Western view, "the world resembles a warehouse of automobile parts. Each item is standard in character, independent of all other items, in its own place, and ordinarily unchanging in its intrinsic nature."[43]

Ecology represents such a radical departure from the traditional Western worldview because it focuses on the relationships between organisms rather than on organisms in isolation from one another and from the elemental environment. Ecology reverses the typically Western focus on the figure at the expense of the ground in the proverbial figure-ground gestalt. Relationships are ontologically upgraded, and classical entities, proportionately, ontologically downgraded. From an ecological point of view, relationships become the primary realities and entities the subordinate realities. Here is why:

From an ecological point of view, an organism has been shaped and molded—in its size, form, viscera, sociology, and psychology—by its interaction with other species. Take the white-tailed deer as an example. Its mouth, teeth, and digestive tract are adapted to the edge-browse it eats, while its musculature, sensory acuity, nervous disposition, and herding proclivities are evolved responses to its predators. Abstractly speaking, the white-tailed deer is almost, but not quite, implied by all the other foci of its matrix. If its habitat could be expressed as a set of propositions, the white-tailed deer would be almost, but not quite, deducible.

The ecological worldview is holistic, then: first, because entities are bound together by a myriad of relationships into a seamless fabric, and second—and more exotically, in the predominant Western way of thinking—because each entity is constituted by a particular and unique junction in a matrix of relationships. Confucius's philosophy can supply an important social correspondent, rich in illustrative anecdotes, concrete analogies, and metaphors, to express and exemplify these very unfamiliar ideas—ideas that are virtually unprecedented in the Western intellectual canon. For example, the *li-yi* complementarity is particularly useful in helping to express the contingent, stochastic aspect of ecological coherency just now alluded to. In precolonial Australia, there were no white-tailed deer. The niche (*li*) that the deer filled in the North American ecosystem was filled in the Australian ecosystem by a species of kangaroo. Similar conditions (generally speaking) prevailed, and therefore analogous relationships between brushy plants, browsers, and carnivores evolved. But the raw material, the organismic *yi*, were different. Australia began its separate evolutionary odyssey with marsupials, not placental mammals. Hence kangaroos evolved, not deer.

By transposing the Confucian social model from the human to the biotic community, the ecological holist is encouraged to add a fourth dimension to the web of life. Ecological relationships are only half the story. The phylogenetic raw material is the other half. Had there not been sauroid survivors from the Cretaceous, our contemporary avifauna would be different from what it is. Although there would be organisms that fly and that exploit the whole spectrum of food resources from nectar to carrion, they would not be birds. The set of ecological niches—the body of *li* in the biotic community—is inherited from the *yi* of the great ancestors of the past: those who ventured and survived. And the survivors today are the organisms that throw themselves fully into the ritual actions of their species and add their own *yi* to drive the engine of evolution.

CONCLUSION

The potential for the development of an explicit indigenous Chinese environmental ethic based on classical Chinese thought is tremendous. And the potential contribution of classical Chinese thought to deep ecology, ecofeminism, and, more generally, to a global ecological consciousness and conscience is equally great. In Confucianism there reposes a philosophy of self-realization which may provide a precedent and pattern for a genuinely ecological Self-realization similar to, but crucially different from, that advocated by Naess, and one that resonates well with the ecofeminist alternative of self-in-relationship advocated by Plumwood. Naess might correct his Deep Ecological concept of Self-realization by turning away from the strict monism of South Asian Vedanta metaphysics and looking farther east, toward China; and there Plumwood might find conceptual resources for articulating her ecofeminist notion of the self.

In fact, the generalization from Confucian social self-realization to an appropriate and genuinely deep-ecological Self-realization may have occurred historically. The Taoist critique of Confucianism expanded the concept of following the *tao* from the social sphere to the whole of nature. A human being is an individuated focus in a network of dynamic, changing relationships—ecological as well as social relationships. Human beings enjoy an interdependence and mutuality with all environing conditions. Perhaps the greatest contribution that classical Chinese thought can make to a global deep-ecological awareness lies in this conception of dynamic, mutually constitutive, internal relatedness. Self-realization may be understood as attunement to the *tao*, but the *tao* is neither transcendent nor static. Each individual's insistent particularity, each person's *te*, reciprocally impresses itself on and conditions the ambient *tao*. Therefore, the despotic strain of Western thought aimed at justifying human tyranny over nature is not simply inverted in Taoism, so that nature is master and humanity slave. Rather, in Taoism the human/nature dualism is subverted, deconstructed. If people are part of nature and nature is relational and processive, then practical environmental ethics consists less in *wu-wei* understood literally as forbearance, and expressed in the popular environmental concept of "nature preservation," than in *wu-wei* understood as noncoercive or cooperative action, expressed in the more recent environmental concept of "sustainable livelihood" through "appropriate technology."

5 Ecological Insights in East Asian Buddhism

Mahayana Buddhism gradually developed in northwest India over a period of several centuries. In Mahayana, the atheism, humanism, and philosophical austerity of the founder was replaced by more conventional religious trappings. The Buddha was elevated to a quasi-divine and even messianic status. A Buddha-nature awaiting self-realization was posited in a variety of living things, and Bodhisattvas, or Buddhas-to-be, abounded. The Bodhisattvas, poised to enter Nirvana, delayed their passage in order to aid the faithful in their own spiritual pilgrimage. A rich and luxuriant cultus evolved. Mahayana offered something like a gospel—the good news that a savior, the Buddha, and a multitude of cosaviors, the Bodhisattvas, existed to cure or ameliorate the sufferings of kings and common people alike.

In the concept of a Buddha-nature within, one may readily detect a Vedantic recidivism in Mahayana Buddhism. But there are two significant twists. The universal pure being in later Buddhism is characterized—reflecting the historical Buddha's very deconstruction of substance—as Emptiness or Void.[1] If the underlying oneness of all things is pure and undifferentiated, it may equally well be represented as absolute being or as absolute nothingness, since in either case it is propertyless and the experience of it qualityless. The Buddha, secondly, did not simply slip off into the Void on attaining enlightenment. He had compassion for his fellow sufferers and benevolently shared with whomsoever his understanding of the path to liberation. Thus in the Mahayana apotheosis of the Buddha—reflecting this conspicuous feature of the character of the historical Buddha—the Buddha-nature at the heart of things is benevolent, a kind of pure, indiscriminate love.

As the more conservative Theravada Buddhism migrated to the south,

Mahayana Buddhism gradually established a foothold in China. While Buddhism was not welcomed by the Confucian establishment in China, it may have struck a sympathetic chord with certain elements in Taoism.[2] For example, in the central Buddhist concept of *sunyata*, or emptiness, Taoists may have seen the Tao, which the *Tao te ching* sometimes characterizes as Nothing: "The myriad creatures in the world are born from Something and Something from Nothing."[3] The *Tao te ching* may also be read to suggest that desire is the cause of unhappiness and frustration and to recommend a cessation of desire, albeit less radical a cessation than in Buddhism, as a key to living well—that is, in accordance with the Tao. Certainly Buddhism was introduced to China through largely Taoist categories and eventually flourished and proliferated there. From its new base in China, it traveled on to Korea and Japan.

Given this monograph's focus on the environmental attitudes and values of major traditional worldviews and representative local indigenous ones, it would be otiose to describe the history and doctrinal nuances of the many Buddhist schools and sects in the Far East—a task about as relevant to environmental ethics as a description of the doctrinal differences between Catholics, Copts, Baptists, and Presbyterians within the overall intellectual milieu of Christianity. A critical gloss of representative schools of thought in which environmental ethics seem implicit would be more appropriate.

HUA-YEN

Joining a growing cadre of comparativists doing environmental philosophy, Francis H. Cook argues that ecology calls into question the discontinuous and object-centered ontology of externally related entities traditional to Western thought. In Cook's opinion, ecology also calls into question other fixtures of the inherited Judeo-Christian/Greco-modern cognitive complex—a representation of the world as created, teleological, hierarchical, and anthropocentric. Ecology, reinforced by parallel ideas in relativity and quantum physics, thus spearheads a conceptual revolution taking place within the Western worldview. Cook imagines that once a hole appears in the predominant Western conceptual dike, a flood will break loose and a "cosmic ecology," anticipated by Hua-yen Buddhism, may engulf us. He suggests that to help articulate the emergent ecological worldview we may repair to the Hua-yen masters.[4]

The central cosmic image of the Hua-yen school of Chinese Buddhism, which dates from the seventh century B.C.E. in China, is the Jewel Net of Indra—a net of infinite dimensions, in each "eye" of which hangs a gem. At first glance, this would not seem to be an especially promising point of departure for the development of an ecological ethic, since it resembles an image used to convey the Vedanta idea that all things are one because they share a common essence—a concept of oneness or unity in nature which, on scrutiny (in chapter 3), does not at all match the oneness or unity in nature posited in ecology. Pursuant to the Vedantic notion, we are asked to think of a sphere of mirrors all facing a point at the center, where a single candle burns. The illumination (*atman*) one finds in each of the mirrors is only a reflection of the same pure—and solely real—flame (*brahman*) burning at the center. But in the Hua-yen image of the Jewel Net of Indra, true to its Buddhist origins, there is no single luminous reality at the center point of the net (nor, for that matter, is a center point of the net mentioned at all). Rather, the mirrorlike facets of each gem reflect all the other jewels in the net. According to Cook, this image represents the typically Mahayana notion of "mutual identity" and "mutual causality," the latter the Buddha's own doctrine of *pratityasamutpada*, or dependent arising.[5]

In its more extreme form, the Hua-yen concept of mutual identity is also a poor analogue of the holism evidenced by ecology, but for a different reason than is the Vedantic concept of substantial identity. Cook explicitly and correctly points out that contemporary ecology and Hua-yen Buddhism share a relation-centered ontology, in which entities are constituted by their relationships rather than the other way around. But as Cook represents the Hua-yen notion, the whole is somehow present in each of its parts, and the annihilation of any of the parts would result in the annihilation of the whole. Forswearing the intensely holistic organismic paradigm of early twentieth-century ecology—a paradigm in which plant and animal associations were represented as supraorganisms, with species as organs and specimens as cells—more recent ecological theory represents ecosystems to be less tightly integrated.[6] But even if we represent an ecosystem by analogy with an organism, it is still unpersuasive to suggest, as Cook does, that with the destruction of any part the whole would be destroyed. If the heart is removed from a human body, the body will die, to be sure; but one can imagine the loss of any number of other parts—a kidney, a limb, a fingernail—which will not result in the death of the body, though in most cases the bodies will be more or less functionally impaired or disfigured. Similarly, while some species are vital to ecosystems, many others are not; and the routine misadventures of specimens are of practically no ecosystemic significance at all.

The Hua-yen concept of mutual identity, strongly interpreted, finds a more convincing analogue in the relational ontology of the new physics—the "cosmic ecology" that Cook envisions as the intellectual wave of the future. In the physicist David Bohm's concept of an implicate order, for example, subatomic entities, the basic building blocks of all other physical things, are local perturbations of a non-Euclidean spacetime continuum.[7] Any rent in such a seamless fabric, a continuum *sensu stricto*, might well mean the destruction of the whole. While in some relative sense an animal or plant may be destroyed, and in an all too absolute sense a species may be extinguished, the relevant wholes—the affected ecosystem and the biosphere—endure. At least, so far. On the other hand, the "annihilation" of a subatomic particle is compensated by an equivalent gain in energy—a shudder, or ripple, as we might think of it, running through the non-Euclidean void at the speed of light. But were the combined (matter-energy) conservation law of physics to be violated and the smallest knot of spacetime utterly destroyed—without a compensatory gain in energy—then the universe as a whole might well disappear.

In its less extreme form, the Hua-yen concept of mutual identity has a metaphorical analogue in ecology. As just noted, early twentieth-century ecology was governed by an organismic paradigm. Cook presses the following argument by organismic analogy. While all the parts of an organism are different, they are nevertheless identical in their very differences, since for each to be what it is, all the others have to be what they are, and all must form a functioning whole:

> The identity of the nose and the left elbow consists in their identity as *conditions* for the whole. Therefore, while the two are different, they are the same; in fact they are identical precisely because they are different. Seen in this light, then, when the nose is understood for what it is, the whole body is known; when we know the nature of the body, we know what the nose is. For this reason, Hua-yen can say that ten thousand Buddhas can be seen preaching on the tip of a single hair. In other words, the one truth which is common to all things (ten thousand Buddhas) is evident in the tip of the hair once we know its place in the whole.[8]

Mutual causality, as Cook interprets it, turns out to be this weaker sense of "mutual identity" by another name. Both follow from a cosmic vision of wholeness and relatedness. The part is the "cause" of the whole and of all the other parts because the parts are internally related. This requires some explanation, but it stands up to scrutiny. For X to be X means that it possesses—or, rather, that it *is*—just this confluence of relations with Y, Z, and so on, *ad infinitum*. Hence in X, as the image of the Jewel Net of Indra perfectly pictures it, all other "things" are present. X is therefore "caused" by all other things. But, since X bears relationships to all other things and these other things are defined by their relationships, then if X were not X, they would not be Y, Z, and so on. Hence X, no matter how humble it may be, is the cause of all other things.

From this theory of mutual causality and mutual identity, Hua-yen Buddhism derives an environmental ethic. The comparative philosopher Steve Odin independently confirms Cook's judgment. According to Odin, the "relational cosmology" of Hua-yen Buddhism

> is codified by the famous doctrinal formulas . . . "interpenetration of part and whole" and . . . "interpenetration of part and part." In such a manner Hua-yen Buddhism has established a compelling ax-iological cosmology according to which, given that everything functions as a causal condition for everything else, there is nothing which is not of value in the great harmony of nature. This view further entails a morality of unconditional compassion and loving kindness for all sentient beings in nature.[9]

As Cook realizes more fully than Odin, this account resonates better with the new physics than with ecology, since in the latter (at least, as presently modeled) there is a good deal that is aleatory. The web of life, to put the point in an alternative figure, is loosely woven of coarse hemp. It is not as finely strung and tightly stretched as Indra's net of jewels. On the other hand, the perfectly turned, energetic subatomic "particles," mutually defined and theoretically well behaved, seem to be nicely captured by the Hua-yen metaphor.

The domains of science are vertically integrated. The organic relationships that are the subject of ecology rest ultimately on the mathematical relationships that are the subject of quantum physics and relativity theory. Ecology and the new physics present interesting theoretical analogues, but they are also related, respectively, as the apex of a pyramid is related to its base.

As to practical philosophy, Hua-yen Buddhism conveys an outlook congenial to environmental ethics. In nature, pain and death are facts of life at the heart of evolutionary and ecological processes. Each organism purchases life at the cost of the death of others. Even plants, autotrophs though they may be, rely on heterotrophs—animals, fungi, and microbes—to recycle the nutrients on which they depend for life. Death is as indirectly necessary to plant life, in other words, as it is directly necessary to the life of the top carnivores. And pain is necessary to the survival of an animal organism, however, unwelcome it may be. A genetically anesthetized animal would have as lethal a birth defect as one born blind or deprived of some other vital sensory function. Attempts to extend standard

Western ethics to nonhuman natural entities and nature as a whole have proved counterproductive from an ecological point of view: Begin with typical moral dualities, such as "pleasure equals good" and "pain equals evil," or "life equals good and death equals evil." Add the ethical axiom that as moral agents it is our duty to maximize good and minimize evil. And then apply these concepts to nature. Standard Western approaches to ethics, extended *simpliciter* to nature, would require us to divide our fellow creatures into good guys and bad guys and condemn the very soul of ecological processes—trophic relationships—as inherently evil, since ecological processes inherently involve pain and death. In the Hua-yen view—which we might regard as a Buddhist spin on the indigenous Chinese polar, not dualistic, conception of opposites—pleasure and pain, life and death, are identical. As Cook comments:

> Both life and death are part of the one ever-changing process which we call being (which is really a "becoming") and thus both are conditions for that being. . . . The real world is a world of lice as well as butterflies, horse piss as well as vintage champagne, and to the person who has truly realized this, one is as good as the other. . . . This is difficult to accept . . . for it demands that one make room not grudgingly or fatalistically, but joyously and with profound gratitude, for the horse urine and lice that do in fact coexist with fine champagne and beautiful butterflies. The [holistic] view sees these as no less real, and no less wonderful, once we have transcended a petty, partial view of existence in which our comfort and unslakable thirst determine what has and has not a right to exist. In the [holistic] universe, which is one organic body of interacting parts, it is an act of self-defeating madness to insist on a never-ending diet of vintage champagne, sunshine, and laughter, and to insist vehemently and with no small amount of hubris that urine, darkness, and tears be banished forever. . . . All that Hua-yen asks is that we realize, and appreciate, that we cannot have one without the other.[10]

TENDAI AND SHINGON

Hua-yen Buddhism came over to Japan as Kegon. Tendai and Shingon are, historically, two other major schools of Japanese Buddhism and among the first to become established in Japan. Both were founded by Japanese contemporaries—Saicho and Kukai, respectively—who brought them directly from China. The corresponding schools in China are T'ien-t'ai and Chen-yen.[11]

The T'ien-t'ai school emphasized the serious study of Mahayana Buddhist texts, in addition to meditation and discipline. The Saddharma-Pundarika, or Lotus Sutra, was supposedly the last of the Buddha's sermons. According to Chi-i, a sixth-century C.E. T'ien-t'ai systematizer of Buddhist doctrine, it was, accordingly, not only final in the temporal sense but final in authority as well. [12] More explicitly than anywhere else, the Lotus Sutra reveals the Buddha as a universal essence—the *bhutatathata*, or Buddha-nature—universally present. In the eighth century, Chan-jan, the ninth patriarch of the T'ien-t'ai school in China and an older contemporary of Saicho and Kukai, was inclined to push Mahayana universalism to its logical conclusions. He argued that

> we may know that the single mind of a single particle of dust comprises the mind-nature of all sentient beings and Buddhas. . . . Therefore, when we speak of all things, why should exception be made in the case of a tiny particle of dust? Why should the substance of the *bhutatathata* pertain exclusively to "us" rather than to "others"? [13]

A correspondingly universal environmental ethic might be mined from Chan-jan's T'ien-t'ai metaphysics, not unlike the environmental ethic mined by contemporary environmental philosophers from A. N. Whitehead's (in some ways) similar metaphysics. [14] In the hands of Saicho and his Tendai successors, in any case, the largely logical and metaphysical concern of Chan-jan—to press Buddhist universalism indiscriminately to the whole of the phenomenal and mundane world, to particles of dust, and so on—became more narrowly (but more interestingly, from the point of view of this monograph) focused on the soteriological significance of the natural environment. Saicho was the first Japanese to use the phrase "the Buddha-nature of trees and rocks." [15]

In China, the Chen-yen sect was in a sense opposite to the T'ien-t'ai. While the latter was inclined to scholarship, doctrinal systematization, and informed meditation as a preparation for gradual enlightenment, the former was more given to efficacious symbolism, ritual, and holy magic—with immediate, more popular religious ends in view. [16] In Japan, the Shingon and Tendai schools became assimilated and more eclectic. However, important differences remained. It is not hard to see in the mind-substance of Chan-jan something very like the *atman-brahman* of Vedantic metaphysics. With the magical identity of symbol and thing symbolized, characteristic of the Chen-yen sect informing his thought, Kukai, the Shingon founder, was less interested in positing an essential substance within phenomenal things (*bhutatathata*) than in establishing an identity between such things and the Buddhist absolute. The difference is subtle but significant. Trees and plants do not merely manifest the *bhutatathata*; rather, such things are, just as they are, Buddhas:

> Even though with the physical eye one might see the coarse form of plants and trees, it is with the Buddha-eye that the subtle color can be seen. Therefore, without any alteration of what is in itself, trees and plants may, unobjectionably, be referred to as Buddha.[17]

Earlier Mahayana philosophers developed the doctrine of three bodies of Buddha-reality: the *dharmakaya*, or body of the cosmic or absolute Buddha, which is identical at one extreme with the essential Void, or *bhutatathata*, and at the other with the *mahavairocana*, or Sun-Buddha, from which all other natures emanate, as sunlight from its central source; the *sambhogakaya*, or body of spiritual bliss, which is the ethereal manifestation of the heavenly Buddhas and the purely spiritual Bodhisattvas; and the *nirmanakaya*, the body of earthly forms or manifestations of the Buddha, of which Siddhartha Gautama was an indisputable example.[18] According to William R. LaFleur, a student of Asian languages and literature, Kukai posited "an identity of the Buddhist Absolute, the *dharmakaya* or 'body of the dharma,' with all forms and things in the phenomenal, mundane world." In other words, Kukai did not argue, as Chan-jan seems to have done, that ordinary things were *nirmanakaya*—that is, earthly forms or manifestations of the Buddha, if not enlightened to that point at least potentially so—but that they were the *dharmakaya*. LaFleur asserts categorically that

> the whole of Kukai's thought seems to be directed toward forging . . . an ontological union of the absolute with the mundane. Therefore, in his view plants and trees [have] Buddha-nature simply because they, along with everything else in the phenomenal world, are ontologically one with the Absolute, the *dharmakaya*. The only real problem is epistemological.[19]

The only real problem, in other words, is that we must awaken ourselves to the Buddha-nature abounding in the natural environment. We must acquire the "Buddha-eye." Thus, in an ironic turn of Buddhist intellectual history, Kukai's thought, beginning with the luxuriant metaphysical efflorescence of Mahayana, at once retrieves something of the Buddha's own affirmation of the ultimacy of the phenomenal and the rejection of the reality of the noumenal, and, at the same time, anticipates the goal of eventual Zen practice. Zen practice, as explored in subsequent discussion, will seem less directed toward stilling desire as a means to *nirvana* than toward cultivating a right way of perceiving the immediate environment as a means to *satori*. However, even if everything in the world is ontologically one with the Absolute, animals and plants are presumably no more aware of their Buddha-nature than unenlightened human beings are; and thus they, like us, must resolve to attain enlightenment, undergo disciplines, and finally realize Buddhahood.

The Lotus Sutra may have suggested a universal Buddha-*nature*, in other words, but it offered the possibility of enlightenment, or Buddha-*hood*, only for all sentient beings. In India, the possibility of enlightenment for sentient beings was intended to be a generous Mahayana extension of the umbrella of salvation, but in China and Japan it appeared as a niggardly limitation. Ryogen, a tenth-century Tendai monk, took up the problem as Saicho and Kukai had left it. He wrote a work entitled "Account of How Plants and Trees Desire Enlightenment, Discipline Themselves, and Attain Buddhahood." In it he expounded an analogy between the life cycle of a plant and the process of enlightenment followed by a human being. When a plant sprouts from its seed, it vows its desire for enlightenment. Because it is rooted in one place and does not speak, it lives, even more perfectly than a monk, a life of ceaseless meditation, discipline, and austerity. It opens itself, through its leaves, to the radiance of the sun, the body of the *mahavairocana*. Its flowering and seeding are the fruits of its enlightenment, its beneficence. Finally, when of itself it withers and dies, without being killed by disease or cut down, it enters into extinction, or *nirvana*. Plants are all Buddhist monks, arising, continuing, changing, and ceasing to be. They not only possess Buddha-nature, undisturbed they attain Buddhahood. Ryogen renders his theory consistent with the Lotus Sutra by including plants among sentient beings: "We must, therefore, regard these as belonging to the classification of sentient beings. Therefore when plants aspire and discipline themselves, sentient beings are doing so."[20]

In the twelfth century, the Tendai scholar Chujin took Ryogen's argument a step further by eliminating its implication that the Buddhahood of plants and trees is (as for human beings) only a potentiality, and that the process of actualization is based on a human paradigm: "As for trees and plants there is no need for them to have or to show the thirty-two marks (of Buddhahood); in their present form—that is by having roots, stems, branches, and leaves, each in its own way has Buddhahood."[21] In LaFleur's view, when Chujin

> sees the Buddhahood of plants resident in their mere possession of roots, stems, branches, and leaves, he is affirming their ordinary mode of existence in the world as one which is in itself an enlightened existence. . . . He does not follow Ryogen in forcing the members of the plant world into a frame of reference based on hu-

man experience [but] permits these members of the natural world to have their own enlightenment in their own way and on their own terms.[22]

Just as Buddhism was inevitably modified by the Confucian and especially by the Taoist intellectual climate of China, on arriving in Japan it was inevitably modified by the Shinto intellectual climate there.[23] Shinto (a word derived from the Chinese *shin tao*, meaning "the way of the higher spirits or gods") pictured a natural world teeming with *kami*, or gods, associated not only with the sky and upper atmosphere but with mountains, streams, lakes, trees, and caverns. The Japanese islands were thought to have been originally inhabited only by *kami*. The eventual human inhabitants, the Japanese, were descended from them. Hence the worship of these nature spirits was also bound up with ancestor worship. Japan, moreover, is a country endowed with an exceptional and haunting natural beauty—a beauty not lost on its populace, who celebrated it in painting and verse.

Perhaps, therefore, it should not be surprising that after several centuries of residence in Japan Indian Buddhism was turned on its head. Sentient beings, condescendingly admitted in India to the long and arduous path to enlightenment, were, in Japan, broadened as a class to include plants as well as animals. And all living natural beings, rather than being regarded by the Japanese Buddhists as at a lower stage of awareness, were elevated to Buddhahood as is. Thus, the Tendai and Shingon spiritual pilgrims might step out of the temple and find themselves surrounded by Bodhisattvas—not invisible graduates of the physical plane but the ordinary living beings of the natural environment. As LaFleur puts this point,

> Chujin's theories . . . made it possible from within a Buddhist context to view natural phenomena as already enlightened; this meant that in some sense, at least, things within nature could be seen as Buddhas and therefore as approximate equivalents—although within another vocabulary—of *kami*.[24]

Japanese Buddhist attitudes and values in regard to nature were expressed not only through the medium of philosophy. They were also articulated through *geido*, or the "*tao* of art." A long tradition of Japanese poets—including Teika, Saigyo, Basho, and Sesshu—captured the delicate Japanese Buddhist religio-aesthetic posture toward nature in a medium accessible to a broad audience. These poets did more, perhaps, than their philosophical colleagues to infuse the popular culture with it. The concept of nature in this tradition has two aspects, according to the philosopher Omine Akira: "nature as companion and nature as Buddha."[25] In the former aspect, sentient beings, à la Ryogen, had Buddha-nature but had not yet attained Buddhahood. As Steve Odin puts it, "mountains and rivers, stones and trees, flowers and birds, all have the potential for enlightenment and tread the path to Buddhahood together."[26] Nature, thus, is the monk's companion on the path to enlightenment. In the latter aspect, à la Chujin, nature is the *dharmakaya*, and natural beings are not so much companions as saviors. Perhaps no Japanese poet better captured this aspect of nature than Saigyo, who wrote *waka*, or thirty-one-syllable verse. Here is an example:

> Long-living pine,
> Of you I ask: everlasting
> Mourning for me and
> Cover my corpse; here's no
> Human to think of me when gone.[27]

Commenting on this poem, LaFleur suggests that the poet is asking the pine to do nothing extraordinary and unnatural.

> Simply by existing in its ordinary mode of being as an evergreen tree it can adequately conceal his corpse from the world and from the elements. . . . Saigyo makes the natural form of the phenomenon an adequate substitute for man's cultic behavior and, as such, attributes to nature a decided preferability as the locus of the sacred.[28]

As to the potential such a view of nature affords for the development of an environmental ethic, one hardly needs to say anything more. If nature is the object of religious veneration and, as both LaFleur and Omine go on to argue, a source of salvation in Japanese traditions of thought—from an aboriginal nature-animism to a nature-oriented Buddhism—then we may expect that, with a sincere revival of those traditions, the Japanese landscape would be respected and used with care.

ZEN

In the course of setting out his enormously influential environmental critique of the Judeo-Christian cognitive complex, the historian Lynn White, Jr., suggests that more positive environmental attitudes and values are found in Zen Buddhism:

> What we do about our ecology [that is, the natural environment] depends on our ideas of the man-nature relationship. More science and more technology are not going to get us out of the present ecologic crisis until we find a new religion, or rethink our old one. The beatniks, who are the basic revolutionaries of our time, show a

sound instinct in their affinity for Zen Buddhism, which conceives of the man-nature relationship as very nearly the mirror image of the Christian view.[29]

White does not elaborate this cryptic remark. He must mean, however, that Zen Buddhism represents the relationship of people to nature opposite to the way it is represented in the Judeo-Christian worldview. In his opinion, the Bible portrays man as having been created in the image of God and as enjoying a rightful dominion over a profane nature. The "mirror image" of that view would represent nature as being quasi-divine and exercising dominion over man.

In Zen, one finds no such portrait of the relationship between man and nature. On the other hand, White is correct to imply that the mid–twentieth-century Western counterculture (calling itself the beat generation in the 1950s) had adopted Zen Buddhism as its epitome of an exotic Eastern alternative to the mainstream Western worldview. The explanation—if the vagaries of fashion in popular culture are ever explicable—for the selection of Zen Buddhism as the Oriental alternative worldview of choice may be that Zen had been rendered more or less accessible to Western academics by D. T. Suzuki and then attractively popularized in the essays of Alan Watts and the poetry of Gary Snyder.[30] The reasons for including a short section on Zen Buddhism here are three. First, Zen does have something unique to contribute to environmental philosophy; second, it remains vital in Japan (and North America); and third, it has, in any case, played an inspirational role in the twentieth-century Western romance with nature—a role somewhat analogous to that played by Hindu philosophy in the nineteenth-century Western romance with nature.

Liberally following White's lead, American environmental writers drew connections between Zen Buddhism and ecology. In a 1973 article entitled "The Ecologist as Zen Master," one wrote that in Zen we find "the interdependence and thus unity of all things, and the consequent artificiality of 'dualistic' thought patterns." After providing a couple of examples of ecological interdependence, the author concludes that "the very study of ecology, then, is the elaboration of Zen's nondualistic thinking."[31] In a better-informed discussion, the Chinese-American political scientist Hwa Yol Jung summed up his assessment of the contribution of Zen to environmental philosophy thusly:

> What then are Zen's potential contributions to today's ecological crisis? In the first place, where the West holds to a technological ethos and an ethic of affluence, Zen offers an aesthetic ethos and an ethic of simplicity and frugality. . . . Zen seeks an active harmony between man and nature. . . . The way of Zen is not to manipulate and control nature, but rather to disclose it as it is.[32]

More recently, Allan Grapard, a distinguished student of Japanese religions, has given academic imprimatur to the association in the popular American mind between Zen and Japanese culture, on the one hand, and between Zen and the mid–twentieth-century environmental movement, on the other. Invoking all the qualifications that any serious scholar would append to such sweeping and oversimple statements, he does not disagree with the casual Western view that Zen is "the school of thought and practice which best represents Japanese culture," and that Zen represents "something akin to the ecological dream of contemporary marginals [that is, Green counterculturalists]."[33]

The word *zen* is the Japanese pronunciation of the Chinese *ch'an*, which is in turn the Chinese rendition of the Sanskrit *dhyana*, which means (roughly) meditation. At the heart of Ch'an/Zen Buddhism is practice, not theory. Indeed, this particular school of Buddhism can be regarded as antitheoretical and even antirational. One could say that it lies at the opposite end of the doctrinal/rational-meditational/intuitional spectrum from the Chen-yen/Shingon school.

The legendary founder of Ch'an in China is Bodhidharma. His name means (roughly) "Enlightened Law" or "Path to Enlightenment," and—if a real person—he arrived from India in the early sixth century C.E. Zen was established in Japan in the late twelfth century. Ch'an enjoyed wide influence in China during the Sung and Yüan dynasties.[34] In Japan, Zen became cultivated by the powerful samurai. However limited, it exerted a profound influence on Japanese culture, artistic and temperamental as well as intellectual, and, as noted, remains vigorous (there and elsewhere) down to the present day.[35]

In the practice of Zen, scriptural study, doctrinal teaching, programmed spiritual development (like the Eightfold Path), and beneficent works are deemphasized. But the central Buddhist institution of a simple and disciplined monastic life is retained. Enlightenment is understood to occur in an instantaneous flash of insight rather than as the culmination of a gradual process of deepened awareness. Such enlightenment, however, is not a matter of grace or happenstance. It follows only upon arduous training with a master, austere living, and long periods of deep meditation.[36]

Though eschewing correct understanding of doctrine as the principal means to enlightenment, Zen practice is rooted nevertheless in basic Buddhist teaching. Suffering is the result of the desire for that which is inherently impermanent—any- and everything under the sun. Liberation from suffering is not the satisfaction but the extinction of desire, resulting from the visceral realization of the emptiness at the core of oneself and of all other things. As the Mahayana interpretation of this emptiness was quasi-substantive—the universal Buddha-nature—then self and nonself are one. Enlightenment, however, is not just to know this fact but to seize it in direct experience. Indeed, given the abstract and paradoxical nature of the truth about reality, such knowing can be as much an obstacle to palpable enlightenment as anything else that might substitute for the real McCoy.[37]

Dogen, one of the greatest of the Zen masters, commented during the thirteenth century on the dialectical relationship between Buddhist doctrine and the direct experience of nature. In a chapter titled "The Voice of Streams and the Form of Mountains," from his major work, *Shobogenzo*, Dogen tells the story of a poet who achieved enlightenment while listening to the nocturnal babbling of a mountain stream. He comments, wryly,

> Is this example of Awakening while hearing a stream of some bene-
> fit to us latecomers? Is it not deplorable—how many times—that
> we have let leak away the possibility of being converted by the nat-
> ural body of the Buddha? But then should we not investigate how
> we listen to streams, how we look at the form of mountains? . . .
> Small indeed is the difference between all those years without
> seeing the Buddha in the mountains and without hearing the Bud-
> dha in streams and this particular night when they were. . . .
> However the question is: what did shock the poet into Awakening?
> Was it the voice of the stream? Or was it the flood of words poured
> over him by his master? I harbor the idea that the talk of his master
> was still echoing in his mind and mixed in an obscure manner with
> the stream.[38]

Zen practice aims not at understanding but at, shall we say, unmediated but nonetheless informed experience. A good deal of Zen teaching is therefore simultaneously designed to frustrate the understanding and awaken the fused consciousness to which Dogen alludes. We might think of Zen meditation and instruction as a two-track ascent. Through meditation, the Zen student tries directly to reach the empty core of his or her being. Meanwhile, the Zen master tries to paralyze the disciple's understanding, in hopes that the conceptual veil separating the disciple from the actual world will fall away. This the master does by assigning *koans* (the famous Zen paradoxes) for the disciple to contemplate, asking apparently answerless questions, answering straightforward questions with nonsensical responses, playing practical jokes, and behaving rudely and sometimes violently.[39]

Zen accordingly has led to a peculiar apprehension of the environment called *satori*. As it appears in Zen poetry—especially well conveyed by the austerity and simplicity of the seventeen-syllable haiku form—*satori* is the very opposite of an otherworldly religious experience. *Satori* is not getting behind the phenomena to experience the characterless ground of being in all things—a clear, pure qualityless state of consciousness describable equally as absolute emptiness and as absolute suchness. *Satori* is, rather, the experience of the seamless unity of the sensory phenomena presented to consciousness. Things are just what they are. But they are not experienced in relation to the experiencer, whose ideas and interests, attitudes and values, divide and distort them. Time and timelessness coalesce. Eternity is arrested in the most fleeting of moments.[40] A famous Basho haiku perfectly captures the essence of this integrated, infinitesimal eternality:

> An old pond, mirror still.
> Quick frog, slanting waterward.
> A liquid plop.

In the final chapter, entitled "Love of Nature," of his book *Zen and Japanese Culture*, D. T. Suzuki connects the Kegon (Hua-yen) doctrines of mutual identity and mutual causality to the natural aesthetic in Zen Buddhism: "The balancing of unit and multiplicity or, better, the merging of self with others in the philosophy of Kegon is absolutely necessary to the aesthetic understanding of Nature."[41] Nature is a seamless continuum, in which each momentary and unsubstantial event arises conditioned by the whole and, in turn, conditioning the whole. Self and world fuse in a field of relationships. Thus according to Suzuki,

> Zen proposes to respect Nature, to love Nature, to live its own life; Zen recognizes that our Nature is one with objective Nature, not in the mathematical sense but in the sense that Nature lives in us and we in Nature. For this reason, Zen asceticism advocates simplicity, frugality, straightforwardness, virility, making no attempt to utilize Nature for selfish purposes.[42]

The Greek word *aisthêsis* means sensory perception, and "aesthetic experience" in English has come to mean a disinterested experience of beauty. In the West, aesthetic experience has been especially occasioned by the disinterested perception of crafted objects—of artifacts made precisely to provoke such an experience both in the artist and in others. Until relatively recently, Westerners went for aesthetic experience primarily to galleries, theaters, and concert halls. In the West, the idea of repairing to nature for aesthetic experience was late to bloom, has been less emphasized, and remains less refined than in the East.[43]

Indeed, Western aesthetic experience of nature is arguably not direct but derived from the aesthetic experience of art. One might say that in the West, historically, Aristotle's famous dictum "Art imitates nature" was in fact reversed. Only nature that imitated art was deemed worthy of aesthetic appreciation. Landscape was valued in nature only after it appeared as a genre of painting. Zen painting and poetry, by contrast, seem less to imitate nature than to capture a direct and primary aesthetic experience of nature—the experience of *satori*.

If the foregoing analysis is correct, in Zen (and in Japanese culture more generally) we may discover a highly developed and cultivated environmental aesthetic—something sorely lacking in the West. Ethics, as noted in the first pages of this monograph, imposes limitations on freedom of action. Aesthetics, by contrast, has none of the burdensome connotations of ethics. The good is a demanding ideal. But the beautiful is seductive. In comparison with environmental ethics, environmental aesthetics opens up possibilities of a freer, more creative human relationship with nature.[44]

The question pressed earlier in this discussion—to what extent does this or that Eastern concept of oneness correspond to the ecological concept of wholeness?—is not appropriate here. *Satori* is not a concept. But the distinctly Zen experience of *satori* could serve as a concrete aesthetic analogue of the unity between man and the environment implied by ecology. For people to cultivate a direct experiential merger with nature—through an aesthetic apprehension of water lilies, frogs, and ponds, say, or of mountain laurel, cherry blossoms, and spring mists—could only represent a clear gain for the cause of environmental awareness.

THE JAPANESE AND THE ENVIRONMENT: A PARADOX

From all that has been written in this chapter, one might well infer that environmental ethics would be flourishing in Japan and that the Japanese would be leading the rest of the world in a crusade for local and global ecological responsibility. But, alas, such is not so. It is true that the uplands of Japan remain forested, and, much to the consternation of the United States government, Japan zealously protects its small-scale, labor-intensive, and environmentally benign agriculture from ruinous foreign competition. Further, Japan has devoted a relatively large part of its landscape to national parks and other protected areas. As a result, rural Japan remains beautiful and, as densely settled countrysides go, relatively healthy, ecologically speaking. But an elaborate sociological study indicates that the Japanese are far less knowledgeable and concerned about wildlife than North Americans are.[45] Japan's industrial areas are notorious for their pollution, as are Japanese cities for smog and grime. Many modern pollution-caused diseases were first discovered in Japan—perhaps most infamously the effects on the human nervous system of heavy metals, which contaminate fish in industrially fouled waters. Japanese logging companies are the principal agents of deforestation in the tropical rain forests of Southeast Asia. Japanese drift-net fishing is impoverishing the world's oceans. And last, but by no means least, the obdurate Japanese taste for whale meat has brought several species of whales to the brink of extinction. (In defense of satisfying that taste, some Japanese have argued that eating whales is part of their culture and that they have as much right to it as, say, the Spanish do to bullfighting. However, this is not supported by Japanese cultural history. Whale meat has been part of the Japanese dietary for scarcely a century.)

To the foregoing litany of the environmental sins of the Japanese I would append a personal anecdote. While walking in the Ginza district of Tokyo in 1989, I came across an ivory shop that openly displayed, in addition to carved pieces of ivory, several whole elephant tusks. As this effrontery suggests, the Japanese are no more sensitive to the plight of the most magnificent of large endangered terrestrial mammals than to that of the most magnificent of large endangered marine mammals. The Japanese government continues to resist efforts to impose a global ban on traffic in ivory, horn, furs, and like commodities—traffic that, if left unstinted, will result in the extinction of some of the world's most charismatic animal species.[46]

How can we understand this enigma?

Allan Grapard suggests that the explanation is simple. Throughout the twentieth century, and even more intensely and profoundly after its defeat in the Second World War, Japan Westernized. "Having imported indiscriminately most of the West's industrial and economic practices, as well as [the] 'cultural' assumptions which accompany these practices, the Japanese have come to face very much the same problems the West is confronted with."[47] Japan rushed to embrace Western technology and promptly forgot its own intellectual culture, Grapard says in effect. Thus nature—beautiful, sacred, and salvific in traditional Japanese thought—was, as in the West, profaned and desecrated:

> Japan turned the century and opened to the West in a catastrophic manner: rejecting much of its past, it emulated the power and discourse of Europe and assimilated in no time the idea that nature is something to be controlled. . . . In the process of industrialization . . . Japan has become a land destroyed and polluted.[48]

Consistent with one of the organizing principles of this book, Grapard believes that Japan can develop an environmental ethic uniquely its own by recovering its intellectual heritage. "The Japanese cultural tradition," he writes, "hides in its deepest recesses a vast storehouse of notions and practices which may be helpful in establishing a culturally grounded ecophilosophy."[49] In his discussion, Grapard explores the potential of Shinto mythology and Zen Buddhism for such a "culturally grounded" Japanese "ecophilosophy." He concludes by stating that "the Japanese could rediscover some fundamental attitudes which could become the basis for developing an environmental ethic, grounded in philosophical systems which had guided Japan for centuries and were forgotten in the aftermath of war."[50]

However, Grapard warns that while the potential for an indigenous environmental ethic in traditional Japanese thought is great, there may be less of a fit with paradigms in contemporary Western environmental ethics than one might suppose. Nature, as conceived in traditional Japanese thought, is heavily vested with cultural elements. As Grapard puts it, a nature-culture "dialectic" has characterized both Shinto and Japanese Buddhism. Therefore, in his view,

> it might be said that what has been termed the "Japanese love of nature" is actually the "Japanese love of cultural transformations and purifications of a world which, if left alone, simply decays." So that the love of culture takes in Japan the form of a love of nature. It may be said that traditional interpreters of Japanese culture have failed to see this point, blinded as they were, perhaps, by a Western romanticism which is out of place.[51]

The alien "Western romanticism" to which Grapard alludes is apparently a love of wild nature on a grand scale—wilderness landscapes, in other words. Exploring the reasons why Japan was not deforested well before the twentieth century, as many other densely populated countries with steep slopes and fragile soils were, the forest historian Conrad Totman rejects the "love of nature" explanation, more bluntly than Grapard, as not only false but a confusion of terms. According to Totman, the "nature" celebrated in traditional Japanese philosophy and poetry

> is an aesthetic abstraction that has little to do with the "nature" of a real ecosystem. The sensibility associated with raising *bonsai*, viewing cherry blossoms, nurturing disciplined ornamental gardens, treasuring painted landscapes, and admiring chrysanthemums is an entirely different order of things from the concerns and feelings involved in policing woodlands and planting trees.[52]

So, apparently, even what most favorably impresses the contemporary environmentalist about Japan—that it has remained green (an "emerald archipelago," as Totman calls it)—owes little if anything to the exalted place of nature in traditional Japanese thought. The contemporary environmentalist sees one "nature" in Japan—forested mountains and traditionally husbanded alluvial valleys, together forming a fairly healthy, functioning ecosystem—while the "nature" so venerated in traditional Japanese art, religion, and philosophy is small in scale, cultivated, abstract, and stylized. Totman notes, "the concerns of those who restored woodlands were emphatically 'practical.' They were concerned with what erosion did to road, village, and cropland. [And] they wanted forests that would meet human material needs."[53]

The French Japanologist Augustin Berque reinforces Grapard's intimations and Totman's blunt declarations that the well-documented traditional Japanese love of nature is not to be confused with contemporary Western environmentalism's love of nature: "As is well known, Japanese culture has paid delicate attention to its natural environment; but this was not environment in general; it was a selection of some places . . . , some plants . . . , some moments of the year . . . , etc., all entangled into certain sets of regular associations."[54]

The Yale environmental sociologist Stephen R. Kellert has empirically confirmed Berque's cultural analysis. According to Kellert, "only a limited Japanese appreciation of nature and wildlife has been identified, and then in a typically narrow emotional, ecological, and intellectual context focusing on single species or aesthetically significant individual natural objects."[55]

Berque explains the twentieth-century Japanese environmental debauchery not as an abandonment of traditional environmental ideals but rather as a function of them. The traditional appreciation only of certain elements of the environment, the association of places with notable persons and events of the past, the patterning of gardens on certain landforms, and the selective appreciation of landscapes via these patterns all conspire to render the Japanese capable of "ignoring for some time an objective environmental change. . . . [Thus] the Japanese could at the same time love and respect nature and beauty, on the one hand, and on the other let their environment become, during the sixties, one of the most polluted and disfigured in the world."[56]

In an analysis complementary to Berque's, Yuriko Saito, a professor of landscape architecture at the Rhode Island School of Design, argues that the evident appreciation of nature exhibited in Japanese gardens has an ironic aspect. The famous garden architects of yore selected what in their view were only the worthiest natural landscapes as motifs and then strove, in re-creating them on a small scale, to improve on them. Hence a garden, a human artifact, might be perceived as a more perfect microcosmic manifestation of the nature of nature than wild, uncultivated nature could ever be. By contrast, real nature might be regarded as a bit shabby and inferior to reconstructed "nature." She argues further that "the Japanese gardeners' obsession with creating the 'natural' look and meticulously maintaining the idealized form and arrangement of each material should be interpreted as a way of exerting power over nature."[57]

This study, let it be remembered, is concerned with exploring the environmental attitudes and values in the world's great and diverse intellectual traditions, not with explaining past environmental behavior, whether good or bad. Its principal purpose is to audit the fund of ecological ideas on which the world's various peoples may draw as we face a common and unprecedented global environmental crisis. Whether or not it was Westernization and an abandonment of their traditional love of nature or the alleged myopia and narcissism of that love which allowed the Japanese to ignore the untoward environmental effects of twentieth-century industrialization is not the issue—at least, not of this monograph. Still less important is whether ecocentric or anthropocentric values preserved Japan's forests. How, rather, may a culturally harmonious, ecologically resonant environmental ethic be constructed from the conceptual materials afforded by Japan's intellectual heritage? That is the pertinent and the only practical question.

The stakes are high. We hope, of course, that the Japanese will keep Japan green. And we hope that they will clean up their polluting industries. But Japan's economic reach has become global in scope and heavy in weight. The severely threatened ecological integrity of the world's oceans and rain forests will depend on the cooperation and the leadership of the Japanese in international conservation initiatives.

And the potential is great. While the much-bruited "love of nature" endemic in popular Japanese culture may be limited in the ways that Grapard, Berque, Saito, Kellert, and Totman have all noted, the intellectual heritage of Japanese Buddhism contains a richer and more imaginative tradition of speculation about the spiritual and moral value of nonhuman natural entities and nature as a whole than any other so far encountered on this world tour. Thus it would not seem farfetched to suppose that Japanese traditions of thought might provide the contemporary Japanese with the intellectual wherewithal to open themselves to the Buddha-nature of the great whales, and to hear in the songs of whales the discourse of enlightened beings, and to want to learn from these Bodhisattvas rather than slaughter them. Similar things might be said about the ancient dipterocarps in the tropical forests of Southeast Asia.

Further, Zen-influenced Japanese garden architecture might be taken as a microcosmic model of the general human relationship with nature. In Japanese gardens, one finds arrangements of grass, streams, shrubbery, and trees so subtle that the gardens hardly appear cultivated at all. Today, as the global human population soars, designated wilderness areas and wildlife reserves are subject to the enormous and eventually (in all probability) irresistible pressure of human encroachment. The old approach to conservation—to designate certain areas as nature preserves and segregate them from human development—is a holding action at best. The foremost problem for contemporary environmental philosophy is to create an ecologically informed environmental ideal that includes human economic activity. One way of stating this shift in basic conservation philosophy is to say that an ideal of a garden planet must, of necessity, replace the ideal of a planet divided sharply but equitably between the natural and the human realms. In the development of this ideal, future conservationists may have much to learn from Zen and Zen-inspired landscape architecture, in which the natural and the cultivated, the human and the nonhuman, are so integrated and harmonized that it is difficult to discern where the one begins and the other ends.

In other words, the peculiar fusion of nature and culture in the Japanese mind may be an asset rather than an obstacle to conservation in the twenty-first century. Contemporary Western conservation philosophy has inherited and perpetuated a radical separation of the human and the natural domains. Historically in the West, "man" has been pitted against nature—the former as hero, the latter as adversary—in an epic struggle for supremacy. Now that we human beings are completing our tragic conquest of nature, conservationists are inclined to reverse the roles, but the dualism itself usually goes unchallenged. In fact, *Homo sapiens* is as much a part of nature as *Loxodonta africana*, and human beings have always modified the environments they inhabit. The problem for conservation in the twenty-first century will be to search for and foster patterns of human use and inhabitation of the natural environment which are mutually enhancing and enriching. Given the success of the Japanese people in intensively using and densely inhabiting a limited and fragile environment over many centuries without destroying either its beauty (albeit partly marred by the devastating postwar industrialization) or its productivity, they may be exceptionally well qualified to take the lead in conserving an analogously small and fragile planet.

The prognosis is good. As Berque notes, a deemphasis of the subjective case is built into the Japanese language and reinforced by the conventions of Japanese literature.[58] As a result, there is a weaker dichotomy between the subjective and the objective—between self and nature and between oneself and other selves—in Japan than in the West. (As Berque also notes, such an observation has been made not only by Westerners about the Japanese but by the Japanese about themselves—from the distinguished philosopher Nishida Kitaro to the many authors of the popular, self-congratulatory *nihonjinron*, or nipponologies, written for domestic consumption.) The Japanese outlook is thus inherently relational and collective. In addition to the welcome capacity for identifying self with environment, and thus personal well-being with environmental well-being, such an outlook has contributed to the vaunted Japanese capacity to act in concert to achieve a common goal.

The political implications of this phenomenological fact about Japanese experience of self in relation to society are reinforced by Japanese political traditions. According to Totman, "Japan today should be an impoverished, slum-ridden, peasant society subsisting on a barren, eroded moonscape characterized by bald mountains and debris-strewn lowlands."[59] Political will is an important element in his explanation of why it is not: Japan's rulers were able to elicit compliance with their forest-conservation policies.

With the death of Emperor Hirohito, and the emergence of Japan during the 1980s as the world's foremost economic superpower, the Meiji Restoration is effectively over. Despite the debacle of the Second World War, the goals of the Meiji have been accomplished. Fritjof Capra has proposed that the next era in Japanese history be called the Ecological Restoration. Should the Japanese become as obsessed about preserving biological diversity and global ecological integrity as they have recently been about pulling off their "economic miracle," we may entertain a real hope that they will succeed in the former enterprise no less decisively than in the latter.

Takashi Kosugi, the chairman of the Committee on Environment in Japan's Diet, basically agrees with many of the conclusions in this chapter. "Many Japanese philosophical traditions," he writes, "reveal a respect for nature. I think that it is time for Japan to reexamine its traditions and redefine them in the context of the current environmental crisis. . . . Traditional concepts of harmony with nature must be broadened and adapted to the new global reality." As to the prospect for Japanese leadership on environmental issues, Kosugi is guardedly optimistic. Japan, he thinks, "is culturally isolated" and inexperienced in such a role. Hence, any bid for global leadership might be misinterpreted as "arrogance" and, against the historical background of the Second World War, "aggression." The environment, however, is one aspect of international relations in which Japan might begin to explore an unfamiliar global responsibility: "I think that the environment is an issue with which Japan can start this process. It is a new arena that has not yet acquired the baggage that security and trade have."[60]

6   Far Western
       Environmental Ethics

This sampler of environmental attitudes and values embedded in the world's major intellectual traditions and selected local indigenous world-views began at the eastern end of the Mediterranean Sea and at the dawn of recorded history. It has moved steadily eastward until reaching the western Pacific rim. Before crossing the Pacific to consider traditional American Indian environmental attitudes and values, it rests in flight briefly to consider the environmental attitudes of the Polynesians—principally represented by the Hawaiians, for whom the best documentary records and the most focused discussion exists.

POLYNESIAN PAGANISM

The Polynesian islands dot a great expanse of the Pacific Ocean which is roughly triangular in shape—from New Zealand at the southwestern corner to Easter Island at the southeastern corner to the Hawaiian archipelago at the apex. The origins of the Polynesians are unknown. Penultimately, they are descended from a horticultural seafaring people who, some three thousand years ago, migrated eastward to Fiji from islands near New Guinea, and then on to Samoa, Tonga, and the other islands in what is now called Western Polynesia. Between one and two thousand years ago, another eastward migration from Samoa peopled the Marquesas, Easter Island, the Society and Cook islands, and finally Hawaii and Aotearoa (New Zealand).[1] Polynesia is united by dialects of a common language and variations of a common material, social, and cognitive culture.

Its cosmogony is among the most distinctive features of Polynesian cognitive culture, and one that is especially germane to this study. Although many popular and local Polynesian origin myths abound (to one of which attention will shortly be given), a more abstract and esoteric "theory" of evolution is extant in both Hawaii and Aotearoa—the northernmost and southernmost enclaves of Polynesians—suggesting a common ancestor in the Society Islands, which are the cultural motherland, as it were, of Eastern Polynesia.[2] An especially detailed expression of this "theory" is given in the *Kumulipo*, a Hawaiian genealogical chant composed in the seventeenth century C.E. for the Big Island chief Kalani-nui-ia-mamao. Its second and third stanzas read, in part:

> From the source in the slime was the earth formed.
> From the source in the dark was the darkness formed. . . .
> The night gave birth.
> Born was Kumulipo [foundation of Darkness] in the night, a male.
> Born was Po'ele [the dark night] in the night, a female.
> Born was the coral polyp.
> Born of him a coral colony emerged.[3]

The *Kumulipo's* translator, Rubellite Johnson, observes that the genealogical origin of species—beginning here, as we see, with the coral polyp—developed in the *Kumulipo* is astoundingly similar to that of modern biology:

> The order of species in the *Kumulipo* is from invertebrates in Chant One to vertebrates in Chant Two. The order of progression is a sequence of forms growing more complex in the scale of evolution from coelenterates (coral polyp, coral), to annelids, nematodes (worms, segmented and unsegmented), echinoderms (asteroids, holothurians, echinoids), and mollusks (sea snails, mussels, i.e., pelycypods; shells, gastropods). . . . The Hawaiian invertebrate phyla and their appearance in the ascending scale of evolutionary complexity correspond rather well to taxonomic norms for invertebrate groupings.[4]

The biological knowledge recorded in the *Kumulipo* was greater than that existing in Europe when James Cook made contact with the Hawaiians in the eighteenth century. Of course, missing from the *Kumulipo* is Darwin's singular nineteenth-century scientific achievement: the concept of natural selection. But that should not be surprising, since natural selection provides a "mechanism"—in the conceptual package of genotypic variation, reproductive excess, competition, and survival of the fittest—driving the process of evolution. From a scientific point of view, the *explanation* of the proliferation and increased complexity of species by natural selection is crucial to the modern *theory* of evolution. However, from an environmental-ethical point of view, whether evolution is blindly driven by natural selection or bootstrapped by reproductive *mana* is neither here nor there. From an environmental-ethical point of view, what is important is the sense of relationship, of kinship, between human and nonhuman life implied in an evolutionary understanding of origins. Reflecting on the implications of the modern theory of evolution for environmental ethics, Aldo Leopold writes,

> It is a century now since Darwin gave us the first glimpse of the origin of species. We know now what was unknown to all the preceding caravan of generations: that men were only fellow voyagers with other creatures in the odyssey of evolution. This new knowledge should have given us, by this time, a sense of kinship with other creatures; a wish to live and let live; a sense of wonder over the magnitude and duration of the biotic enterprise.[5]

Kinship was extremely important to the traditional Polynesians. One's status in the highly organized and stratified society of ancient Hawaii, for example, was determined by genealogy, and anyone of note could name his or her ancestors back thirty or more generations.[6] In most traditional stratified societies, such genealogical tracings terminate in divinity. What is most remarkable about the *Kumulipo* is that it begins *beyond* the gods, with chaos or night itself, and moves on to "primitive" ancestral life forms, thus linking the royal scion by blood relationship not only with the divine powers above and beyond nature but with the myriads of kinds in the immediate natural environment.

Such continuity between "man" and nature as represented in the *Kumulipo* is augmented by a peculiar Polynesian form of animism. A Maori genealogical chant recorded in the nineteenth century by the British anthropologist Richard Taylor begins not with night but with the prior birth of bodiless consciousness:

> From the conception the increase,
> From the increase the swelling,
> From the swelling the thought,
> From the thought the remembrance,
> From the remembrance, the consciousness, the desire.
> The word became fruitful;
> It dwelt with the feeble glimmering;
> It brought forth night.[7]

This chant (linked with the *Kumulipo* by the cosmogonic importance of night) seems to imply that nature, for the Polynesian, is shot through from its very inception with life and consciousness.

Furthermore, the four principal Hawaiian gods—Kane, Kanaloa, Ku, and Lono—were each manifested by a wide variety of species. These mul-

tiple forms are called the *kino lau* of the gods. The scholar E. S. C. Handy
writes, "Probably if we knew in its entirety the ancient Hawaiian teachings
about nature and creation, it would be found that every natural phenomenon and form of life was thought to be an embodiment of a particular god
or demigod."[8] Hence, for the traditional Hawaiian, the environing life
forms were not only alive and conscious but also sacred, as manifestations
of the gods.

Even the Old Testament, a written history presented as one continuous
narrative, contains two inconsistent creation myths lying head to foot in
its first chapters, as noted earlier in this study. So it should not be surprising that in addition to the extremely sophisticated creation account in Hawaiian and Maori genealogical chants, we might find more popular, less
abstract, more typical origin myths among other Polynesian oral traditions. In one popular story, the demigod Maui fished up the Hawaiian
Islands.[9] In perhaps the most widely credited epic tradition, a mother figure, Papa, and a sky-father, Wakea, were parents first of the Big Island and
the island of Maui. Their first human child was a daughter, Ho'ohokukalani. Through an involved series of circumstances, Wakea mates with
Ho'ohokukalani, and she gives birth to Haloa the taro plant, the staple food
of the Polynesians; Haloa the chief, progenitor of the Hawaiian chiefs and
people; and the islands of Lanai and Molokai. Reunited with Wakea, Papa
completes the (pro)creation by giving birth to the islands of Oahu, Kauai,
Niihau, and Kahoolawe. So the Hawaiian people are represented as the
younger siblings of their major food source, the taro; and both the taro and
the people are children of Earth and Sky. Right down to the present, the
Hawaiians call themselves *kama'aina*—children of the land.

A most interesting and cogent environmental ethical interpretation has
been given to this myth by the Hawaiian scholar Lilikala Kame'eleihiwa:

> In traditional Hawaiian society as in the rest of Polynesia, it is
> the duty of younger siblings and junior lineages to love, honor, and
> serve their elders. This is the practice that defines the Hawaiian re-
> lationship to [the land and to] the taro that feeds the Hawaiian
> people. Thus the . . . concepts of *aloha 'aina*, or love of the land,
> and *malama 'aina*, or serving and caring for the land, stem from
> the traditional model. . . . The Hawaiian does not desire to con-
> quer his elder brother, the land, but to take care of it, to cultivate it
> properly, and make it beautiful with neat gardens and careful hus-
> bandry.

Kame'eleihiwa apparently alludes here to the despotic reading of Genesis at the core of the prevailing Western worldview (reviewed in chapter 2) as a foil for the Hawaiian worldview. She goes on:

Moreover, throughout Polynesia it is the reciprocal duty of the elder siblings to feed the younger ones as well as love and care for them. The relationship is thereby further defined; it is the land and the taro which feeds, clothes, and shelters its younger brothers and sisters, the Hawaiian people. So long as Hawaiians love, serve, and honor their elders, the elders will continue to do the same for them, as well as provide them with all their physical needs. Clearly, by this equation it is the duty of Hawaiians to *malama 'aina*, and as a result of this proper behavior the land will *malama* Hawaiians. In Hawaiian this perfect harmony is known as *pono*, which is often translated into English as "righteousness," but really refers to the universe being in perfect balance. [10]

However, everything was not all *aloha* and *malama 'aina* in Paradise before the arrival of the Europeans. Warfare, for one thing, was not uncommon; and Ku, the war god, demanded human sacrifice. Everyday life, moreover, was fettered by all sorts of *kapus* (taboos—a word of Polynesian origin). Further, Polynesian society was stratified into a strict hierarchy, which was basically feudal in form. Each island in the Hawaiian chain was divided into districts, subdistricts, farms, fields, and patches. Commoners worked the land and sea. Their activities were overseen and coordinated by several echelons of lesser *ali'i*, or chieftains, who reported to those above them, who in turn reported to the *ali'i nui*, or high chiefs. The *ali'i* exacted a tribute from the commoners—a portion of the fruits of their labor, which was amassed by the paramount chief, the *mo'i*, from whom it trickled back down to the petty aristocracy. The *ali'i nui* were considered to possess so much *mana* that they were divine. Attending such persons were personal *kapus* (a commoner's shadow, for example, might not fall on a high chief), the violation of which could be punished instantly by death.

Kame'eleihiwa also offers a most perceptive socio-environmental interpretation of the *kapu* system—at first glance a system that may seem wholly arbitrary and irrational. The Wakea-Papa myth also accounts for the institution of the *'aikapu*, or sacred eating (literally, "eating taboos")— taboos that stand at the foundation of the *kapu* system—according to which men and women eat apart and certain foods are forbidden to women. As Kame'eleihiwa sees it, the *'aikapu* symbolizes "the male imposition of order upon the chaotic nature of the female earth." [11] She suggests that it is a system of order both unnatural ("contrary to normal human behavior") and effected by violence. The whole system of *kapus*—from the *'aikapu* to the deadly personal *kapus* of the gods and high chiefs—provided the basis of the social order on which the economy depended.

The limits of the Polynesian resource base were palpable. Moreover,

these remote Pacific islands—many of them, like the Hawaiian chain, geo-
logically young—had no native land mammals and precious few other indigenous foodstuffs. (The Polynesians brought their cultivars, and the pig,
the dog, and the rat—the last no doubt inadvertently—with them to new
lands in their voyaging canoes.) While the fishing—a watery form of
hunting and gathering—was excellent, the land could not support the
gathering and hunting methods of the native peoples of North and South
America. Horticulture and aquaculture were the only viable methods of
getting an ample livelihood from the land. Taro cultivation (especially) and
fish ponds require a considerable amount of organization and engineering.
Fields have to be situated properly, terraces and irrigation sluices built and
maintained, and so on.

Settling truly virgin lands with ideal climates and largely free of predatory, parasitic, and disease organisms, the newly arrived Polynesian pilgrims (not known for sexual continence) must have multiplied rapidly.
Soon there would have been selective pressures favoring a social system
maximizing efficiency in the production of food. Besides managerial organization in the production of taro, breadfruit, bananas, coconuts, tapa,
fishing nets, canoes, and so on, political organization was necessary.
Boundaries had to be established and policed, water rights assigned, and
the like.

In addition to favoring a social system that could support and maintain
a highly organized bureaucratic and managerial infrastructure, conditions
also favored the development of militarism. Among the chief preoccupa-
tions of the *ali'i* was war. Significantly, a principal *kino lau* of Ku was Ku-
ka-'ai-moku—Ku-the-eater-of-islands, or (more freely translated) Ku-
the-island-conqueror. The relative isolation of each district—at least, on
the larger islands—by mountain ranges and lava ridges mirrored the absolute separation of each island by the ocean. Each district on the Big Island
of Hawaii, for example, was ruled by an independent *mo'i*, who could re-
lieve internal pressure for more arable land only by conquering a neighboring district. Each paramount chief, therefore, had to be constantly on
watch for the ambitions of the others, as well as for opportunities to expand
his own fiefdom.

In the mythopoeic representation of these prosaic facts of life, the main
way for the *ali'i nui* to remain *pono* was scrupulously to keep the *'aikapu*.
The intracultural perception of such observances was that the gods smiled
on the righteous chief and made his lands bountiful and his people prosperous. Similarly, crop failure and other natural disasters were sure signs
that the chief had lost favor with the gods—presumably because, know-

ingly or unknowingly, he had broken a *kapu*. In such circumstances, he was ripe for overthrow. But the symbolism, in any case, is altogether transparent. The *'aikapu*, and the *kapu* system generally, is the religious analogue of social structure as it divides women from men and commoner from aristocrat and surrounds males, and, in particular, the ranks of *ali'i*, from lower to higher with proportional degrees of *mana* and mystery, and thus with social status and political power and authority.

For the purposes of this monograph, the key point is that the land itself was part of this social structure—its abiding foundation. The social order and the natural order were integrated. As the paramount chief, so highborn and *mana*full as to be a god on earth, is at the pinnacle of the social order, so he is also at the pinnacle of the natural order. On the death of one chief and before the installation of a successor, the social order and the natural order revert to chaos. The *kapus* are broken: women eat pork, bananas, coconuts, and other male foods, and violate the sanctity of the *heiaus* (temples). Men eat with women. People go forth naked and copulate in public.[12] And the land is imagined to die. Indeed, it is not at all farfetched to suppose that in the midst of such social chaos the productivity of the land, absent the organization and discipline needed to maintain it, will falter: the irrigation systems become clogged with silt, weeds take over the taro patches, lianas climb over the fruit trees, and so on. When the next *mo'i* comes to power, he must deliberately and publicly reinstate the *'aikapu*. With that act, social order and discipline are restored and the land comes back to life.

The environmental ethic implicit in this religious representation of social-natural order is clear and immediate, albeit quite unlike anything encountered elsewhere in this study. Imagine a pyramid with the primary productive resource, the land itself, at the bottom. Over this is a layer of imported food plants, principally taro. Next is a human layer of commoners who work the land; immediately above them, land stewards, called *konohiki*, who coordinate and direct the work; above the land stewards come administrators of the *ahupua'a*, the subdistrict (usually a wedge-shaped valley bordered on two sides by ridges and on the third by the sea); and above them the administrators of the district, or *'okana*, which is ruled and protected by the *mo'i* and his retinue.

Food flows up from the bottom. And organization, defense against human attack and the wrath of the gods, and *mana* all flow down from the top. The measure of the health of the system is the sustained productivity of the land. The principal goal of the *ali'i nui* is *malama 'aina* and the principal means is *pono* behavior. In this model we have a socio-religious analogue of an agro-ecosystem—that is, an agricultural system modeled on an ecosystem. Compare this representation of the Hawaiian socio-agro-ecosystem with Aldo Leopold's image of a natural ecosystem:

> Plants absorb energy from the sun. This energy flows through a circuit called the biota, which may be represented by a pyramid consisting of layers. The bottom layer is the soil. A plant layer rests on the soil, an insect layer on the plants, a bird and rodent layer on the insects, and so on up through various animal groups to the apex layer, which consists of the larger carnivores. . . .
>
> Land, then, is not merely soil; it is a fountain of energy flowing through a circuit of soils, plants, and animals. Food chains are the living channels which conduct energy upward; death and decay return it to the soil. The circuit is not closed; some energy is dissipated in decay, some is added by absorption from the air, some is stored in soils, peats, and long-lived forests; but it is a sustained circuit, like a slowly augmented revolving fund of life.[13]

In the mythopoeic representation of the Hawaiian socio-agro-ecosystem, *mana* is the analogue of solar energy flowing through the circuit of land, taro and other food plants, and the several strata of human consumers. At the apex is the paramount chief, who, though not the source of this mystic energy, is its principal mediator or conduit into the system. When the chief is in his place, assiduously observing the *'aikapu* (that is, symbolically maintaining social order), religiously attending to his religious duties, and pursuing a prudent foreign policy—living *pono*, in short—the *mana* flows uninterrupted down through the ranks into the common people, their garden plants, and into the land itself. It is returned in the form of food, which flows back in the opposite direction—"a sustained circuit, like a slowly augmented revolving fund of life."

Underlying this text is a subtext on which depends the Hawaiian and more generally the Polynesian socio-agro-ecosystem. "Land . . . is not merely soil"; neither is it properly a commodity. According to Kame'eleihiwa, the traditional Hawaiian, pressured by the Europeans and Americans to sell them real estate, believed that buying and selling land "was equivalent to buying and selling one's elder brother."[14] After Kamehameha the First united all the Hawaiian islands, nominally he owned all the land. But the king, at the apex of the land pyramid from which all the people drew their sustenance, was its ultimate steward, not its owner. In truth, no one "owned" the land. Individual land ownership was not an operative concept in the traditional Hawaiian worldview.

In the case of the Maori, ancestral collective land tenure—in contradistinction to the modern Lockean concept of individual land ownership—is even more clearly pronounced. The Maori were no less devoted to genealogy than were the Hawaiians, but used it chiefly to divide themselves into tribes and subtribes rather than into gentry and commonality.[15] Each tribe traced its lineage back to an ancestor who had come in a voyaging canoe to Aotearoa from Hawaiki, the mythical (and controversial) place of origin.[16]

New Zealand is a much larger landmass than all of Hawaii. It lies in temperate latitudes, and the indigenous natural resources, both terrestrial and marine, found by the Polynesians on their arrival were richer and more diverse. Hence there was less pressure to cultivate the land intensively and efficiently, and (correlatively) less pressure to evolve a highly organized and hierarchical society. Tribal lines divided the people laterally rather than stratifying them vertically, and individuals experienced a greater sense of identity with a tribe, subtribe, and extended family. Ancestral lands, tribal identity, and individual identity thus merged in the traditional Maori mind. The New Zealand scholar E. M. K. Douglas writes,

> In the Maori consciousness, land . . . was their mother and ancestor, it was viewed as an integral part of their personal and group identity. . . . Land is personified, the mountains, hills, and rivers are named, [and] referred to as ancestors. As an ancestor, land embodies the spirit of the tribe and each individual descendent of the tribe. . . . Land is seen as the source of tribal and individual identity.[17]

From the prevailing Western point of view, land ownership is regarded as more an economic than a philosophic concern. But the modern Western concept of individual land ownership was specifically crafted and defended by the English philosopher John Locke. It has since become so ingrained in the Western worldview that it is perceived to be less an optional cultural idea than an empirical natural relationship.[18] Locke argued that when an individual "mixes" labor with a wild piece of land—clearing it of rank vegetation and planting it to crops—its natural productivity multiplies. Thus the individual has a right to enclose it and exclude others; in short, to make private property of it. When land becomes private property, it may be alienated—transferred, bequeathed, divested, bought, and sold. The environmental repercussions of this seventeenth-century Western conceptual novelty are momentous. One may husband the land, taking care not to kill the goose that lays the golden egg, and pass it on to one's offspring in full productive capacity. Or one may pursue another strategy. One may overwork, mine, or strip the land—thus drawing from it not a living but a windfall profit—sell or abandon it, move away, and leave the land in a ruined condition.

An individual's lifetime is finite. Thus, it is "rational" for the individual in atomized Western society to provide for a limited lifetime by short-term, high-profit exploitation of real private property—by strip-mining it, clear-cutting it, or whatever. In the Maori concept of land ownership, however, the tribe, not the individual, "owns" the land. A tribal community endures, if not forever, at least indefinitely. Moreover, a tribe's identity—among the Maori, anyway—is merged with a particular landscape; and an individual's identity is merged with the tribe. Thus, for the Maori, dislocation from ancestral lands is loss of tribal and hence of personal identity. Therefore, ruinous use of ancestral lands becomes unthinkable—or, at least, not a rational alternative. Correlatively, sustainable development, from a traditional Maori point of view, is the only kind of development that makes good sense.

The Australian Deep Ecologist Warwick Fox has eloquently anticipated these un-Lockean observations:

> We have a philosophical tradition in the West that says that if a person "mixes" their labour with some aspect of the environment then the product of that interaction becomes their *property*. . . . In the case of the Maori people, however, what they have traditionally "mixed" with their environment is not so much their labour as the contents of their mind, psychology, self, soul, or spirit—call it what you will. . . . As a cultural generalization, we can say that whereas we Westerners have invested ourselves in our property, Maori and many other indigenous peoples have invested themselves in their landscapes.[19]

To sum up, the traditional Hawaiians did not have a merely implicit environmental ethic, they actually expressed the concept—*malama 'aina*—in their language. The physical appearance of the land itself, their organized subsistence, the hierarchical structure of their society, their mythology—all correspond to the "trophic-dynamic" model of an ecosystem. Complementing this mytho-ecology, the ancient Hawaiians also achieved a mytho-evolutionary understanding of themselves in relationship to the rest of the natural world, fostering a sense of their kinship with all other forms of life. Moreover, for the Hawaiians, and for the Polynesians more generally, land was held in common, not owned by autonomous individuals. Therefore, the idea of individual gain through unsustainable exploitation of land was not thinkable. Finally, in the case of Hawaii, the robust health of the land, under conditions of dense settlement and intense cultivation, before European disruption of the tightly integrated Polynesian belief system, social organization, means of subsistence, and system of land tenure, mutely attests to the efficacy of the Polynesian land ethic.

AMERICAN INDIAN LAND WISDOM

More than ten thousand years ago, Asiatic big-game hunters wandered across the Bering land bridge into the Western Hemisphere. These so-called Paleo-Indians were the ancestors of the American Indians, who eventually became a distinct race. There is, of course, no such thing as *the* American Indian worldview. North American Indian peoples, to say nothing of those in South America, were divided by hundreds of mutually unintelligible dialects of several distinct language stems, and they inhabited and culturally adapted to biomes ranging from dense wet cypress forests dripping with Spanish moss in the southeastern quarter of the continent to hot dry deserts in its southwestern quarter, and from rich grassy prairies in the Great Plains to the barren tundra of the far north. For each tribe there were a cycle of myths and a set of ceremonies, and from these materials one might abstract for each a particular view of nature.

However, recognition of the diversity and variety of American Indian cultures should not obscure a complementary unity to be found among them. Despite great differences, there were common characteristics that culturally united the American Indian peoples. The comparative theologian Joseph Epes Brown claims that

> this common binding thread is found in beliefs and attitudes held by the people in the quality of their relationships to the natural environment. All American Indian peoples possessed what has been called a metaphysic of nature; and manifest a reverence for the myriad forms and forces of the natural world specific to their immediate environment; and for all, their rich complexes of rites and ceremonies are expressed in terms which have references to or utilize the forms of the natural world.[20]

The historian Calvin Martin confirms Brown's conjecture:

> What we are dealing with is two issues: the ideology of Indian land-use and the practical results of that ideology. Actually, there was a great diversity of ideologies, reflecting distinct cultural and ecological contexts. It is thus more than a little artificial to identify a single, monolithic ideology, as though all Native Americans were traditionally inspired by a universal ethos. Still, there were certain elements which many if not all these ideologies seemed to share, the most outstanding being a genuine respect for the welfare of other life-forms.[21]

The religious genius of Nicholas Black Elk, a Lakota (or Sioux) shaman, and the poetic genius of John G. Neihardt combined to create *Black Elk Speaks: Being the Life Story of a Holy Man of the Oglala Sioux*, a masterpiece of American literature, published in 1932.[22] American Indian activist Vine Deloria, Jr., recently observed that *Black Elk Speaks* has been "elevated . . . to the status of an American Indian Bible."[23] Echoing Deloria's observation, the scholar Raymond J. DeMallie comments that "Black Elk's teachings appear to be evolving into a consensual American Indian theological canon."[24] In addition to the environmental attitudes and values native to the Lakota of the Great Plains (attitudes and values which are increasingly also the touchstone of a latter-day Pan-Indian belief system), the very different environmental attitudes and values implicit in the worldview of the forest Indians of the Great Lakes region, represented by the Ojibwa, are also considered in this chapter.

Lakota Shamanism

There is some similarity between the most basic elements of the Lakota worldview and the Polynesian origin myth of Wakea and Papa. Wakea is a sky-father and Papa a cosmic mother. According to Lakota cosmology, the sky is also a father, but the earth is a mother. Thus, unlike the Hawaiian worldview, in which the landmasses are offspring, the Lakota worldview represents the land itself as the procreative matrix. In the words of Black Elk (as interpreted by Neihardt), "Is not the sky a father and the earth a mother, and are not all living things with feet or wings or roots their children?" And, again, he speaks of "the earth, from whom we came and at whose breast we suck as babies all our lives, along with all the animals and birds and trees and grasses."[25]

As Lilikala Kame'eleihiwa points out, if a people believe themselves to have been born of divine, cosmic parents, then the other beings believed to have been born of the same parents will explicitly or implicitly be regarded as siblings. In Black Elk's narrative account of the Lakota worldview, the relationship is explicit. The prayerful prologue of *Black Elk Speaks* begins with these words:

> My friend, I am going to tell you the story of my life, as
> you wish; and if it were only the story of my life I think I would
> not tell it; for what is one man that he should make much of his
> winters, even when they bend him like a heavy snow? So many
> men have lived and shall live that story, to be grass upon the
> hills.
>
> It is the story of all life that is holy and is good to tell, and of us

two-leggeds sharing it with the four-leggeds and the wings of the
air and all green things; for these are children of one mother and
their father is one spirit.

And it ends with these:

Hear me four quarters of the world—a relative I am! Give me
the strength to walk the soft earth a relative to all that is! . . .
Great Spirit, Great Spirit, my Grandfather, all over the earth the
faces of living things are all alike. With tenderness have these come
up out of the ground. Look upon these faces of children without
number and with children in their arms that they may face the
winds and walk the good road to the day of quiet.[26]

Notice that for Black Elk the only essential difference between human
beings, birds, and beasts is their different modes of locomotion. The "two-
leggeds," "four-leggeds" and "the wings of the air," and all the plants "are
children of one mother and their father is one spirit." Therefore, "the faces
of living things are all alike." That is, all living things are kin; they share
a common parentage and heritage. Black Elk's principal prayer is to "walk
the soft earth a relative to all that is"—a kinsman of all living things and
a child of the earth and sky.

It is hard to imagine a simpler foundation for an environmental ethic
than this. To provide an analysis where none is needed, one may say that
the Lakota worldview pictures nature as a large extended family, and therefore mutual duties and obligations analogous to those governing family relations should also govern human relations with the earth and sky and with
all the other forms of life.

Sky and earth are father and mother; therefore, a filial piety should be
exhibited in one's relations with one's cosmic parents. This mother-earth
ethical precept was articulated by the Wanapum spiritual leader Smohalla,
who was under pressure to cede territory and adopt a Euro-American life-
style:

You ask me to plow the ground. Shall I take a knife and tear my
mother's bosom? You ask me to dig for stone. Shall I dig under her
skin for bones? You ask me to cut grass and make hay and sell it,
and be rich like white men. But how dare I cut off my mother's
hair?[27]

Relations between species should, in sum, be relations of mutual care
and mutual dependency. Hunting-gathering Plains Indians felt no practical
contradiction between their need to appropriate animals and plants for
their survival and their belief that animals and plants were their siblings.

Mutual care and mutual dependency imply mutual sacrifice. Provided that plants and animals were taken in response to genuine need and with demonstrative respect for the feelings of the victims, and that care was taken not to waste the harvest, then the Plains Indians—at least, in their view—did nothing that contradicted their family-model environmental ethic. Wooden Leg, a nineteenth-century Cheyenne (the Cheyenne were neighbors of the Lakota and shared their basic outlook), puts this point nicely and embellishes it with a small detail:

> The old Indian teaching was that it was wrong to tear loose from its place on the earth anything that may be growing there. It may be cut off, but it should not be uprooted. The trees and the grass have spirits. Whenever one of such growths may be destroyed by some good Indian, his act is done in sadness and with a prayer for forgiveness because of his necessities, the same as we were taught to do in killing animals for food and skin.[28]

Despite the simplicity and directness of what one might call the Lakota familial environmental ethic, Lakota natural philosophy was not lacking in abstract sophistication. Besides the sky-father and earth-mother, Black Elk also refers in kinship terms to the Great Spirit—as "Grandfather" (significantly, note well, not as "Father")—in the remarks quoted above. He mentions, further, "the four quarters of the world." The full text of Black Elk's prayer and the narrative in which it is embedded explain the sacred pipe and its adornments, which symbolize all the essential elements of the Lakota cosmos: in addition to the sky and the earth, Black Elk prays to the spirit-winds associated with the cardinal points of the compass—south, west, north, and east—each of which represents a "power" (growth, death, strength, and wisdom, respectively) symbolized by an associated color (yellow, blue, white, and red, respectively).

As Black Elk says, however, the six major spirits—sky, earth, south, west, north, and east—"are only one Spirit after all": the Great Spirit. The relationship between the Great Spirit, the four quarters, sky, earth, and the myriad other spirits and powers animating the Lakota world is best described as panentheism. Pantheism—"all-[is]-God," literally translated—is the view that nature collectively is divine. Panentheism—"all-[is]-*in*-God"—is the view that the divine both transcends and is immanent in all things. Here is how John Fire Lame Deer, an Oglala Sioux shaman of a generation or so younger than Black Elk, attempted to capture the particular Lakota spin on this theological option:

> Nothing is so small and unimportant but it has a spirit given it by Wakan Tanka [the Great Spirit—or, more carefully rendered, the

Great Mystery]. Tunkan is what you might call a stone god, but he is also a part of the Great Spirit. The gods are separate beings but they are all united in Wakan Tanka. It is hard to understand—something like the Holy Trinity. . . . The Spirit split itself up into stones, trees, tiny insects even, making them all *wakan* by His ever-presence. And in turn all these myriads of things which make up the universe flowing back to their source, united in one Grandfather Spirit.[29]

Thus in the Lakota worldview we find a deeper metaphysical concept of natural unity, reinforcing the straightforward familial environmental ethic. Though expressed in very different terms, the Lakota pantheistic principle of oneness among all creatures great and small is not altogether unlike the concept of *atman-brahman* or *bhutatathata* in the Hindu and Mahayana Buddhist philosophies, respectively. For the Lakota, in each thing—be it animal, vegetable, or mineral—hides a splinter of the Great Spirit, animating it and giving it life and consciousness.

There is no evidence that the Lakota holy men pursued the logical and psychological implications of this idea anywhere near as far as the thinkers of South and East Asia. Nor is there evidence to suggest that any Lakota were in the least interested in transcending their fragmentary state of spirit-being and achieving an experiential unity with the Great Spirit. To be sure, the Lakota shamans practiced a kind of spiritual regimen—the Vision Quest—which involved fasting and isolation, but the successful experiential terminus of this practice was nothing like *nirvana, satori,* or enlightenment. Rather, its aim was contact with a power broker from the spirit world in the form of a bird, animal, or natural phenomenon (such as thunder), experienced in an altered state of consciousness like a dream or hallucination. This difference may reflect not only a temperamental difference between the occidental Indians and the oriental; it may also reflect a slight but significant metaphysical difference in their respective concepts or principles of unity. The Great Spirit both stands apart from and at the same time "splits itself up into . . . the myriad of things which make up the universe" (the very definition of panentheism). Therefore, to "flow back to the source," as Lame Deer styles the process of death and spiritual recycling, would not be to merge oneself with an undifferentiated state of being-consciousness, since the Great Spirit is, in its transcendental mode, not undifferentiated.

Neither is there any evidence that anything quite like *ahimsa* characterizes the Lakota environmental ethic. To be sure, the Lakota respect other forms of life, and that respect flows directly from their worldview. But the Lakota expression of respect for the other fully conscious beings abounding in their universe has nothing of the passivity or of the patronizing and pitying quality of *ahimsa* about it. That may be because the Lakota do not regard themselves as in any way morally superior to or more spiritually advanced than other natural beings. Nor does their own future welfare depend on not accumulating bad *karma*. Traditional American Indians seem to have had no compunction about taking the lives of animals and plants, under the conditions mentioned above. But as evidenced by the kinship terms used to address animals and plants, they regarded nonhuman life-forms as, if anything, superior to themselves. Indeed, animals and plants, in permitting themselves to be taken for legitimate human needs, are said to "pity" people and to voluntarily sacrifice themselves for the sake of their younger siblings, the human beings.

As noted, the Lakota worldview represents a more or less conventional profile of American Indian natural philosophy—for contemporary American Indians as well as for non-Indians. The Pulitizer Prize–winning American Indian poet, novelist, and scholar N. Scott Momaday supports this generalization: " 'The earth is our mother. The sky is our father.' This concept of nature, which is at the center of the Native American worldview, is familiar to us all. But it may well be that we do not understand entirely what that concept is in its ethical and philosophical implications." Momaday then goes on to draw out those implications, and concludes, "Very old in the Native American worldview is the conviction that the earth is vital, that there is a spiritual dimension to it, a dimension in which man rightly exists. It follows logically that there are ethical imperatives in this matter."[30]

As also noted, American Indian traditions of thought are at least as varied as the environments of the North American continent. Fortunately for all concerned, the Polynesian people of Hawaii were not discovered by Europeans until the mid–eighteenth century. The Western Enlightenment was at its height, and while Western colonialists were certainly not universally disposed to indulge Hawaiian "superstitions," at least there was some recognition of the existence of a Polynesian intellectual culture— which was recorded even as it was being eroded by missionization and other less deliberate but no less abrasive forces. Much was lost, but not nearly as much as was lost of American Indian cultures, which suffered three centuries of foreign hostility, intellectual pollution, and neglect before there existed any systematic and sympathetic interest in recording them. Hence, just what the American Indian environmental attitudes and values were before the European landfall is a highly problematic and to some extent speculative matter.

A strong case can be made against the authenticity of the consensual American Indian theology canonized in *Black Elk Speaks*: First, John G. Neihardt, a neo-Romantic poet, had his own agenda and may have insinuated his own impression of Indian ideas into the words of Black Elk. Adding to doubts on this score, Black Elk spoke no English. His actual words—spoken on the wind and gone forever—were translated by his son, Benjamin, and recorded by Neihardt's daughters, Enid and Hilda. And second, Black Elk had been converted to Catholicism and had spent thirty years as a catechist working on behalf of the Church to spread the gospel among other Indians.[31] One may therefore doubt the authenticity of *Black Elk Speaks* even if Benjamin Black Elk's translation were entirely true, Enid and Hilda Neihardt's record entirely accurate, and Neihardt's redaction entirely faithful. Old Black Elk may have created a syncretic religious vision—a blend of the religions of the pipe and the cross—in which Mother Earth is a transposed Virgin Mary and the union of Father Sky and the four quarters in the Great Spirit is an inspiration based on the Holy Trinity (as Lame Deer's remark suggests).

Questions about the authenticity of *Black Elk Speaks* have been recently resolved, however, by Raymond DeMallie, who has reviewed the transcripts from which Neihardt worked and found that, consistent with Neihardt's professed intention to act as a conduit and not to use Black Elk as a spokesman for his own views, *Black Elk Speaks* is remarkably faithful to the transcribed record—at least, of Benjamin Black Elk's translation of his father's oral narrative.[32] And comparing the Lakota worldview represented in *Black Elk Speaks* (and the raw transcriptions on which the book was based) with *Lakota Belief and Ritual*, an earlier ethnographic record by James R. Walker, one finds that they agree in most details and certainly in overall structure.[33]

However, even if *Black Elk Speaks* gives us a completely faithful record of the Lakota worldview, the irony remains that that worldview is invidiously tainted with Western influence—if not influence from Western ideas, then influence from Western "technology." The religion of the pipe was of recent origin among the Lakota, even by their own account. It was associated with the ephemeral culture of the mounted buffalo hunter, which began with the appearance of the Spanish horse on the plains of North America and ended ("in bloody snow") with the massacre at Wounded Knee. There is little doubt that the Lakota worldview outlined here and widely known in its general contours grew out of and is continuous with a genuinely aboriginal American Indian outlook. As received, however, it can hardly represent an *ancient* American Indian land wisdom.

Ojibwa Totemism

The natural environment of the mounted Plains Indian and that of the pedestrian forest Indian, such as the Ojibwa, differed profoundly. On the Great Plains, the buffalo hunters navigated through a sea of grass. Theirs was a spacious universe dominated by sky and earth. Up/down/north/ south/east/west were the principal parameters of experience. By contrast, in the forests of the North American continent people meandered along foot trails and on rivers in canoes beneath an unbroken canopy of leaves. The Great Spirit was a distant and impersonal reality, while closer at hand a multitude of spirit beings animated the rich and diverse natural environment.

The economy of the Plains horse culture was focused on a single game species. The buffalo provided meat and grease, clothing and shelter, bone tools and ornaments. And in the mytho-history of the Lakota oral tradition, Buffalo Cow Woman gave the first sacred pipe (which is still extant) to the people.[34] From a scientific historical perspective, this suggests that the worldview symbolized by the pipe and its adornments originated, at least in its received details, with the commencement of mounted buffalo hunting.

The economy of the forest Indian, on the other hand, was spread over a wide variety of resources seasonally exploited. In the spring and summer, tribes gathered in fishing villages, planted gardens of corn, squash, and beans, and gathered wild roots, fruits, nuts, and berries. In the winter, family units scattered into the forest depths and hunted migrating waterfowl, resident deer, and other game, and trapped beaver and other furbearers.[35]

During long winter nights throughout the woods around Lake Superior, the Ojibwa elders retold rich cycles of stories. These were the principal vehicle for schooling the young in the Ojibwa worldview. In a nineteenth-century history of his people, George Copway writes,

> The Ojibways have a great fund of legends, stories, and historical
> tales, the relating and hearing of which, form a vast fund of winter
> evening instruction and amusement. Some of these stories are
> most exciting and so intensely interesting, that I have seen children
> during their relation, whose tears would flow most plentifully, and
> their breasts heave with thoughts too big for utterance. Night after
> night for weeks have I sat and eagerly listened to these stories. The
> days following, the characters would haunt me at every step, and
> every moving leaf would seem to be the voice of a spirit.[36]

In the Nanabushu cycle, Ojibwa social ethics are taught by negative example. Nanabushu, the Great Hare, is the Ojibwa culture hero, and a trickster figure. Nanabushu is continually up to some mischief, and because of it continually coming to grief. He attempts to lie, cheat, steal, and imitate the ways of other creatures without having been blessed with their natures and talents. And he always suffers the consequences of his errant ways, usually getting a second chance to do things the right way and to succeed in the end. Thus the social values and the natural penalty for their transgression are conveyed among the Ojibwa.[37]

Other stories also set out an explicit environmental ethic. In the Ojibwa stories, the flora and fauna are not simply impersonal natural resources to be exploited. Rather, animals and plants are portrayed as nonhuman persons living in their own families and societies. The representation of the relations between human persons and animal and plant persons is modeled on intertribal exchange. Just as one tribe may commerce with another— trading, say, obsidian arrowheads for copper ornaments—so animals are portrayed as enthusiastic trading partners with human beings. The animals willingly exchange their flesh and fur for the artifacts and cultivars that only human beings can produce.

Key to this mythic representation of animal-human exchange is the belief that if the bones of the slain animals are not broken, burned, or fed to dogs, and if they are returned to the element from which the animals were taken—to the earth, in the case of bear bones; to the water, in the case of beaver bones; and so on—then the animals will return to life. The slain animals' spirits are imagined to come into the lodges of the people as dinner guests and to observe and partake of the feast made of their soft parts. Then their bones, returned whole to the forest or the stream, are reclothed in flesh and fur and the literally reincarnated animals go back to their dens and lodges with warm memories of their visit to enjoy their "gifts."

In general, the stories stress the need to respect and honor the spirits of animals and plants. They censure wanton slaughter, cruelty, waste, and above all the ill disposition of bones. Each species was imagined to be tended by a spirit warden, or master. These keepers of the game occasionally revealed themselves as large white specimens. If a hunter broke the rules of interspecies trade, the keeper of the injured species would find out and would withhold further specimens from the offender or sometimes visit a harsher reprisal on him. The animals were bound by corresponding obligations. If a hunter extended an animal all the appropriate courtesies and offered the appropriate tokens of exchange, then the animal was obliged to surrender itself to his weapons.[38] As the anthropologist Frank Speck summed it up,

The hunter's virtue lies in respecting the souls of the animals necessarily killed, in treating their remains in prescribed manner, and
in particular making as much use of the carcass as is possible. . . .
The animals slain under the proper conditions and treated with the
consideration due them return to life again and again. They furthermore indicate their whereabouts to the "good" hunter in
dreams, resigning themselves to his weapons in a free spirit of self-
sacrifice.[39]

The Ojibwa stories often involve marriage between a human being and
an animal. Correlatively, transformations of outward appearance are commonplace: people become beavers and bears, and vice versa. To a Western
audience these stories may seem strange, and almost indecipherable. But
their subliminal message to the magic-oriented mind of the forest hunter-
gatherer is clear. Just as intertribal social relations and mutual goodwill
were cemented by intermarriage between tribes, so the interspecies social
relations and mutual goodwill—on which the Ojibwa felt their survival to
depend—were cemented by intermarriage between species in the ambiguous past/present of story time. Often the human spouse in such an interspecies marriage will return after a while to his or her own people with
information about the species to which he or she is wed—not information
that, like military intelligence, is useful to one party seeking to take advantage of another but information having to do with the social sensibilities of the alien species or with its mortuary requirements. The moral of a
story called "The Woman Who Married a Beaver" is this:

Thereupon she plainly told the story of what happened to her while
she lived with the beavers. She never ate a beaver. . . . And she
was wont to say: "Never speak you ill of a beaver! Should you
speak ill of a beaver, you will not be able to kill one."
    Therefore such was what the people always did; they never
spoke ill of the beaver, especially when they intended hunting
them. . . . Just the same as the feelings of one who is disliked, so is
the feeling of the beaver. And he who never speaks ill of a beaver is
very much loved by it; in the same way as people often love one
another, so is one held in the mind of the beaver; particularly lucky
then is one at killing beavers.[40]

If the Lakota worldview represents nature on the model of a large family, the Ojibwa worldview represents nature on the model of a multinational community. Calvin Martin expresses the Ojibwa representation of
nature most succinctly:

Nature, as conceived by the traditional Ojibwa, was a congeries of
societies. Every animal, fish, and plant . . . functioned in a society

that was parallel in all respects to man's. Wildlife and plant life had homes and families just as man did.[41]

In the Lakota worldview, the ideal pattern of interaction between human beings and other life-forms is understood to be like the interaction between members of a large healthy family—mutually dependent and mutually supporting. In the Ojibwa worldview, the ideal pattern or interaction between human beings and other life-forms is understood to be somewhat less intimate—more a matter of mutual obligation and mutual benefit, with a distinct quid-pro-quo dimension. Human beings, wildlife, and plant life were trading partners in a multispecies economy of nature.

The economy-of-nature metaphor was the first in a historical series of metaphors governing thought in ecology. It was originally introduced as a working model in proto-ecology in the eighteenth century, by no less important a figure than Linnaeus. In the ecology of the late nineteenth and early twentieth centuries, Linnaeus's paradigm was eclipsed for a time by an organismic metaphor, in which plants and animals were regarded as cells in supraorganisms and ecology was understood as a kind of exophysiology. The economy-of-nature metaphor was revived and renewed by the great British ecologist Charles Elton, who introduced the concept of the "biotic community" as a working model in ecology in the 1920s. The major sectors in Elton's model of nature's economy are the producers (plants), the consumers (animals), and the decomposers (fungi and bacteria). Further, there exist various community types: wetlands, grasslands, forests, deserts, and so on. Each species fills a niche in a particular biotic community—or, as Elton sometimes puts it, each species performs a "role," or even has a "profession," in one or another biotic community.[42]

Elton's ecological "community concept" became the fulcrum of Aldo Leopold's land ethic, which is the prototype of contemporary environmental ethics. Working from Charles Darwin's scenario of the origin and development of morality in human evolution, Leopold wrote,

> An ethic ecologically is a limitation on freedom of action in the struggle for existence. An ethic, philosophically, is a differentiation of social from antisocial conduct. These are two definitions of one thing. The thing has its origin in the tendency of interdependent individuals to evolve modes of cooperation. . . . All ethics so far evolved rest upon a single premise: that the individual is a member of a community of interdependent parts. . . . The land ethic simply enlarges the boundaries of the community to include soils, waters, plants, and animals, or collectively: the land. . . . In short, a land ethic changes the role of *Homo sapiens* from conqueror of the land

community to plain member and citizen of it. It implies respect for his fellow members and also respect for the community as such.[43]

The Ojibwa land ethic, as it might now be rather technically styled, rests on the same general concept as Leopold's. Human beings, plants, and animals, if not soils and waters, are members of a single, tightly integrated economy of nature, or biotic community. Human beings are not properly "conquerors of the land community"; neither ought we to be stewards of it. Rather, we should assume the role, as Leopold would have it, merely of "plain members and citizens" of the land community. In the Ojibwa land ethic, as in Leopold's, human beings ought principally to respect their fellow members of the biotic community. Respect is expressed in the variety of attitudes and behaviors just now indicated. In addition to a respectful attitude, respect for plants and animals is evidenced by giving animals payment for their bodies, taking care not to cause them unnecessary suffering, and carefully disposing of their skeletal remains so that they may return to life; and by neither overharvesting nor wasting plants.

Of course, the representation of the personal-social order of nature among the Ojibwa is vastly different from that of contemporary ecologists. The former is mythic and anthropomorphic, while the latter is scientific and self-consciously analogical. Nevertheless, when the mythic and scientific detail is stripped away, an identical abstract structure—an essentially social structure—is revealed as the core conceptual model of both the totemic natural community of the Ojibwa and the biologists' economy of nature. In form, the Ojibwa land ethic and the land ethic of Aldo Leopold are identical.

SUMMARY

From the outset of the twentieth-century ecologic crisis, environmentalists have looked to "the" American Indian as a guru who could show them how to relate more positively to a despised and wounded natural world. In *The Quiet Crisis*, Stewart Udall portrays American Indians (with an ill-chosen metaphor) as "pioneer ecologists." Udall was inspired by Henry David Thoreau, who, apparently under the influence of the "noble savage" element in the Romantic cognitive complex, had declared the American Indian to be a "child of nature."[44]

Not surprisingly, critics of the current environmental mystique surrounding American Indians have suspected that the Indian's status as custodian of a special land wisdom is neo-Romantic nonsense with an environmental spin. These suspicions have been recently abetted by the sordid "Seattle affair"—the revelation that the famous "speech" (or "letter," as it is sometimes known) of the nineteenth-century Suquamish chief Seattle, which contains a number of environmental pieties, is a forgery composed in the 1970s by a professor of English literature at the University of Texas named Ted Perry.[45] (Perry meant no harm. He had been commissioned by the Southern Baptist Convention to provide a voice-over narration for a documentary on the pollution of the American landscape, called *Home*. Perry used an account of Seattle's supposed words at the signing of the Point Elliott Treaty of 1855, written down twenty-five years later by the physician Henry Smith, who claimed to have been there—embellishing and rearranging it. The Baptist producers, however, did not credit Perry as the author of the narration. His script was transcribed and published under Seattle's name alone, and was subsequently reprinted literally thousands of times.)

The debate over whether or not an environmental ethic was part of the cognitive cultures indigenous to North America has largely proceeded a priori—that is, without benefit of reference to specific Native American intellectual traditions. But when we do put the proposition that American Indians had an environmental ethic to the test of comparison with those of their beliefs preserved in cultural materials, we find that it is confirmed. At least among some traditional cultures—those of the Lakota and the Ojibwa, representative plains and woodland peoples, respectively—there is indisputably an environmental ethic to be found. The Lakota and the Ojibwa environmental ethics, moreover, differ quite dramatically from each other, the former being a kinship environmental ethic and the latter a community environmental ethic (as one might characterize them). Both are, however, capable of adaptation to the prevailing intellectual climate of the twentieth century, and thus relevant and useful in helping us deal with the contemporary environmental crisis. Like the Lakota, Charles Darwin—our modern Hesiod, the author of our contemporary origin myth—portrays other living things as our kin. And the extensions of evolutionary theory confirm, in a general sense, the Lakota intuition that all plants and animals are children of the earth and the sky—the former supplying the materials from which we are made, the latter the energy (sunlight) by which the earthy elements are synthesized into complex organic entities. Furthermore, current ecological theory, like that of the Ojibwa, represents human beings, plants, and animals all as members of one biotic community. We depend on plants and animals for goods and services, and they depend on us for their very existence—since without our respecting them and their needs in something like the way that the traditional Ojibwa did, many of them will be driven to extinction.

Though there has been much less ballyhoo by environmentalists about traditional Polynesian environmental attitudes and values—except perhaps in contemporary Polynesia—we find that an indigenous environmental ethic also existed in Hawaii and Aotearoa. In Hawaii, a complex agro-ecosystem was supported by a hierarchical social structure and a corresponding belief system in which the health and sustained productivity of the land and surrounding sea were correlated with care for the land (*malama 'aina*) and the maintenance of social discipline and order (*'aikapu*). A mythic equivalent of solar energy (*mana*) was imagined to flow through the land and the people, provided that its conduits remained open and free from pollution by unwise and mean-spirited (un*pono*) behavior. In Aotearoa, the structural elements of a Maori environmental ethic are an intense identity of the individual with the tribe and the tribe with a region of the land, and the consequent institution of collective land tenure.

7   South American Eco-eroticism

NORTH-SOUTH COMPARATIVE PHILOSOPHY

Comparative philosophy is a relatively new discipline, which was initially limited to a comparison of the rich intellectual traditions of the East and West.[1] Many pitfalls, however, lay in the way of even such an apparently straightforward dialogue. The most salient follow.

The Western intellectual tradition's distinct tributaries and various backwaters notwithstanding, its ideas historically flowed together to form a main channel of thought. In the East, on the other hand, while several intellectual currents are connected by canals, as it were, and thus intermingle, the sources are many and arise in distinct lands, cultures, and peoples. Thus it soon became apparent that East-West comparative philosophy was actually a multilateral exchange.

Then there is the problem of translation. Sanskrit and Greek are cognate languages, and the latter is an ancestor of modern European tongues. Japanese and French, Chinese and English are related only to the extent that each in both pairs is a human language. Can one, therefore, ever hope to capture the nuances of, for example, the Japanese Buddhist concept of *mu* in English, or, translating the other way, the unsubtle but abstract British Empiricist concept of "sense data" in Japanese? Or can one, to take another couple of examples, hope to make the Confucian virtue of *jen* intelligible to a francophone or to express the condition of Existential angst in an ideogram (or two)?

Perhaps the most insidious of all the snares set to entrap the intrepid comparativist is the possibility that conventional intellectual categories like religion, philosophy, history, and science and all their subdivisions—theology, metaphysics, epistemology, physics, cosmology, ethics, and so on—are endemically Western, and that similarly to divide the intellectual efflorescences of the East is to misrepresent them from the get-go.

It has been the posture of this discussion to celebrate the polymorphism of human cognitive constructs and to stress the differences between the various traditions of thought, West and East, that have been visited: between Judeo-Christian creation theology and Greco-modern atomic materialism; between Hinduism, Jainism, and Buddhism; between Brahman and the Tao. And, while acknowledging that the mutual incommensurability of languages phylogenetically remote from one another is a barrier to mutual understanding, it has also been an assumption of this discussion that the basic ideas of the world's various cognitive complexes can be translated adequately enough to explore, in a rough-and-ready way, the environmental attitudes and values implicit in each. Finally, throughout, tendentious intellectual categories have been avoided. "Worldview" has been preferred to "metaphysics," "tradition of thought" to "philosophy," and so on.

By this means, the comparative enterprise has been further extended along the East-West axis, encompassing the environmental attitudes and values of representative Pacific and North American peoples, who may not have produced a library of philosophy but who nevertheless look on the world through finely ground conceptual lenses. This review of environmental ethics in cognitive complexes cannot be accused of "civilizationism." But so far it can certainly be accused of another bias—"Northern Hemispherism."

In other contexts, such a bias might go unnoticed and unremedied. Increasingly, however, our gravest environmental concerns—especially the "biodiversity crisis," the current episode of abrupt and massive species extinction—have turned the spotlight of attention on more southerly latitudes. What are the environmental ethics, if any there be, indigenous to South America, to sub-Saharan Africa, and to Australia which could be revived and adapted in their native regions? How might their rhythms and timbres contribute to the chorus of voices around the world singing of a harmony with nature? A whirlwind global tour such as this can hope to make only a few ports of call on the south side of the equator. But initiating a North-South intellectual cross-fertilization seems as important and fruitful a field for comparative philosophy today as the opening of an East-West dialogue was a century ago.

SOUTH AMERICAN ECOLOGIES OF MIND

Of the two Americas, the southern continent, though more populous on the eve of European discovery in 1492, is the least well known—ethnologically as well as in practically any other domain of inquiry.[2] Further, the ethnographic record is least complete in the very region on which most environmental concern has been lately lavished—the Amazon Basin. The Amazon is the beneficiary of intense environmental concern because it is unusually rich in species, unusually fragile, and recently the object of violent assault. Until the mid–twentieth century, the Amazon Basin was an ethnological terra incognita, for the same reason that its ecosystem was not until then subjected to wholesale economic conversion. The region is too vast, the forest too dense and forbidding, the rivers too many and too mighty to have been brought under the iron heel of progress until chain saws, bulldozers, airplanes, outboard motors, and other instruments of subjugation had become sufficiently powerful and available. Anthropological study was thwarted by the same physical barriers, and also by the reluctance of the Amazonians to submit to examination by outsiders. Many of the indigenous cultures of the Amazon Basin have survived into the twentieth century in a pristine condition, though now, tragically, they are succumbing to the juggernaut of ruthless industrial development no less rapidly and terminally than the trees and other denizens of the rain forests. A brief window of ethnographic opportunity has thus opened up. Well-trained anthropologists have been able to gain access to and systematically study Stone Age peoples, whose cultures remained intact well into the age of mature social science before becoming polluted with Western technologies, habits, and beliefs (or, if resistant to change, before being violently exterminated).

Ethnographers with an ecological outlook are the kind of guides that would be ideal for this leg of our global journey. Though not nearly as large as the North American ethnographic literature, there are a number of fascinating studies of South American peoples, including those of the Amazon region. Most are concerned, however, principally with patterns of subsistence, cultural infrastructure, and social organization and mores—as befits social science—or with language, music, and mythology, the "literature" of nonliterate peoples. Hardly any of these studies are concerned with environmental attitudes and values. However, one Colombian ethnographer, Geraldo Reichel-Dolmatoff, has concentrated on the environmental attitudes and values of one Amazonian people, the Tukano. Because Reichel-Dolmatoff's studies so directly address the concerns of this monograph, the home of the Tukano, in the watershed of the Vaupés River (a major tributary of the Negro, which is in turn a major tributary of the Amazon) shall be visited first.

A new strategy to preserve the species-rich moist tropical forests is taking shape. "Sustainable development," as it is called, is intended to complement, not replace, the more familiar effort to preserve biological diversity through the creation of national parks, wilderness areas, and nature reserves. The idea is to adapt human economic activity to existing ecosystems rather than to destroy those ecosystems and replace them with (often imported) domesticated crops and livestock. We are just beginning to fully appreciate the fact that the biologically rich and diverse New World—its northern and southern continents, and its tropical and temperate latitudes—was not an unpeopled wilderness when the Europeans discovered it.[3] The New World was thoroughly, if not densely, populated.[4] And its human inhabitants were active managers of their natural resources—not "primitive" nomadic foragers taking what nature freely provided. Their management methods were so artful that, like all masterly technique, little of the craft was discernible in the outcome. Hence, the New World looked untouched by the hand of man to the European invaders, who had manhandled their own landscapes. Not only did the aborigines of North and South America not destroy the ecosystems they inhabited, arguably they improved them by objective measures of biological productivity and diversity.[5]

Attention has been lately paid to the complex sustainable economy of the Kayapo Indians, who live in the Xingu watershed of the Amazon Basin, as a model for the sustainable development of the entire region. The Kayapo have also recently emerged as leaders of those Amazonian indigenes who are resisting the destruction of their forest home. They have successfully thwarted efforts—by Euro-Brazilian squatters, land speculators, gold miners, and timber operators, among others—to trespass on their territories.[6] And the Kayapo organized a celebrated showdown with the government of Brazil and the World Bank which ended in the withdrawal of plans for a dam at Altamira that would have flooded much of their homeland.[7] As the anthropologist Terrence Turner comments, "At the level of international environmentalist politics, the Kayapo are now an established presence."[8]

The Tukano, though they cultivate manioc, consider themselves to live mostly by hunting and fishing.[9] The Kayapo, by contrast, subsist primarily on the produce of their gardens and managed forests, although they also gather, fish, and hunt. The Tukano live deep in the rainy, densely forested northwest Amazon, the Kayapo in the drier, forest-savannah margin in the southeast. The Tukano speak an Arawakan language, the Kayapo a language of the Gê family.[10] The Tukano are patrilineal and virilocal, the Kayapo matrilineal and uxorilocal.[11] Together these two peoples provide representative and complementary views from the rain forest.

Tukano Systems Theory

In the Tukano worldview, one encounters several of the major conceptual elements found in the northerly Far Western cultures visited in the previous chapter. But the feeling of déjà vu is soon dispelled when one realizes that these elements are combined so as to form an intellectual gestalt quite unlike anything yet encountered. Like the Lakota, the Tukano find a male procreative deity in the sky—namely, the sun. Like the Ojibwa, they believe that game animals are conserved by a spirit warden, that disease or other personal and collective misfortunes may be visited on the profligate hunter, and that the principal duty of their shamans is to communicate and intercede with the animal spirits and spirit masters. And like the old Hawaiians, the Tukano envision a power or energy—a kind of *mana*—flowing through the world.

But we find nothing resembling the portrait of nature as a vast family of siblings parented by a Father Sky and Mother Earth, and a corresponding kinship environmental ethic, as among the Lakota. Nor do we find a representation of nature as a congeries of plant and animal societies and a corresponding community environmental ethic, as among the Ojibwa. And we find nothing at all like the socioenvironmental pyramid that epitomizes the Hawaiian worldview among the egalitarian Tukano, or anything resembling the Hawaiian mandate to *malama 'aina* (care for the land). Though the principal elements are familiar, we encounter among the Tukano a completely novel worldview. It is a worldview, however, that resonates no less well with modern ecology than do those it resembles in certain respects.

Most cultures that subsist primarily through gathering and hunting must frequently move their encampments, because they soon deplete their residential environs of resources. The Tukano are an exception to this rule, inhabiting a territory bounded on all sides by other Indians or mestizos, who do not brook trespass. They live in small widely spaced permanent settlements each consisting of a *maloca* (a large, well-built structure with a thatched roof and mat interior as well as exterior walls, housing four to eight nuclear families) situated on a watercourse near land suitable for manioc cultivation.[12] Indeed, according to the anthropologist Janet Chernela, "the Tukano demonstrate a greater density of settlement than do Amerindian populations elsewhere in Amazonia."[13] Hence the Tukano must be even more wary of prodigality than other hunter-gatherers—who tend to be prudent managers in any case.

The impotency of Western-style rational conservation doctrine—the "wise use" of "natural resources" for "the greatest good of the greatest number for the longest time"—is painfully apparent in the United States and other industrialized countries. While a public shout of righteous indignation is raised in Europe and North America over the destruction of tropical rain forest in Central and South America, the last stands of redwood forest and old-growth temperate rain forest in the Pacific Northwest are being clear-cut, and acid rain is damaging the woodlands of countries bounding the North and Baltic seas. The Tukano demonstrate a thorough practical and empirical knowledge of their forest habitat, but their principles of conservation are formulated in the more powerful and obligatory language of myth and morality.

Tukano cosmogony begins with twin brothers, the sun and moon.[14] The two are rivals, and the sun constantly vanquishes or humiliates the moon. As befits his superiority, the sun created the rest of the world—the earth, with its forests and rivers, its animals and plants, its spirits and demons, and lastly its people. One may notice not only the similarities already mentioned with other Far Western intellectual systems but also that the structure of the cosmos in the Tukano worldview is not unlike that in early Greek mythology, as preserved in Hesiod's *Theogony*. For Hesiod, the flat disk-shaped earth is equidistant between the vault of heaven and the antipodal bowl of Tartarus. The Tukano also conceive of the sky-lidded earth as disk-shaped, with an underworld beneath it.[15] There is, however, a difference worth mentioning: the Tukano underworld is the paradisiacal home of good souls, rather than the dank abode of the damned.[16]

For the Tukano, the sun's act of creation was not a unique event. Creation is an ongoing process, though neither a cumulative nor an evolving one. The sun, that is, is not adding more and more kinds of things to the world or replacing those that once existed with different kinds; rather (not surprising for a people living right on the equator) the creation is imagined to be subject to decay and so must be re-created or rejuvenated by the sun's energy. Aside from the absence of a sense of evolutionary change, Tukano intuition is certainly corroborated by science on this point. Solar energy drives all life processes on the earth, and without its constant flow the living world would quickly atrophy. But quite unlike anything familiar to science—albeit admirably serving, as we shall see, to help keep the people within the limits of their resources—the vital solar flux is imagined by the Tukano to be the deity's seminal fluid fertilizing a largely feminine earth.[17]

There is another point on which the Tukano view is at odds with science. In the scientific view, while the movement of "nutrients"—the materials from which living things are organized—is cyclical (discounting some downhill wash), the flow of energy (discounting its accumulation in fossil deposits) is continuous and strictly linear, from solar source to galactic sink.[18] In the Tukano view, the generative heat of the sun is limited and flows cyclically through a circuit of soils, plants, and animals. According to Reichel-Dolmatoff, "man may remove what he needs only under certain conditions and must convert this quantum of 'borrowed' energy into an essence which can be reincorporated into the circuit." People remove what they need primarily through hunting and gathering—that is, through the food quest. But since the energy in edible plants and animals is ultimately of a sexual nature, it may be stored and returned through sexual continence. Thus for the Tukano, "food and sex are closely related and are symbolically equivalent."[19]

To stay within the carrying capacity of their environment without switching to more efficient and intensive means of subsistence, a hunting-gathering people must limit population growth. Without a central authority to penalize overreproduction (as in China today) or some more democratic system of mutual coercion mutually agreed on, a population explosion constantly threatens to disrupt the people/resource equilibrium of a commons. Free-for-all rational individualism in the reproductive sector no less than in the productive, as the human ecologist Garrett Hardin has so eloquently argued, leads to tragedy.[20] The Tukano system of birth control combines several methods—social, pharmaceutical, and mythopoeic. For example, parents are forbidden to copulate during the entire time that their newborn child is breastfeeding—a period of three years or more.[21] Tukano women also ingest herbal concoctions that render them temporarily sterile, and couples with many children are openly criticized as socially irresponsible.[22] Moreover, for some days before going hunting, men must, in order to insure success, undertake a rigorous ritual preparation that includes abstention from sexual relations, nor may they even "have had any dreams with an erotic content."[23] In short, "Uncontrolled multiplication; large families; and voracious, omnivorous appetites are condemned by most Tukanoans, who are ever so diet-conscious and preoccupied with population control."[24] In what might be called Tukano systems theory, hunters must balance the food energy they take from the environment by conserving the sex energy they might otherwise spend in conjugal divertissements. Thus do the Tukano keep population growth in check.

Thus also do they restrain themselves from overhunting. Hunting is not a casual productive activity, and certainly not a sport. It is hedged about by all sorts of burdensome requirements in addition to the periods of celibacy mentioned above—practices intended to curry favor with the "Master of Animals."[25] Further, some forehunting activities are designed to seduce the game that the supernatural gamekeeper has been cajoled into releasing from his hidden sanctuaries—for the Tukano hunter, like his North American counterpart, also imagines himself romancing his prey. If the hunter impeccably carries out the prescribed rigmarole, the Gamekeeper will parcel out some animals, and those that the hunter courts will submit of their own accord. Intimately tied in with their celestial mythology, the Tukano even impose closed hunting seasons on themselves. Each

species of game—tapir, deer, peccary, monkey—is associated with a con-
stellation and can be hunted only after its stars have risen over the horizon.[26]

Finally, the Tukano have instituted food restrictions. On this occasion
or that, a man or woman may not eat this or that food, thus further selectively lessening the pressure on limited resources. For example, a man
whose wife is pregnant should not eat tapir, peccary, or monkey, as his con-
suming the meat of these animals is believed to endanger the future health
of his unborn child.[27] All rites of passage and other ceremonial occasions
involve dietary restrictions for a period of time.[28] Some foods are unsuit-
able to some social subgroups. For example, "children, expectant mothers,
and women who are still nursing a baby must not eat the meat of such forest animals as tapir, deer, peccary, woolly monkey, curassow, trumpeter
bird, or tortoise."[29] And, because food and sex are symbolically equated,
sexual prohibitions, such as rules proscribing incest and prescribing exog-
amy, are associated with dietary prohibitions.

If a Tukano should violate these venereal, venatic, and phagic taboos, he
or she runs the risk of getting sick. Sickness is a universal human experience, but how sickness is understood is far from universal. Each culture explains sickness through the concepts provided by its larger worldview. A
culture's etiology of disease is, in fact, one way—perhaps even the best
way—to identify its fundamental constitutive notions. In modern Western
medical theory, disease is ascribed to a variety of unseen (at least, unseen
by the naked eye) material causes—viruses, chemical carcinogens, bacteria, broken or misspelled genes, and so on—all of which affect our bodies
in either mechanical or chemical ways. That is because the modern Western worldview is materialistic, mechanical, and reductive. It explains the
functions and malfunctions of macroscopic organisms in terms of micro-
scopic material—from atoms to microorganisms. In Tukano medical theory, disease is also ascribed to a variety of unseen causes—the spirits of
slain game animals and their spirit warden, other spirits and demons, and
human witchcraft.

And in every culture the cures indicated for various symptoms are commensurate with the putative causes. Commensurate with the materialistic,
mechanical, and reductive medical etiology prevailing in the West and consistent with the prevailing general Western worldview, cures are effected
by surgery (the very essence of a mechanical remedy) or by medicines that
mechanically or chemically attack invading pathogens. A principal function of the Tukano *payé*, or shaman, is to diagnose and cure disease. As the
Tukano believe that a spirit, an animal, or another person magically causes

the victim's discomfort, the cure, as one might expect, directly addresses the cause. But since the Tukano do not believe that a person, animal, or spirit normally inflicts disease on a victim arbitrarily, countermagic is not the usual prescription. Rather, the victim is believed to have provoked retribution by breaching a taboo or neglecting a duty, and part of the diagnosis is to determine what the patient has done or left undone to attract the malevolent attention of some pathogenic agent. Overhunting, the eating of forbidden foods, and incest, adultery, or other sexual misconduct are common causes of patients' complaints. The wrong must be righted and the offended entity propitiated before the patient can get well.[30]

Western medicine is not only materialistic, mechanical, and reductive in the ways just mentioned, it is also paradigmatically atomistic. Individual persons, conceived of as social atoms, get sick, and unless they communicate their viruses or bacteria to others, society in general and the larger environment are not thought to be involved in the illness itself or in its cure. The Tukano, by contrast, conceive of individuals as embedded in society and society as embedded in the environment. Hence an individual's state of ill health is a symptom less of organic malfunction than of socioenvironmental disturbance. For the sick person to be healed, the disturbance that he or she created must first be corrected and socioenvironmental harmony restored. On this point, Reichel-Dolmatoff is especially emphatic:

> The delicate balance existing within the natural environment, between nature and society, and within society itself, constitutes a series of systems in which any disturbance, however slight, is bound to affect the whole. . . . To the shaman it is therefore of the essence to diagnose correctly the causes of illness, to identify the exact quality of the inadequate relationship (be it adultery, overhunting, or any other overindulgence or waste), and then to redress the balance by communicating with the spirits and by establishing reconciliatory contacts with the game animals. . . . It might be said then that a Tukano shaman does not have individual patients; his task is to cure a social malfunctioning. The diseased organism of the patient is secondary in importance and will be treated eventually, both empirically and ritually, but what really counts is the reestablishment of the rules that will avoid overhunting, the depletion of certain plant resources, and unchecked population increase.[31]

The Tukano believe, according to Reichel-Dolmatoff, that "deep in the forest are ghostly abodes wherein game-animal spirits dwell under the care of the Master of Animals."[32] The cultural anthropologist Christine Hugh-

Jones adds that these "mystical houses appear to ordinary people as out-crops of rock, each one associated with a particular species."[33] And, Reichel-Dolmatoff continues,

> These "hill-houses," as shamans call them, have a womblike char-acter. They are places where game animals are said to multiply and from whence they emerge to roam in the forest; they are the spirit houses inside which a continuous process of gestation is going on. Shamans say that they visit these places during their narcotic trances because they must converse with the Master of Animals in order to ask him to release some of his charges so that the hunters may kill them. . . . The shaman will not ask for individual ani-mals, but rather for herds or troops of certain species [for which] he must always recompense the Master of Animals.

These shamanic visits represent "an ecological stocktaking and a bal-ancing of books."[34] The Tukano shaman thus wields enormous power. He is in effect the community-resource czar—an "ecological broker."[35] His concern for the feelings of animal and plant spirits and their spiritual over-seer translates, empirically, into imposing restrictions on the taking of an-imals and plants for human purposes, not only for food but for other uses as well. The shaman—all in the course of his magical divination, com-munication, and intercession—must acquire an intimate knowledge of the proximate forest's biotic community to become proficient in his art. Thus, empirically speaking, he represents a living encyclopedia of vernacular botany, zoology, and ecology. Lay members of Tukano society must accede to the limitations he imposes on their economic, social, and sexual activi-ties. If they do not, they may, or so they believe, sicken and die.

Geraldo Reichel-Dolmatoff's comparison of the Tukano worldview to a contemporary ecological representation of nature is explicit and deliberate. Reichel-Dolmatoff understands ecology, first of all, to be an expression, in the domain of biology, of a more general "systems theory." He takes a systems-theoretical approach to his own field, anthropology—an approach he credits Gregory Bateson with pioneering. In a systems-theoretical ap-proach, the anthropologist attempts not only to see cultural elements like mythology, kinship, and the division of labor as interrelated and integral parts of a whole, functional society but also to fit the society, as it is pe-culiarly constituted, into the larger system—the natural environment. Further, no element is exclusively cause and none exclusively effect. In other words, although certainly a society's size, structure, and economy is adapted to the exigencies of its environment, the natural environment doesn't determine a people's mode of subsistence and social organization; just as certainly, the environment is affected by the cultural peculiarities of its resident *Homo sapiens*. And finally, he interprets the Tukano worldview as itself a systems theory. That is, the Tukano, as Reichel-Dolmatoff has represented them, view their world not exactly as an ecosystem, in the precise scientific sense of the word, but as a system that corresponds rather nicely with an ecological description of nature.[36]

How so? Well, because, as in the ecosystem paradigm in ecology, the Tukano portray people, plants, animals, soils, and waters to be eddies in the stream of solar energy flowing through terrestrial nature. As Reichel-Dolmatoff succinctly puts it, Tukano cosmology and myth

> together with the ritual behavior derived from them, represent in all respects a set of ecological principles and . . . these formulate a system of social and economic rules that have a highly adaptive value in the continuous endeavor to maintain a viable equilibrium between the resources of the environment and the demands of society.[37]

In addition to a Tukano ecological worldview—which he expressly contrasts with ones that "describe Man's Place in Nature in terms of dominion, of mastery over a subordinate environment"—Reichel-Dolmatoff also posits a Tukano environmental ethic.[38] It is constituted by the "social and economic rules"—that is, by the venereal, venatic, and phagic restrictions just mentioned—derived from the "ecological principles."

Recent developments in ecology may cast a shadow on Reichel-Dolmatoff's representation of ecological systems-theory. He seems to assume that nature, unless upset by human beings, will remain in a state of equilibrium. And he portrays Tukano medical practice as bent on restoring a humanly disrupted "balance of nature." Ecologists today see nature as more loosely integrated than they formerly did, and now believe that constant change—evolutionary, climatic, successional, and stochastic—rather than static equilibrium, is nature's norm.[39]

The practical implications of such a pendulum swing in scientific opinion must be cautiously drawn, however. Normal evolutionary and climatic changes are so slow as to be imperceptible to human observers, and even one complete cycle of the plant succession may take several human generations to complete. The tropical rain forests are among the oldest and most stable (albeit among the most fragile) ecosystems on earth. Until recently, they have changed only very gradually, and less radically than ecosystems in the temperate latitudes. A healthy respect for biosocial balances and equilibria, however subject to scientific qualification these notions may be, has served the Tukano well for many generations in their forest habitat. As the Amazon region is integrated into the economies of the nation-states that claim it, and into the global economy, much can be learned from the Tukano about how to live successfully in and with its extensive rain forest. The empirical knowledge of their ecosystem which the Tukano have assembled during their long tenure is itself a valuable natural resource. And just as in North America, where the native Indian environmental philosophies are a neglected resource now much needed by all modern North Americans, so learning from the ecological worldviews and environmental ethics of the native Indians of South America may help all the people of that continent to inhabit it gracefully and symbiotically.

Kayapo Agro-ecology

Along the north-flowing Rio Xingu and its tributaries live the Kayapo, a Gê group. The Gê are united not only by a common linguistic stem but by common cultural traits. Until their populations were reduced by European diseases and their traditional way of life disrupted by the encroachment of Euro-Brazilians, the Gê lived for most of the year in large, self-sufficient villages of about two thousand people, centered around two men's houses, which served both as daytime hangouts for the mature males and as dormitories for the juveniles.[40] Gê households are typically uxorilocal. Well before puberty, boys leave their families and go to live in a men's house, where they will remain for more than a decade. Upon marrying, a Gê husband moves in with his wife's family, and the couple continues to reside in her home. The Gê sons-in-law supply fish and game for the extended family into which they marry, and each is socially suborned to his wife's parents. Except for the clearing of plots—heavy and dangerous work, performed by men during the dry season—gardening is women's work.[41]

The history of ethnographic literature on the Gê, including the Kayapo, provides a revealing study in progressive rehabilitation. In the earlier literature, the Gê were presented as anomalies.[42] Their societies, the main focus of anthropological attention, were discovered to be large and complex and their ceremonies many and rich. But their economies were considered more primitive than those of the socially less complicated native peoples living almost exclusively by agriculture in the fertile floodplains of the larger rivers in the basin. Most Gê live in what was considered a "marginal" (figuratively as well as literally speaking) ecotone, and hunt and gather as well as farm. Two unfounded assumptions were involved in the anomaly theory. One is that hunting and gathering is a more primitive, less desirable way of life. And the other is that the ecotone of the forest-savannah margin is a marginal habitat for human beings.

Hunting (including fishing) and gathering prized vegetable foods and medicines more than a day's walk from home is the province of men, and more esteemed by them than gardening. From the Gê point of view, people who live exclusively by agriculture are in a more degenerate estate than themselves, since, in such a condition, men must do women's work. Some modern theorists share their perception, and suggest that agriculture originated as a response to overpopulation—cultivation being a more intensive (and laborious) use of land in a shrinking territory—and is a way of life that hunter-gatherers are forced by circumstance reluctantly to adopt, rather than an enlightened choice they rush to embrace.[43] As to the second assumption, the forest-savannah margin is in fact a biologically richer and more productive habitat than either pure forest or pure savannah. According to Terrence Turner,

> the margin between the forest and the savannah, the preferred site of Gê villages, is a distinct ecozone richer in floral and faunal resources than either the savannah or the tropical forests in themselves, [and] the Gê mixed economy, in making use of all three zones, is actually far more complex and sophisticated in the range of resources it exploits, and thus richer in productive potential, than the more narrowly based economies of either the forest or the savannah tribes.[44]

The traditional Gê had plenty of arable land at their disposal, as their villages were very widely spaced (100–150 kilometers being the average distance between them). And swidden horticulture is their most important and reliable subsistence activity, its produce accounting for more than half the Gê larder. Turner argues that therefore the seasonal hunting-gathering trek, undertaken during part of each year by the Gê, is motivated more by social than by economic imperatives: It gives the men a chance to be men.[45] Further, contrary to the jaundiced view of earlier investigators, who noticed only its small scale, Turner observes that "Gê horticulture has an unusually varied repertoire of crops."[46]

The varied, complex, and sophisticated patterns of Kayapo subsistence have, still more recently, been closely observed and widely publicized. For more than a decade, the anthropologist Darrell Posey has studied Kayapo land-management practices. Posey soon realized that the Kayapo inhabitation of their environment was more complex and sophisticated than even Turner had thought, and so organized the ongoing "Kayapo project"—a research initiative in which scientists from a number of disciplines would study with the Kayapo and transpose the extensive Kayapo botany, zoology, and ecology into the framework of international science. As Posey notes, "The world is threatened not just with the loss of tropical ecosystems but with the loss of the peoples who know how to use them, whose ideas and knowledge may be the richest of all tropical resources."[47] And as Turner notes, "indigenous forest-dwelling peoples are not just a passive part of the problem but an active part of the solution."[48] The methods of Kayapo integrated resources management emerging from this research were reported in the *New York Times*, on April 3, 1990.[49]

To the casual observer, the Kayapo may appear to be ordinary swidden cultivators—slashing, burning, planting, harvesting, and, after the few years it takes for the nutrient-poor tropical soils to become exhausted and overrun with rank weeds, moving on to repeat the cycle. Such farmers, who make up in numbers for what they lack in individual destructive power, have been identified as major contributors to the deforestation of the moist tropics—as well they might be, since swidden cultivation is also undertaken by exogenous peasants who have been driven off their ancestral lands by the consolidation of their small holds into large plantations geared to the export market.[50] But one Kayapo family, in its fifty-year corporate lifetime, may clear only ten hectares of forest.[51] Moreover, a Kayapo swidden will remain productive throughout its fallow, and when the land finally returns to canopy forest it will have been enriched by the process.

That process begins with the choice of soil, the suitability of which is determined by its vegetative cover (indicative of surface and subsoil types), color, texture, tilth, and drainage. Before the trees are cut and burned, underbrush is cleared and tubers—manioc, sweet potatoes, and yams—are planted. The trees are felled in a radial pattern to form a circular clearing, and they are allowed to dry for two or three months before they are burned. Burning takes place just before the start of the rainy season. The pre-burn plantings, which have by then established good roots, take up nutrients from the ashes with the first rains, and they are ready for harvest almost immediately. The remaining crops are planted in distinct concentric zones. The central sector of the plot is reserved for the starchy staples, like manioc and sweet potatoes. The intermediate zone, in which the nutrients are most concentrated, is devoted to a diverse mix of plants such as yams, maize, beans, melons, squash, cotton, and tobacco. On the periphery are fast-growing fruit trees (such as banana and papaya), palms, medicinal herbs, and certain plants that, in a variety of ways, help control insect pests.[52]

As the plot ages and its ashy nutrients are depleted, the Kayapo cultivate it differently. Corn, beans, and the other middle-sector crops are no longer planted. The staple root-crop zone is expanded outward from the center, and the fruit trees, palms, and medicinal herbs move in from the forest edge. When the plot is finally allowed to be retaken by trees, the Kayapo seed it with species that bear fruits and nuts (edible by monkeys and other wildlife as well as by people) or that are useful in other ways—for building materials, thatch, fiber, and so on. A fallow field thus eventually becomes both an agroforest, harvestable in perpetuity, and a game park, where quarry is concentrated, attracted there by their favorite foods, which have been deliberately planted for them.[53]

This method of game baiting has been extended by the Kayapo onto the animal-rich savannahs, where they have developed islands of forest called *apêtê*.[54] According to Posey, the *apêtê*

> are some of the most ingenious aspects of Kayapo resource management . . . created by the Indians in piles of a planting medium prepared from termite and ant nests mixed with compost. Small *apêtê* are expanded to many hectares over the decades. A complete survey of sample *apêtê* revealed that 98 percent of the plants found in them had at least one use; well over two-thirds had multiple uses. Equally amazing is that these forest islands are composed of botanical resources taken from an area the size of Western Europe. Many of the species are used to attract wildlife and are included in the [af]forestation process so that older *apêtê* abound in useful birds, reptiles, rodents, and other mammals.[55]

The cultural geographer Susanna Hecht and the left-leaning journalist Alexander Cockburn point out that Kayapo agricultural processes ("process" is the operative word, since for the Kayapo a garden is not a static thing; each year it is different from the garden of the year before) are structurally similar to unmanaged ecological processes following nonanthropogenic disturbances, such as wind-felled trees or lightning-ignited fires. A Kayapo swidden imitates natural ecological succession, and each sere in the cultivated series has a mixture of species similar to those in the corresponding sere of an uncultivated series. After the forest trees are felled and burned, the Kayapo

> then plant short-cycle crops such as corn, beans, melons, and squash [which] rapidly cover large areas, along with longer-cycle crops that can be harvested anywhere from six months to two years after the planting. In their use of short-cycle, light-tolerant species that gradually give way to woody fruits, the principles of succession are maintained. The grasses, corn, the fast-growing vines, the squashes, sweet potatoes, and melons all mirror the types of plant families found in early succession. The role of weedy *solanum* is taken on by their domesticated cousins—peppers. The ubiquitous euphorbia of successional vegetation find their analogs in manioc. . . . The rapid uptake of nutrients by plants that root at different depths and have life cycles of different lengths mimics what

happens in [unmanaged] plant succession in the tropics. Short-lived plants are gradually replaced with longer-lived species. [Finally,] the Kayapo stimulate forest succession in their fallows by making sure that their agricultural sites incorporate the necessary elements to recuperate forests, which are often as valuable to them as the agriculture.[56]

The Kayapo help the forest recuperate by deliberately planting native species whose seeds may have been destroyed by the fires, in addition to particularly desirable trees and shrubs; by weeding out less useful species; by protecting others (especially palms); by pruning, fertilizing, and so on. Like the savannah *apêtê*, the fallow swiddens thus become living resource caches as well as game parks.[57]

Eager to complete the rehabilitation of the Kayapo and other peoples of the forest, who have hitherto been demeaned as backward and primitive by earlier generations of ethnologists, and to lay a foundation for the patenting of native intellectual property, Hecht and Cockburn write enthusiastically of native "science." Certainly, the Kayapo and other peoples of the forest have an intimate and extensive knowledge of their overwhelmingly complex environments. And certainly they should share in the profits when their knowledge is exploited by pharmaceutical houses and seed companies. If knowledge is science, the Kayapo are scientists of the first water. "Science," however, also suggests a certain conceptual organization of a body of knowledge and critical evaluation of its theoretical scaffolding. Since the Kayapo conceptual organization of their knowledge is not the same as that characterizing Western science, it is misleading to label Kayapo native knowledge "science" and leave it at that.

Ailton Krenak, a Botocudos Indian from the Rio Doce valley, was raised in the rain forest and then migrated to the city at the age of eighteen. He learned to read and write, and, now in his thirties, works as a journalist in São Paulo. He reminds us that

> when talking of native science it's impossible to separate it out of
> its context. If I pull one of the shells off a bracelet, the entirety is
> less beautiful, and the shell itself, however beautiful, has less
> meaning. We can miss so much of what a shell actually is if we cut
> it away from myths, practices, the people who discovered and
> named the shell and other shells, and the rituals and stories and se-
> crets of that shell. That's only one part of the bracelet, and that
> shell—let's say it's agriculture—is only one part of the special
> knowledge we have about nature.[58]

The literature provides us with a goodly sample of the rituals, stories, and secrets associated with various elements of Kayapo environmental knowledge.[59] As among the Tukano, shamanic craft is closely linked with resource management. The Kayapo shaman determines, for example, the exact moments for slashing, burning, and planting by the coming into flower of certain trees, the movement of fishes and animals, and the position of constellations.[60] These signs, however, are linked symbolically or through myths with the activities they auger; and the setting of fires and planting of seeds are ceremonial as well as pragmatic acts. Consistent with the pattern and scope of this monograph, however, we must be content with a summary of the configuration of the bracelet—that is, the overall Kayapo Gê worldview.

Comparative ethnometaphysics reveals a remarkable amount of intellectual diffusion across language barriers. One would think that technologies and behaviors would cross such barriers more readily than ideas, since ideas live exclusively in language and material artifacts and ways of doing things are open to observation and imitation. But that does not seem to be the case. For example, the traditional Gê owned no dogs (indeed, had no word for "dog") and did no loom-weaving, as did the "higher" riverine peoples of Amazonia.[61] But a review of Gê mythology turns up cosmological ideas that would seem familiar to the Arawakan Tukano, clear across the basin. One cannot help thinking that such singular notions have somehow circulated throughout Amazonia just as the notions of a Great Spirit and a comic culture hero, like Coyote or Nanabushu, were widespread among North American peoples speaking mutually unintelligible tongues.

The universe, according to the Gê, consists of three or more tiers, all but the bottom one serving as the sky for the tier beneath it.[62] This notion of a stratified cosmos is vaguely reminiscent of the origin myths of the Hopi and other pueblo peoples of North America. The pueblo peoples, however, imagined themselves to have arrived on this, the fourth and highest world, by emerging through a hole in the ground from the third, which they had entered in a similar way from the second, and so on from the first.[63] The Gê, on the contrary, think that they formerly lived a paradisiac life beyond the sky that hangs above this world. Then, a precocious hunter among them, digging into an armadillo burrow, broke through the floor of the upper world and discovered this one. Finding it irresistible, the ancestors of the Gê descended to the earth by means of a rope. A third world, beneath this one, was later discovered by another hunter in the same way (digging for armadillo), but, though briefly visited, the world below remains unpeopled either by the living or the dead (the latter having no special abode). The Kayapo believe that the stars are relatives of theirs who did not climb down from the sky to the earth.[64]

Little more is said about the heavenly bodies except for the sun and the moon, whose exploits the Gê remember in a whole cycle of stories. The sun and moon are not twins, as among the Tukano and many other South American aboriginals; rather they are portrayed as "friends" of each other, though implacable enemies would seem to be a more accurate description. Fully fourteen narratives dealing with conflict between the strong (and therefore usually victorious) sun and the weak (and therefore usually humiliated) moon have been collected by Johannes Wilbert in his two-volume *Folk Literature of the Gê Indians*. In these stories, the sun and moon adventure about the earth, creating sundry entities and setting up various ways of doing things. Their tasks completed, they depart the earth and return to the sky. Scholars argue over whether or not the Gê possess a "solar religion" and recognize a "true sun god" or if the sun is just one of a dichotomous pair of culture heroes, majority opinion favoring the latter alternative.[65] However that may be, the sun does not appear to be the source of a seminal energy in Gê cosmology, as it is in Tukano—although a substance functionally equivalent to seminal energy but having no connection with the sun may exist in Gê thought, as we shall see.

The Gê do not think that darkness is primary or aboriginal—that which would exist in the absence of light and its embodiments, the sun and moon. Rather, they believe that it was obtained from the Lord of Darkness by a Kayapo hunter, who carelessly let it out of the calabash container in which it had been kept by its original owner. (Hapless missionaries to the Gê did not get very far into the Bible, which begins with the proposition that darkness prevailed until God created light, before provoking cosmological quarrels with the people they hoped to instruct.[66]) Gê mythology also addresses the human acquisition of fire, which the sun and moon brought to earth with them but kept in their possession, returning with it to the sky. The Kayapo credit Bebgororoti, the being of thunder and lightning, with teaching them how to produce fire by twirling sticks. Without fire, people had been able to eat only raw fish, fruit, rotten wood, leaves, and fungi. Along with the secret of making fire with which to cook them, Bebgororoti also gave the people certain crops.[67]

Or his daughter did. Bebgororoti was wed (logically enough) to the rain. Their daughter, Na-Kra ("rain child"), quarreled with her mother, and then left the sky home of her parents for earth, where a young Indian found and befriended her. He concealed her—some stories say in a calabash, others in a basket—and slipped her into his house. At night he let her out of her container to sleep with him. After a time, Na-Kra was discovered by the youth's parents, who cut her hair and painted her red with the juice of the roucou vine and black with the genipa fruit to make her look

Kayapo. Now formally naturalized and married, she found the limited Kayapo diet tiresome and pined for the good foods she had enjoyed on high. So, she decided to visit her erstwhile home and bring back some of its cultivars. She instructed her husband to prepare a swidden in the forest, and away she went. Her mode of travel is so singular that it is worth pausing to describe: Her husband bent a tall buriti palm to the ground, and she sat in its crown; when he let it go, she was catapulted back into the sky. After a long wait, and some fear that the Rain Child had gone home for good, the young Indian was reunited with his wife, who returned bearing sweet potatoes, yams, manioc, squash, and bananas.[68]

This apparently simple story is rich in Kayapo agro-ecological information. Cultivars are indeed children of the rain, since the rains germinate their seeds and nourish their growth. They are associatively female, because they are planted, tended, and harvested by Kayapo women. As Kayapo swiddens are prepared to the specifications of the women who own them by their male consorts, Na-Kra instructs her young husband to clear a field for her in the forest. After an absence of uncertain length, people anxiously await the return of the food-making rain, which seems to have gone back where it came from. As just mentioned, it was Bebgororoti who taught people how to start fires for themselves—quite naturally, since lightning is a frequent cause of fires. Garden plants are also associated with Bebgororoti as firegiver, since in the tropics fires are necessary to fertilize the soil in which they will be sown. The first rumbles of thunder announce the advent of the rainy season—the time to plant—further associating Bebgororoti with cultivars.

No doubt someone with firsthand knowledge of the environment and horticultural practices of the Kayapo could mine this story and many others for more nuggets of agro-ecological wisdom. It is cursorily analyzed here—in accordance with the "syntagmatic" or "context-sensitive" method set out by Terrence Turner—as an example of the way empirical knowledge is framed and recorded by the Kayapo in their mytho-cosmology.[69]

The extent to which Gê cosmology correlates with an ecosystemic worldview seems not to have been explored in the literature. That may be in part because Gê studies have been influenced far more by the ultramodern "structuralism" (and its dialectical development by anthropologists such as Turner) articulated by Claude Lévi-Strauss, who worked among the Gê, than by the postmodern systems theory of Gregory Bateson. But in a wonderful book titled *Vital Souls*, Jon Christopher Crocker, who studied with Lévi-Strauss, hints of a systems representation of the environment, managed by shamans, among the Gê-speaking Bororo, who live upriver from the Kayapo—a portrayal not unlike Reichel-Dolmatoff's of Tukano mytho-ecology.

The Bororo call nature spirits *bope,* and the vital substance that animates all beings *raka*. This *raka* seems not to be directly related to the sun or to its energy, but it is paradigmatically present in bodily fluids—especially in blood and in both male and female sexual secretions. Living beings are charged with it at birth, gain it as they mature, then slowly expend it during the course of their productive and reproductive careers, and die once it becomes exhausted. According to Crocker, "one of the most central tenets of Bororo cosmology is . . . that the sustenance of any organic life requires the diminution of other life and that those who create new life from their own bodies are endowed with the awesome capacity to destroy existing forms."[70] This sounds familiar.

Bororo life revolves around—and, indeed, depends on—careful adherence to a "food code that prescribes orderly relationships between men [in the generic sense, including women and children] and *bope*." This code

> has the nature of a contract or covenant in which, if human society carries out its obligations to *bope*, they in turn will ensure fertility, natural plenty, and long untroubled life. These obligations center on behaving in certain ways toward a large set of animals and plants, and especially on conveying to the *bope* their rightful share of these foods, through the intermediary of the shaman.[71]

The Bororo *bope* are not the wardens of these edible animals and plants but competitive consumers of them. Nevertheless, the empirical outcome is the same: shamanic monitoring and regulation of consumption. The *bope* eat their rightful share via the village shaman, whom they possess for that purpose and for the purpose of diagnosing and curing the afflictions of which they themselves are the cause. It is remarkable how much the physical appearance of the Bororo *bope* resembles the Tukano Master of Animals, whom Reichel-Dolmatoff describes as "a dwarflike spirit-being with marked phallic attributes," detectable by his rank odor, and fond of prodigiously copulating with young women.[72] According to Crocker, "In their essential condition the *bope* are homunculi about a meter high [and] give off a strong reek." And they are lustful in the extreme—so much so that "one of the most reiterated elements in a young girl's moral education is the necessity of sleeping on her side, with her legs tightly closed, so as to frustrate the *bope's* desires."[73]

Crocker provides a droll account of his attempt to discover the rationale behind the *bope ure* (the foods of the *bope*) classification. Not all foods are included. The living Bororo have inherited the food code they follow, however, and could no more tell Crocker exactly why only such and such a plant or animal and not another was *bope ure* than the Amish can say why some modern technologies are prohibited and others are not. After following one false lead after another, he comes to the conclusion that the common denominator of the *bope ure* is that the plants and animals so classified are all "vulnerable and defenseless."[74] The same foods are the preferred foods of the Bororo.

A Reichel-Dolmatoffian ecological analysis is irresistible. Those vulnerable and defenseless plants and animals of which the Bororo are especially fond would soon be exterminated unless their consumption were restrained. They are conserved by being declared *bope ure*. Thus their consumption may be monitored by a shaman, who, consulting the *bope*, can proscribe them if his divinations and diagnoses indicate the necessity of doing so. The people obey their shamans in respect to the taking, preparing, and eating of *bope ure* because they fear that if they do not, the *bope* will make them sick or cause them to die. As Crocker reports,

> The myth states that the *bope* may legitimately be offended if one of "their" animals is wounded and escapes the hunter . . . especially if the animal is hurt severely enough so that it later dies never to be properly delivered up to the *bope*. *This idea actively constrains Bororo hunting.* I have often seen Bororo refuse to shoot at one of the *bope ure* if there seemed to be any chance that they could not wound it mortally or successfully pursue it later. . . . And, if far from the village and lacking a shaman in their company, hunters will refuse to kill any kind of *bope ure* whatsoever, owing to the difficulties in obtaining the necessary shamanistic intervention. . . .
>
> None of this should be taken to indicate that the Bororo fail to pursue these restricted species with any less vigor and skill than they devote to the hunting of other quarry. On the contrary, the meat of the *bope ure* is considered to be the best tasting of all game, as well as vital for the maintenance of the *raka* of the hunters and their relatives. . . . In short, the *bope ure* are the epitome of things that are dangerous but good to consume. And they are perfectly suited to human diet, if only the rules surrounding them are properly obeyed.[75] [Emphasis added.]

Bororo mytho-ecology parallels Tukano even in relating potent food and potent sex: "The Bororo draw [an] equation between eating and copulating."[76] This may be because the division of productive labor between the sexes is as rigid and, to them, as natural as the division of reproductive labor; because marital relations also are restrained by rules and taboos requiring both periodic abstinence and a restricted diet; and because the distribution of *raka*-rich *bope ure* follows the same pattern as exogamous exchange of spouses between moieties.

According to Terrence Turner, the Kayapo also see

> society and its members . . . as appropriating and channeling natural energy, and are thus dependent on the ability of the natural world (meaning the forest, animals, birds, rivers, and fish) to reproduce itself and continue as a great reservoir and source of the energy society must continually draw upon to live.[77]

If, on the basis of this and other similarities, one can safely generalize from the Bororo Gê to the Kayapo Gê, resource exploitation is managed by a central authority. In effect, the tribal commons is enclosed and made a property. It is owned by the *bope*—the spirits, by whatever name. The shaman serves as the medium of communication between the spiritual and social realms. He is the spirits' steward, who regulates the use of their lands and their animals and plants. The spirits are omniscient, and no infraction of the rules—the rigors of which serve to inhibit overconsumption and overpopulation—escapes their notice. And they requite even the most picayune and unintended infractions of their apparently arbitrary and whimsical requirements with the most frightful punishment, sickness unto death.

CONCLUSION

Among the most promising new conservation stratagems for the Amazon rain forest is the proposed creation in it of extractive reserves. An extractive reserve differs from a national park or nature reserve by not excluding economic activities. It differs from a typical World Bank–financed industrial-development project by conserving, not converting, the forest. Extractive activities include rubber tapping, Brazil-nut gathering, fishing, Indian-style swidden agriculture, medicine-plant harvesting, selective logging, and a variety of other traditional and innovative ways of using the many and varied renewable resources that the region produces just as it is and just as its former human denizens have made it to be. The Kayapo have led the way, among Amazonian Indians, in this conservation strategy as in so many others, declaring "part of the Kayapo Indigenous Area xtractive reserve' closed to all ecologically destructive forms of tim- d mineral exploitation."[78]

xtractive reserve would be a commons. As Hecht and Cockburn

These reserves would recognize the use rights of the local population, but the holdings would not be privately owned. They would be collective 'condominium rights' or long-term leases. . . . This model was the first formal expression of a *land*-management program founded in the extractive economy and history of Amazonia.[79]

But how to avoid the tragedy of the commons?

Ailton Krenak suggests that if the concept of extractive reserves expresses the traditional economy and history of Amazonia in a vocabulary understandable in the political debates and economic accounting of modern nation-states, then the reserves might also draw on indigenous intellectual resources to formulate an equally intelligible means of effective corporate management. As Krenak puts it, "How does one guarantee a reserve's effective occupation? Imagine if all the people in Amazonia decided in the next decade that they didn't want to treat the places they lived as a commodity but rather as a sacred place!"[80] The notion of a "sacred place" has universal currency, from Mecca to Mauna Loa. Perhaps the review provided here of representative Amazonian worldviews will indicate the sort of intellectual traditions on which the people of Amazonia might draw in giving foundation, specificity, and substance to Krenak's call for a revival and contemporary application of a distinctly Amazonian idea of sacred place.

8 African
Biocommunitarianism
and Australian Dreamtime

THE AFRICAN SCENE

A Paradox

While less rich in sheer numbers of living species than tropical South America, tropical Africa is the richest place on earth for what conservation biologists call "charismatic megafauna."[1] Indeed, the mere mention of Africa conjures images in the mind's eye of wildebeests, springboks, hippopotami, rhinoceroses, zebras, giraffes, elephants, ostriches, flamingos, crocodiles, lions, leopards, cheetahs, monkeys, baboons, gorillas, chimpanzees, and many many other kinds of animals. On the other hand, mention of African culture evokes no thoughts of indigenous African environmental ethics. Nor have contemporary scholars looked to African intellectual traditions, as they have to Zen Buddhism, Taoism, and American Indian thought, when casting about for conceptual resources from which to construct an exotic environmental philosophy.

This combination of circumstances is at once paradoxical and discomfiting. How could African peoples be blessed with such a wonderful complement of fellow voyagers in the odyssey of evolution and not have mirrored that singular environmental endowment in their several cultural worldviews? Perhaps they have, and both the popular new environmental movement and scholars in the even newer field of comparative environmental ethics have simply neglected African ecophilosophy.

Of course, all of us *Homo sapiens* are Africans. Our species is one ng the indigenous charismatic megafauna incubated in Africa. We d shoulder to shoulder with our phylogenetic first cousins, the go- d chimpanzees. After our African genesis, we gradually dispersed it the world. Perhaps for those of us in the diaspora the reverence for the wildlife of Africa is like reverence for the things of home. It would be surprising to learn that our fellow Africans whose forebears remained at home during the past hundred thousand years did not share those feelings and incorporate them in their philosophies and religions.

Given these reflections, one may be stunned to discover that, generally speaking, indigenous African religions tend to be both monotheistic and anthropocentric. Most posit the existence of a high God, both literally and figuratively speaking, who created the world. And most hold that the world was created with all its creatures for the sake of humanity. Apparently reinforcing anthropocentrism is ancestor worship—the belief nearly ubiquitous in Africa that the spirits of dead relatives haunt the living and must be ritually honored, served, and propitiated.

According to the distinguished British student of African religions Geoffrey Parrinder, "most African peoples have clear beliefs in a supreme God."[2] The African philosopher J. S. Mbiti goes beyond generalization to universalization. He states categorically that "All African peoples believe in God."[3]

As to anthropocentrism, Noel Q. King makes the following claim:

> Having studied these systems [of African thought] in all of their diversity, a student is able to recognize their unity and can only then legitimately look for a paradigm, a pattern. . . . The point of departure is anthropocentric; the central and ultimate concern is with woman and man, their fullness of being and power, their health in the widest sense.[4]

On this score, Mbiti is both emphatic and once again universal in delivering his opinion:

> The creator of the universe, God, is outside and beyond it. . . . [and] in African myths of creation, man puts himself at the centre of the universe . . . [thus] he consequently sees the universe from that perspective. It is as if the whole world exists for man's sake. Therefore the African peoples look for the usefulness (or otherwise) of the universe to man. This means both what the world can do for man, and how man can use the world for his own good. This attitude toward the universe is deeply ingrained in African peoples. For that reason many people, for example, have divided animals into those which man can eat and those which he cannot eat. Others look at plants in terms of what can be eaten by people, what can be used for curative or medical purposes, what can be used for building, fire, and so on.[5]

Even Africans who regularly hunt for a living take an anthropocentric stance toward the environment. The Lele are village dwellers and subsist primarily on the maize cultivated by the female members of the tribe, but the ritual and psychological life of the Lele centers on hunting. Yet, according to the British anthropologist Mary Douglas,

> they frequently dwell on the distinction between humans and animals, emphasizing the superiority of the former and their right to exploit the latter. . . . Of God, Njambi, they say that he has created men and animals, rivers and all things. The relation of God to men is like that of their owner to his slaves. He orders them, protects them, sets their affairs straight, and avenges injustice. Animals of the forest are also under God's power, though they have been given to the Lele for food.

This way of thinking, Douglas notes, has ominous consequences for wildlife conservation: "Game protection laws enforced by the Administration [of the Belgian Congo in the 1940s and 1950s] strike the Lele as an impious contravening of God's act, since he originally gave all the animals in the forest to their ancestors to hunt and kill."[6]

Apparently, therefore, Africa looms as a big blank spot on the world map of indigenous environmental ethics for a very good reason. African thought orbits, seemingly, around human interests. Hence one might expect to distill from it no more than a weak and indirect environmental ethic, similar to the type of ecologically enlightened utilitarianism, focused on long-range human welfare, briefly sketched in chapter 1. Or perhaps one could develop a distinctly African stewardship environmental ethic grounded in African monotheism, similar to that developed in chapter 2 from the core belief—of Judaism, Christianity, and Islam—in God, the Creator of Heaven and Earth.

While Christianity and Islam, especially the latter, are well established in Africa, the monotheism described in the scholarly literature on indigenous African religions has a flavor all its own. And the anthropocentrism characteristic of Western utilitarianism drags in its train a lot of conceptual baggage that seems out of place in an African context. African peoples are traditionally tribal, and the typically African sense of self is bound up with family, clan, village, tribe, and, more recently, nation. To such folk, the individualistic moral ontology of utilitarianism and its associated concepts of enlightened rational self-interest, and the aggregate welfare of social atoms, each pursuing his or her own idiosyncratic "preference satisfaction," would seem foreign and incomprehensible.

However that may be, finding some environmental ethic (or ethics) consonant with African experience and ideas is a dire necessity. As the human population of Africa explodes, civil wars and the degradation of arable land have created widespread famine. Paralleling this human tragedy, the future of Africa's magnificent wild heritage is becoming ever more desperate. Notoriously, African elephants and rhinoceroses are ruthlessly slaughtered by poachers for ivory and horn. Poachers also take a toll on the populations of African ungulates. Growing numbers of farmers and herders encroach on wildlife habitat, and come into conflict with lions and other top African carnivores, with the usual outcome—the predators are purged to make the country safe for cattle. Some environmental ethic, resonant with Africa's age-old intellectual chords and rhythms, is badly needed to help stem this tide of biocide.

The solution to Africa's environmental problems is, of course, complex and multifaceted. Any effective strategy would involve much more than finding conceptual foundations in indigenous African ideas for environmental ethics. Fostering the development of African environmental ethics can contribute, though importantly, only to a single root of Africa's many and synergistic environmental problems.

Human population growth, for example, needs to be curbed in Africa, as elsewhere. But the notion that exponential human population increase can be controlled by broadcasting sex education and birth-control technology is naive. Human fertility is conditioned by cultural, economic, political, and social forces, all of which must be addressed before I.U.D.s or birth-control pills will be accepted. Patterns of natural-resource use and development are equally conditioned by cultural, economic, political, and social forces. Africa, in short, desperately needs human rights, women's liberation, health care, and sustainable development as an economic alternative to reproductive wealth, wildlife exploitation, and forest destruction. Hopefully, parallel work on these other fronts will complement the African environmental ethics suggested here.

The Unity in Diversity of African Thought

For many centuries, the Africans north of the Sahara, from Morocco to Egypt, have been of predominantly Arab descent and predominantly Muslim in outlook. As this global inventory of actual and potential indigenous environmental ethics is necessarily unnuanced, the environmental attitudes and values native to North Africa can be considered covered in chapter 2's section on Islam.

Like Christianity, Islam is an aggressive, intellectually colonizing worldview. On the continent of Africa, before the perfection of medieval transport (the camel caravan) and modern mechanized transport, the formidable Sahara Desert represented a natural barrier to human information exchange—both genetic and cultural—and the inroads of Islam were limited to Arabic centers of trade on equatorial Africa's east coast. As commerce across the Sahara was established in the eleventh and twelfth centuries, and North African Muslims increasingly frequented the Sahel, or sub-Saharan region of Africa (now including Senegal, Mali, Niger, Chad, and the Sudan), Islam predictably spread to the interior of tropical melanotic Africa.[7] Further south, as the savannah thickens to bush and the bush gives way to the forests of moist equatorial Africa, the influence and purity of Islam diminishes. Islam becomes more and more mixed with traditional African beliefs, rites, and customs. The belt of rain forest girdling central Africa constitutes a second natural barrier to human cultural diffusion, and has historically served to limit the spread of Islam to the southerly latitudes of the continent.

Christianity has enjoyed a longer but much weaker tenure in Africa. By the fourth century it had spread south into Ethiopia, but that's about as far as it got until the era of aggressive European colonialism. During the heyday of European empire in Africa, conversion to Christianity was a necessity for upward mobility in the native petite bourgeoisie created by the colonial regimes. Conversion to Christianity also meant conversion to the full spectrum—medical, educational, political—of Western beliefs, attitudes, and values. Living, so to speak, by European colonialism, the growth and vigor of Christianity stagnated with African independence. In postcolonial Africa, Christianity remains a minority family of religions, mixed with and enriched by native beliefs and rituals. Many of the new and often ephemeral cults and sects, the springing up of which has been a curious aspect of recent African religious experience, exhibit Christian foundations and motifs to one degree or another.[8]

When one turns from the relative simplicity and familiarity of North African and Sahelian Islam and Ethiopian Christianity to consider indigenous African worldviews, one is overwhelmed and bewildered by the diversity of African languages, cultures, and religions. The distinguished student of African religions E. Thomas Lawson points out that in the Niger-Congo language family alone there are over nine hundred distinct tongues, each having numerous dialects, and that traditional native African social structures range from small bands of gatherer-hunters to large kingdoms, and from small encampments and villages to ancient cities with thousands of inhabitants.[9]

On the other hand, many scholars, while keenly aware of Africa's cultural diversity, have insisted on a complementary unity. Putative unity in diversity has been approached in two ways. Geoffrey Parrinder and J. S. Mbiti both find lowest common denominators in African belief systems, as just illustrated (indeed, in the case of the latter, universal denominators).

Another approach, more typical of the social sciences than the humanities, attempts to construct a cognitive taxonomy, or "typology," by means of which the myriad tribal mythologies of Africa can be categorized, abstracted, and organized by genera and species. This half of chapter 8, following the example set in the discussion of North American Indian environmental attitudes and values, will note the authoritative claims that there are common themes in indigenous African belief systems and then pursue them in detail through reference to specific representatives.[10]

Yoruba Anthropo-theology

The Yoruba are an agricultural people of equatorial West Africa, whose traditional tribal territory today lies mostly in Nigeria. They are well covered in the literature on African culture and belief and well represent their region of the continent intellectually. Warranting mention is the fact that elements of Yoruba belief may be found in Brazil, Jamaica, Haiti, Cuba, and the United States, having crossed the Atlantic with the slave trade.[10]

As noted, most African belief systems include a high God. The Yoruba name for the Supreme Being is *Olorun* or *Olodumaré*, the names meaning, in different dialects, "Owner-of-the-Sky."[11] The conceptual difference just hinted at between the typically African notion of God and the Judeo-Christian Jehovah and Muslim Allah can be understood by noting a manifest difference. So fundamental to Jewish, Christian, and Muslim religious practice is the locus of worship—the synagogue, temple, church, or mosque—that we scarcely pause to note its significance. In these related religions indigenous to the Middle East, the high God is the only God and the direct source of human blessing, grace, misfortune, and so on. God, by whatever name, is the central actor in history, from the initial creation of the universe to the vagaries of daily weather. Hence, God is the direct object of worship and prayer. But Olorun/Olodumaré has "no shrines . . . erected in his honor, no rituals . . . directed toward him, no sacrifices . . . made to placate him."[12] According to Parrinder, this is typical: "The general picture in Africa is that regular communal prayers to God are rare. Temples and priests are few, and found only among certain tribes."[13] Yoruba religious sites (shrines, temples, and the like) and religious practice (prayers, rituals, divination, and sacrifice) are far from rare, but center on a variety of subordinate spirits—called the *orisa*—instead of on the high God. According to Noel King, comparativists have thus been led to declare Olorun/Olodumaré "otiose, 'superfluous, out of circuit, supernumerary.'"[14]

Naturally, there has been scholarly speculation about this religious happenstance. According to one hypothesis, belief in a Supreme Being is not native to tropical Africa. It was gradually acquired from the literary religions of the Middle East over many centuries of incidental cultural contact and diffusion.[15] Eventually, belief in a Supreme Being was tacked onto—or, to shift metaphors, papered over—the many forms of polyspiritualism native to the region, or so this story goes. Therefore, lip service is paid to the (originally foreign) high God throughout Africa, while sincere, genuinely native ritual service to the indigenous gods proceeds as before, hardly affected by the intellectually alien accretion.

According to a hypothesis favored by J. S. Mbiti and also the African scholars Joseph B. Danqua and E. Bolaji Idowu, however, belief in a high God is as indigenous to Africa as it is widespread. Further, the cult spirits are not separate entities existing apart from the Supreme Being. They are, rather, Spinozistic modes and attributes of the one high God.[16] As Christians manage to believe in one God and three divine persons—Father, Son, and Holy Spirit—so the Yoruba believe in one divinity, Olorun/Olodumaré, who has multiple personalities and manifestations: the *orisa*. One or another of the *orisa* may have particular sites of worship, be addressed in prayer or sacrifice, and ritually served, depending on locale, season, and circumstance. Thus Olorun/Olodumaré is, according to this hypothesis, hardly neglected in actual Yoruba religious practice. On the contrary, all prayers, services, sacrifices, and rites are ultimately addressed to him in his various guises.

Behind both these hypotheses lurks a questionable assumption: that monotheism is more advanced and sophisticated than polytheism and polyspiritualism (or "fetishism," as the latter practice was often called in an African context). This assumption originated in the Enlightenment, first advanced, in 1760, by the French scholar Charles de Brosses, who argued that fetishism was typical of a primitive human religious consciousness. In the nineteenth century, the French sociologist Auguste Comte and the British anthropologist E. B. Tylor historicized and Darwinized de Brosses' theory, speculating that human religion first took the form of animistic nature worship, from which there evolved polytheism, followed by monotheism—the end point of progress in religion, as "civilization," preceded in turn by "savagery" and "barbarism," was the end point in social evolution.[17]

The first of these two hypotheses about why the Supreme Being in African religions is a *"deus remotus"* assumes that African peoples are too primitive to have arrived at monotheism on their own and thus their professed belief in a high God is necessarily imported. The second hypothesis does not challenge the assumption that monotheism is the more advanced and sophisticated religious alternative; rather it attempts to liken to Western monotheism what appears to be a hierarchical spiritual cosmology—a belief system that includes a remote, aloof, high God, subordinate spirits, and the souls of the deceased.

As this study is not burdened by a monotheistic bias, the Yoruba pantheon will simply be taken at face value. Why should monotheism be regarded as any less primitive than animism? It apparently arose, at least in its familiar Judeo-Christian-Islamic form, largely because a single group of people insisted that their particular tribal divinity was superior to the ones that their neighbors, such as the Canaanites, worshipped. The earliest biblical texts suggest that Yahweh considered himself to be one of many gods, ruling over one of many peoples, the Hebrews. As time went on, the Israelites elevated *their* god to the status of the *only* god.

Fundamental to Yoruba cosmology is a division between sky (*orun*) and earth (*aiye*). Chief of the sky spirits is, of course, the remote and unapproachable Olorun, its "owner." The *orisa* and/or (as shall be elaborated forthwith) the departed ancestors are also residents of the sky. The number of *orisa* is large and indeterminate. Some are worshiped only by one clan in one village; others restrict their influence to but one region of Yorubaland; still others are known to all Yoruba.

Myth, of course, is never entirely systematic or internally consistent, and one should not be exasperated if in addition to Olorun/Olodumaré the Yoruba should also speak of another spirit who had a hand in creation, *Orisa-nla*, also called *Obatala*. This being seems to be next in the hierarchy of sky dwellers, and in some quarters is particularly associated with the shaping of the human body.

Orunmila is the chief god of divination—though one may inquire of other spirits about things hidden from human ken, like the future, the cause of illness, lost objects, and so on.

Esu is a complex Yoruba spirit whom the Christian and Muslim missionaries identified with Satan. This unfortunate association seems to have arisen because Esu tries to trick people into misconduct, as does the Christian-Muslim devil. (Anthropologists draw a parallel of their own, to the "trickster" figures like Coyote and Nanabushu in American Indian narrative cycles.) Unlike the devil, however, Esu's intent is good, not evil; he provides people with the occasion to exercise self-restraint, or, if they succumb to temptation, to expiate their miscreancy through sacrifices to the gods. Esu also mediates between the people and the spirits on high. According to E. Thomas Lawson,

> It is precisely because Esu contains within himself forces both
> good and evil, both reverence and irreverence, and encourages both
> worship and giving offense that he is able to mediate between
> heaven and earth. It is his contrary qualities that make it possible
> for him to assume the key role of mediator between the many lev-

els of power conceived of in Yoruba thought, particularly between the worlds of divine and human power.[18]

In *Shango*, one finally comes upon a being in the Yoruba pantheon who seems to be a bona fide nature spirit; he is the storm god, whose most powerful manifestation is thunder and lightning. Among his symbols are rams and the double-headed axe. The rivers are his wives.

Ogun is also plausibly interpreted as a nature spirit. He is associated with wild animals and the hunt and with iron. His personality is violent and impulsive.

The ecological alter ego of Ogun is *Orisa-oko*, the peaceful and benign god of farming and cultivation.

The Yoruba, it would seem significant for this study, also believe that the earth is a maternal goddess, *Ilé*. For reasons that remain obscure, small-pox was (until eliminated) believed to be the "arm" or sanction imposed by Ilé on those who did not respect her.

Scholarly comment on the environmental implications of Yoruba—and, more generally, African—belief is limited and often contradictory. For example, affecting a composite voice of native "African traditionalists and scholars," Noel King remarks, in a discussion of the Yoruba cult of Ogun:

> Perhaps that is why the complex metallurgical processes and alloys discovered by African smiths were used in sacred ceremonies and regalia rather than in firearms and engines. Iron helped not only our warriors but also our farmers and mighty migrations across the continent. Even so, in our traditional times we did not rape the earth and the forest, nor look on the trees, forests, rivers, and mountains as enemies against whom to wage war.

Doubtless this last sentence represents a not so thinly veiled allusion to the sort of Judeo-Christian-Islamic environmental despotism discussed in chapter 2 of this monograph. Only a few paragraphs later, in describing the cult of Ilé, King writes, now in his own voice and perhaps either gainsaying the claim just quoted or highlighting the difference between "traditional times" and modern times,

> It is unfortunately not true that modern Yoruba respect the earth more than their Western counterparts. They too are willing to refuse to face pollution so long as they go on benefiting from modernization and development. But this story of Earth and her power reminds them and us what defiance of Earth and what eco-logical disaster mean.[19]

In any case, even from the scant information recounted here, one can see that the representative Yoruba cannot be simply assimilated to Judeo-

Christian-Islamic monotheism. Therefore—given the very un-Western hierarchical pantheon, headed by a remote high God—a corresponding stewardship environmental ethic would not seem fitting. On the other hand, the *orisa* are on the whole not exactly nature spirits either, such as those encountered among native North Americans; thus an animist environmental ethic similar to that found in traditional Sioux or Ojibwa culture would appear no less forced and implausible.

Indeed, Yoruba belief does not fit into any of the three classic nineteenth-century religious categories just mentioned—monotheism, polytheism, and animism (or fetishism). The *orisa* seem more like deified ancestors than like "gods" or personified forms and forces of nature, even when they are linked with aspects of nature. Perhaps "ancestor worship" lies at the core of typically African systems of belief.

J. S. Mbiti, however, takes umbrage at this term, with some justification: "The departed, whether parents, brothers, sisters, or children, form part of the family, and therefore must be kept in touch with their living relatives." This is done through rituals and ceremonies. According to Mbiti, "Worship is the wrong word to apply in this situation; and Africans themselves know that they are not 'worshipping' the departed members of their family."[20] On the other hand, Mbiti acknowledges that the departed spirits of "a few national heroes might become deified," in which case, of course, such ancestors might legitimately be said to be worshiped.[21] While such a point of departure seems most unpromising for the development of indigenous African environmental ethics, the concept of "self"—what it means to be a human person—giving rise as it does to the need for the dead to remain close to the living in spirit and to the deification of some special ancestors, may prove fruitful in this regard.

For example, who is Shango, the storm god of thunder and lightning? He began life as a powerful Yoruba king of the city of Oyo. As such, he magically commanded lightning, which he used to defend his kingdom and control its quarreling factions. According to one legend, Shango was forced to abdicate his throne; according to another, he accidentally destroyed his subjects with an errant thunderbolt; but all agree that, disgraced, he wound up hanging himself in the forest. His devotees believe that thereupon he ascended to heaven and became the storm god. Their ritual exclamation after a thunderclap is "the king did not hang."[22]

Who is Obatala? He was a son of Olorun the sky owner, who burdened him with certain responsibilities in the process of creation. In discharging them he grew tired and thirsty and so drank too much palm wine. His duties were taken over by Oduduwa, another son of Olorun. After conflict between the people that Obatala made and those that Oduduwa made,

Obatala returned to the city of Ife, as its fourth (evidently human) king. In this mythic cycle, an essentially human king is not deified, rather an essentially divine ancestor is humanized.

According to Lawson,

> The "deified ancestors" are tied not to particular families but to the history of the cities or to important factors in the development of Yoruba culture. These ancestors have shrines not simply in the home but in the towns, often throughout the country. . . . Sango [and] Orisa-oko . . . are examples of ancestors who have attained a very special status in Yoruba religion.[23]

Typical of the African outlook, the Yoruba worldview is this-worldly, not otherworldly. Since the dead are not packed off to another world, they remain concerned with and involved in the affairs of the living. (In this regard it is perhaps worth remembering that spirits reside in the sky, not in a realm beyond it.) Relations with socially important and influential relatives are maintained after they are deceased. The ritual nature of these relations has given rise to the common though somewhat misleading characterization of them as "ancestor worship."

But ancestor worship is a natural response to something in addition to the problem of what to do about the spirits of the dead when there is no Other World for them to go to. It is a natural response to a peculiar sense of personal identity or sense of self. Personal identity in Yoruba thinking is far more corporate than in modern Western atomic individualism. Mbiti has succinctly expressed the African view: "Whatever happens to the individual happens to the whole group, and whatever happens to the whole group happens to the individual."[24] Expressing the same thought more formally, the sociologist of religion Benjamin C. Ray writes, "African philosophy tends to define persons in terms of the social groups to which they belong. A person is thought of first of all as a *constituent* of a particular community, for it is the community that defines who he is and who he may become."[25]

An African's identity, nevertheless, is not confined to his or her role in the community. African social psychology is not modeled on the anthill, the beehive, or the termite colony. Each individual is a distinct person, with his or her unique blend of personality, needs, desires, talents, and destiny. But, far more vividly than in the modern Western worldview, individuality is not only counterbalanced by community identity but one's unique individuality is defined in part by one's social relationships and expressed through social interaction.

This idea is especially reinforced by one aspect of Yoruba ancestor worship. The *ori* is the inner substance of an individual's essence—his or her soul, as it were. But the *ori* is also understood to be "the partial rebirth or reincarnation of a patrilineal ancestor."[26] Hence, what individuates one— one's *ori*—is drawn from a communal pool of personalities. Throughout one's life, one lives both as and for oneself and reexpresses the essence and destiny of a forebear. As Ray puts it, "Freedom and individuality are always balanced by destiny and community, and these in turn are balanced by natural and supernatural powers. Every person is a *nexus* of interacting elements of the self and the world which shape and are shaped by his behavior."[27] [Emphasis added.]

In this notion of embedded individuality—of individuality as a nexus of communal relationships—we may have the germ of an African environmental ethic. Add to the intense sense of social embeddedness an equally vivid sense of embeddedness in the *biotic* community, and anthropocentric African communitarianism might then be transformed into a nonanthropocentric African environmentalism. Indeed, traditional Africans may be better prepared to respond to contemporary ecology's story of a natural economy and social order than those of us who remain in the grip of the modern Western worldview. The traditional African is accustomed to think of personal identity and destiny as intimately bound up with community, while "the Western notion of individualism—the idea that men are essentially independent of their social and historical circumstances," as Ray characterizes it, may prevent unregenerately modern Westerners from internalizing the moral implications of ecology.[28]

A San Etiquette of Freedom

"San" is the preferred name of the south-central African people often called "bushmen," of which the Kalahari Desert !Kung are the best known. Because until very recently they lived exclusively by foraging, the San have been celebrated subjects of anthropological study. They have also come to popular attention in an entertaining South African film called *The Gods Must be Crazy* (1980). While the film lays no claim to documentary truth, it strikes some nebulous environmental-ethical chords. Of all indigenous African peoples, the San may be an exception to the general nonassociation of traditional African cultures with responsible environmental attitudes and values.

Nonetheless, one looks in vain through the anthropological and ethnographic literature on the San for evidence of a sense of gratitude toward fellow members of the biotic community similar to that expressed by the North American Ojibwa, who also lived close to nature in a hunting-gathering estate. Neither does one find descriptions of San hunting magic aimed at seducing the game and cajoling it into voluntarily surrendering itself to the suppliant human hunter. Confirming the generalizations of

Parrinder and Mbiti, even the geographically, racially, culturally, and lin-guistically isolated San express a belief in a high God and the continued involvement of dead relatives in the affairs of the living.[29] And their magic is primarily medical in purpose.[30]

More particularly disappointing—especially when compared with the respectful attitude of North American hunters toward their prey—the San go out of their way to "insult the meat," according to the distinguished an-thropologist Richard B. Lee. If a hunter hits a gemsbok with a poisoned arrow (the principal means among the San for killing game), the animal will flee and may not die until the following day. Meanwhile, the hunter returns to camp and sits in silence by his fire until asked by someone about his luck. Then "he replies quietly, 'Ah, I'm no good for hunting. I saw nothing at all . . . maybe just a tiny one.'" *This* announces his success. The next day a party of tribesmen will help the hunter track down the kill. Before cutting it up and carrying it away, the others say something like "You mean you have dragged us all the way out here to make us cart home your pile of bones?" The hunter must agree and say something like "You're right, this one is not worth the effort. Let's just cook the liver for strength and leave the rest for the hyenas."[31]

Such banter is not gratuitous; it humbles successful hunters. In an egal-itarian society composed nevertheless of persons of unequal skills, arro-gance is unacceptable. Insulting the meat is the San way of nipping nim-rodic pride in the bud. It thus facilitates important social goals. But one could not imagine the equally egalitarian Ojibwa saying such things, how-ever socially serviceable, for fear of offending the spirits of the game ani-mals or their spirit wardens.

On the other hand, the Afrikaans writer and filmmaker Laurens Van der Post, who observed San hunters at their work in the Kalahari, points out that they are neither wanton nor cruel killers:

> I've never seen killing which seemed more innocent. It was killing
> in order to live. On their faces there was always an expression of
> profound relief and gratitude when the hunter's quest had been ful-
> filled. There was also a desire to complete the killing as quickly as
> possible. . . . I've watched their faces many times when perform-
> ing this deed and I could see only the strain of the hunt, the signs
> of the fatigue of running all day under a cloudless sky in a high
> temperature, together with a kind of dedicated expression; but no
> gloating or killing for the sake of killing. In the whole process they
> seemed to call on unbelievable reserves of spirit and energy.[32]

The San seem to be no less matter-of-fact in their relations with super-natural entities. They believe in a creator high God who is, according to Lee, characteristically remote and inaccessible.[33] They also believe in a lower god who is something of a trickster. According to the folklorist Megan Biesele, this god began life as a human being and "later ascended to the sky and became divine." The stories of Kauha-the-trickster's tricks "are heard with anything but awed reverence. Instead, amused indignation greets the outrageous or bumbling adventures."[34]

Both Lee and Biesele report that according to San myth in the beginning all creatures were human beings, "persons of the early race."[35] In their originally human condition, moreover, the creatures who were eventually transformed into animals exhibited the personality traits that presently typify their species. One may immediately infer from this mythic particular that the San personify animal behavior. They regard the unusually diverse wildlife in their environment as a community of subjects—a community composed of beings animated by essentially the same consciousness enjoyed by a human being. This inference is confirmed by empirical studies of San beliefs about wildlife.[36] The San worldview puts human and nonhuman beings on the same metaphysical and psychological plane, the institution of insulting the meat notwithstanding. In some practical sense, therefore, the San regard themselves as "plain members and citizens" of the biotic community.

Van der Post captures the implication of the San sense of a shared subjectivity quite vividly:

> In the Bushman's knowing, no matter how practical, there was a dimension [that] could almost be called mystical. For instance, he seemed to *know* what it actually felt like to be an elephant, a lion, an antelope, a steenbuck, a lizard, a striped mouse, mantis, baobab tree, yellow-crested cobra, or starry-eyed amaryllis, to mention only a few of the brilliant multitudes through which he so nimbly moved. . . . His world was one without secrets between one form of being and another. As I tried to form a picture of what he was really like, it came to me that he was back in the moment . . . when birds, beasts, plants, trees, and men shared a common tongue, and the whole world, night and day, resounded like the surf of a coral sea with universal conversation.[37]

For the San, success in hunting seems to be premised simply and squarely on skill and luck. As to skill, the San are perhaps most renowned for their ability to track and to read spoor. They are also very knowledgeable about animal behavior.[38] As to luck, that depends on the whereabouts of the game, which in turns depends on the moods, whims, and wiles of the beasts themselves, who are apparently believed to be no less interested in self-preservation than properly human human beings are. In comparison with their North American counterparts, San hunter-gatherers seem to be members of a less enchanted, more everyday biotic community—

though, as in Van der Post's vivid evocation, one no less inwardly alive and shot through with subjectivity.

The difference may lie in the prehistoric human ecology of Africa and North America. In Africa, predatory *Homo sapiens* coevolved with the other fauna of the continent. In pre-Columbian North America, *Homo sapiens* were recent immigrants (by evolutionary measures of time), who encountered innocent, inexperienced populations of game. The encounter apparently led to tragedy—to the extinction of more than thirty genera of North American fauna and to a consequent post-Pleistocene New World human population explosion and crash.[39] The cultural evolution of explicit North American environmental ethics, such as that of the Ojibwa, may have been a dialectical response to this debacle.

Despite enthusiastic hunting by indigenous *Homo sapiens*, Africa retained into the historical period its populations of elephants, zebras, and camels, while similar fauna were extirpated in North America. In Africa the animals may have taken care of themselves—may have evolved defensive measures adequate to insure their species' survival. If so, there would have been no cause, as there was in North America, for the cultural evolution of explicit indigenous environmental ethics. In any case, according to Richard Lee, "Whatever the nature of their gods and ghosts, the !Kung do not spend their time in philosophical discourse (except when anthropologists prod them). They are more concerned with the concrete matters of life and death, health and illness in their daily lives."[40]

However little reflection the traditional San may give the matter, they behave as though they regarded themselves as plain members and citizens of the biotic community. A window into San biocommunitarianism is provided by Elizabeth Marshall Thomas in a 1990 essay in *The New Yorker*. She writes,

> What mattered to the integrity of the environment was that human hunter-gatherers had been there long enough to count as ecologically indigenous. . . . The ecosystem absorbed the impact of its people, who in vast areas of the Kalahari are the only primates, as it absorbed the impact of, say, its lions.[41]

A major—and beneficial—impact of its people on the Kalahari ecosystem was secondary but critical. The San set fires, and the fire regime in the Kalahari is a principal determinant of the structure of the floral community, favoring grasses and suppressing thornbushes.[42] Because the former are palatable and nutritious for the antelope and other grazers, the traditional human population was indeed the keystone species, in large measure responsible for a productive, diverse, and healthy biotic community.

The focus of Thomas's discussion, however, is not on the general human ecology of the Kalahari but on the mutual cultural adaptation between two of the region's species, its people and its lions. Over many generations, the San and their leonine neighbors worked out a protocol for sharing a territory, its water, and its game—a protocol culturally transmitted by both parties. After recent and radical changes overtook the area—mainly the incursion of Bantu cattle ranches and the creation of Etosha National Park, in Namibia, from which all people, including the indigenous San, are excluded—a primate-feline etiquette going back perhaps thousands of years has been lost.

For example, people did not hunt lions nor lions people. If a chance encounter between a person and a lion occurred in the bush, it was proper to "walk purposefully and obliquely away." If a group of curious lions came upon a human encampment or a human kill site, the people would assert their property rights by speaking firmly to the intruders and, if necessary, chase them away by throwing clumps of sod in their direction. Living near the same water hole in the dry season, the lions and people would drink and draw water at different times of day. The lions "came and went quietly. They didn't roar near [the water hole]. They never lay viewing it all day. . . . And no lion ever left a scat by the water." For their part, the people "used the water hole with care. They didn't pollute it or sit around it, but drew water and left."[43]

All this Thomas observed in the 1950s and then believed it simply to be in the "nature" of lions. Returning to the area in the 1980s, after the near eradication of the San culture, she found a generation of lions very differently disposed toward human beings. On one occasion, she was chased by two adolescent males. On another, she was stalked by two lionesses. On a third, she returned to her equipment to find a lioness snooping around it. She did then as she had been taught by the indigenes thirty years earlier and tossed a pebble at the beast while asking it firmly but respectfully to leave. The big cat charged, and Thomas barely escaped to the safety of her vehicle. From these latter-day experiences, she realized that the patterns of human-lion interaction she had earlier experienced were learned, not innate. Young lions for several generations had not observed older members of their prides interacting with human beings and so had not themselves acquired the old ways. This was Thomas's reaction:

> I was flabbergasted. . . . No such thing would have ever happened
> at Gautsha [a water hole in the Kalahari]. The Juwasi [a San
> subgroup] would not for one moment have tolerated being chased
> by lions. . . . The people were gone and the old way was finished.
> If the authorities had decided that the park would be more natural

without lions, and had removed them, their absence would not have been more glaring than the absence of the hunter-gatherers after half a million years.[44]

However little the San folkloric record may reflect their respect for fellow members of the biotic community, the ecological and ethological records testify to an accommodation both with the game and with other predators. The prey species remained abundant. They were not overhunted. The San venatic equipment was simple, fit only for securing enough meat to supplement a diet consisting mostly of vegetable foodstuffs.[45] Continued development even of Stone Age technology is certainly conceivable. Why was it not pursued? Nor did the San attempt to eradicate species such as lions, leopards, and hyenas, which competed with the San for game. Here again, a systematic campaign of removal is conceivable, even with Stone Age weapons. Again, why was it not pursued? One can only assume that the San, as suggested by their scanty cosmogony, regarded themselves as one with the other fauna and practiced a quiet policy of live and let live with their nonhuman neighbors.

An African Afterword

The San sensitively and beautifully painted their quarry on rocks. Of one such painting of an eland bull Van der Post remarks that "he was painted as only a Bushman, who had a deep identification with the eland, could have painted him."[46] The ecological significance of such rock painting, of Dogon and Yoruba sculpture, of the African drum and the African dance are beyond the philosopher's power to state and illuminate (at least, beyond this philosopher's power to do so). One sees, hears, and feels in these nonverbal modes of human expression an attunement of African peoples to Africa's timbres and rhythms. What potential have they for an African environmental ethic? How much of Africa's human responsiveness to the land and care for its creatures is implicit, habitual, lived, rather than explicitly codified? In the unspoken and unthought realm of human knowing, there may repose African resources for an indigenous environmental conscience that other researchers using very different methods may one day disclose.

AUSTRALIAN ABORIGINAL CONSERVATORS

The aboriginal peoples of Australia are also sometimes referred to as bushmen. And indeed, they have more than a few things in common with the San. The Australian aborigines were (and some still are) traditional hunter-gatherers, with all that that implies economically and socially.[47]

The majority still live in arid environments. Ancestors play a prominent role in their belief systems. And the beings in their native mythologies were at first human and later took on animal form.

From the perspective of this study, however, the bushmen of Africa and the bushmen of Australia differ profoundly in their verbally manifest environmental attitudes and values. While the San seem to have been well integrated into the interspecies community of the Kalahari Desert and to have remained in balance with their nonhuman neighbors, San mythology lacks elaborately articulated paradigms of interspecies relationships and— unlike San painting—does not celebrate or sanctify the landscape. In contrast, the Australian aborigines verbally as well as graphically express a very intimate and morally charged sense of relationship with other species and with the topography of their territories. Accordingly, Australian aboriginal thought is beginning to attract the same sort of attention from contemporary environmentalists that North American Indian thought has enjoyed. Most notably, perhaps, the nature-poet laureate of the United States, Gary Snyder, has touched on the ecophilosophical significance of Australian aboriginal attitudes toward nature in his book of beautiful essays, *The Practice of the Wild.*

At first glance, like Africa, Australia confronts the casual student with a bewildering diversity of native peoples—about five hundred tribes (defined as a group of people speaking a mutually intelligible language), according to the dean of Australian anthropology, A. P. Elkin.[48] But a closer look reveals an anthropological commonality greater than in Africa or, for that matter, in the Americas. All native Australians are of one racial stock. All were foragers, practicing no gardening or herding. Further, Australian languages and social structures have many similar features. As Elkin puts it, "The Aborigines are one people. Their tribal languages, in spite of differences of structure and vocabulary, have a common base. Likewise, the economic and social organization of all the tribes, being based on food gathering and hunting, perforce have much in common."[49]

One also finds an amazing unity in the cognitive culture of Australian aboriginals. According to David H. Bennett, an Australian philosopher who has begun the process of seriously assessing the environmental attitudes and values of the aborigines,

> there are strong similarities among all groups across the continent. All groups, for example, have remarkably similar cosmological beliefs about the origin of their particular ancestral beings [and] all groups have ceremonies for the maintenance of species in their country.

The principal differences lie in the details—"in the events and characters in myths relating the same story [and] in ritual practices."[50]

Therefore, on this, the final stop of the ecological-ethics tour vehicle, it would seem appropriate to sketch the Australian aboriginal worldview in profile, illustrating it by reference to this or that tribal detail, since in its general features it seems to have been virtually omnipresent on the continent. The environmental attitudes and values implicit in this composite native Australian belief system may then be spelled out.

Elements of an Australian Worldview

Australian aboriginal mythology is referred to as "The Dreaming" or "Dreamtime"—alternative translations of the Aranda word *alcheringa*.[51] The contemporary convention of capitalizing these terms indicates that they are better understood as proper names than as descriptive nouns. "The Dreaming," read literally, suggests that Australian aboriginal mythology originated in and was sustained by dreams. However, while dreams per se seem to play a vital part in the spiritual life of native Australia, their role is not as large as the name would suggest.[52] "Dreamtime" seems to be the less misleading term, since the reference is to a special sort of time—the familiar time of the mythic human mind, a time that is at once long past and existing alongside the present, perhaps as dreams exist parallel to waking experience. Elkin captures its dual sense of both long ago and right now, and its similarity to dreams: "the eternal dream-time—a time which is past and yet present, partaking of the nature of the dream-life, unfettered by the limitations set by time and space."[53] Gary Snyder characterizes Dreamtime as "the mode of the eternal moment of creating, of being, as contrasted with the mode of cause and effect in time." And he has insightfully suggested further similarities between dreams proper and Dreamtime, "a time of fluidity, shape-shifting interspecies conversation and intersexuality." In this realm there occurred "radically creative moves, whole landscapes being altered."[54]

In the beginning, there was the sky and the land. But the land was featureless. "Culture heroes" or "ancestral beings" traveled the land along specific routes or "tracks." As they went, they transformed it, establishing hills here, ravines there, water holes yonder, and other topographical formations. The Australian religions scholar Nancy Munn reports that in Walbiri mythology "the ancestor first dreams his . . . travels—the country, the songs and everything he makes—inside his head before they are externalized."[55] The doings of these mythic beings at various sites along their travel routes also establish the rites and ceremonies for their human progeny to reenact on location, so to speak. How the ancestral beings did the things they did, like cooking animals in their skins and observing incest taboos, establishes "the Laws" (mores) of the tribes. Part of what it means to be an aboriginal person is to observe the Law.[56] As another Australian religions scholar, R. M. Berndt, sums it up,

> The mythical beings are believed to have been responsible not only for creating the natural species, which included man, and much of the physiographic features of the country associated with them. Importantly also, in this context, they are believed to have established an Aboriginal way of life, its social institutions and patterns of activity.[57]

The ancestral beings were human but also had the characteristics of various animals—such as the emu, kangaroo, bandicoot, or red flying fox—into which they would eventually transform themselves. When their walkabouts were complete, each ancestral being "went down" or "in" at a certain spot.[58]

Such spots are called "increase sites." There the spiritual power, essence, or life force of the ancestor permanently resides. From that site are born both the animals whose specific form the ancestral being assumed and the people who also happen to be its progeny. Since these culture heroes are the ancestors both of certain people and of certain animals, those people and those animals are of one kind, so to speak. Thus arises Australian aboriginal totemism. Some people are emus, some are kangaroos, others bandicoots, still others red flying foxes, and so on. Berndt has expressed this concept thusly:

> A mythic symbol, in the form of a creature or some associated manifestation, animates a foetus, bringing with it a life-force emanating from the Dreaming. This symbol, or "totem" as it is sometimes called, serves as an agent, a manifestation of that bond. In doing so, it underlines the belief that he, or she, has the *same* being. In some areas, he or she is regarded as the living representation of a particular mythic character.[59]

It is necessary to stress the site and species particularity of the ancestral beings. Each mythic person in the Dreamtime is associated with its peculiar species and its particular increase site, though other sites may be associated with its wanderings and doings. David Bennett notes, "For example, if in Aranda country there is a water hole that is the [increase] site of Karora, the bandicoot, then that is the source for bandicoots and humans of the bandicoot totem. It is not a site, for example, of green parrots or red flying foxes."[60] In some instances, the particularity may extend to individual spirits. According to Elkin:

> [The increase site] is in a sense animated; life can go forth from it, whether this be thought of as a generalized power which in one case will operate in kangaroos and in another in wallabies, and so on, or as the abode or source of *individual* kangaroo spirits or lives which are ritually sent forth to be incarnated.[61]

In theory, the assignment of a totem to an individual may be based on one of several principles. For example, a North American Indian tribe may be comprised of a number of subgroups, each one designated by its totem—the crane clan, the bear clan, and so on—in which case a person's totemic identity is determined by patrilineal (or sometimes matrilineal) descent. In Australia, a person's totem is most commonly determined by the locale in which he or she is conceived. If a woman notices that she is pregnant while traveling outside the area occupied by her clan, then the child's totem will be determined by the ancestral being who "went down" nearby. The logic is simple and straightforward. Since the ancestral beings are either the source of new life in their regions or have generated spiritual effluences awaiting incarnation, the mother's womb will have been quickened by the local ancestral being, or by a "spirit child" thereof, at the time of conception. And, as Australian aboriginal thinking involves no ideas of sperm and ovum, the moment that an ambient spirit child has entered a woman's womb is indicated by morning sickness, foetal movement, or other physical signs of pregnancy.[62]

However, for the most part, the members of one group will all belong to the same local totem. And it falls to them to maintain the sacred sites marking the adventures along the tracks of the ancestral being who went down in their territory, even when these places happen to be in the vicinity of another ancestral being's increase site. They must also perform a cycle of rites and ceremonies, the patterns for which were set out by the actions of their ancestral being. Most important, at the increase site of their totemic ancestor, they must perform the annual "increase ceremony."

The purpose of an increase ceremony is to ensure the plentifulness of a species—the totem species of the group performing the ceremony. The object is not to bring about an occurrence contrary to the usual workings of nature but to assist and encourage the natural course of events.[63] The traditional Australian aboriginals believe that the neglect of increase ceremonies will result in abnormal declines in the respective species populations. Such declines, when they occur, are blamed on those totemites who

must have been derelict in their duties. The efficacy of the increase ceremonies, the other ceremonies, and the Law manifest the same principle in
Australian aboriginal thought—the rejuvenation by means of reenactment of the events of the past. Thus continuity of all life through time can
be maintained, and both the order of human society and the order of nature, in which human society is embedded and on which it depends, can be
preserved.

Elkin provides a brief description of a typical increase ceremony:

> If the hero were connected, for example, with the kangaroo, having
> it for his totem and possibly being able to adopt its form, he might
> have performed ceremonies for the increase of kangaroos at one
> place and left a great stone not only to mark the site but also as a
> storehouse of kangaroo life or spirits. . . . Such a site is henceforth
> sacred. It is a channel from the creative and eternal dream-time.
> The creative power is brought into operation and causes the in-
> crease, for example, in this case, of kangaroos, by the care bestowed
> on, and the rituals performed at, the site. . . . The performer or
> performers say, "Let there be plenty of kangaroo here and there,"
> and so on. . . . In the simplest form they blow powder from the
> stone, throw stones from the sacred heap, or take a mixture of pow-
> dered stone or earth and blood from the sacred place and deposit it
> in the countries where an increase of the species is desired and
> should normally occur.[64]

In addition to maintaining the totemic species population, the persons
whose totem the species is are forbidden at times to kill and eat members
of that species, or may eat only ceremonial morsels on ritual occasions.
"For most groups," according to Bennett, "the totem may not be eaten or
harmed in certain seasons or at certain locations."[65] And other taboos may
restrict a person's activities in respect to his or her totem species, or in respect to the totems of certain classifications of kin.

As this brief sketch suggests, Australian aboriginal mythology is extremely rich, subtle, and complex. Indeed, Australian aborigines seem to
have been at the opposite end of the spectrum of inclination to abstract
speculation from their African counterparts. Aboriginal Australia evidently has consisted of a checkerboard of tribes and subgroups sharing a
mythic worldview that is deeply rooted in the topography of the continent.
Each local community provides a single tile, or small collection of tiles, in
a single mosaic of ideas laid out on the landscape. Say that a certain cave is
alleged in the mythology to have been excavated by one of the ancestral
beings. As there indeed it lies, yawning in front of you, the landscape itself
mutely verifies the myth. And the myth in its totality is the integrated ag-

gregate of each tribe's special knowledge and lore. As Elkin puts it, each group

> is the custodian of a particular chapter of the myth and of the particular rites and sites associated with that chapter. . . . Each local cult-group is responsible for one, sometimes for a few, of these rites and sites, but as it requires for its sustenance the regular increase of other species, the rites and sites for which it does not possess, it is dependent on the ceremonial knowledge, sites, and activities of other local cult-groups for its own life. As this is mutual, we see that the cult-life is a vast system of ritual cooperation binding together local groups and also tribes.[66]

The Dreamtime is also a map of the countryside. As the mythology celebrates the wanderings of the ancestral beings, the several cycles of songs coordinate the deeds of the heroes with landmarks. In journeying from place to place through the literally roadless outback, an aboriginal follows the tracks of an ancestral being, navigating from sacred site—distinguished by peculiar geographical features—to sacred site by means of the relevant song. Gary Snyder was particularly impressed with this aspect of the Dreamtime when he visited Australia. Each of the "special places" to which he was taken by his aboriginal guides was "out of the ordinary, fantastic even, and sometimes rich with life." Snyder mentions a place with "several unique boulders, each face and facet a surprise." He was charmed by "a sudden opening out of a hidden steep defile where two cliffs meet with just a little sandbed between, and some green bushes, some parrots calling . . . [and by] a water hole you wouldn't guess was there, where a thirty-foot blade of rock stands on end, balancing."[67]

Camped for the night, Snyder's native companions would recite Dreamtime journey songs. "Each night they'd start the evening saying, 'What will we sing?' and get a reply like 'Let's sing the walk up to Darwin.'" He then asks his reader to

> remember a time when you journeyed on foot over hundreds of miles, walking fast and often traveling at night, traveling night-long and napping in the acacia shade during the day, and these stories were told to you as you went. In your travels with an older person you were given a map you could memorize, full of lore and song, and also practical information. Off by yourself you could sing those songs to bring yourself back. And you could maybe travel to a place that you had never been, steering only by the songs you had learned.[68]

With a little less personal touch, the Australian comparative sociologist Annette Hamilton confirms Snyder's anecdotal account:

Aboriginal people find their way unerringly through trackless wastes not because they understand how to navigate by the stars but because they have encoded in their memories the names of all the watering places from one end of their living range to the other in song verses that tell of mythical travels of creative ancestral powers. These verses name the places where water and sometimes other resources will be found and include information on their physical appearance and the directions from one to another.[69]

An Australian Environmental Ethic

If an environmental philosopher were to make up a "traditional" world-view from which environmental ethical implications would follow, he or she would find it hard to come up with anything more apt than what the Australian aboriginal peoples have actually articulated. Theirs is a world-view that at once unites human beings with the land and with the other forms of life on the land. As the Australian anthropologist Deborah Bird Rose observes, aboriginal Australian peoples

> believe that human life exists within the broader context of a living and conscious cosmos. Humans' responsibility lies in actions that nurture and enhance human life, the life of other species (plants and animals) and the relationships among humans and between humans and others. Other animal species are believed to be acting responsibly. People, other animals, and other categories of beings are moral agents. The whole cosmos is maintained through the conscious and responsible actions of different forms of life.[70]

Citing the "noble savage" fallacy, skeptics will nonetheless almost certainly dismiss the work of those contemporary anthropologists and environmental philosophers who have begun to draw out the environmental ethical implications of Australian aboriginal thought—just as such skeptics have dismissed similar work focused on American Indian thought.[71] There is no reason to think, however, that the anthropologists who worked among American Indians during the first half of the twentieth century, such as Frank Speck and Irving Hallowell, had strong but covert environmentalist biases that they projected on the peoples they studied; they lived and worked long before the advent of popular environmentalism. Yet it was Speck, in the 1930s, who first spoke of "savage savers" and "aboriginal conservators" and who characterized the American Indian hunting-gathering way of life as "a holy occupation."[72] And it was Hallowell who first described the Algonkian social representation of nature together with its moral dimensions.[73] That A. P. Elkin was a "greenie," as the Australians sometimes call Down Under environmentalists, is even less likely. Yet in his magnum opus, *The Australian Aborigines,* also published in the 1930s, Elkin frequently comments on the extraordinarily subtle and sensitive Australian aboriginal attitudes toward nature. For example, he remarks that totemism "unites them with nature's activities and species" and is "based on the belief that man and natural species participate in a common life," leading to a worldview in which a "unity of man and nature is expressed."[74] Anticipating the passionate "respect for nature" environmental ethic of the contemporary ecophilosopher Paul W. Taylor, Elkin states that "the Aborigine . . . brings nature into his social and ritual life [and] adopts an attitude of respect towards it."[75]

The Australian aboriginal mind seems to have been deeply conservative—not, of course, in the contemporary political sense of the term but in its literal sense. In the Dreamtime, the past is in some way also the future, since the continued order of human life and of nature is perpetuated through the ritual reenactment of the heroic age. As Elkin succinctly puts it, "Sanctity, sanction, and life arise from the heroic and life-giving past. Conservatism and the maintenance of continuity with the past play an important part in the life . . . of the Aborigines."[76] Confirming Elkin, Berndt holds that "the 'deities' were not only creators but the stimulators of continuity: their power, released through human rituals, ensures the maintenance of the status quo."[77] Since natural features of the landscape are the enduring monuments to the deeds of the ancestral beings, then maintaining continuity with the past entails conserving the distinctive topography of Australia, be it forest, savannah, or desert.

One might therefore expect that contemporary Australian aboriginal groups would be at the forefront of resistance to land-defacing development in Australia. And according to Annette Hamilton, they are: From the aboriginal point of view, the acceptability of a development scheme

> depends on the nature of the development, where it is, and what level of local transformations may be expected. Is the proposed development going to affect a large and significant sacred site or complex? Will it involve going under the ground in a limited way (oil wells) or in a large way (open-cut mining)? Will it involve roads that cut across traditional ritual pathways for carrying ceremonial objects from place to place? Will it involve towers that overlook vast areas including sacred sites and tracks? Will it cut across dreaming tracks in such a way as to "break" them?[78]

Hamilton raises the question of whether or not one can legitimately speak of "management" by traditional Australian aboriginal peoples as well as conservancy. Though they did not cultivate crops or herd animals, Australian aborigines judiciously employed fire to promote the kind of vegetation useful to themselves and to other animal species.[79] Moreover, there is considerable support for the view that the spectrum of behaviors and behavioral limitations surrounding totemism helped to prevent the overexploitation of native species. If by "management" one means the conscious adaptation of means to ends, then the Dreaming was not management. But like the social representation of nature among the Ojibwa and the seminal representation of energy flows among the Tukano, the Australian Dreamtime seems to have been a crucial element in the ecological adaptation of the people to the land.

More than anyone else, David Bennett has concerned himself with the specifically environmental attitudes and values implicit in Australian aboriginal thought. He thinks that indeed there existed a "conservation effect," especially in regard to native beliefs and associated practices, that prohibited the overuse of economically exploited species. As Bennett characterizes Australian aboriginal taboos concerning other species, they seem functionally equivalent to the game laws enacted by Europeans and their cultural progeny.

Bennett believes that the Aranda and other groups placed a severe restriction on eating one's own totem species not out of respect either for the species or its several specimens but out of respect for one's future spirit children, who may currently be inhabiting the bodies of one's totem, and for one's ancestors. (Only a token amount of totem meat, as in the Christian eucharist, he claims, may be consumed on ceremonial occasions—although during periods of protracted drought the taboo on nonritual consumption by totemites could be violated with impunity.) But he argues that the effect of this prohibition—whether or not it was consciously motivated—was conservation: "In a land with relatively few individuals of some species, prohibiting a segment of the human population from eating that species eases the pressure of human predation and promotes the continued existence of that species."[80]

Further, the increase site itself and its environs were "posted," so to speak, and no hunting or gathering of anything was allowed in the precinct of the sanctum sanctorum. It also had to be approached along the ritual track that the ancestral being had established, and sometimes, according to Bennett, "the proper approach extends to walking backwards." In any case, the conservation effect of this taboo was the creation of "game reserves."[81] On this point, Bennett has the support of the Australian anthropologist T. G. H. Strehlow, who comments that "many of the finest water holes . . . provided inviolable sanctuaries for kangaroo," and "while there is no evidence to show that the Aranda *pmara kutata* [increase sites] had intentionally been created as game reserves," that was in fact the result.[82]

In line with Strehlow's suggestion that there may have been a program of game management encoded in the geomancy of the Australian aborigines, the Australian zoologist A. E. Newsome found that "in Aranda mythology, the major totemic sites for the red kangaroo coincide with the most favorable habitat for the species."[83] Totemic sites in places where there is no habitat for the totem species are not likely to have been instituted in the mythology. One would hardly expect to find an increase site for, say, waterfowl miles from the nearest water. So a coincidence such as Newsome notes is not really noteworthy. Rather, what is notable is the prohibition of exploitation in the best habitat. "The coincidence of myth and reality indicates an underlying ecological base to the mythology and its high adaptiveness in that it was unlikely to fail," Newsome awkwardly concludes.[84]

Another basic technique of European and Euro-American "rational" or "scientific" game management is the establishment of "closed seasons," coinciding with the nesting of fowl, the suckling of mammals, and so on. David Bennett reports that among the aborigines of central Australia, "between the performance of an increase ceremony and the time when the ceremony is considered to have had its effect, eating the totemic species is normally restricted."[85] The time when the ceremony is considered to have had its effect presumably is the time when the young actually start to appear. So here again one finds a "coincidence of myth and reality," to employ Newsome's infelicitous phrase.

Bennett's pioneering discussion of Australian aboriginal environmental ethics is vitiated to some extent by his assumption that a proper environmental ethic should follow the lead of the Australian animal-liberation theorist Peter Singer and extend human rights to individual animals. He believes that he is leveling a serious criticism of the view that Australian aboriginal culture included an environmental ethic when he points out that the manifest concern of the people and the "conservation effect" of their mythology inclines toward the preservation and increase of the species, not the welfare of the individual kangaroo, emu, or whatever. Bennett's curious ethnocentrism is evident in the following comment:

> One of the main reasons for formulating an interspecies ethic is to abate practices *we* consider cruel. . . . The question of cruelty is not even raised for Aborigines. . . . The attitude of concern for the species, but not necessarily the individual, is the reverse of a general trend in *Western* thinking. At least in recent times, Western thought has emphasized the individual.[86] [Emphasis added.]

One reason for formulating an interspecies ethic may be to abate practices that Westerners like Bennett consider cruel, but that is certainly not one of the main reasons for doing so. The main reasons for formulating an interspecies ethic are to preserve species, which the world is losing at an abnormal rate, and more generally to abate practices destructive of other aspects of the environment. And these desiderata the Australian aboriginal worldview seems admirably adapted, if not actually designed, to achieve. Deborah Rose is more on target, in comparing an Australian aboriginal environmental ethic to the holistic Leopold land ethic rather than to an ethic primarily concerned with minimizing animal suffering.[87] Undeniably and unequivocally, Australian aboriginal totemism and associated increase ceremonies evidence a keen sense of kinship with and mutual dependency on other creatures, and express a concern for the flourishing of species populations. No less certainly, Australian aboriginal thought manifests a deep and abiding investment in place. The importance of "storied residence" for a "contextualized" environmental ethic has been stressed in the recent literature of environmental ethics and Deep Ecology.

For example, the American environmental philosopher Holmes Rolston, III, maintains that "an environmental ethic does not want merely to abstract out universals, if such there are, from all this drama of life, formulating some set of duties applicable across the whole." Then—without reference to (and almost certainly without a thought for) Australian aboriginal belief—he continues in terms that nevertheless evoke the mythogeography of aboriginal Australia:

> An ethic is not just a theory but a track through the world. . . . If a holistic ethic is really to incorporate the whole story, it must systematically embed itself in historical eventfulness, or else it will not really be objective. It will not be appropriate, well-adapted to the way humans actually fit their niches. . . . An environmental ethic needs roots in locality and in specific appreciation of natural kinds—not always rooted in a single place, but moving through particular regions and tracks of nature so as to make a narrative career, a storied residence.[88]

And one might say without undue exaggeration that for Gary Snyder "a sense of place" lies at the foundation of any genuine and practical environmental ethic. Bennett writes, "Land gives Aborigines their identity. They are at home."[89] Snyder's warm and personal portrait of his aboriginal hosts and their historically eventful storied residence in their Australian homelands brings vividly to life Bennett's dry declaration. Snyder writes:

> Our place is part of what we are. Yet even a "place" has a kind of fluidity: it passes through space and time—"ceremonial time". . . . It is not enough just to "love nature" or to want to

"be in harmony with Gaia." Our relation to our natural world takes place in a *place*, and it must be grounded in information and experience.[90]

Perhaps more clearly and vividly than any other peoples on the planet, the Australian aboriginals have articulated their sense of self in terms of place. According to the Australian environmental philosopher Val Plumwood,

> Aboriginal culture [is] a model of bioregionalism. Identity is not connected to nature as a general abstract category (as urged upon us by the proponents of Deep Ecology), but to particular areas of land, just as the connection one has to close relatives is highly particularistic and involves special attachments and obligations not held to humankind in general. And in complete contrast to Western views of land and nature as only accidentally related to self and as interchangeable means to human satisfaction, the land is conceptualized as just as essentially related to self as kin are, and its loss may be as deeply grieved for and felt as the death of kin.[91]

As this chapter ends, I pause to think of my own "place," my own spirit land. I find myself falling into a mode of consciousness that is human and natural, yet a mode of consciousness so unmodern and un-Western that imaginative immersion in a worldview from the other side of the earth is required to awaken it in me. I wonder what it would be like to stand in reverential silence in the fastness of a particular and familiar crane marsh and think to myself—and feel in my bones—that out of this watery wild both came I and the big birds trumpeting over the tamaracks. This place is the Crane, and I am a crane. Or so I dream.

9   A Postmodern Evolutionary-Ecological Environmental Ethic

WHAT IS POSTMODERNISM?

Postmodernism is modish (no conundrum intended). It is also ambiguous.

On the one hand, *deconstructive* postmodernism claims that all religious and philosophical worldviews are fabricated to justify the power of a dominant élite. None is true. And a person's preference for and loyalty to this one or that depends on how well it serves his or her interests. Deconstructive postmodernism is both nihilistic and cynical.

On the other hand, *reconstructive* postmodernism is creative and optimistic. It aims to clear away the rubble and rubbish of the dilapidated modern worldview founded on now-defunct modern classical science, and, in its stead, to rebuild from foundations constituted by the "new physics" (relativity and quantum theory) and the "new biology" (the theory of evolution and ecology).

Modern natural philosophy—essentially, classical mechanics—has been overturned by the new physics. Everything else modern—the social contract between egoistic social atoms, economic reductionism (including both capitalism and anticapitalistic Marxism), preference utilitarianism, and so on—which has orbited about modern natural philosophy has been left without a center. Because reconstructive postmodernists can't be quite sure what modernity's successor will turn out to be, they remain cautious and call this interregnum "postmodernism," while they wait for "organicism," or "systems theory," or some such label to take hold.

In 1989, the ecofeminist philosopher Jim Cheney took a deconstructive "postmodern turn" in the field of environmental philosophy and ethics.[1] According to Cheney, with the "demise of modernism" there has occurred a "shattering into a world of difference, the postmodern world."[2] No reconstruction is possible, in his opinion, since Cartesian certainty is most

185

certainly unobtainable and the underlying political agenda of all intellectual constructs has been exposed. And further, no reconstruction is desirable, since any comprehensive worldview represents a "totalizing" package of concepts which would "colonize" other systems of thought. Deconstructive postmodernists are content to deconstruct the old texts and declare that there will be no new master narratives, no new *New Organons*, *Meditations*, or *Principias* to set the course for generations to come.

As this book consists of a global sampler of traditional and indigenous environmental attitudes and values, one might expect it to close with a resounding endorsement of deconstructive postmodernism and the pluralism it implies. Certainly this book recognizes and celebrates cultural diversity and intellectual pluralism. But untempered pluralism, especially if harnessed to deconstructive postmodernism, courts conflict rather than mutual understanding and cooperation. The endpoint of untempered "claims of otherness and an ethic of difference," so warmly endorsed by Cheney, is the violent ethnic conflict now plaguing the world.[3] A unity and harmony in multiplicity must be achieved, if our common environmental crisis is to be cooperatively—and successfully—addressed. What is needed is a Rosetta stone of environmental philosophy to translate one indigenous environmental ethic into another, if we are to avoid balkanizing environmental philosophy. Or, to continue shifting metaphors, we need a conductor's score in addition to charts for all the individual players, if we are to orchestrate effectively all the world's voices singing of a human harmony with nature.

Biological diversity is a good thing. So is cultural diversity. They are, moreover, intimately linked. Cultural diversity is a reflection of biological diversity, a fact more clearly recognized by tribal totemism than by contemporary social science. The same forces—transnational corporations, Green Revolution agriculture, and a global market, among others—driving cultural homogenization and impoverishment also drive biological homogenization and impoverishment. And the conservation of cultural diversity is instrumental in the conservation of biological diversity. Since the life-ways of foragers and vernacular agriculturalists are so thoroughly integrated into their local biotic communities, culture conservation is tantamount to biological conservation.

The myriads of species that make up biological diversity do not, however, exist in isolation from one another. Each is integrated into an ecosystem. How, analogously, might we unite the environmental ethics of the world's many cultures into a systemic whole? That is the principal task for this penultimate chapter. The ecofeminist philosopher Karen Warren has suggested an appropriately feminine metaphor for the union—or "solidarity," more precisely—of diverse ecofeminist "voices": a patchwork quilt.[4] But the colors in a patchwork quilt may clash, and the whole will then have no systemic integration or integrity. A patternless patchwork quilt is a poor analogue of an ecosystem. We want a genuine multicultural network of environmental ethics, rather than an eclectic and conflictive patchwork.

Hence the "postmodernism" of this chapter's title is of the reconstructive sort. And the evolutionary-ecological environmental ethic founded on such a postmodernism is intended to embrace and unite, as well as complement, the traditional and indigenous environmental ethics so far reviewed. We must be keenly aware of human differences, and we must defend cultural diversity as ardently as we defend biological diversity. But we must also be aware of what unites the world's diverse cultures, no less keenly than we are aware of the ecological relationships binding the myriads of species into hierarchically nested ecosystems.

THE ONE-MANY PROBLEM

An oft-repeated refrain of this study has been that there is one species of *Homo* but many peoples; one planet but many worlds. The modern scientific worldview, however, has partly unified the planet intellectually, making it—to some extent—one world as well as one planet. Science is Western in provenance, as the historical sketch in the next section of this chapter suggests, but science is now also international in practice and influence. The modern scientific worldview has become a cognitive lingua franca. It coexists and often insidiously intermingles with the many and diverse traditional cultural worlds. Thus, it is one of the ties that unite them.

We all live in distinct bioregions, each with its characteristic climate, topography, flora, and fauna. But the shores of all continents and islands are washed by one ocean, and we all inhale one atmosphere. Similarly, we all inhabit distinct traditional cultural worlds, each with its characteristic ontology, epistemology, cosmology, aesthetics, and ethics. But, for better or worse, Western ideas have become a pervasive cognitive ether that nearly everyone breathes in—more or less deeply. The curricula of secondary schools and universities from China to Brazil and from Tanzania to Canada include standard biology, physics, and chemistry along with indigenous culture studies. Further, the hardware icons of the modern Western scientific worldview are ubiquitous. And they invade the most intimate aspects of the lives of all but the most remote and isolated of the earth's peoples. Airplanes fly over the Kalahari Desert; Land Rovers crisscross the Serengeti Plain; chain saws buzz in the forests of Borneo; snowmobiles ply the frozen Yukon; diesel-powered ships anchor off remote Pitcairn Island; hydroelectric impoundments flood vast reaches of the Amazon Basin.

Machines, no matter in what cultural context they may be found and no matter what traditional agendas they may be employed to serve, are microcosms of the Newtonian macrocosm. They embody the modern scientific paradigm, and constantly, remorselessly reiterate and validate it. Vaccinations put the stamp of the modern scientific worldview on the shoulders of infants in Africa; intrauterine birth-control devices insert the modern scientific worldview into the wombs of women in India; when the Shining Path guerrillas of Peru grasp AK-47 assault rifles, they grasp the modern scientific worldview. When such technologies as these "work," they confirm the "truth" and the power of the ideas that engendered them and which they manifest.

The irony, of course, is that, theoretically speaking, the "modern" scientific paradigm is now obsolete. A new postmodern natural philosophy has been taking shape during the whole of the twentieth century. From a postmodern scientific point of view, the mechanico-industrial transmogrification of nature appears to be a grotesque and dangerous outrage, requiring us to develop an environmental ethic to temper its effects. And while the modern Western worldview and its associated values represent a hostile intellectual climate for the development of a direct or nonanthropocentric environmental ethic, the emerging postmodern paradigm promises to be much more hospitable to such an enterprise. The central section of this chapter is devoted, therefore, to the construction of a postmodern evolutionary and ecological environmental ethic, which is offered both as a complement to and a touchstone for the indigenous environmental ethics sketched in the preceding chapters.

How, more precisely, is the postmodern evolutionary-ecological environmental ethic here constructed related to the foregoing traditional and indigenous environmental ethics? What exactly do "complement" and especially "touchstone" mean?

The "land ethic" developed in this chapter is a sister to those in the preceding chapters. But it is more than that. It is not just one option among many, standing alongside, say, the Jain *ahimsa* environmental ethic, and appealing only to members of a specific sect or culture. It is a sister environmental ethic, but it is also proffered as a universal environmental ethic, with globally acceptable credentials, underwriting and reinforcing each of the others. Further, it is also intended to serve as a standard for evaluating the others.

Mindful of Jim Cheney's condemnation of totalizing and colonizing discourse, one might well wonder if such claims on behalf of the land ethic were not an arrogant assertion of philosophical imperialism, a bid for intellectual hegemony. Notice that throughout this book an evolutionary and ecological worldview has implicitly served as a standard for evaluating the environmental attitudes and values associated with traditional cultural worldviews. For example, in chapter 3, Hindu substantive holism was found to be a problematic basis for environmental ethics, because it differed significantly from the systemic holism characteristic of ecology. For another example, in chapter 6, the woodland American Indian concept of multispecies socioeconomic exchanges was touted, because it was, abstractly speaking, identical to the ecological concept of a biotic community, which is foundational to the Leopold land ethic. The implicit normative appeal to an evolutionary-ecological worldview and its associated environmental ethic may here and now be explicitly acknowledged. But is such an appeal warranted? Can it be justified?

Since science is Western in provenance, one cannot pretend that a scientifically grounded environmental ethic is culture-neutral. But science is now practiced internationally, with only the slightest culture-specific variations from nation to nation. These variations are so slight, in fact, that expressions like "Japanese science" or "Indian science" refer not to different and mutually unintelligible species of thought but to the international science going on in Japan or India, largely untouched by Shintoism or Hinduism. One can fairly assert that at least the ever-evolving scientific worldview enjoys genuine international currency.

The postmodern evolutionary-ecological environmental ethic here outlined may therefore make a claim to universality simply to the extent that its scientific foundations are universally endorsed—whether openly and enthusiastically or sub rosa. As just noted, the ubiquity of education in science and the ubiquity of modern and now postmodern technology, which is the fruit of Western science, has, for better or worse, inoculated all other cultures with Western attitudes and values. Citizens of Iran watching a fundamentalist ayatollah fulminate against Western ideas and values on TV receive contradictory messages. One message is conveyed by the words of the speaker, the other by the medium of communication, which is an object lesson (so to speak) in Western ideas and ideals. For the citizens of Iran, an evolutionary-ecological land ethic could be both a sister to the Islamic stewardship environmental ethic and a reinforcement of it, grounded in a contemporary science that, however much a fundamentalist regime may rail against it, has wormed its way into the contemporary Persian mind.

Certainly no worldview can claim to be absolutely and finally true. We human beings are prisoners of our imaginations and cognitive constructs.

We cannot step outside our minds to see if our ideas correspond to Reality with a capital "R." Hence we cannot know the Truth with a capital "T." No worldview is epistemologically privileged in the sense that it alone is certifiably true and all the others are false. It follows that traditional cultural worldviews cannot be said to have a share in *truth* only to the extent that they jibe with science. So how can an evolutionary-ecological worldview be presumed to serve as a standard for assessing the credibility of the others?

Though they may be considered neither true nor false, worldviews are neverthless subject to rational criticism and comparative epistemological evaluation. One worldview may consistently comprehend more of human experience than another. If so, it may make a peremptory claim on our credulity, or at least on our intellectual allegiance. Or to express the same thought negatively, a worldview that cannot accommodate the full range of human experience, or cannot do so coherently, fails to capture our intellectual allegiance and may be eclipsed by a more inclusive one. And over the course of human history our range of experience has grown enormously and is constantly expanding, more rapidly now than ever.

To take a familiar example, neither of the biblical origin myths discussed in chapter 2, if literally construed, can accommodate a certain set of experiences not enjoyed by Bronze and Iron Age Hebrews, indeed not enjoyed by anyone until very recently. Close observation of fossils in sedimentary rocks and of other geological phenomena made it impossible for a few thoughtful people in the late eighteenth century to credit the idea that the world had suddenly come into being about six thousand years ago. Charles Darwin consolidated a competing origin myth, which embraced these experiences and coherently united them with others (such as the many family resemblances among living species). The publication of his unbiblical uncreation story stimulated learned debate, which had the effect of familiarizing educated opinion makers in the West and its colonial outposts with "the fossil record" and other formerly obscure phenomena. Eventually, the whole literal worldview sketched in Genesis became itself a fossil—an extinct worldview preserved in the textual sediments of the Old Testament (and in the minds of die-hard Islamic, Jewish, and Christian fundamentalists).

Scientists, moreover, scrutinize one another's work. Skepticism and faultfinding are cardinal scientific virtues. One measure of a genuinely scientific hypothesis is its logical linkage to novel experience that will either confirm (but never finally prove) or contradict it. If, in the course of their investigations, scientists stumble on phenomena that contemporaneous scientific theory cannot account for, such phenomena are not simply ignored—at least, not if they keep intruding; certainly they are not deliberately suppressed. The old master narratives are first stretched to accommodate the new experiences. When the familiar theoretical constructs burst at the seams, patches are added. Finally, the old scientific paradigms become hopelessly rent and tattered. Then a rare opportunity opens up that begs for genius. A Copernicus, a Darwin, an Einstein steps forward to reweave the entire tapestry of scientific thought. Thus new, ever more subtle, sophisticated, and comprehensive scientific paradigms arise to replace the older ones.

The scientific worldview is, therefore, epistemologically privileged—not because it and it alone is uniquely true but because it is self-consciously self-critical. Hence, the evolutionary-ecological environmental ethic—shortly to be elaborated—may stake a coattail claim to epistemological privilege, since it is grounded in the epistemologically privileged reconstructive postmodern scientific worldview.

Today we live in the dim light of the dawn of a brand new Western natural philosophy. Ours is a time of great anxiety, because the old Western natural philosophy—articulated most paradigmatically by Galileo, Descartes, Locke, and Newton—has fallen apart and the shape of the new has not become entirely clear even to the most sharp-sighted visionaries. By the same token, ours is also a moment of great opportunity. Contemporary philosophers can help give shape to the Western worldview that future intellectual historians will date to the beginning of the third millennium C.E.

In this process, traditional non-Western worldviews can play an important role. Val Plumwood argues that they can provide a multiplicity of critical perspectives, bringing to light "areas that we may have failed to see as important" and deep assumptions that might otherwise go unnoticed.[5] Fritjof Capra has argued that there exist profound similarities between the new physics and traditional non-Western worldviews, especially those of Asia.[6] While Capra naïvely treated "Eastern philosophy" as if it were a monolithic historically and culturally unified tradition of thought like Western philosophy, he nevertheless struck a note of truth. The "new science," shaped as much by evolutionary and especially ecological biology as by relativity and quantum physics, though growing directly out of the old, has laid the foundations for a very un-Western Western worldview of the future.

However revolutionary, the new science is expressed in the same abstract language as the old. The new physics is not completely accessible to anyone without training in advanced mathematics. The new biology is also liberally laced with mathematical formulas, tables, graphs, and equations. A few philosophically gifted high priests of science struggle to convey something of the sweeping and profound intellectual implications of the arcane new doctrines and rites over which they preside. Albert Einstein, Werner Heisenberg, and Erwin Schrödinger, for example, have been effective popularizers as well as principal architects of the new physics. Perhaps no one has been a more successful communicator of the philosophical implications of the new biology than the ecologist Aldo Leopold.

But the articulation and dissemination of something so general, multifaceted, and fundamental as a new picture of nature, human nature, and the relationship between the two cannot be effected by a few able writers in each relevant scientific field. The process of worldview poièsis is gradual, cumulative, and ongoing. Generalizing Capra's insight, and correcting for the limitations of his *Tao of Physics*, we may confidently say that there are interesting similarities between the ideas of the new science and non-Western traditions of thought. Indigenous worldviews around the globe can contribute a fund of symbols, images, metaphors, similes, analogies, stories, and myths to advance the process of articulating the new postmodern scientific worldview. Thus the contemporary custodians of traditional and indigenous non-Western systems of ideas can be cocreators of a new master narrative for the rainbow race of the global village. They have a vital role to play. Historically, the reconstructed postmodern worldview will be Western. Substantively, it will not. It will be more Buddhist than Platonic, more Kayapoan than Cartesian.

In this way, indigenous environmental ethics may complement a postmodern evolutionary-ecological environmental ethic as well as vice versa. We may anticipate a global intellectual dialogue, synthesis, and amalgamation to emerge, rather than an era of Western philosophical hegemony, or—just as bad—an era of intellectual balkanization, bickering, intolerance, and ethnic cleansing: the bitter fruit of claims of absolute "otherness" and irreconcilable "difference."

Note that the comparative dialogue here envisioned is a far cry from the caricature, drawn by some writers, of starry-eyed Western environmentalists hoping to convert the West to the ecological attitudes and values of various non-Western cultures. Deborah Bird Rose, for example, warns of

> the possibility that people who perceive a lack in their own culture will be drawn to a romantic and nostalgic glorification of other cultures and seek to transplant another culture's ethical system into their own. The attempt is misguided. Every culture is the product of particular beings living particular lives within the particular options and constraints of their own received traditions, their mode of production and so on.[7]

No such transplantation is suggested here. Nevertheless, even the more limited and careful cross-fertilization envisioned here has been severely criticized. "Mining" the "conceptual resources" of indigenous intellectual traditions for insights and images that will help articulate the environmental attitudes and values latent in the emerging postmodern scientific worldview is a reprehensible kind of philosophical colonialism, according to the comparativist Gerald James Larson—a kind that differs from but is related to the colonizing about which Cheney complains.[8]

Is comparative environmental philosophy guilty of "stealing the discourse of the other"? Such a charge, however politically fashionable, is preposterous. Things of the mind are not diminished when they are shared. When the conquistadors took New World gold back to Spain, the New World indigenes were the poorer. Would that the Spanish had taken New World ideas back instead! Quite the contrary: the conquistadors were as anxious to export their own ideas as to import the physical riches of the peoples they subjected. Let us not be deterred by caricatures of comparative environmental philosophy. Let us drop these unpersuasive charges of intellectual piracy and instead seek a mutually enriching fair trade in ideas—East and West, North and South.

Rose warns that "the attempt to appropriate another culture's ethical system is self-defeating because it is self-contradictory: the act of appropriation is so lacking in the respect which is the basis of the desired ethic that the appropriation becomes annihilation."[9] A moment's reflection suggests that this charge, too, is just so much politically fashionable rhetoric. The "act of appropriation" is on the face of it an indication of respect rather than disrespect—imitation being the sincerest form of flattery. Neither are things of the mind debased when they are shared. Again, quite the contrary: favorable comparison with the emerging postmodern scientific worldview—which is what this study attempts—validates traditional and indigenous intellectual achievements. It gives them new meaning, dignity, and power.

A GENEALOGY OF SCIENCE

Science, in the current sense of the word, is a legacy of the Western intellectual tradition. In the West, the first philosophy, temporally speaking, was natural philosophy. And "modern" science, which came into its own in the seventeenth century C.E., is just Western natural philosophy consolidated and united by a universally accepted paradigm (the mechanical paradigm), method (the inductive-hypothetical-deductive-experimental method), and division into areas of inquiry (astronomy, astrophysics, physics, physical chemistry, chemistry, biochemistry, biology, and the rest).

The West's first philosophical question was, Of what is the world composed? It was asked by Thales of Miletus, if we may infer the question from his answer—to wit, water. Thales did not allege that this answer was a truth revealed to him by the gods; it was an idea of his own devising. Hence his "hypothesis" invited criticism.

Thales' immediate intellectual successor, Anaximander, argued that if everything was composed of water, then everything would be wet; indeed, it would seem that if everything was composed of water there would be nothing but water. Hence the *archê*—the underlying substance from which all things come to be and into which they are all finally resolved—must be the *apeiron*, the "indeterminate," or "indefinite." Anaximander did not question the implicit assumption that there was an ultimate stuff or that such stuff was unitary. He argued, rather, that it must be a neutral mix of opposite qualities—hot and cold, wet and dry. Hypostatized and systematized by Empedocles, these opposites became the four classical "elements"—fire, earth, water, and air.

Nevertheless, the severe Greek intellectual requirement, explicitly articulated by Parmenides, that Being be absolutely one and unchanging obviously could not be satisfied by a theory positing the irreducible reality of four things. The atomic theory of matter, proposed by Leucippus and refined by Democritus, came very near to passing muster, however. To be sure, the atoms theorized by Leucippus and Democritus were many—indeed, infinite in number—and constantly moving. But each atom meets Parmenides' specifications for Being, since each, considered by itself, is one, internally unchanging, motionless, eternal, and spatially limited: An atom is not generated; it will not be destroyed; and throughout its infinite career it will change not one iota. More abstractly considered, though, the atoms collectively are not irreducible. In a sense, space is the ultimate, genuinely one Reality—the true *archê* of the atomic theory. The atomists seem to have thought of space as binary. A volume of space, in other words, may be either "on" or "off." The scattered small volumes of positive or "on" space are the atoms. Between them is negative or "off" space, the void.

That the classical atoms, in any case, are quintessentially spatial entities is confirmed by the primary qualities assigned them by the ancient architects of the atomic theory. The atoms do not differ from one another substantively, and they are all colorless, odorless, and flavorless. They differ only in shape, relative size, and the speed with which they spatially translate, or move from point to point. Manifest change is attributable to the association and dissociation of the impassive but promiscuous atoms, while manifest qualities like color and sound are attributable to the effect of the differing geometrical properties of the atoms and their states of motion on our errant senses.

Because Aristotle preferred the theory of Empedocles to that of Democritus, the qualitative elemental quartet of earth, air, fire, and water dominated European natural philosophy during its gradual recovery from the European Dark Age, when Aristotle was taken to be the final authority on every secular subject. After the Renaissance, the atomic theory of matter was revived, and finally was institutionalized by Isaac Newton in his modern mechanical natural philosophy—the philosophy around which modern science coalesced. The classical atom was significantly revised only in the twentieth century, as part of the paradigm shift from the modern Newtonian mechanical natural philosophy to the postmodern Einsteinean-Heisenbergian Unified Field natural philosophy. Today's subatomic "particles" are often imagined to be simply smaller versions of their ancient prototypes, with more exotic mathematical characteristics. That is at best an uncritical and ill-informed imposition of past ideas on the present. However that may be, from Thales to Niels Bohr the question "Of what is the world composed?" has been a central preoccupation driving Western inquiry into nature. While work on the problem has not gone on uninterrupted, from the sixth century B.C.E. down to the present the problem itself has remained exactly the same, and each thinker who has seriously taken it up has built directly on the work of his or her predecessors in the tradition.

A second central question driving Western inquiry into nature was first posed by Heraclitus. More important, he thought, than the question about the stuff of which things are composed is the question about the order of natural processes. Water is evaporated by the sun from the sea and falls to the earth again as rain; day follows night and night day; the stars revolve about the heavens in a wonderfully regular way, while the planets (literally, "wanderers," in Greek), including the sun and the moon, move in an intricate and regular but devilishly complex pattern. What is the Logos governing natural phenomena? Heraclitus asked. He thought that it was evidently "out there" at work in nature as a transcendent principle, but he believed that it was also "in here," at the core of the human psyche. In other words, he suggested that human reason and the laws of nature are isomorphic. The world is, in short, logical; therefore, we can know through self-knowledge what is out there ordering the cosmos—by exploring what is in here, the rational essence of the human soul.

Although Pythagoras lived before Heraclitus and was contemned by him, Pythagoras's mathematical explorations lent detail to Heraclitus's insight. Mathematics is the exfoliation of both logic and the Logos—that is, human reason within and the order of nature without. According to Plato, Pythagoras was a veritable Prometheus, who stole the most potent of secrets from the gods—not fire but mathematics, the key to knowing the order of nature. Descartes and Galileo revived the Pythagorean-Platonic doctrine that the order of nature was logical and, more particularly, expressible in the language of numbers. Newton institutionalized it in modern science, as he institutionalized atomism, by inventing the calculus, a mathematical language that expresses the mechanical interactions among the atoms (or material "corpuscles," as they were sometimes called).

The third central question driving Western inquiry into nature was not so much first posed as first provoked by Parmenides. Parmenides, scorning sensory experience, argued that Being was not only one and eternal but also necessarily motionless. His Milesian predecessors seem to have assumed that the *archê* was self-moving and thus alive. Parmenides created the first crisis in Western proto-science: Reason seemed to require the existence of a blankly unitary static reality, while the senses disclosed a multifarious moving reality. The post-Parmenidean Greek natural philosophers took it as their task to "save the appearances"—that is, to reconcile logic and sensory experience, enabling natural philosophy to go forward. Therefore, they did not accede to the arguments of Parmenides and his disciple Zeno that motion was irrational. But they did feel constrained to account for the existence of otherwise aberrant motion by expressly positing a moving force or forces. According to Anaxagoras, the moving force was Mind, and according to Empedocles there were two such forces alternately moving inert matter—Love and Strife. According to Newton, while atoms possessed kinetic energy, which they exchanged through collisions with one another, the primary natural force was gravity (a bloodless version of the first of Empedocles's forces)—an attraction of all the corpuscles for one another.

The pursuit of the mathematical form of the order of nature and the force or forces of nature has been as constant a feature of Western natural philosophy as the pursuit of the problem of the nature of nature's material substance. Some contemporary scientists imagine themselves to be nearing the end of their triple quest, as theoreticians draw nearer to unifying mathematically the four fundamental forces of nature—electromagnetism, the weak force (these two were recently combined), the strong force, and gravity—in a final Theory of Everything.

In the first chapter of this monograph, the historical roots of our ecological crisis—to echo Lynn White, Jr.'s felicitous phrase—were traced less to the Judeo-Christian tradition, as he did, than to Greco-modern natural philosophy. The Greek natural philosophers supplied the conceptual materials from which the modern scientific paradigm was forged; and that paradigm—classical mechanics—in turn inspired and informed the modern Industrial Revolution and what Aldo Leopold called "the Machine Age."[10] The global reach of the environmental crisis does not invalidate White's insight that its historical roots lie in the West. Rather, the ubiquity of the crisis only testifies to the insidiousness of the modern Western worldview and its associated values. That Japan is a country as noted for its industrial pollution as for its tea gardens does not argue either that ideas are impotent or that Japanese intellectual traditions do not, as supposed, encourage a harmony of people with nature. That the modern Japanese have been environmentally insensitive indicates, rather, the degree to which Japanese culture has been Westernized. And the same could be said about India, China, or any other formerly non-Western society.

THE POSTMODERN SCIENTIFIC REVOLUTION

Although we may be able to apprehend the world through a variety of conceptual frames of reference, we cannot apprehend it independently of any conceptual frame of reference whatsoever. The emerging postmodern scientific worldview has its roots in a tradition of Western natural philosophy more than twenty-five hundred years old. It has, however, through its own internal dialectic, burst out of its distinctly Western conceptual cachet. To be sure, postmodern science is continuous with modern science and thus with premodern Western natural philosophy. The same central tripartite quest drives it. And more or less the same scientific method that disciplined inquiry in modern science disciplines inquiry in postmodern science. Modern and postmodern science differ in the substantive worldview or paradigm each presents, not in the questions regarded as worth pursuing or the method used to pursue them.

Moreover, the philosophical specifics of the new scientific paradigm seem very un-Western in spirit and substance. As Niels Bohr suggested back in the 1930s, there exist interesting similarities—such as the logic of complementarity—between the new physics and some Asian philosophies.[11] To underscore his point, he emblazoned the *yin-yang* symbol on his coat of arms. Both because science has become an international currency of ideas and because the postmodern scientific worldview is decidedly untraditional—un-Western—in its cognitive details, the postmodern evolutionary and ecological environmental ethic here envisioned may be considered to be part of an intellectual global commons. An environmental ethic grounded in a postmodern scientific worldview, therefore, need not be received in non-Western cultures as yet another Western import or imposition. Though a by-product of a dialectical development in Western nat-

ural philosophy or science, an evolutionary and ecological environmental
ethic is cognitively consonant with non-Western traditions of thought—
ironically, perhaps even more so than it is with the Western tradition.

In the modern Western worldview, nature is pictured as a vast mechanism. The postmodern (and, in a sense, also post-Western) worldview is
still very much in the gestation stage, and so cannot be as definitively characterized. But from all indications, nature will be pictured in the eventual
consolidated postmodern worldview more as a vast organism than as a vast
mechanism. In any case, it seems clear that in the emerging worldview,
from the macrocosmic family of galaxies to the microcosmic dance of
quanta, including the middle-size terrestrial environment we inhabit, nature is systemically unified by a hierarchy of internal relations.

To characterize a paradigm shift in science as a "scientific revolution" is
a little misleading. "Scientific revolution" suggests an ideological coup
d'état in which one party of natural philosophers seizes the professorships
and directorships from the incumbent party of natural philosophers and establishes a new regime among the scientific foot soldiers. The process is,
for one thing, much more gradual than the revolution metaphor suggests,
and for another, it is not philosophically arbitrary. A reigning paradigm is
given up very reluctantly and only for the most compelling of reasons: because it cannot embrace all the phenomena, or, in the phraseology of the
ancients, because it cannot save all the appearances. The Ptolemaic paradigm in premodern astronomy was simply unable to cope with the ever-
increasing accuracy of the observed motions of the planets, no matter how
ingeniously it was fine-tuned. It was relinquished gradually and with considerable trauma, not only because the entire edifice of Aristotelian dynamics was swept away with it but also because Christianity had entangled
itself with the geocentric picture of the world.

The Newtonian paradigm, for all its untoward moral, spiritual, and environmental consequences, is intellectually elegant and thus enormously
appealing from a scientific point of view. Pure Euclidean space; absolute,
equably flowing time; aggregates of material particles moving implacably
along straight lines, deflected only by collisions with other such bodies or
by the gravitational force—all this is easy to imagine and straightforward
to model mathematically. Many scientists today seem deeply to regret the
passing of the Newtonian world model, to yearn for its imaginability and
familiarity, and to backslide into a mechanical mode of thinking when not
called to account. (The continuing references to the dynamic and often
ephemeral subatomic knots of spacetime as "particles" is a case in point.)
But certain fundamental phenomena just cannot be made to fit the me-

chanical mold—the wave/particle ambiguity in subatomic physics, the quantization of light, its constant speed, and so on.

Scientists in the vanguard of a "revolution," moreover, try to maintain as much continuity with the obsolescing natural philosophy as possible. For example, in addition to retaining circular planetary orbits, Copernicus retained the outermost sphere of the fixed stars of the Ptolemaic system. While he argued that the earth was a planet, it never occurred to him to argue that the planets might execute any but circular motions, or that the sun might be a star. For an example from the more recent revolution, Albert Einstein relativized, warped, and integrated space and time, but refused, notoriously, to accept the Heisenberg Uncertainty Principle and the indeterminacy and insubstantiality it implied. Furthermore, a scientist faithful to the old paradigm will inadvertently contribute to the emergence of the new. The Danish astronomer Tycho Brahe, for example, supplied the observational data that enabled Johannes Kepler to complete the Copernican model of the solar system, but Brahe himself refused to accept the Copernican paradigm.

A NATURAL HISTORY OF ENVIRONMENTAL ETHICS

To shift from astronomy and physics, the central theater of the postmodern scientific "revolution," to biology, a more peripheral battleground: Charles Darwin likewise brought biology, the last bastion of Aristotelian science, into line with the modern mechanical philosophy, but at once planted the seeds for its defection to the organicism of the future.

From the point of view of Aristotelian biology, species were as eternal and unchanging as the heavens. Darwin's central concept, natural selection, provided a mechanism for the origin, change, and extinction of species. Organisms reproduce excessively; the progeny compete for scarce resources; those with competitive advantages survive and reproduce, thus increasing the frequency of their characteristics in subsequent generations. New species gradually evolve as the environment mechanically and impersonally winnows the unfit from the population and favors the better adapted.

But when *Homo sapiens* is set in this scene, as Darwin did in his second great work, *The Descent of Man*, then our species becomes a part of nature, a creature among creatures (or, rather, an evolvant among evolvants). Descartes, the aptly christened "father" of modern philosophy, had rigorously segregated man from nature. By bringing human beings onto the evolutionary stage, Darwin effected a man-nature reunion. As Aldo Leopold poignantly put it, Darwin's theory of evolution "should have given us, by this time, a sense of kinship with fellow-creatures; a wish to live and let live; a sense of wonder over the magnitude and duration of the biotic enterprise."[12]

Darwin's evolutionary epic not only undermines the Cartesian dogma that our fellow creatures are soulless automata. More profoundly, it undermines a cornerstone of the Cartesian modernist epistemology—viz., that we human beings are essentially disembodied passive observers of nature. From a Darwinian perspective, reason is a survival tool. Like the elephant's trunk or the giraffe's neck, reason is only a hypertrophic extension of a generic animal endowment, not, as Descartes believed, a special divine instrument of clear and distinct ideas—the same ideas in accordance with which God designed nature. Darwin thus set the stage for the great epistemological upheaval of postmodern physics, in which the observer, as a physical being, invariably affects and is affected by the physical object of observation, and always observes from a finite and immersed, rather than from a synoptic and privileged, point of view.

Darwin's account of the origin and development of ethics, treated here as a foundation for an evolutionary and ecological environmental ethic, is indisputably modern in its assumptions, but was given a definite postmodern spin by Aldo Leopold. Darwin recognized that however great man's inhumanity to man may be, ethics nevertheless exist. Even the most disillusioned and misanthropic observer of the human drama must acknowledge that human self-restraint, kindness, generosity, and even self-sacrifice exist no less certainly than human indifference, inconsiderateness, and unspeakable cruelty. All debate about "man's inhumanity to man" must be about the relative proportion of inhumanity to kindness, since no one can doubt that altruism exists, however attenuated or infrequent.

But how is it possible to account for the existence of selflessness? Assuming an evolutionary point of view, one would suppose that treachery and aggression would be of great advantage to individuals competing for the limited means to life, and that therefore such characteristics would be represented in ever-increasing magnitude in future generations. As time goes on, we should see less and less rather than—as Darwin himself believed—more and more inclination toward "moral" behavior. At this late date, in any event, all human beings—indeed, all animals—should be thoroughly rapacious and utterly merciless. Even the words "kindness," "pity," "generosity," "benevolence," and the like should have no currency in our language, since the dispositions they name should have been nipped in the bud by the remorseless and impersonal principle of natural selection.

A century earlier than Darwin, David Hume—an anti-Enlightenment skeptic who was nonetheless firmly ensnared by the modern paradigm—insisted that morality, though informed by matters of fact and cause-effect reasoning, is rooted ultimately in feeling. Just as we are moved to act in our own self-interest, and in the (reproductive) interest of the species, by powerful passions and desires, so we are moved to act in the interest of others, and in the interest of society *per se*, by opposing passions and emotions—such as sympathy, love, and patriotism. Likewise, Hume's younger contemporary Adam Smith rested his own philosophy of ethics on a very similar "theory of moral sentiments."

Darwin supplied an evolutionary derivation for the moral psychology Hume and Smith had described but could not explain. He begins with the observation that for many species, and especially for mammal species, prolonged parental care is necessary to ensure reproductive success; and that such care is motivated by a strong instinct, experienced as a strong emotion that adult mammals (in some species, perhaps only the females) feel for their offspring—parental (or maternal) love. Love, thus, can have been naturally selected, as it contributes to *inclusive* fitness—not to individual longevity, necessarily, but to successful reproduction.

Darwin then argued that "parental and filial affections" permitted the formation of small social units. The survival advantages to the individual of lifelong membership in a protective social unit like a family group are obvious and would tend to conserve more expansive variations of the parent-child emotional bond, such as affection for other kin—siblings, uncles, aunts, cousins, and so on. Those individuals in whom these affections were strongest would form the most closely knit extended family and clan bonds. These and similar "social sentiments" or "social instincts," such as the "all-important emotion of sympathy," Darwin reasoned, "will have been increased through natural selection; for those communities which included the greatest number of the most sympathetic members would flourish best and rear the greatest number of offspring."[13]

As clan competes with clan, the principle of natural selection, which at first would seem to lead to greater intolerance and rapacity, actually leads instead, Darwin suggests, to increased affection, kindness, and sympathy—for now the struggle for limited resources is understood to be carried on collectively, and groups with "the greatest number of the most sympathetic members" may be supposed to out-compete those whose members are quarrelsome and disagreeable. "No tribe," Darwin tells us, "could hold together if murder, robbery, treachery, &c., were common; consequently such crimes within the limits of the same tribe 'are branded with everlasting infamy'; but excite no such sentiment beyond these limits."[14] Such socially destructive acts were labeled "evil," and were socially proscribed. Thus a rudimentary tribal ethic came into being.

Darwin's own resolution to the Darwinian paradox represented by the existence of morality is simple and straightforward. Morality evolved among human beings, and perhaps something very similar (a kind of proto-ethics) evolved among other highly developed mammalian species, as a means to social cohesion. Thus, not only was there selective pressure for more intense sympathy and affection within group boundaries but there was also selective pressure for more widely cast social sentiments, since as one internally loyal and cooperative group competes with others, the largest will win out. Darwin concludes his scenario of ethical evolution thusly:

> As man advances in civilization, . . . small tribes are united into larger communities [and] the simplest reason would tell each individual that he ought to extend his social instincts and sympathies to all the members of the same nation though personally unknown to him [and unrelated to him genetically]. This point being once reached, there is only an artificial barrier to prevent his sympathies extending to the men of all nations and races. If, indeed, such men are separated from him by great differences of appearance and habits, experience unfortunately shews us how long it is, before we look at them as our fellow-creatures.[15]

And, it should be noted, Darwin even extends ethics beyond the species barrier, foreshadowing the eventual effort to construct nonanthropocentric moral philosophies. According to Darwin,

> sympathy beyond the confines of man, that is, humanity to the lower animals, seems to be one of the latest moral acquisitions. . . . This virtue, one of the noblest with which man is endowed, seems to arise incidentally from our sympathies becoming more tender and widely diffused until they are extended to all sentient beings.[16]

For Darwin, notice, humanity to *all* sentient beings is an *incidental* extension of our sympathies. Why? Because in the absence of an ecological worldview only some of the "lower" animals are conceivably members of human society. Pets are, as it were, honorary family members, and other domestic animals, as the philosopher Mary Midgley points out, are longstanding members of a "mixed [human/animal] community."[17] But absent an ecological understanding of nature, and especially the ecological concept of a biotic community, the vast majority of animals (which are wild), to say nothing of plants, remain putative social outlanders, and, as such, exempt from moral consideration.

Darwin could not have perceived nature through the lens of ecology, because the conceptual elements of ecology are embedded in the basic evolutionary biology that Darwin pioneered. Functional relationships among organic beings are conceivable apart from evolutionary biology—by analogy with the functional relationships among the parts of a machine, for example. But Darwin's idea that species adapt to and are sculpted by a multitude of environmental conditions brings the complex of a species' relationships to other species and also to temperature, humidity, acidity, and all the other inorganic facets of its niche sharply to the forefront of attention.

In the 1920s, Charles Elton captured the relationally integrated view of nature presented by the new but rapidly maturing science of ecology in a metaphor—one that has become so ingrained that ecologists sometimes forget that it is in fact only a metaphor. According to Elton, plants and animals are united into biotic communities. Just as in human societies all sorts of specialized roles or professions "evolved"—farmers, manufacturers, teamsters, merchants, priests, doctors, teachers, lawyers—so in nature's economy analogous roles or "professions" evolved, in respect to which species specialized. As the human economy is divisible into major sectors, the economy of nature is divisible into producers, consumers, and decomposers. And each of these major divisions is subdivided into myriads of specializations. Among the plant "producers," or autotrophs, are annuals and perennials, short-lived algae and long-lived evergreens, water-loving and drought-resistant species, and so on and on; among the animals—the consumers—are herbivores, omnivores, carnivores, and carrion-eaters; among the decomposers are fungi and bacteria. Together they form one community of competing and cooperating citizens.

Although Darwin himself envisioned the spillover of the moral sentiments beyond the species barrier to all sentient beings, it fell to Aldo Leopold to erect a full-blown nonanthropocentric environmental ethic on Darwin's basic biosocial account of the origin and evolution of ethics. Leopold integrated Elton's ecological model with Darwin's construction of the evolution of ethics to create a nonanthropocentric environmental ethic, or "land ethic," as he called it.

He begins by putting Darwin's theory of the origin and evolution of ethics in a nutshell: "An ethic, biologically, is a limitation on freedom of action in the struggle for existence. An ethic, philosophically, is a differentiation of social from antisocial conduct." Leopold goes on to draw a generalization from Darwin's natural history of ethics: Since "these are two definitions of one thing . . . [and] the thing has its origins in the tendency for interdependent individuals or groups to evolve modes of cooperation, . . . all ethics so far evolved rest upon a single premise: that the individual is a member of a community of interdependent parts."[18]

Immediately he adds the novel Eltonian element to this essentially Darwinian generalization. In addition to various strata of human societies—extended families, clans, gens, nations, nation-states, and the human race—ecology has revealed that we are also members of a hierarchy of biotic communities: our specific bioregions, biomes, and Gaia herself, the global or planetary ecosystem. Thus, according to Leopold, "the land ethic simply [reflects this enlargement of] the boundaries of the community to include soils, waters, plants, and animals, or collectively: the land." Practically speaking, "a land ethic changes the role of *Homo sapiens* from conqueror of the land community to plain member and citizen of it. It implies respect for his fellow members, and also respect for the community as such."[19]

When represented, as they are in ecology—as fellow members of a biotic community—soils, waters, plants, and animals stimulate our social instincts and sympathies. They bring into play our moral sentiments. Accordingly, we extend these fellow members moral consideration; we grant them moral entitlement; we enfranchise them ethically. Individually and collectively, they command our respect.

How exactly to translate these abstract principles of the land ethic into practical precepts generally follows from its overall theoretical structure. If ethics evolve as means to social cohesion and stability, then the precepts of ethics should reflect the organization of the societies to which each is correlative. Extended families and tribes are different kinds of social institutions, although the former are embedded in the latter. Hence our duties to our fellow tribespersons are not the same as our duties to members of our own families. We are obliged to support family members, for example, in their infancy and old age, but we have no such obligations—at least, none so categorical—in respect to our fellow citizens. And our duties to the members of our own nation-states are different from those we owe to human beings of other countries. We pay taxes to defend our fellow citizens against military aggression, for example, but we usually feel compelled to offer only moral support to citizens of other nation-states when they are threatened—as the inaction of the United States and other military powers in the recent central Asian and African ethnic conflicts indicates.

Similarly, our duties to the members of our own biotic communities are decidedly distinct and very different from the duties devolving to us from all our other social relationships—since the biotic community is only a metaphorical community, the structure of which is radically different from any of our actual societies, no matter how small and intimate or diffuse and impersonal. Murder, robbery, and treachery may be branded with everlasting infamy within both the savage tribe and the global village. But since eating and being eaten lie at the very center of the structure of the biotic community, an evolutionary and ecological environmental ethic could hardly condemn predation as murder, browsing and grazing as robbery, and nature's many ingenious devices to seduce and deceive the unwary into performing various interspecies services (pollination, for example) as treachery.

Generally speaking, the emphasis of the land ethic, in comparison with our various properly social ethics, is more holistic than individualistic. To be sure, one feels an obligation to one's family as such—as for example not to disgrace the family name—as well as to one's mother, father, siblings, and offspring, but family duties focus more on family members than on the family per se. One also feels an obligation to one's nation-state in addition to its members severally. Indeed, honoring one's obligation to one's country has a name of its own: "patriotism." But again, one's primary obligations run to one's fellow citizens at the national stage of social evolution. An adequate and practicable environmental ethic, on the other hand, reverses the relative weight placed on part and whole in our familiar social ethics. It is concerned less with sorting out the mutual obligations among specimens than with preserving species. Individual specimens ought to be respected, but specimens can claim no legitimate right to life in an economy of nature in which one being purchases life only at the expense of the life of others. In addition to preserving species, an evolutionary and ecological ethic is concerned with preserving natural processes and other biotic wholes. It is concerned with safeguarding genetic diversity and with preserving a substantial and widely distributed sample of the hierarchy of ecosystems—from ten-acre ponds and forty-acre woodlots to vast moist tropical forests, deserts, temperate prairies, subarctic steppes, and arctic tundra. Its ultimate concern is to ensure the health and integrity of the biosphere as a whole. As Aldo Leopold expresses the summary moral maxim—the golden rule—of the land ethic: "A thing is right when it tends to preserve the integrity, stability, and beauty of the biotic *community*. It is wrong when it tends otherwise."[20] [Emphasis added.]

THE POSTMODERN CREDENTIALS
OF THE LEOPOLD LAND ETHIC

As we see, the land ethic rests explicitly on Darwin's account of the evolution of ethics; and Darwin's natural history of ethics, in turn, rests explicitly on Hume's and Smith's theory of the moral sentiments. And the proposition that morality is rooted in our affections—that ethics ultimately spring from our subjective feelings, as Hume and Smith proposed—takes for granted the radical Cartesian distinction between subject and object. One could thus fairly argue that the evolutionary and ecological ethic sketched here, following Leopold, remains imprisoned by Descartes' dualism—the very castle keep of the modern scientific paradigm.

Granted. But even though the Aldo Leopold land ethic is built on distinctly modern foundations, it opens out upon the prospect of a fully postmodern environmental ethical ideal. In his vision of nature as an integrated community and an organic whole, Leopold points beyond the bifurcated Cartesian-Newtonian model of nature. A telling ambiguity pervades Leopold's discussion. To expose it, to diagnose it, is to deconstruct the land ethic and recast it in a fully postmodern form.

Why, one might ask, should we accept an evolutionary and ecological ethic? Leopold writes, "The extension of ethics to . . . [the] environment is, if I read the evidence correctly, an evolutionary possibility and an ecological necessity."[21] It is an evolutionary possibility for the reasons already elaborated—that is, because ecology portrays nature as a biotic community and we are evolved to respond morally to the communities to which we perceive ourselves as belonging and to their members. It is an ecological necessity because "the path to social expediency is not discernible to the average individual."[22] Thus the land ethic, though putatively grounded in the other-oriented moral sentiments, is ultimately justified in terms of collective human self-interest, in terms of "social expediency." The point is this: Unless we evolve a nonanthropocentric environmental ethic, *Homo sapiens* may not be around for very much longer. Ours is a gravely self-endangered species, and adopting an environmental ethic that subordinates human excesses to the good of the whole biotic community may be, paradoxically and ironically, our only hope for an extended tenure on the planet.

This air of paradox is removed when we come to see the full implications of ecology for an understanding of self, and, by extension, of self-interest. From an ecological point of view, oneself is a nexus of strands in the web of life. More formally, any entity (oneself included), from an ecological point of view, is a node in a matrix of internal relations. Reflecting on these metaphysical implications of ecology, the ecologist Paul Shepard was led to exclaim that "relationships of things are as real as the things" and to endorse Alan Watts's Zen-inspired declaration that "the world is your body."[23] Pushed a step further, ecology, in tandem with the new physics, may even be taken to imply not merely that relationships of things are as real as the things but that relationships are *more* real than things—that is, that things are just the focus of a complex of relationships, however abstract this may seem.

From the perspective of contemporary biology, species adapt to a niche in an ecosystem. Their actual relationships to other organisms (to predators, to prey, to parasites and disease organisms) and to physical and chemical conditions (to temperature, radiation, salinity, wind, soil, and water pH) literally mold their outward forms, their metabolic processes, and even their psychological and mental capacities. A specimen is, in effect, a summation of its species' historical adaptive relationship to the environment. To convey a very un-Aristotelian thought in an Aristotelian manner of speech, one might say that from an ecological perspective relations are "prior to" the things related, and the systemic wholes woven from these relations are prior to their component parts. Ecosystemic wholes are logically prior to their component species because the nature of the part is determined by its relationship to the whole. Or, to express the thought more simply and concretely, a species has the particular characteristics that it has because those characteristics evolved by way of its adaptation to a niche in an ecosystem.

One might argue that ecology, even so, is not prepared per se to deny outright the primary reality of atomic and molecular matter, no matter how completely organismic entities dissolve into a field of ecological relationships. However, if we take advantage of the way quantum theory resolves the erstwhile solid and immutable atoms of matter composing the molecules, which in turn compose the cells of organic bodies, into ephemeral quanta, then we may say quite confidently that organisms are in their entire structure—from subatomic microcosm to ecosystemic macrocosm—relational entities.

Gary Snyder captured this vertical integration of metaphysical ideas in a poem:

> Eating the living germs of grasses
> Eating the ova of large birds . . .
> Drawing on life of living
>   clustered points of light spun
>   out of space
> hidden in the grape.[24]

In these lines, "clustered points of light spun out of space" apparently alludes to the dynamic configurations of the microcosm—the quantum knots in the universal spacetime field. In the ecosystemic macrocosm, the grape itself is a "knot in the biospherical net of intrinsic relations," to quote Deep Ecologist Arne Naess.[25] Thus the grape, through and through, from ecosystemic macrocosm to subatomic microcosm, is less a freestanding thing than a multitiered nexus in a complex and hierarchical network of relations.

In any case, from an ecological/quantum-theoretical point of view, one cannot draw sharp boundaries, as did Democritus and Newton, between one thing and another, and, as Descartes did, between self and world. Hence a nonanthropocentric environmental ethic, fully ecologized, so to speak, turns out to be a form of enlightened—or, better, embedded—collective human self-interest, after all. Nonanthropocentrism thus comes full circle back to anthropocentrism, though to an anthropocentrism, one must hasten to say, thoroughly informed—and therefore thoroughly transformed—by ecology.

As noted in chapter 3, Arne Naess has called this process of ecological enlightenment Self-realization. The capital "S" is important, because it distinguishes this special ecological sense of Self-realization from the narrowly self-absorbed sort of self-realization that was the hallmark of the Reagan decade of the twentieth century—a sense of self-realization with which we are all too painfully familiar. While Naess himself sometimes confounds the ecometaphysical foundations of his Deep Ecological sense of Self-realization with the substantive monism of Hinduism, the Australian Deep Ecologist John Seed expresses Naess's expansive notion of Self-realization in metaphysically more appropriate terms, as well as more succinctly and concretely:

> As the implications of evolution and ecology are internalized . . .
> there is an identification with all life. . . . Alienation subsides. . . .
> "I am protecting the rain forest" develops to "I am part of the rain
> forest protecting myself. I am that part of the rain forest recently
> emerged into thinking."[26]

Just as the embedded, collective human self-interest implied by ecological Self-realization must be distinguished from superficially similar ideas in Advaita Vedanta, so it must be distinguished from the pedestrian concept of enlightened collective human self-interest familiar in utilitarianism, the modern secular ethic of choice. Utilitarians assume that self and other are clearly and distinctly distinct. One must grudgingly respect the interests of "others" if one expects others to respect one's own interests, and if an orderly society with all its benefits is to be preserved. But from the perspective of ecometaphysics, while others retain their identity and integrity, oneself and others are mutually defining and interdependent. Thus, since ecology conceptually relates self and other, embedded self-interest is not equivalent to reciprocal altruism or quid pro quo. John Seed is not protecting the rain forest because he realizes "he" needs "it" to survive. That is true. We do need the planet's rain forests to survive. One could also say that we need our families and our jobs to survive. But that is not the only (and maybe not even the most) important reason we take so much care to safeguard them. We each do so because, for each of us, meaningful work and intimate, meaningful relationships make us the persons we are. If by some calamity we are stripped bare of these, we may survive as "individuals," but just as surely we may lose our identities. But we are embedded no less in ecological than in social and professional communities, albeit in a more attenuated way. Therefore, we must be solicitous of ecological conservation for reasons of enlightened self-interest, since our survival as a species depends on a functioning biosphere. But, just as surely, we ought to care about the natural environment for reasons of embedded self-interest, since our identity as individuals as well as our collective identity as a species depends on the integrity both of our local bioregions and of the whole biosphere.

Here then is a genuinely postmodern, scientifically informed and constructed theory for environmental ethics. It is genuinely postmodern because its conceptual foundations are not Cartesian. The dualisms of subject and object, self and other are transcended. It is offered as a global intellectual commons. Though it grows directly out of the Western tradition of natural philosophy, its actual intellectual content is more Eastern than Western. It posits a unity in nature which has more affinities with Hua-yen than with Parmenidean monism. And it posits a Wattsian connectivity between self and world which is much more foreign to the West's intellectual past than to that of many indigenous cultures, especially those that are totemic.

CONCLUDING REMARKS

As we enter the twenty-first century, we find that each of us inhabits at least two cultures—a local culture and a global or international culture. Earlier chapters of this monograph have explored the conceptual elements for environmental ethics in the intellectual dimensions of selected indigenous cultural traditions around the world. This chapter has explored the conceptual elements for environmental ethics in the international intellectual milieu of twenty-first-century science. Happily, the emerging global scientific worldview is not as conceptually dissonant with the world's many indigenous intellectual traditions—at least, not with those reviewed herein—as its predecessor, the mechanical worldview. Thus an international environmental ethic firmly grounded in ecology and buttressed by the new physics will complement, rather than clash with, the environmental ethics implicit in the world's many indigenous traditions of thought.

Although this study has so far focused exclusively on ideas and ideals, its motivation is ultimately practical. As its first chapter more fully explained, ideas shape the stage on which the human drama is enacted, and ideals serve as both the ends and the norms of human behavior. Surely, the twentieth century has been the most dizzying and paradoxical of all in human history. During the twentieth century, we have witnessed the most abject human misery and the most spectacular human achievement, the most debased human depravity and the most exalted human nobility. The physical legacy we bequeath to the future is equally extreme and contradictory. Human life has been at once enormously improved by the century's technological achievements and enormously debased and impoverished. Conserving the human benefits and minimizing the environmental costs of modern technology will head the global agenda of the twenty-first century. As a first step, we will require a revised understanding of the theater of human action—a new constructive postmodern worldview—and a revised set of ideals, among them a new postmodern environmental ethic. To construct a genuinely postmodern environmental ethic—an ethic that respects diversity and the wonderful variety of past human culture—we must try to bring the intellectual elements of the earth's many indigenous cultural traditions into a complementary and concordant relationship with those of postmodern international science. This chapter has been devoted to suggesting a theoretical foundation for that project.

10 Traditional Environmental Ethics in Action

As Aristotle first observed, ethics is the most directly practical branch of philosophy. And it was concern about the dire environmental crisis that motivated the systematic study and development of ecological ethics which began around the middle of the twentieth century. Environmental philosophers cannot rest content with the charming intellectual exercise of theory-building. Theories of environmental ethics must prove themselves to be applicable and efficacious in the context of current environmental concerns. The Aldo Leopold land ethic has become the secular bible of the contemporary North American conservation movement.[1] So at least one environmental ethic has proved applicable and efficacious. This chapter will focus on how three representative traditional environmental ethics, outlined in previous chapters, are being applied in the real world by real people to actual environmental problems.

The dialectical debate in the late 1960s and early 1970s about the environmental attitudes and values embedded in the Judeo-Christian tradition—a debate stimulated by Lynn White, Jr.,'s notorious essay, "The Historical Roots of Our Ecologic Crisis"—set the precedent for this monograph.[2] What are the environmental attitudes and values embedded in the world's other traditional and indigenous cognitive cultures? That question has motivated and organized this book. And the way that the environmental attitudes and values embedded in the Judeo-Christian worldview were identified, criticized, and positively reinterpreted served as a model for a similar gloss of Islam, Hinduism, Taoism, and the rest.

The tenth and final chapter will be modeled on the design of the whole. Returning to the (for most readers) familiar Judeo-Christian complex of ideas, this chapter documents how its reconstructed environmental ethic is being effectively applied by believers on the ground to local environmental concerns. That discussion is followed by analogous reviews of how the environmental ethics implicit in two other of the world's important traditions of thought—Hinduism and Buddhism—are also being worked out on the ground.

THE STEWARDSHIP ENVIRONMENTAL ETHIC IN ACTION

By 1980, the Judeo-Christian stewardship environmental ethic had become virtually institutionalized in the United States. The Book of Leviticus 25:23—"Land must not be sold in perpetuity, for the land belongs to me. And to me you are only strangers and guests"—inspired the title of a statement by a regional conference of Catholic bishops on land issues, *Strangers and Guests*. Among the "principles of land stewardship" that the bishops identified were the following: "the land is God's"; "people are God's stewards on the land"; "the land should be conserved and restored"; "land-use planning must consider social and environmental impacts"; "land use should be appropriate to land quality"; and "the land should provide [only] a moderate living."[3]

In 1982, the American Lutheran Church adopted "a statement of comment and council" titled *The Land: God's Giving, Our Caring*, described as "a study document on the theology of the land." Cryptically alluding to the academic debate about the interpretation of Genesis 1:26–28, the Lutheran statement declares:

> Creation in general is given to the care of humankind in general. "Dominion" is not lordship over the rest of nature in any conquering sense, but living in harmony with, caring for the earth in responsibility before God. We are lovingly, gently to "till and keep" the land (Gen. 2:15).

A central tenet of the Lutheran theology of the land is that

> people are free to use and enjoy and benefit from the land, but not to possess it. God retains ownership (Ps. 24:1; Lev. 25:23). Humankind serves as God's caretakers on the land, God's stewards of what remains God's. We are given the land conditionally, in a sort of tenancy. We have use rights only—but that's enough.[4]

Based in Minneapolis, the Land Stewardship Project is working directly with farmers and other members of Midwestern rural communities to conserve and husband farmland and its environing ecological milieu. As the name of the organization suggests, its work is directly cast in terms of the Judeo-Christian worldview—the operative worldview of most of the people to whom the Land Stewardship Project reaches out. Just what is this organization accomplishing by its appeal to the Judeo-Christian steward-ship environmental ethic? Here is a brief review.

Encouraged by the "greening" of the churches, Ron Kroese founded the Land Stewardship Project in 1982, to address the downward spiral of deterioration in farmland and farm life diagnosed in Wendell Berry's masterly *The Unsettling of America*.[5] The foundation of an effective response to rural environmental degradation, Kroese believed, lay in the dissemination of a "land ethic" in the rural community.[6] Though Kroese consciously borrowed the phrase from Aldo Leopold (who was himself no stranger to farmers), the environmental ethic he wound up promulgating was grounded less in the controversial ideas of *The Descent of Man* and the "biotic community" concept of ecology than in the conventional ideas found at the beginning of the Old Testament.

During its first few years, the Land Stewardship Project focused mostly on dialogue and mutual education. "Stewardship ethics" meetings were convened in small-town church basements. To graphically communicate the stewardship ethic in a way that was not overly didactic and off-putting, Nancy Paddock, the editor of the Land Stewardship Project's newsletter, wrote a one-act play titled "Planting in the Dust," about the social and environmental aspects of the deepening farm crisis.[7] The play features a farm woman named Annie, who is trying to establish harmony within her family, with the land, and with her rural community. Annie raises questions about an ethical relationship of people to the land which she never definitively answers. The group discussion after the performance thus becomes the principal vehicle of consciousness-raising and empowerment.

During these discussions, Kroese and his associates listened as carefully as they talked. They began with the premise that Midwestern farmers were acutely aware of the deterioration in pasture and cropland, in rural communities, in farm families' quality of life, and that these farmers had given careful thought to the reasons for such deterioration. And they also began with the premise that farmers, perhaps more than most craftspersons, cared about the medium in which they worked—soils, waters, plants, and animals—as well as about turning a profit. In each place they visited, they asked, What are the forces that "contribute to good land stewardship and those that detract from it?"[8]

As to forces detracting from good land stewardship, two answers kept recurring. First, federal farm programs create disincentives for conservation practices, an example being price supports for row crops. And second, the university extension system promotes the "modern" industrial motif of agriculture aggressively and exclusively. Consequently, genuine husbandry is punished, and farmers who, despite the economic disincentives, want to practice it have nowhere to turn for technical information and support. The Land Stewardship Project has responded with a Public Policy Program and a Stewardship Farming Program.[9] The latter is at the heart of the project's mission.

The goal of the Stewardship Farming Program is to convert as many farmers as possible to methods that halt soil erosion; that begin to rebuild the proper physical structure, chemical content, chemical balance, and microbiota of the soil; and that do not pollute the domestic and natural environments with toxins. Project staff members knowledgeable in such methods work with farmers who would like to reduce both their overall costs and also the health risk to themselves and their families posed by chemical fertilizers, pesticides, and herbicides; improve the quality of their product; and restore the health and integrity of their soils and waters.

In addition to providing technical information and expertise, the Stewardship Farming Program helps organize a social infrastructure. Regional advisory boards are formed composed of men and women respected for their standing in the community and their concern for the environment. Participating farmers join together in Sustainable Farming Associations and hold regular home meetings to share information and provide themselves with a supporting community. Despite the wide dispersal of people on the landscape—or perhaps because of it, since one cannot lose oneself in an anonymous crowd—social pressures in the rural Midwest can be unrelenting. Deviating from accepted norms, agricultural as well as cultural, can attract intense notoriety and suspicion. Therefore, feeling that they are alone in experimenting with alternatives to so-called conventional agriculture can discourage a farm family from trying again in the face of failure, or even from trying at all. Moral support among peers can be as important to would-be stewardship farmers as receiving technical assistance. But since sustainable agriculture is a practice and not an ideology, these regional associations do not recruit members on the basis of doctrinal purity, nor are they in the business of proselytizing. Rather, the organizational effort is far more pragmatic—aimed at providing moral support, to be sure, but also at expanding the human experience and resources necessary to solve the problems of weed control without herbicides, crop yield without synthetic fertilizer, and so on.[10]

The message gets out by word of mouth; "conventional" farmers stuck in the rut of industrial agriculture hear the success stories of neighbors who no longer handle poisonous chemicals, who have saved money on "inputs," and who have gotten a premium price for their product on the organic-foods market. The Land Stewardship Project, in cooperation with the Sustainable Farming Associations it has fostered, organizes field days, in which on-farm demonstrations of manure composting, controlled grazing, intercropping, and other environmentally benign agricultural methods are demonstrated. On these occasions, farmers committed to making the transition to organic agriculture, as well as those who remain skeptical, can see for themselves how well their neighbors' experiments are working.

Again and again, farmers participating in the Land Stewardship Project's Stewardship Farming Program express their commitment and motivation in terms of the Judeo-Christian stewardship environmental ethic. Examples follow.

Mike Rupprecht began a field-day demonstration on his farm by quoting from Psalms 24:1: "The earth is the Lord's and the fullness thereof, the world and those who dwell therein." Then he declared, "What the Bible says is what I believe. And that gives me the inspiration to make changes on my farm. The land belongs to the Lord, and He has entrusted me to take care of it. I am working to do the best job I can."[11]

According to dairy farmer Ted Tews, "God is the owner and we are just the managers. He created a perfect earth. I don't always farm perfectly, but that's what I strive for."[12]

Dave Schonberg is perhaps as explicit about the motivation for his endorsement of good husbandry as anyone could be:

> My worldview is the Christian worldview. I am a Christian. And by this I mean that I embrace the basic teachings of the Bible. Different authors have helped us to see that soil care is part of being a good Christian. How we take care of the soil may be perceived differently by different Christians. They're not always going to agree on what is the best way, but I think most Christians will agree that the Creator is concerned about His Creation and that we should also be concerned about it and try to take care of the things that He has entrusted to us.[13]

Girard Radermacher expresses his stewardship ethic this way:

> Our working with the soil and everything we have comes from God. We are to preserve it and save it, rather than try to get all we can out of it. In the first place, I don't really own the land, I'm just using it. It still belongs to our Creator. And I feel that when I leave this farm, I should have it in better shape than when I started. Otherwise, I didn't do anything. And our work is really working with the Lord, because it is all His gifts that He has given us.

His wife, Mary, adds,

We are just the stewards here, just the workers, the caretakers for the time being. And I don't feel that we can use it to make a lot of money, because then money has become our God instead of the Creator that created this land that we are living off of. Just so we can make a living and get by and be comfortable about it is what I'm after.[14]

Overhauling agricultural practices can be accomplished incrementally on each family farm, field by field, method by method. And an agrarian revolution can also occur incrementally, farm by farm. One whole and stable farm may be nothing but a drop in the agricultural bucket, but the water in the bucket is composed of all the drops; as each drop changes quality, so eventually does the whole bucket of water.

Affecting change in federal agricultural policy, however, cannot be accomplished in quite the same way. The vote of one enlightened member of Congress means nothing if he or she is not in the majority. Hence, the Land Stewardship Project's Public Policy Program had to take a different tack from its Stewardship Farming Program. Rather than working to persuade member of congress by member of Congress to resist the overwhelming economic and political influence of Big Business and Big Government on behalf of industrial agriculture, the Land Stewardship Project has joined with other groups in a broad-based coalition to lobby against those aspects of federal agricultural policy which actively discourage genuine land husbandry. The Sustainable Agriculture Working Group, a twenty-five-member consortium, jointly develops policy proposals and presses for their enactment in Washington.[15]

The Land Stewardship Project is concerned not only with public policy but with corporate policy as well. As crippling debt conspired with falling prices and falling land values, many Midwestern farmers went bankrupt, and their farms were repossessed by large financial institutions. This was the fate of the well-run Hauk farm in Wabasha County, Minnesota. It passed into the hands of the John Hancock Insurance Company, which allowed a renter to bulldoze terraces, thereby destroying in a few days' time twenty-five years' worth of soil-conservation efforts. The Land Stewardship Project made an example of the Hancock handling of the Hauk farm. Angry letters-to-the-editor were written, people cashed in their John Hancock life-insurance policies, protest rallies and demonstrations were held, testimony was taken, lawsuits were filed, all of which brought national attention to the abuses of farmland by absentee institutional owners. Eventually, insurance companies were compelled by law to require their lessees to continue in-place conservation practices on the farms they repossessed. Unfortunately, the Land Stewardship Project is powerless to stop farm foreclosures or to make sure that financial institutions resell family farms to farm families.[16]

The Land Stewardship Project also works to prevent farmland from being "developed"—converted into suburbs, shopping malls, and parking lots—when urban areas, such as Minneapolis/St. Paul, sprawl. The project's Metro Farm Program followed the bottom-up organizational pattern that had worked so well in rural areas. Meetings of farmers whose land was threatened by unruly suburban growth were held in church basements. Helen DiMichiel, a project staff member, composed a new discussion-starting drama, "Turn Here Sweet Corn." Action committees formed. Initiatives were placed on ballots. Eventually, ordinances protecting farmland from development pressures were successfully enacted.[17]

Consistent with the grass-roots philosophy of initiating positive change, the Land Stewardship Project asked its active constituents to help set long-range goals as the organization embarked on its second decade. Dispersal and diversity were the watchwords. Constituents envisioned "dispersal of animals from feedlots to individual farms and dispersal of people from concentrated urban areas to rural areas," hoping eventually to see "a greater variety of cultivated crops and more [wild] species of plants and animals" as well as "more complex rural communities in terms of race, ethnic heritage, gender, age, and work." Perhaps the most revealing directive the constituents communicated to the organization's board and staff, from the point of view of this study, was "to do more with churches to help build a stewardship ethic in society as a whole." Constituents hoped that the American rural landscape of the future would consist of

> smaller more diverse farms, a growing number of people on the land, and livestock spread out across the countryside; perhaps three to four farms per section anchoring revitalized rural communities set in environments of clean water, clean air, and healthy soil; and smaller cities, with plenty of farmland nearby producing food for local consumption.[18]

The emphasis on diversity generally—and particularly the emphasis on "dispersal of animals" from feedlot concentrations back to the farmscape—reveals the degree to which the ecological worldview has penetrated the philosophy of stewardship farming. The agro-ecologist Wes Jackson argues that agriculture should mimic a natural ecosystem as nearly as possible.[19] All future farms should become, indeed, agro-ecosystems. Biological diversity, of course, is a hallmark of healthy ecosystems. And all ecosystems are characterized by food chains and the recycling of nutrients. Animals are thus essential parts of an agro-ecosystem, converting alfalfa and other grasses that people can't eat into high-quality human foods. And just as important, they are an essential part of a closed nutrient cycle, since their manures supply an organic fertilizer.

THE HINDU ENVIRONMENTAL ETHIC IN ACTION

The Chipko movement in northern India draws on the political-action principles of Mohandas Gandhi and the foundational ideas of Hindu philosophy in organizing Indian villagers to resist environmentally destructive industrial forestry and other top-down "development" schemes that enrich an urban élite at the expense of local people and their age-old patterns of sustainable subsistence. Born in the early 1970s, Chipko is venerable in comparison with other grass-roots environmental movements around the world.[20] But over the past twenty years the Chipko movement has met with unparalleled success, winning virtually all its major confrontations with government bureaucrats and commercial profiteers, who regularly conspire to mine the forest and dispossess the common people.[21] Perhaps Chipko's most spectacular political success was convincing Prime Minister Indira Gandhi to proclaim, in 1981, a fifteen-year moratorium on logging in the Himalayan forests of the State of Uttar Pradesh.[22] To gauge the measure of that achievement, North Americans might ask themselves what chance the Association of Forest Service Employees for Environmental Ethics in the United States might have of convincing President Bill Clinton to seek a ban on logging for fifteen years in the old-growth forests of the Pacific Northwest.

The contemporary saga of Chipko is well documented and makes fascinating reading. It has all the elements of a heroic folk legend: hill people, rebuked and scorned, organizing to fight neglect, injustice, and dispossession; deception and surprise tactics on the part of officials, matched by discovery and swift nocturnal maneuvering; death-defying women at the front lines of conflict; confrontation with armed policemen; imported lowland laborers changing sides and joining the mountain villagers in an expression of cross-regional peasant solidarity; a charismatic leader in the ancient tradition of Indian asceticism and martyrdom vowing to fast to the death; bards composing rally songs and immortalizing the movement in stirring poetry; and, finally, internal struggles for power and control of the movement's direction, goals, and future. Here space permits only a sampling of the details of this remarkable story.

In Hindi, *chipko* means "to hug" or "to embrace." By all accounts, the first contemporary Chipko action—taken in the literal sense of hugging trees so as to stand in the way of the axe—occurred near the town of Gopeshwar, in the Mandal forest, in 1973. Gopeshwar is located in the northern part of Uttar Pradesh, an area known historically as Uttarakhand, "the most sacred region of the holy Himalaya, the source and watershed of the Ganges River."[23] The federal Forest Department had denied a village co-op—the Dasholi Society for Village Self-rule—permission to cut a few ash trees in order to make farm implements to sell on the regional market. To its shock and chagrin, the co-op learned that a sporting-goods corporation located in distant Allahabad had been allotted ash trees in order to manufacture tennis racquets for the export market.[24] This blatant injustice moved the villagers to action. Chandi Prasad Bhatt, a follower of Gandhi and a local organizer and activist, came up with the idea. "Let them know they will not fell a single tree without felling one of us first," he declared. "When their men raise their axes, we will embrace [*chipko*] the trees to protect them!"[25]

During the early years of British colonial rule, India's forests were raided willy-nilly for timber to make railroad ties, ships' masts, and the like. So rapidly did the trees disappear that the British overlords imposed forest-enclosure laws, restricting their exploitation. Priority was given to foreign concessionaires to harvest trees, and competing indigenous village users were denied access. After independence, the same policies were continued in the name of economic development and progress.[26]

Traditional villagers feed green leaves and grass to farm animals, whose dung supplies fertilizer for food crops. They cook with dry twigs and branches collected from the forest floor. They lightly and selectively extract timber to make farm implements and build frames for stone houses. And they gather large amounts of fruit, nuts, fibers, and medicinal herbs for personal consumption and local markets. Himalayan peoples have inhabited and used forests in this communal fashion for many generations without destroying them.[27] By contrast, clear-cutting forests for timber and pulp on a commercial scale has well-known adverse social and ecological consequences: Because its resource base is expunged, the tried and true traditional way of life is threatened. And because the hillsides are denuded, upland soils erode, streams overflow and then dry up, lowlands are flooded, and rivers and reservoirs fill with silt.

The 1970 flood in the Alakananda Valley crystallized the nascent ecological consciousness of the village people. Water rushing off the skinned mountains inundated 100 square kilometers of farmland, washed away roads and bridges, carried off buses and trucks, destroyed houses and outbuildings, and killed hundreds of people and domestic animals.[28] The Alakananda flood made the environmental costs of the national forest policy starkly evident to the people it affected—though not to distant government officials. Thus, even before the Gopeshwar *satyagraha* (militant noncooperation), the people of the Indian Himalaya had begun to resist as well as resent the appropriation of their forests.[29]

Bhatt's inspiration to *chipko* the trees, according to the environmentalists Jayanata Bandyopadhyay and Vandana Shiva, had been anticipated a year earlier in verse by the folk poet Ghanshyam Raturi, who wrote, "Embrace the trees and / Save them from being felled; / The property of our hills, / Save them from being looted."[30] Whether consciously or not, first Raturi (in words), then Bhatt (in deed as well as word) gave contemporary expression to a method of resistance which was "old in Indian culture."[31] The most famous historic precedent occurred in the eighteenth century, when members of the Bishnoi sect embraced their sacred Kherji trees to prevent the Maharaja of Jodhpur's axemen from chopping them down. On that heroic occasion, 363 people were axe-murdered in an attempt to save a montane forest.[32] (One may infer that some moral progress has occurred since the Bishnoi slaughter, for so far no contemporary Chipko activist has been hacked to death by zealous loggers.) Right down to the present, "the Bishnoi community continues to protect trees and animals with the same fervor," according to the political scientist O. P. Dwivedi, who believes that "their community is the best example of a true Hindu-based ritual defense of the environment in India."[33]

The power and reach of Chipko soon spread. The sporting-goods company was asked to take its allotment of ash trees from another forest, near the village of Phata. When word reached Bhatt in Gopeshwar, he informed his Phata counterpart, who organized a huge protest demonstration there, once again thwarting the commercial-governmental axis.[34]

Auctioned to a timber company, the Reni forest, near the village of Josimath, was scheduled to be clear-cut in March 1974. After the Chipko movement announced its opposition, the Forest Department resorted to duplicity. The village men were called away on a pretext, and Bhatt was decoyed to another site. Skirting the village during the night, forest workers made for the condemned woods. A little girl noticed their movements and ran to tell Gaura Devi, the head of the village women's club, who mobilized her cohorts and confronted the laborers the next morning. She told them, "Brothers, this forest is our home. From it we satisfy so many of our needs. Do not axe it. If you do, landslides will ruin our homes and fields."[35] One of the men brandished a pistol, but "Gaura Devi stood in front of him, bared her breast, and told him he would have to shoot her before she would allow the forest to be cut."[36] From that point on, the Chipko movement was a force to be reckoned with. Time and again, stumpage sales to timber companies were massively and successfully resisted.

The Chipko movement draws not only on traditional heroic precedents, such as the martyrdom of the people of Bishnoi, but on traditional Hindu religious beliefs as well. In 1977, the Adwani forest was scheduled to be felled. Women from nearby villages tied sacred threads to the marked trees, signifying the sanctity of all forms of life. For seven days, women from fifteen villages maintained watch. On that occasion, according to the sociologist Ramachandra Guha, "a reading of the *Bhagavad Gita* was organized"; and according to Bandyopadhyay and Shiva, "discourses on the role of forests in Indian life from ancient texts went on nonstop."[37]

Unfortunately, Guha does not detail the intellectual substance of these "readings"; nor do Bandyopadhyay and Shiva disclose the nature of the "discourses" to which they refer. But the Sanskrit scholar Sankar Sen Gupta points out that "the whole of one hymn (X. 97) of the *Rig Veda* is devoted to the singing of the praises of the properties of plants." He notes further that "the entire ancient Indian literature right from the *Vedas*, the *Puranas*, the *Ramayana*, the *Mahabharata* and the *Gita* to the works of Kalidasa and Tagore teem with praise for trees." And finally he adds a theological observation of his own: "The God [Brahman] who exists in this universe, in water, in fire, also exists in large trees."[38] O. P. Dwivedi confirms Gupta's analysis of the *Rig Veda* and adds,

> During the period of the great epics and Puranas, the Hindu respect for flora expanded further. Trees were considered as being animate and feeling happiness and sorrow. It is still popularly believed that every tree has a *vriksa-devata*, or "tree deity," that is worshipped with prayers and offerings of water, flowers, sweets, and encircled by sacred threads.[39]

Deterred for the time being, the contractors returned to the Adwani forest, this time with two truckloads of armed police, who intended to cordon off the timber sale and prevent the Chipko-organized locals from entering the woods to interfere with the operation. But they were foiled again. The villagers had already explained their position to the loggers, and when the contractors and their police escort arrived each tree was being hugged by three volunteers. It was here in the Adwani forest, according to Bandyopadhyay and Shiva, who chronicle the event, "that the ecological slogan 'What do the forests bear? Soil, water, and pure air' was born."[40]

Two years later, Bhatt's mentor, Sunderlal Bahuguna, was called in when a large felling was planned in the Badyargahr region. In the tradition of Indian religious asceticism, he went on a hunger strike, which rallied the local populace. "The act of protest," according to Guha, "was seen as having moral-religious sanction."[41] Over three thousand men, women, and children—one for every condemned chir pine in the forest—stood vigil, day and night. After a week and a half, Bahuguna, still refusing to eat, was jailed by the police. His arrest only stiffened the resolve of the people. Again, a reading of the *Bhagavad Gita* was begun. Fearing the moral power of ancient scriptural ideas, an official tried to stop the reading, only to be "firmly told that all the *Vedas* were written in the forest."[42] Finally, three weeks after it began, the protest ended when the contractors capitulated.

Gandhi's ideas inform the Chipko movement through the following line of descent: Mira Behn (Madeleine Slade) and Sarala Behn (Catherine Heilman) were both "close associates of Gandhi's."[43] The former was among the first to analyze the adverse ecological effects of deforestation in the Himalaya, and the latter established an ashram in the area "for the education of hill women."[44] Sunderlal Bahuguna, in turn, joined Gandhi's independence struggle when he was only thirteen years old, and afterward was a junior associate of Mira and Sarala Behn in the Himalaya.[45] Finally, Bahuguna recruited Chandi Prasad Bhatt to work in the ongoing post-Independence struggle for grass-roots "development based upon justice and ecological stability."[46]

The *Bhagavad Gita* exerted a powerful influence on Gandhi. How he connected his manifestly social and political work with traditional Hindu thought is indicated in the introduction to his translation of this Indian religious classic. According to Gandhi, "Man is not at peace with himself till he has become like unto God. The endeavor to reach this state is the supreme, the only ambition worth having. And this is self-realization." By self-realization, Gandhi refers to the union of *atman* with *brahman*, one of the most fundamental tenets of Advaita Vedanta (as outlined in chapter 3). He continues:

> This self-realization is the subject of the *Gita*, as it is of all scriptures. But its author surely did not write it to establish that doctrine. The object of the *Gita* appears to me to be that of showing the most excellent way to attain self-realization. . . . That matchless remedy is renunciation of fruits of action.[47]

By taking one's work for one's own and dedicating the fruits of that work to the world, one may best achieve *moksha* (liberation), in Gandhi's view.

In chapter 3, the substantive being at the core of all natural phenomena, in Hindu thought, was identified as *brahman*. Interpreting the worldview animating the Chipko movement, Vandana Shiva articulates the substantive monism at the very foundation of Hindu thought in alternative terms. Shiva identifies the being or reality at the core of all phenomena as *prakriti*. "Nature as *prakriti*," she writes, "is inherently active, a powerful, productive force in the dialectic of the creation, renewal, and substance of *all* life."[48] But as the concept of nature in European thought may have two complementary senses—on the one hand, *natura naturata*, nature in its infinite plurality, diversity, and change, and, on the other, *natura naturans*, the nature, the essence of natural phenomena—so the concept of *prakriti*, in Indian thought may have a similar duality of meaning. Shiva evidently understands *prakriti* in the sense of *natura naturans*. A similar interpretation is also offered by O. P. Dwivedi. According to Dwivedi, "both God and *prakriti* (nature) was to be one and the same."[49] But whether the principle of identity among all things is understood as the more dynamic *prakriti* or the more quiescent *brahman* makes little difference in practice. Farmers participating in the Land Stewardship Project's Stewardship Farming Program in the Midwestern United States do not all cite the same biblical texts as ultimate grounds for their farming practices. Nor are they schooled in the philosophical fine points of the Judeo-Christian stewardship environmental ethic. Similarly, Chipko activists are united by the basic Hindu worldview no matter how idiosyncratically articulated. After all is said and done, they feel an identity between themselves and the trees they embrace.

The Chipko movement positions itself in clear and uncompromising opposition to conventional neocolonial development schemes, in which local resources are ravaged to supply foreign markets with lumber, minerals, luxury foods, and the like, to make money for an urban entrepreneurial élite, and to generate low-interest World Bank loans and foreign exchange for the pleasure and profit of the federal government and its functionaries. The Chipko movement, however, is divided over the question of what positive alternative to such "maldevelopment" it should offer to its constituents.[50]

Chandi Prasad Bhatt, who, before the birth of Chipko, was a leader of the Dasholi Society for Village Self-rule, envisions a proliferation of locally owned and operated small-scale labor-intensive enterprises similar to his own Gopeshwar co-op. The Dasholi Society for Village Self-rule had managed, against all odds, to operate a small resin and turpentine distillery, to collect and market medicinal herbs, and to manufacture agricultural implements (the latter enterprise being the one that led to the original tree-hugging confrontation with the forces of conventional development and to the birth of the movement).[51] Bhatt's plan involves twenty-seven villages working together on "a program of conservation and development ranging from forestry to beekeeping, from establishment of child-care centers to promotion of solar cookers and small-scale industries, including local sawmills."[52]

The central goal of Bhatt's program is just and sustainable development. During the British raj and the subsequent reign of federal and state bureaucrats and technocrats, economic development had enriched foreigners and an Indian élite, at the expense of local people and their natural resources and natural environment. Bhatt works to return natural resources to their traditional custodians and to initiate economic exploitation of those resources in ways that will generate steady employment and a modest income for local people now and in perpetuity. Since he envisions sustainable as well as just development, his program necessarily involves conservation, which—in the context of the Chipko movement—consists primarily of popular environmental education and planting economically useful trees.[53]

At first hearing, one could hardly fault such a program. But the Chipko faction led by Sunderlal Bahuguna does fault it, especially the sawmills. Compare the first articulation of the goal of what soon became the Chipko movement by the poet Raturi, "The property of our hills, / Save them from being looted," with the slogan that emerged from the Adwani action, "What do the forests bear? Soil, water, and pure air." In 1972, the trees were perceived primarily as "property"—natural resources. The central issue was Whose property—the sporting-goods company's or the villagers'? By 1977, forests had become something more than a *resource*. People realized that they were a *source*—the source and very foundation of life: of soil, water, and pure air. Thus Bahuguna opposes all tree cutting and industrial development of forest "resources," no matter how localized, just, and sustainable. In his view, "Soil, water, and pure air, uniquely offered by forests, are surely more valuable than resin, timber, and foreign exchange. Whether the latter even benefits local people is another matter."[54] Drawing on the distinction set out by Arne Naess in 1973, Bandyopadhyay and Shiva suggest that "the differences between the two activists [Bahuguna and Bhatt] is not unexpected and is universally faced as the difference between deep ecology and [shallow] environmentalism."[55]

A fair question for Bahuguna is How will the village people make a living? If not by way of Bhatt's program of just and sustainable development, then by what means will hill families survive and thrive? The suspicion Bahuguna expresses about the value of "foreign exchange"—hard currency, in other words—hints at an answer. According to Bandyopadhyay and Shiva, Bhatt "explains poverty as the absence of processing industries and recommends solutions in technology transfer."[56] But poverty may be measured in terms of diminishing quality of life as well as in terms of diminishing income, in terms of poor health as well as in terms of a poor purse, in terms of the loss of familial and social integrity as well as in terms of joblessness, and in terms of environmental degradation as well as in terms of low purchasing power. As an alternative to Bhatt's tacit acceptance of the "dominant development paradigm"—as characterized by Bandyopadhyay and Shiva—"albeit with environmental adjustments," Bahuguna's program would have the people of Uttarakhand return to the livelihood that served them well enough until 1962, when roads opened their mountain Shangri-la to outside exploitation.[57] Traditionally, the isolated and self-sufficient people of the Indian Himalaya grew their own staple foods; and from the standing forest they obtained fodder for their animals, materials for tools and houses, fuel wood, fruits, nuts, fiber, and herbal medicines.

Not only does the Chipko movement's future hang in the balance—between Bhatt's reform environmentalism and Bahuguna's deep ecology—but ownership of its past is disputed as well. Though Bhatt and Bahuguna have been at its forefront from the start, some chroniclers—Vandana Shiva, most prominently—have insisted that Chipko is primarily a women's movement, indeed, a feminist movement. Of himself and Bhatt Bahuguna often says, "We are the runners and messengers—the real leaders are the women," according to Shiva.[58] As to leadership, Gaura Devi, the heroine of the Reni campaign, has as strong a claim as anyone. And numbers of women have swelled the ranks of Chipko foot soldiers. Ramachandra Guha, however, disputes such assertions, insisting that "despite the important role played by women, it would be simplistic to characterize Chipko as a feminist movement. In several instances, especially the early mobilizations at Mandal and Phata, it was men who took the initiative in protecting forests."[59] And Gerald Berreman observes, more circumspectly, that "men are involved as well as women, in similar ways and to a similar extent" in the Chipko movement.[60]

More light is shed on this debate if attention is shifted away from the extent of participation by either gender to the question of whose interests, men's or women's, are best advanced by the Chipko movement. Formulating the issue this way reveals, moreover, an interesting and illuminating parallel between male interests versus female interests and the different economic paradigms—associated with Bhatt and Bahuguna, respectively—that divide the movement.

In India, as in many traditional cultures, work is segregated along gender lines. In Uttarakhand, women's work includes hauling water, gathering firewood, and fetching fodder for livestock. As the monetary economy has mixed with the traditional subsistence economy, men have taken on the role of money-makers, thus shifting even more of the burden of the traditional subsistence economy onto the shoulders of women. As wood gatherers, water haulers, and fodder fetchers, women thus have a more immediate interest in the well-being of the forests. More generally, as conservators of the traditional subsistence economy, women have a greater stake in the conservation of the environmental status quo ante, to which the traditional economy is exquisitely adapted. Still more generally and abstractly, the sphere of production is typically male, as the ecofeminist intellectual historian Carolyn Merchant points out, while the sphere of reproduction—not only biological reproduction but social and cultural reproduction as well—is typically female. [61]

Ironically, Guha provides the evidence that undermines his astigmatic objections to the feminist appropriation of the Chipko movement. The men of the village of Dungri-Paintoli, he writes,

> wanted to sell their oak forest to the Horticulture Department,
> which intended to establish a potato farm on the land. If the forest,
> the only good one for miles around, had been cut, the women
> would have had to walk a long distance every day to collect fuel and
> fodder. When the women voiced their opposition, it went un-
> heeded. . . . Lured by promises of better communications and
> other "modern" facilities, the men hoped to make some quick
> money. [62]

In the opinion of the Dungri-Paintoli women, Guha goes on, "agriculture and animal rearing was entirely dependent on them." Chipko activists intervened on behalf of these women and saved the forest for their convenience. Clearly, in this case of open conflict between the interests of village men and village women, the Chipko movement served the latter. Generalizing, Guha notes that

> hill women are in fact aware that they are the repository of local
> tradition. In the orbit of the household, women often take decisions
> that are rarely challenged by men. In the act of embracing the
> trees, therefore, they are acting not merely as women but as bear-
> ers of continuity with the past in a community threatened with
> fragmentation. [63]

When men join women in embracing the trees, they too are acting as bearers of continuity with the past. Thus, quite apart from who leads and who follows and which gender is more numerously represented at demonstrations and confrontations, Chipko may be rightly understood as a feminist movement. The movement promotes the interest of village women in maintaining the traditional subsistence economy and sometimes thwarts the interest of men in making a fast rupee. Moreover, the interests of hill women coincide with the health and integrity of both the social and natural orders.

O. P. Dwivedi nicely sums up the feminist claim on the Chipko movement:

> Women have not only seen how their men would not mind destroying nature in order to get money while they had to walk miles in search of firewood, fodder, and other grazing materials, but, being more religious, they are also more sensitive to injunctions such as *ahimsa*. In a sense, the Chipko movement is a kind of feminist movement to protect nature from the greed of men. In the Himalayan areas, the pivot of the family is the woman. It is the woman who worries most about nature and its conservation in order that its resources are available for her family's sustenance [while] men go away to distant places in search of jobs, leaving women and old people behind.[64]

Therefore, not surprisingly, the feminist historians of the Chipko movement more warmly endorse Bahuguna's deep ecological—and deeply conservative—vision of its future rather than Bhatt's more male-oriented progressive vision of money-making turpentine factories and sawmills scattered throughout Uttarakhand. Shiva persuasively argues that maldevelopment and the modern scientific worldview are intimately associated. And she clearly articulates the convergence of traditional worldviews, especially those of India, with the emerging postmodern scientific worldview: "Today, with new ecological awareness, ecologists the world over turn to the beliefs of . . . indigenous peoples as a special source of learning how to live in harmony with nature."[65]

THE BUDDHIST ENVIRONMENTAL ETHIC IN ACTION

The Sri Lanka Sarvodaya Movement

Though himself deeply steeped in Hindu thought, Mohandas Gandhi was primarily a social activist and statesman, not a philosopher or theologian. As such, he was ecumenical, freely enlisting the spiritual and moral energies of all religious worldviews in the cause of social justice and local autonomy. Thus it should not surprise us that the figure of Gandhi also stands at the fountainhead of a Buddhist self-help movement in Sri Lanka.

In 1958, Ahangamage Tudor Ariyaratne, a science teacher in Colombo, took his privileged students to an impoverished village to *shramadana* ("give work")—building roads, cleaning wells, digging latrines. So beneficial was the fruit of the work to the villagers and the experience of giving work to the students that the idea caught on. In the years following, Ariyaratne involved more of his students, other upper-class schools began *shramadana* programs, and villages that had been helped began helping others in turn. Deciding to make the eradication of misery in Sri Lanka his life's vocation, Ariyaratne went to India to study the methods of Gandhi's close associate Vinoba Bhave. He returned with a clear vision of a nationwide movement. Adopting the familiar name of the Gandhian program of local self-help, the Sri Lanka Sarvodaya movement was born. By 1972, the movement had become so successful that international support enabled Ariyaratne to resign his teaching post and devote all his energies to his true calling.[66]

About 70 percent of Sri Lanka's population is Buddhist, and the country is filled with temples, monasteries, and large statues of the Enlightened One. The sight of saffron-robed monks and nuns is commonplace. Though the idea of *sarvodaya* ("awakening of all") is originally Gandhian—and thus was intended to inspire a universal awakening of social and political consciousness—for Buddhists it has deep spiritual resonance as well. As Ariyaratne expresses it, "The person himself must awaken to his true needs and true strengths if the society is to prosper without conflict and injustice. From the wisdom embodied in our religious traditions we can cull principles for that kind of personal and collective awakening."[67]

Among the principles culled from Buddhism and reinterpreted by Sarvodaya workers to fit current conditions are the fundamental Four Noble Truths (discussed in chapter 4). The First—that we find ourselves in a condition of suffering—requires little elaboration or interpretation in the context of contemporary rural Sri Lanka. By beginning with that quintessential Buddhist observation, villagers can focus on the specific manifestations of suffering in their midst, such as hunger, disease, and conflict. The Second Noble Truth is that craving is the cause of suffering. Craving is interpreted in the Buddhist Sarvodaya movement as the personal greed, self-centeredness, and mutual distrust that has divided (and conquered) communities in Sri Lanka since the colonial epoch and is now exacerbated by neocolonial capitalist ideology. The Third Noble Truth is that to cease to crave is to cease to suffer. By throwing off the insidious oppression of the Western economic doctrine—that greed is good and that competitive entrepreneurship leads to an ever-increasing level of consumption (for those who are successful)—Buddhist Sarvodaya workers argue that a community can recover its former vigor, unity, and decency. Through an essentially spiritual and moral recovery, it can once again become genuinely prosperous, healthy, and whole. Finally, the Fourth Noble Truth—that the way to overcome suffering is to follow the Eightfold Path—translates into a direct and concrete agenda of community action. The Buddhist/Deep Ecologist writer/activist Joanna Macy explains:

> Right Understanding and Right Intention arise as we understand the systemic nature of life, the interdependence between self and other, mind and body; and Right Speech arises when we give expression to this with honesty and compassion. Right Action, Right Livelihood, and Right Effort are no longer abstract notions, but become as immediate and tangible as today's collaboration in cleaning the village well or digging latrines, and Right Mindfulness is given a similarly social thrust . . . [to] "stay open and alert to the needs of the village . . . to enter the minds of the people."[68]

Above all, the golden rule of Buddhist practice—to follow the Middle Path, between the extremes of indulgence and asceticism—is given a contemporary social and political spin by Ariyaratne. He distinguishes between needs and wants, and also between poverty and misery. Poverty is having little money and few worldly goods. Misery is living in a degraded environment, in the midst of squalor and lawlessness, homeless, starving, without sanitation or health care. There is no shame—indeed, there can be much merit—in poverty. A long life without monetary wealth and a plethora of material possessions may be led with dignity and pride. But there is no virtue in human misery. Human needs must be satisfied. In the Buddhist gospel according to Ariyaratne, wants, however, are entirely superfluous. Indeed, advertising-manufactured desires—for tobacco, alcohol, and other intoxicants; cars and motorcycles; televisions and other electronic gadgets; tight blue jeans and other foreign fashions in clothing; and so on—can be very destructive in a Third World setting:

> The "basic need" is our first economic objective, not growth, not increasing per-capita income. This talk about growth and no-growth is nonsense when there is no value attached to the whole thing. You should not ask the question "How much has the economy grown?" You should ask, "How many people are now getting a balanced meal?" You know a lot of wealth goes into unnecessary, wasteful consumption. But in the old societies, when the primary needs are satisfied, they then build works of art and architecture.[69]

In the Buddhist tradition of naming sets of important things and numbering their elements for easy mnemonic retrieval, Ariyaratne has identified "Ten Basic Needs." They are (1) water, (2) food, (3) housing, (4) clothing, (5) health care, (6) communication, (7) fuel, (8) education, (9) a clean, safe, beautiful environment, and (10) a spiritual and cultural life.[70] The Sarvodaya movement is organized to help Sri Lankan village people meet these needs by drawing on local resources—natural and human, social and religious.

Among the first things people do with the encouragement, help, and organizing skills of Sarvodaya workers is build roads, clean public wells, and dig latrines. Personally experiencing the power of cooperative effort in achieving such immediate and concrete common infrastructural goals enables people to envision and undertake more sophisticated and ambitious projects, such as forming local marketing cooperatives and credit unions. Sarvodaya has also assisted villages in building schools and libraries, providing legal aid and conflict-resolution services, and initiating immunization and nutrition programs.[71]

Ariyaratne's philosophy of development is also a typically Buddhist middle path between the extremes identified with the two Chipko theorists, as described by Bandyopadhyay and Shiva and discussed in the preceding section of this chapter. Chandi Prasad Bhatt conceives of development as a transfer of resource control and technology to rural people, who may then earn money from low-tech, labor-intensive industries supplying milled lumber, turpentine, tennis racquets, and other products for markets ranging from local to global in reach. Sunderlal Bahuguna, on the other hand, rejects the concept of "development," which he considers to be a neo-colonial euphemism for the insinuation of foreign values and life-styles into indigenous cultures. In his view, a market economy and its associated values—whether the "benefits" are distributed justly or not—leads inexorably to the destruction both of nature and of traditional societies. As an alternative, Bahuguna recommends a return to the traditional subsistence economy that served rural people for generations without destroying the integrity, stability, and beauty of their natural environments. Like Bahuguna, Ariyaratne is deeply suspicious of the international economy. But, like Bhatt, he favors village-level development, provided that it is not only sustainable (in the sense of prudently managing renewable resources) but marked by "appropriate technologies" and geared to meeting local, regional, and national needs, not foreign demands. According to Ariyaratne,

> Maybe a handful of people in Sri Lanka, a really insignificant minority, have benefited from the economic development in trade with the West that has taken place in the past few years, while the poor people are becoming poorer and the numbers of the poor are increasing. . . . International trade should be restricted, because the injustice this international economic order produces cannot satisfy basic needs of clothing and shelter but satisfies the greed of

rich people in rich countries. And we in the poor countries get cash in return, and this cash is once again spent to buy media-created wants, desires created entirely by advertising media. It's a vicious cycle. What I would advocate is to totally de-link from this international economic system.[72]

The method suggested by Ariyaratne for de-linking Sri Lanka from the international economic order is direct, simple, and effective—reneging on all foreign debt.[73] That is an ingenious as well as a radical solution, for then the international economic order will of itself bring about his goal of economic independence for Sri Lanka, by punitively ostracizing the country. But his economic vision for Sri Lanka does not involve an atavistic return to premodern modes of subsistence. Rather, Ariyaratne envisions a postmodern economic order involving new but appropriate technologies supplying local, regional, and national markets. Among the technological innovations fostered by the Sri Lanka Sarvodaya movement are windmills, electricity generators that run on biogas extracted from human feces, gravity-fed water systems, a mortar for mud-walled houses made from banana-tree juice, and a roofing material made from palm fibers.[74]

The Sri Lankan Sarvodaya movement is less directly focused on environmental conservation than on bottom-up sustainable development. But a clean, safe, and beautiful environment is one of the aforementioned Ten Basic Needs identified by Ariyaratne. And built into the concept of appropriate technology is environmental compatibility. To qualify as appropriate, a proposed technology must, at the very least, not pollute or otherwise degrade the natural environment. Windmills for drawing water or generating electricity are an example of an environmentally benign technology. Better still would be a technology that removed an environmental bad while producing a human good, such as a device that converts human wastes into a fuel gas.

Furthermore, *pratityasamutpada*, or "dependent co-arising" ("the most central and distinctive doctrine" of Buddhism, as Macy characterizes it), is given an ecological interpretation in the movement. From the perspective of the postmodern scientific worldview, successful social and economic development must be sensitively situated in a natural matrix. According to Macy, the traditional Buddhist idea of *pratityasamutpada* facilitates a genuinely ecological way of thinking about development: "Because reality is seen as dependently co-arising, or systemic in nature, each and every act is understood to have an effect on the larger web of life, and the process of development is perceived as being multidimensional."[75]

Undercutting the efforts and success of the Sarvodaya movement in Sri Lanka is the armed conflict between the Tamils, Hindus who migrated from

India and live mostly in the northern part of the island, and the indigenous Sinhalese. The hostility between these two populations is usually chalked up to seething ethnic hatreds going back centuries and compounded by religious intolerance; the conflict appears analogous to the situation in the former Yugoslavia. Ariyaratne, however, has a different analysis. In his view, the fighting is not the result of two sets of traditional cultural belief systems coming into conflict, but just the opposite. The repression and violence pervading Sri Lanka result from "a gradual breakdown of spiritual, moral, and cultural values" on both sides.[76]

> During the last decade, a frantic attempt was made by the government and the local and multinational economic sectors toward material affluence. . . . Earning money and spending money was promoted as the most fundamental value of life. . . . Naturally, violence became a part of the structure first, and later it came to the community where not only personal disputes but also political disputes came to be settled by armed power. The so-called ethnic conflict was only a symptom.[77]

Ariyaratne believes that when the violence runs its course, the people, both Tamil and Sinhalese, "will turn to the nonviolent alternatives offered by Sarvodaya."[78]

Buddhist Forest Conservation in Thailand

As in Sri Lanka, Buddhism has enjoyed a long and secure tenure in Thailand. Ninety-five percent of the population is Buddhist. And in Thailand, as in Sri Lanka, Buddhist institutions, monuments, and symbols abound. Buddhism is the state religion. Nearly thirty-seven thousand temples accommodate more than three hundred thousand Buddhist monks and nuns.

For ten thousand or more years, Thailand was covered by several varieties of moist and seasonal tropical forest.[79] The international market for lumber and other wood products has, however, reduced Thai forests by 75 percent in only fifty years.[80] With deforestation have come, of course, the familiar and tragic social and environmental consequences. The backcountry folk have been dispossessed of their lands and their life-ways and the insidious cycle of floods, erosion, and drought has ensued. Gradually, through painful experience, ecological awareness has grown—first among the people most immediately affected by deforestation, and finally among those in positions of political power and economic privilege. The disastrous floods of November 1988 represented the final moment of truth. Thousands of logs washed down hillsides, demolishing villages and paddies. Within months, the government responded by declaring a moratorium on logging throughout the country.[81]

Rural Thai activists have culled different Buddhist principles from those culled by the Sri Lankan movement, to address a different set of circumstances. Traditionally, Sri Lanka was an agrarian country, so much so that it was once referred to as "the Granary of the East."[82] Thailand, on the other hand, was traditionally a country of small valley villages nestled among forested highlands. To save the trees, and thus the integrity of the natural environment, ecologically enlightened Thai monks have adapted the arboreal imagery and symbolism in classical Buddhism. The comparative philosopher Carla Deicke elaborates: "the Buddha was born at the base of a tree, died at the base of a tree, achieved enlightenment at the base of a tree, and gave most of his teachings while seated beneath trees."[83] Among the additional austerities vowed by the solitary "forest monks" of Thailand is to dwell at the base of a tree.[84] Thus their lives are thought to more closely resemble that of the Buddha.

Thailand's forest monks have become leaders in a grass-roots movement to save Thailand's remaining forests and to begin to restore those that have been cut down and sold off. The doctrine of *karma* naturally leads the Buddhist believer to the practice of accumulating merit, for the sake of future lives and eventually for the sake of attaining *nirvana*. Traditionally, accumulating merit meant giving alms to the temple and discharging other distinctly religious duties in addition to faithful adherence to the *dharma*, or body of Buddhist ethical teachings. Thailand's forest monks have reoriented these religious duties and moral responsibilities to include environmental protection and restoration.[85] By tradition, for example, Thai villagers offer robes, money, and food to their temple several times a year. One abbot now asks that people offer to plant tree saplings instead. On the first occasion of this request, three thousand rural Thai Buddhists planted a hundred thousand trees. "In this way," Deicke comments, "villagers are beginning to believe that environmental guardianship can be an integral part of their religious customs, as well as a facet of their Buddhist philosophy."[86]

One particularly ingenious technique of reorienting religious feelings from traditional human beneficiaries to novel natural ones was invented by Phra Khrumanat, a forest monk working in Phayao province. He began the practice of ordaining trees. The idea occurred to him, Deicke recounts,

> when a man who attempted to fell a large old tree on temple grounds died suddenly and unaccountably. Village elders explained the incident as a case of sacrilege: because the tree was very old and had been showered with religious blessings from temple ceremonies for many years, it had become a holy being. In addition, inhabitants of the northern provinces (of which Phayao is one) have

traditionally believed that the largest and oldest trees in any grove are inhabited by spirits and must be treated with respect and fear.[87]

The arboreal ordination ceremony involves wrapping trees with saffron-colored monk's robes and performing the customary religious rites. Thus trees become holy entities. To cut ordained trees down would not just be like murdering monks; that's what it would actually be. When Khrumanat's tree-ordination ceremonies received media attention, people thought he was crazy. But it worked. While, as just noted, logging is now illegal in many parts of Thailand, the ban is poorly enforced. Encountering trees swathed in one of the most sacred, powerful, and ubiquitous emblems of Buddhism, tree poachers have been deterred, despite the absence (complicitous or not) of forest wardens. Tree ordination is now practiced all over the country and has filled a void left by inadequate law enforcement.[88]

CONCLUSION

As this chapter suggests, purely secular programs—bureaucratic, technological, legal, or educational—aimed at achieving environmental conservation may remain ineffective unless the environmental ethics latent in traditional worldviews animate and reinforce them. Forest preservation and restoration in Thailand and India exemplifies the important role that environmental ethics creatively (re)constructed from regional intellectual traditions can play in the contemporary global environmental network.

And so this book ends with an allusion—the word "*network*"—to an image drawn from Buddhist thought: the Jewel Net of Indra, discussed in chapter 5. The world's indigenous and traditional systems of thought must create a network of environmental ethics—each a jewel, with its own unique color and composition, reflecting the light of all the others. Connecting all the eyes of this biospherical network of recovered traditional and indigenous environmental ethics—binding them into a coherent whole—is a common thread, the emerging postmodern worldview and its associated evolutionary-ecological environmental ethic. This common thread taps into a different facet of each: into the Buddha-nature of plants and trees here, dependent co-arising there, and *ahimsa* yonder; into Australian aboriginal increase ceremonies; into the North American Indian Great Spirit and Mother Earth, with all their children, the two-leggeds, the four-leggeds, the wings of the air, the myriad faces of green things; into the *Bhagavad Gita*, the *Tao te ching*, the Torah, the *Kumulipo*. As citizens of one planet and as denizens of its many cultural worlds, we hold the fate of the earth in our hands. And of all the means available to save it, none are so powerful or so resourceful as our collective stock of traditional ideas and ideals.

Notes

1.   INTRODUCTION: THE NOTION OF AND NEED FOR
ENVIRONMENTAL ETHICS

1. An elegant and influential example is Geraldo Reichel-Dolmatoff, "Cosmology as Ecological Analysis: A View from the Rain Forest," *Man* 12 (new series, 1976) 2: 307–318. For an overview of the literature and a discussion, see N. L. Jamieson and G. W. Lovelace, "Cultural Values and Human Ecology: Some Initial Considerations" in K. L. Hutterer, A. T. Rambo, and G. W. Lovelace, *Cultural Values and Human Ecology in Southeast Asia*, Michigan Papers on South and Southeast Asia (Ann Arbor: University of Michigan, 1985), and J. Baird Callicott, "American Indian Land Wisdom: Sorting Out the Issues," *Journal of Forest History* 33 (1989): 35–42.

2. Aldo Leopold, *A Sand County Almanac* (New York: Oxford University Press, 1949), p. 202.

3. Ibid., p. 207.

4. See Clifford Geertz, "Ethos, World View, and the Analysis of Sacred Symbols" in Clifford Geertz, ed., *The Interpretations of Cultures* (New York: Basic Books, 1973), pp. 126–141, for a discussion of the relationship in living cultures between ought and is, value and fact, ethos and worldview. See also J. Baird Callicott, "Hume's Is/Ought Dichotomy and the Relation of Ecology to Leopold's Land Ethic," *Environmental Ethics* 4 (1982): 311–328, and "Just the Facts, Ma'am," *The Environmental Professional* 9 (1987): 279–288, for a theoretical discussion of the relationship.

5. See, for example, Richard B. Norgaard, "Economics as Mechanics and the Demise of Biological Diversity," *Ecological Modelling* 38 (1987): 107–121; Marty Strange, *Family Farming: A New Economic Vision* (Lincoln: University of Nebraska Press, 1988); Robert C. Paelke, *Environmentalism and the Future of American Politics* (New Haven: Yale University

Press, 1989); Christopher D. Stone, *The Gnat Is Older than the Man: Global Environment and Human Agenda* (Princeton: Princeton University Press, 1993).

6. Karen J. Warren, "The Power and the Promise of Ecological Feminism," *Environmental Ethics* 12 (1990): 125–146.

7. See Susan Griffin, *Woman and Nature: The Roaring Inside Her* (New York: Harper & Row, 1978).

8. See Vandana Shiva, *Staying Alive: Women, Ecology, and Development* (London: Zed Books, 1989).

9. The phrase "materially . . . equivalent" does not mean here what it means in formal logic.

10. See, for example, Daniel A. Guthrie, "Primitive Man's Relationship to Nature," *BioScience* 21 (1971): 721–723.

11. See Paul S. Martin, "The Discovery of America," *Science* 179 (1973): 969–974.

12. See W. C. Lowdermilk, *Conquest of the Land Through Seven Thousand Years*, Agricultural Information Bulletin, no. 99, revised edition (Washington, D.C.: Soil Conservation Service, U.S. Department of Agriculture, 1975).

13. See Jonathan Schell, *The Fate of the Earth* (New York: Alfred A. Knopf, 1982).

14. See Henry Shue, *Basic Rights: Subsistence, Affluence, and U.S. Foreign Policy* (Princeton: Princeton University Press, 1980).

15. See John Passmore, *Man's Responsibility for Nature: Ecological Problems and Western Traditions* (New York: Charles Scribner's Sons, 1974) and H. J. McClosky, *Ecological Ethics and Politics* (Totowa, N.J.: Rowan & Littlefield, 1983), for arguments for such an approach.

16. James K. Mitchell, *Human Dimensions of Environmental Hazards: Complexity, Disparity and the Search for Guidance* (unpublished ms., 1988), is a programmatic study.

17. David W. Ehrenfeld, "The Conservation of Non-resources," *American Scientist* 64 (1976): 648.

18. See Christopher D. Stone, *Should Trees Have Standing?: Toward Legal Rights for Natural Objects* (Los Altos, Calif.: William Kaufman, 1974). For a discussion see G. E. Varner, "Do Species Have Standing?" *Environmental Ethics* 9 (1987): 57–72.

2.   THE HISTORICAL ROOTS OF WESTERN EUROPEAN ENVIRONMENTAL ATTITUDES AND VALUES

1. *The Holy Bible*, King James, et al., eds. (London, 1611 / New York: The World Publishing Company, 1952).

2. The classic critique is Lynn White, Jr., "The Historical Roots of Our Ecologic Crisis," *Science* 155 (1967): 1203–1207.

3. James Barr, "Man and Nature: The Ecological Controversy and the Old Testament," *Bulletin of the John Rylands Library* 55 (1972): 20.

4. Lynn White, Jr., and his fellow critics provoked a veritable flood of apologetic literature too vast to cite in its entirety. James Barr's "Man and Nature: The Ecological Controversy and the Old Testament," *Bulletin of the John Rylands Library* 55 (1972): 9–32, is a personal favorite of mine. Francis Schaeffer, *Pollution and the Death of Man: The Christian View of Ecology* (New York: Hodder & Stoughton, 1970), represents a Protestant response; Albert J. Fritsch, S.J., *Environmental Ethics: Choices for Concerned Citizens* (New York: Doubleday/Anchor, 1980), represents a Catholic response; and see David W. Ehrenfeld and Philip J. Bently, "Judaism and the Practice of Stewardship," *Judaism* 34 (1985): 301–311.

5. That Genesis 1:28 was read by the Puritans as the "first commandment" of God to man is argued by Roderick Nash in *Wilderness and the American Mind* (New Haven: Yale University Press, 1967).

6. See Arthur Weiser, *The Old Testament: Its Formation and Development*, D. Barton, trans. (New York: Association Press, 1961).

7. For a full discussion, see J. Baird Callicott, "Genesis and John Muir," *ReVision* 12 (Winter 1990): 31–47.

8. See J. Donald Hughes, *Ecology in Ancient Civilizations* (Albuquerque: University of New Mexico Press, 1975); Hwa Yol Jung, "The Orphic Voice and Ecology," *Environmental Ethics* 3 (1981): 329–340; Michael F. Zimmerman, "Toward a Heideggerian Ethos for Radical Environmentalism," *Environmental Ethics* 5 (1983): 99–131.

9. J. Donald Hughes, "The Environmental Ethics of the Pythagoreans," *Environmental Ethics* 2 (1980): 195–213.

10. Empedocles, *Purifications*, DK 31 B 121, in *An Introduction to Early Greek Philosophy*, John Mansley Robinson, trans. (New York: Houghton Mifflin, 1968), p. 152.

11. Thomas S. Kuhn, *The Copernican Revolution: Planetary Astronomy and the Development of Western Thought* (Cambridge: Harvard University Press, 1957), p. 237.

12. Indeed, at 3:4 the Quran declares itself to be both ambiguous in part and unambiguous in part: "It is He who has revealed to you the Koran. Some of its verses are precise in meaning . . . and others are ambiguous." Al Quran, S. V. M. Ahmad Ali, ed., N. J. Dawood, trans. (Karachi: Sterling Printing Press, 1964).

13. As to the creative raw material, see the Quran, chap. 95, for clots; elsewhere, it's potter's clay.

14. 31:20 reads, "Allah has subjected to you all that the heavens and the earth contain and lavished on you both His visible and unseen favors."

15. In 2:30, Allah says, "I am placing on the earth one that shall rule as my Deputy."

16. Fazlur Raman, *Major Themes in the Qur'an* (Minneapolis: Bibliotheca Islamica, 1980).

17. Abou Bakr Ahmed Ba Kadar, Abdul Latif Tawfik El Shirazy Al Sabbagh, Mohamed Al Sayyed Al Glenid, Mawil Y. Izzi Deen, *Islamic Principles for the Conservation of the Natural Environment* (Gland, Switzerland: International Union for Conservation of Nature and Natural Resources, 1983), p. 13.

18. Iqtidar H. Zaidi, "On the Ethics of Man's Interaction with the Environment: An Islamic Approach," *Environmental Ethics* 3 (1981): 41. Zaidi cites 2:284.

19. Kadar, et al., *Islamic Principles*, p. 13.

20. Mawil Y. Izzi Deen, "Islamic Environmental Ethic, Law, and Society," in J. Ronald Engel and Joan Gibb Engel, eds., *Ethics of Environment and Development: Global Challenge and International Response* (Tucson: University of Arizona Press, 1990), p. 191.

21. Ibid., p. 190.

22. Ibid.

23. See Abdal-Aziz Kamil, *Islam and the Race Question* (Paris: UNESCO, 1970).

24. Ehrenfeld and Bently, "Judaism and the Practice of Stewardship," p. 303.

25. Ikhwan al-Safa (the Pure Brethren), *The Case of the Animals versus Man Before the King of the Jinn*, Lynn Evan Goodman, trans. (Boston: Twayne Publishers, 1978), pp. 53–54.

26. Ibid., p. 54.

27. See Kamil, *Islam and the Race Question*.

28. See Zaidi, "On the Ethics of Man's Interaction."

29. Robert Graves, *The Greek Myths*, vol. 1 (Baltimore: Penguin Books, 1955), p. 11.

30. Ibid., p. 12.

31. Riane Eisler, *The Chalice and the Blade: Our History, Our Future* (San Francisco: Harper & Row, 1987).

32. The quotation is from Elinor W. Gadon, *The Once and Future Goddess: A Symbol for Our Time* (San Francisco: Harper & Row, 1989).

33. See Marija Gimbutas, *The Goddesses and Gods of Old Europe, 6500–3500 B.C.: Myths and Cult Images* (Berkeley, Los Angeles, London: University of California Press, 1982).

34. See Ynestra King, "The Ecology of Feminism and the Feminism of Ecology," in Judith Plant, ed., *Healing the Wounds: The Promise of Ecofeminism* (Philadelphia: New Society Publishers, 1989).

35. Gadon, *The Once and Future Goddess*, p. xv.

36. Charlene Spretnak, *States of Grace: The Recovery of Meaning in the Postmodern Age* (San Francisco: HarperSanFrancisco, 1991), p. 134.

37. James E. Lovelock, *Gaia: A New Look at Life on Earth* (New York: Oxford University Press, 1979), p. vi.

38. Ibid., chap. 2.

39. For a discussion, see Stephen H. Schneider and Penelope J. Boston, eds., *Scientists on Gaia* (Boston: The MIT Press, 1991).

40. James E. Lovelock, *The Ages of Gaia: A Biography of Our Living Earth* (New York: W. W. Norton, 1988).

41. Aldo Leopold, "Some Fundamentals of Conservation in the Southwest," in Susan L. Flader and J. Baird Callicott, eds., *The River of the Mother of God and Other Essays by Aldo Leopold* (Madison: University of Wisconsin Press, 1991), p. 95.

42. Ibid.

3.   ENVIRONMENTAL ATTITUDES AND VALUES IN SOUTH ASIAN
INTELLECTUAL TRADITIONS

1. Elinor W. Gadon, *The Once and Future Goddess: A Symbol for Our Time* (San Francisco: Harper & Row, 1989), pp. xi, xiii.

2. See Ainslee T. Embree, *The Hindu Tradition* (New York: Modern Library, 1966).

3. See R. C. Majumdar, ed., *The History and Culture of the Indian People* (London: George Allen & Unwin, Ltd., 1951).

4. See R. Gordon Wasson, *Soma: Divine Mushroom of Immortality* (New York: Harcourt Brace, 1969).

5. See D. D. Kosambi, *Ancient India* (New York: Pantheon Books, 1965).

6. See Franklin Edgerton, *The Beginnings of Indian Philosophy* (Cambridge: Harvard University Press, 1965).

7. See Mircea Eliade, *Yoga: Immortality and Freedom* (New York: Pantheon Books, 1958).

8. See W. K. C. Guthrie, *A History of Greek Philosophy*, vol. 1 (Cambridge: Cambridge University Press, 1962).

9. See Eliade, *Yoga*.

10. See A. B. Keith, *The Religion and Philosophy of the Vedas and Upanishads* (Cambridge: Harvard University Press, 1920).

11. Rajagopal Ryali, "Eastern-Mystical Perspectives on Environment," in Dave Stefferson, Walter Herrscher, and Robert S. Cook, eds., *Ethics for Environment: Three Religious Strategies* (Green Bay: University of Wisconsin Press–GB, 1973), pp. 47–48.

12. Ibid., p. 49.

13. Ibid.

14. Ibid., p. 50. Ryali cites Donald K. Swearer, "Ecological Perspectives from Asian Religions" (unpublished ms., n.d.), p. 1.

15. Eliot Deutsch, "Vedanta and Ecology," in T. M. P. Mahadevan, ed., *Indian Philosophical Annual* 16 (1970): 3–4.

16. O. P. Dwivedi, "*Satyagraha* for Conservation: Awakening the Spirit of Hinduism," in J. Ronald Engel and Joan Gibb Engel, *Ethics of Environment and Development: Global Challenge and International Response* (Tucson: University of Arizona Press, 1990), p. 206.

17. Arne Naess, "The Shallow and the Deep, Long-Range Ecology Movement: A Summary," *Inquiry* 16 (1973): 95–100.

18. See Warwick Fox, *Toward a Transpersonal Ecology: Developing New Foundations for Environmentalism* (Boston: Shambhala, 1990).

19. Arne Naess, "Self-realization: An Ecological Approach to Being in the World," in John Seed, Joanna Macy, Pat Fleming, and Arne Naess, eds., *Thinking Like a Mountain: Towards a Council of All Beings* (Philadelphia: New Society Publishers, 1988), pp. 24–25. Naess cites an earlier book of his from which he has requoted Gandhi: Arne Naess, *Gandhi and Group Conflict* (Oslo: Universitetsforlaget, 1974), p. 35.

20. Fritjof Capra, *The Tao of Physics: An Exploration of the Parallels between Modern Physics and Eastern Mysticism* (Boulder: Shambhala, 1975).

21. Arne Naess, *Ecology, Community, and Life-style: Outline of an Ecosophy*, David Rothenberg, trans. and ed. (Cambridge: Cambridge University Press, 1989), p. 165.

22. Fox, *Toward a Transpersonal Ecology*, p. 232.

23. See Albert Schweitzer, *Philosophy and Civilization*, John Naish, trans. (London: A. & C. Black, 1923), and Arthur Schopenhauer, *The World as Will and Idea*, R. B. Haldane and J. Kemp, trans. (Garden City, N.Y.: Doubleday, 1961).

24. See Arthur Schopenhauer, "Transcendent Considerations Concerning the Will as Thing in Itself," Richard Taylor, ed. (New York: Frederick Unger, 1962), pp. 33–42.

25. Eliot Deutsch, "A Metaphysical Grounding for Natural Reverence: East-West," in J. Baird Callicott and Roger T. Ames, eds., *Nature in Asian Traditions of Thought: Essays in Environmental Philosophy* (Albany: State University of New York Press, 1989), pp. 262–263.

26. Sankara is quoted by Deutsch, without citation, in "Vedanta and Ecology," p. 1.

27. See A. B. Keith, *The Samkhya System* (Calcutta: Association Press, 1918).

28. Christopher Chapple, "Noninjury to Animals: Jaina and Buddhist Perspectives," in Tom Regan, ed., *Animal Sacrifices: Religious Perspectives on the Use of Animals in Science* (Philadelphia: Temple University Press, 1986), p. 215.

29. Herman Jacobi, trans., *Jaina Sutras* (Delhi: Motilal Banarsiddas, 1973), I.2.3.

30. Translated and quoted by Nathmal Tatia, *Studies in Jaina Philosophy* (Banaras: Jain Cultural Research Society, 1951), p. 18.

31. Christopher Chapple, "Contemporary Jaina and Hindu Responses to the Ecological Crisis," paper presented at the 1990 meeting of the College Theology Society, Loyola University, New Orleans, p. 6.

32. Christopher Chapple, *Nonviolence to Animals, Earth, and Self in Asian Traditions* (Albany: State University of New York Press, 1993).

33. See, for example, Eugene C. Hargrove, *The Animal Rights/Environmental Ethics Debate: The Environmental Perspective* (Albany: State University of New York Press, 1992).

34. Chapple, "Contemporary Jaina and Hindu Responses," p. 7.

35. See Kerry Brown, "Prime Minister Dedicates Jain Declaration to Nature," in *The New Road: The Bulletin of the WWF Network on Conservation and Religion* 19 (May–July 1991): 1.

36. Quoted by Kerry Brown, "Jains Celebrate First Environment Day," *The New Road* 23 (April–May 1992): 2.

37. L. M. Singhvi, *The Jain Declaration on Nature* (Cincinnati: Federation of Jain Associations of North America, n.d.), p. 7.

38. See A. Fourcher, *The Life of Buddha*, S. B. Boas, trans. (Middletown, Conn.: Wesleyan University Press, 1963).

39. See Arthur L. Herman, *An Introduction to Buddhist Thought* (Washington, D.C.: University Press of America, 1984).

40. See Edward J. Thomas, *The Life of the Buddha as Legend and History*, 3d ed. (London: Kegan Paul, Trench, Trubner & Co., 1949).

41. G. F. Allen, *The Buddha's Philosophy* (London: Macmillan & Co. Ltd., 1959).

42. *Sacred Books of the East*, vol. 11, *Buddhist Suttas*, T. W. Rhys Davids, trans. (Oxford: The Clarendon Press, 1881), p. 148.

43. See Thomas, *The Life of the Buddha*.

44. Ibid., p. 148.

45. Ibid., p. 149.

46. See L. d.l. V. Poussin, *The Way to Nirvana* (Cambridge: Cambridge University Press, 1917).

47. See E. A. Burtt, ed., *The Teachings of the Compassionate Buddha* (New York: Mentor, 1955).

48. David J. Kalupahana, "Toward a Middle Path of Survival," in *Nature in Asian Traditions of Thought*, p. 252.

49. David Edward Shaner, "The Japanese Experience of Nature," in *Nature in Asian Traditions of Thought*, pp. 169–171.

50. Ienaga Saburo, "The Development of the Concept of Religious Nature in Japanese Thought," translated and quoted by William R. LaFleur, "Saigyo and the Buddhist Value of Nature," in *Nature in Asian Traditions of Thought*, p. 204.

51. Saigyo, untitled, translated and quoted by LaFleur, "Saigyo and the Buddhist Value of Nature," p. 204.

52. These questions were touched on in a debate running for centuries in Chinese and Japanese Buddhism. See LaFleur, "Saigyo and the Buddhist Value of Nature."

53. Walt Whitman, "Walt Whitman," in *Leaves of Grass* (Philadelphia: McKay, 1900), pp. 62–63.

54. Chapple, *Nonviolence to Animals, Earth, and Self.*

55. Nancy Nash, "The Buddhist Perception of Nature Project," in Shann Davies, ed., *Tree of Life: Buddhism and Protection of Nature* (Hong Kong: Buddhist Perception of Nature Project), pp. 31–33.

56. Bhikku Bodhi, "Foreword," in Klas Sandell, ed., *Buddhist Perspectives on the Ecocrisis* (Kandy, Sri Lanka: Buddhist Publication Society, 1987), p. vii.

4. TRADITIONAL EAST ASIAN DEEP ECOLOGY

1. See J. Baird Callicott, "Conceptual Resources for Asian Traditions of Thought: A Propaedeutic," *Philosophy East and West* 37 (1987): 115–130.

2. George Sessions is quoted by Donald Worster in a review of Michael P. Cohen, *The Pathless Way: John Muir and American Wilderness* (Madison: University of Wisconsin Press, 1984), *Environmental Ethics* 10 (1988): 268.

3. Chang Chung-yuan, *Creativity and Taoism: A Study of Chinese Philosophy, Art, and Poetry* (London: Julian Press, 1963).

4. Richard Sylvan and David H. Bennett, "Taoism and Deep Ecology," *The Ecologist* 18 (1988): 148.

5. Lao Tzu, *Tao te ching*, D. C. Lau, trans. (Harmondsworth: Penguin Books, 1963), LXXX, p. 142.

6. See Holmes Rolston III, "Can We and Ought We to Follow Nature?," *Environmental Ethics* 3 (1981): 7–30.

7. Roger T. Ames, "Taoism and the Androgynous Ideal," in R. V. Guisso and S. Johanessen, eds., *Women in China* (Youngstown, N.Y.: Philo Press, 1981), p. 27.

8. D. C. Lau, "Introduction," in Lao Tzu, *Tao te ching*, p. 25.

9. David L. Hall and Roger T. Ames, *Thinking Through Confucius* (Albany: State University of New York Press, 1987).

10. I owe this analogy to Roger T. Ames, personal communication.

11. See Tu Wei-ming, "The Continuity of Being: Chinese Visions of Nature," in J. Baird Callicott and Roger T. Ames, eds., *Nature in Asian Traditions of Thought: Essays in Environmental Philosophy* (Albany: State University of New York Press, 1989), pp. 67–78.

12. See Roger T. Ames, "Putting the Te Back into Taoism," in *Nature*

in Asian Traditions of Thought, pp. 113–143. Ames directs us to David L. Hall, *Eros and Irony: A Prelude to Philosophical Anarchism* (Albany: State University of New York Press, 1982).

13. See D. C. Lau, trans., *Chinese Classics: Tao te ching* (Hong Kong: Chinese University Press, 1982).

14. See Ames, "Putting the Te Back."

15. David L. Hall, "On Seeking a Change of Environment," in *Nature in Asian Traditions of Thought*, p. 108.

16. See Hall, "On Seeking a Change," and Ames, "Putting the Te Back."

17. See Aldo Leopold, "The Farmer as a Conservationist," *American Forests* 45 (1939): 294–299, 316, 323, for a modern environmental illustration of this Taoist ideal.

18. See Russell Goodman, "Taoism and Ecology," *Environmental Ethics* 2 (1980): 73–80.

19. D. C. Lau, "Introduction," in Lao Tzu, *Tao te ching*, p. 12.

20. See Karen J. Warren, "The Power and the Promise of Ecological Feminism," *Environmental Ethics* 12 (1990): 125–146.

21. See Riane Eisler, *The Chalice and the Blade: Our History, Our Future* (San Francisco: Harper & Row, 1987).

22. Lao Tzu, *Tao te ching*, XXVIII, p. 85.

23. Ibid., LXXVI, p. 138.

24. Ibid., LXXVIII, p. 140.

25. See D. C. Lau, "Introduction," in Lao Tzu, *Tao te ching*, pp. 7–52.

26. See H. G. Creel, *Confucius, The Man and the Myth* (New York: John Day, 1949).

27. Roger T. Ames, "Taoist Ethics," in Lawrence Becker, ed., *Encyclopedia of Ethics* (New York: Garland Publishing Company, 1992), pp. 1226–1227.

28. See Roger T. Ames, *The Art of Rulership: A Study in Ancient Chinese Political Thought* (Honolulu: University of Hawaii Press, 1983).

29. For differing interpretations of these virtues, see Tu Wei-ming, *Humanity and Self-Cultivation: Essays in Confucian Thought* (Berkeley: Asian Humanities Press, 1979), and Hall and Ames, *Thinking Through Confucius*.

30. See Ames, *The Art of Rulership*.

31. Hall and Ames, *Thinking Through Confucius*, pp. 86–87.

32. See John Shrylock, *The Origin and Development of the State Cult of Confucius* (New York: The Century Company, 1932).

33. J. Donald Hughes, "Mencius's Prescriptions for Ancient Chinese Environmental Problems" (unpublished ms., 1989), pp. 2–3. Hughes cites *Mencius* (2.A.1.), D. C. Lau, trans. (London: Penguin Books, 1970), p. 85.

34. Hughes, "Mencius's Prescriptions," p. 8.

35. Hall and Ames, *Thinking Through Confucius*, p. 85.

36. See Arthur Waley, *The Analects of Confucius*, Book X (Boston: Houghton Mifflin, 1938).

37. Hall and Ames, *Thinking Through Confucius*, p. 90.

38. Ibid., p. 94.

39. Ibid., p. 100.

40. See Kenneth Goodpaster, "On Being Morally Considerable," *Journal of Philosophy* 75 (1978): 306–325.

41. Val Plumwood, "Nature, Self, and Gender: Feminism, Environmental Philosophy, and the Critique of Rationalism," *Hypatia* 6 (1991): 20.

42. See Paul Shepard, "A Theory of the Value of Hunting," *Twenty-Fourth North American Wildlife Conference* (1957): 505–506.

43. Anthony Quinton, "The Right Stuff," *The New York Review of Books* (December 5, 1985), p. 52.

5. ECOLOGICAL INSIGHTS IN EAST ASIAN BUDDHISM

1. Bhikku Yen-kiat, *Mahayana Buddhism* (Bangkok: Debsriharis, 1961).

2. Kenneth K. S. Chen, *Buddhism in China: An Historical Survey* (Princeton: Princeton University Press, 1964).

3. Lao Tzu, *Tao te ching*, D. C. Lau, trans. (Harmondsworth: Penguin Books, 1963), XL, p. 101.

4. Francis H. Cook, "The Jewel Net of Indra," in J. Baird Callicott and Roger T. Ames, eds., *Nature in Asian Traditions of Thought: Essays in Environmental Philosophy* (Albany: State University of New York Press, 1989), pp. 213–229.

5. Ibid., p. 214.

6. See Robert P. McIntosh, *The Background of Ecology: Concept and Theory* (Cambridge: Cambridge University Press, 1985).

7. David Bohm, *Wholeness and the Implicate Order* (London: Routledge & Kegan Paul, 1983).

8. Cook, "Jewel Net," p. 221.

9. Steve Odin, "The Japanese Concept of Nature in Relation to the Environmental Ethics and Conservation Aesthetics of Aldo Leopold," *Environmental Ethics* 13 (1991): 354.

10. Cook, "Jewel Net," pp. 222, 226.

11. See Alicia and Daigan Matsunage, *Foundations of Japanese Buddhism: vol. 1, The Aristocratic Age* (Los Angeles: Buddhist Books International, 1976).

12. See Chen, *Buddhism in China*.

13. Fung Yu-lan, *A History of Chinese Philosophy*, vol. 2, Derk Bodde, trans. (Princeton: Princeton University Press, 1953), p. 385.

14. See Charles Birch and John B. Cobb, *The Liberation of Life: From the Cell to the Community* (Cambridge: Cambridge University Press, 1981), and Susan Armstrong-Buck, "Whitehead's Metaphysical System as a Foundation for Environmental Ethics," *Environmental Ethics* 8 (1986): 241–259.

15. Miyamoto Shoson, "The Authorship and Significance as a Theory of the Buddha-nature of the Phrase 'Plants, Trees, and Earth All Become Buddha,'" *Journal of Indian and Buddhist Studies* 9 (1961): 696, translated and quoted by William R. LaFleur, "Saigyo and the Buddhist Value of Nature," in *Nature in Asian Traditions of Thought*, p. 186.

16. See Chen, *Buddhism in China.*

17. Kukai, "Record of Secret Treasury," translated and quoted by LaFleur, "Saigyo and the Buddhist Value of Nature," p. 187.

18. See Edward J. Thomas, *The History of Buddhist Thought* (New York: Alfred A. Knopf, 1933).

19. LaFleur, "Saigyo and the Buddhist Value of Nature," p. 187.

20. Ryogen, "An Account of How Plants and Trees Desire Enlightenment, Discipline Themselves, and Attain Buddhahood," translated and quoted by LaFleur, "Saigyo and the Buddhist Value of Nature," p. 190.

21. Chujin, *Kanko Ruiju*, translated and quoted by LaFleur, "Saigyo and the Buddhist Value of Nature," p. 192.

22. LaFleur, "Saigyo and the Buddhist Value of Nature," pp. 195–196.

23. A strong case for a long history of Shinto-Buddhist syncretism is made by Allan G. Grapard, "Japan's Ignored Cultural Revolution: The Separation of Shinto and Buddhist Divinities in Meiji and a Case Study: Tonomine," *History of Religions* 23 (1984): 240–265.

24. LaFleur, "Saigyo and the Buddhist Value of Nature," p. 196.

25. Omine Akira, "Probing the Japanese Concept of Nature," Dennis Hirota, trans., *Chanoyu Quarterly: Tea and the Arts of Japan* 51 (1987): 7.

26. Odin, "The Japanese Concept of Nature," p. 357.

27. William R. LaFleur, *Mirror for the Moon: A Selection of Poems by Saigyo (1118–1190)* (New York: New Directions, 1978), p. 60.

28. LaFleur, "Saigyo and the Buddhist Value of Nature," p. 200.

29. Lynn White, Jr., "The Historical Roots of Our Ecologic Crisis," *Science* 155 (1976): 1206.

30. See, for example, D. T. Suzuki, *Essays in Zen Buddhism*, 3 vols. (London: Luzak, 1927, 1933, 1934); and Alan W. Watts, *The Way of Zen* (New York: Pantheon Books, 1957).

31. D. Barash, "The Ecologist as Zen Master," *American Midland Naturalist* 89 (1973): 214–215.

32. Hwa Yol Jung, "Ecology, Zen, and Western Religious Thought," *Christian Century* 89 (1972): 1154–1155.

33. Allan G. Grapard, "Nature and Culture in Japan," in Michael Tobias, ed., *Deep Ecology* (San Marcos, Calif.: Avant Books, 1984), p. 247.

34. See Chen, *Buddhism in China.*

35. See Heinrich Dumoulin, *A History of Zen Buddhism,* Paul Preachey, trans. (New York: Pantheon Books, 1963).

36. See D. T. Suzuki, *Training of the Zen Buddhist Monk* (Kyoto: Eastern Zen Buddhist Society, 1934).

37. See Christian Humphries, *Zen Buddhism* (London: Allen & Unwin, 1958).

38. Quoted from Grapard, "Nature and Culture in Japan," p. 250.

39. See Alan W. Watts, *The Spirit of Zen* (New York: Grove Press, 1958).

40. See D. T. Suzuki, *Introduction to Zen Buddhism* (London: Rider, 1947).

41. D. T. Suzuki, *Zen and Japanese Culture* (Princeton: Princeton University Press, 1959), p. 354.

42. Ibid., pp. 351–352.

43. See J. Baird Callicott, "The Land Aesthetic," in J. Baird Callicott, ed., *Companion to A Sand County Almanac: Interpretive and Critical Essays* (Madison: University of Wisconsin Press, 1987), pp. 157–171.

44. See J. Baird Callicott, "Leopold's Land Aesthetic," in J. Baird Callicott, *In Defense of the Land Ethic* (Albany: State University of New York Press, 1989), pp. 239–247.

45. J. Sutherland and D. Britton, *National Parks of Japan* (Tokyo: Kodansha International, 1985).

46. Stephen R. Kellert, "Japanese Perceptions of Wildlife," *Conservation Biology* 5 (1991): 297–308.

47. Grapard, "Nature and Culture in Japan," p. 240.

48. Ibid., p. 254.

49. Ibid., p. 241.

50. Ibid., p. 255.

51. Ibid., p. 243.

52. Conrad Totman, *The Green Archipelago: Forestry in Preindustrial Japan* (Berkeley, Los Angeles, London: University of California Press, 1989), p. 179.

53. Ibid., p. 181.

54. Augustin Berque, "Identification of the Self in the Medial Process," in Nancy Rosenberger, ed., *Conceptions of the Self in Japan* (Cambridge: Cambridge University Press, 1992), pp. 97–98.

55. Kellert, "Japanese Perceptions," p. 306.

56. Berque, "Identification of the Self," p. 7.

57. Yuriko Saito, abstract of "Japanese Garden: The Art of Improving Nature," paper presented to the sixty-sixth meeting of the American Philosophical Association–Pacific Division, March 1992.

58. Augustin Berque, "The Sense of Nature and Its Relation to Space in Japan," in Joy Hendry and Jonathan Webber, eds., *Interpreting Japanese*

Society: Anthropological Approaches (Oxford: Jaso Occasional Papers, no. 5, 1986).

59. Totman, *The Green Archipelago*, p. 1.

60. Takashi Kosugi, "Reflections on the Prospect of Japanese Environmental Leadership" Carnegie Council on Ethics and International Affairs, Japan Programs Occasional Papers, no. 2, pp. 2–3.

6.   FAR WESTERN ENVIRONMENTAL ETHICS

1. See Peter Bellwood, *The Polynesians: Prehistory of an Island People* (London: Thames & Hudson, 1978).

2. See Robert Wood Williamson, *Religion and Cosmic Beliefs of Central Polynesia*, vol. 1 (Cambridge: Cambridge University Press, 1933).

3. Rubellite Kawena Johnson, *Kumulipo: Hawaiian Hymn of Creation* (Honolulu: Topgallant Press, 1981), p. 45.

4. Ibid., pp. 4–5.

5. Aldo Leopold, *A Sand County Almanac* (New York: Oxford University Press, 1949), p. 109.

6. See David Malo, *Hawaiian Antiquities*, Nathaniel B. Emerson, trans. (Honolulu: Bishop Museum Press, 1971).

7. Richard Taylor, *Te Ika a Maui, or New Zealand and Its Inhabitants* (London: George Allen & Unwin, Ltd., 1970), p. 109.

8. E. S. C. Handy, "Traces of Totemism in Polynesia," *Journal of the Polynesian Society* 77 (1968): 44.

9. See Martha Warren Beckwith, *Hawaiian Mythology* (Honolulu: University of Hawaii Press, 1970).

10. Lilikala Kame'eleihiwa, *Land and the Promise of Capitalism: A Dilemma for the Hawaiian Chiefs of the 1848 Mahele* (unpublished University of Hawaii Ph.D. dissertation), pp. 33–34.

11. Ibid., p. 48.

12. See Samuel M. Kamakau, *Ruling Chiefs of Hawaii* (Honolulu: Kamehameha Schools Press, 1961).

13. Leopold, *Sand County*, pp. 215–216.

14. Kame'eleihiwa, *Land*, p. 46.

15. See D. R. Simmons, *The Great New Zealand Myth: A Study in the Discovery of the Origin of the Maori* (Wellington: A. H. and A. W. Reed, 1976).

16. See Margaret Orbell, *Hawaiki: A New Approach to Maori Tradition* (Christchurch: University of Canterbury Press, 1985).

17. E. M. K. Douglas, "Land and Maori Identity in Contemporary New Zealand," *Plural Studies* 15 (1984): 33–51.

18. See Eugene C. Hargrove, "Anglo-American Land Use Attitudes," *Environmental Ethics* 2 (1980): 121–148.

19. Warwick Fox, "Comments Arising out of Discussions at 'The

Search for Common Ground: New Directions in Environmental Decision-Making' Conference, Massey University [New Zealand], 30 May–1 June 1990" (unpublished ms., 1990).

20. Joseph E. Brown, "Modes of Contemplation through Action: North American Indians," *Main Currents of Modern Thought* 30 (1973–1974): 60.

21. Calvin Martin, *Keepers of the Game: Indian-Animal Relationships and the Fur Trade* (Berkeley, Los Angeles, London: University of California Press, 1978), p. 186.

22. "Sioux" is a French name, derived from shortening *Nadoweisiw*, the Ojibwa name for the Lakota. Before being pushed out onto the Great Plains by the Ojibwa and other more easterly tribes, the pedestrian Lakota inhabited the woodlands and oak savannahs of northwestern Wisconsin.

23. Vine Deloria, Jr., quoted in Raymond J. DeMallie, *The Sixth Grandfather: Black Elk's Teachings as Given to John G. Neihardt* (Lincoln: University of Nebraska Press, 1984), p. xx.

24. Raymond J. DeMallie, *The Sixth Grandfather*, p. 80.

25. John G. Neihardt, *Black Elk Speaks: Being the Life Story of a Holy Man of the Oglala Sioux* (Lincoln: University of Nebraska Press, 1961), p. 3.

26. Ibid., pp. 1, 6.

27. James Mooney, "The Ghost Dance Religion and the Sioux Outbreak of 1890," *Fourteenth Annual Report of the Bureau of Ethnology, 1892–1893* (Washington, D.C., 1896). See Sam D. Gill, *Mother Earth: An American Story* (Chicago: University of Chicago Press, 1987) for context and critical discussion.

28. Brown, "Modes of Contemplation through Action," p. 61.

29. Richard Erdoes, *Lame Deer: Seeker of Visions* (New York: Simon & Schuster, 1976), pp. 102–103.

30. N. Scott Momaday, "A First American Views His Land," *National Geographic* (July 1976): 14, 18.

31. See DeMallie, *The Sixth Grandfather*.

32. Ibid.

33. James R. Walker, *Lakota Belief and Ritual*, Raymond J. DeMallie and Elaine A. Jahner, eds. (Lincoln: University of Nebraska Press, 1980).

34. See Neihardt, *Black Elk Speaks*, and Erdoes, *Lame Deer*.

35. See Adrian Tanner, *Bringing Home Animals: Religious Ideology and Mode of Production of the Misstassini Cree* (New York: St. Martin's Press, 1979).

36. George Copway, *The Traditional History and Characteristic Sketches of the Ojibway Nation* (London: Charles Gilpin, 1850), p. 95.

37. See William Jones, *Ojibwa Texts*, parts 1 and 2 (New York: American Ethnological Society, 1917, 1919).

38. See Martin, *Keepers of the Game*.

39. Frank G. Speck, "Savage Savers," *Frontiers* 4 (October 1939): 23.

40. Thomas W. Overholt and J. Baird Callicott, *Clothed-in-Fur and Other Tales* (Washington, D.C.: University Press of America, 1982).

41. Martin, *Keepers of the Game*, p. 71.

42. See Donald Worster, *Nature's Economy: The Roots of Ecology* (Garden City, N.Y.: Anchor Books, 1979).

43. Leopold, *Sand County*, pp. 202–204.

44. As reported by Roderick Nash, *Wilderness and the American Mind* (New Haven: Yale University Press, 1967), p. 92.

45. See Rudolph Kaiser, "Chief Seattle's Speech(es): American Origins and European Reception," in Brian Swann and Arnold Krupat, eds., *Recovering the Word: Essays on Native American Literature* (Berkeley, Los Angeles, London: University of California Press, 1987), pp. 497–536.

7. SOUTH AMERICAN ECO-EROTICISM

1. Gerald James Larson and Eliot Deutsch, eds., *Interpreting Across Boundaries: New Essays in Comparative Philosophy* (Princeton: Princeton University Press, 1988).

2. See Patricia J. Lyon, ed., *Native South Americans: Ethnology of the Least Known Continent* (Boston: Little, Brown, 1974); for population estimates, see William M. Deneven, ed., *The Native Population of the Americas in 1492*, 2d ed. (Madison: University of Wisconsin Press, 1992). The population of South America at the end of the fifteenth century is estimated to have been a whopping six times as great as the population of North America north of Mexico. The Amazon Basin alone is estimated to have had a population more than twice as large as the population of North America north of Mexico.

3. See William M. Deneven, "The Pristine Myth: The Landscape of the Americas in 1492," *Annals of the Association of American Geographers* 82: 369–385.

4. Deneven, "The Pristine Myth," p. 370, reports recent estimates of a hemispheric population between forty and eighty million in 1492.

5. See Arturo Gomez-Pompa and Andrea Kaus, "Taming the Wilderness Myth," *BioScience* 42 (1992): 271–279.

6. Terrence S. Turner, "The Role of Indigenous Peoples in the Environmental Crisis: The Example of the Kayapo of the Brazilian Amazon," *Perspectives in Biology and Medicine* 36 (1993): 526–545.

7. *The Kayapo: Out of the Forest* (documentary by M. Becham, Grenada Television International, 1989).

8. Turner, "Role of Indigenous Peoples," p. 542.

9. Geraldo Reichel-Dolmatoff, *Amazonian Cosmos: The Sexual and Religious Symbolism of the Tukano Indians* (Chicago: University of Chicago Press, 1971), p. 11, reports that the Tukano "emphatically insist that they

are hunters" and that in their view "the life of a hunter is the only fit one for a man."

10. See Aryon Dall 'Inga Rodrigues, "Linguistic Groups of Amazonia," in Lyon, ed., *Native South Americans*, pp. 51–58.

11. Christine Hugh-Jones, *From the Milk River: Spatial and Temporal Processes in Northwest Amazonia* (Cambridge: Cambridge University Press, 1979); Terrence S. Turner, "Kinship, Household, and Community among the Kayapo," in David Maybury-Lewis, ed., *Dialectical Societies: The Gê and Bororo of Central Brazil* (Cambridge: Harvard University Press, 1979), pp. 179–217.

12. Reichel-Dolmatoff, *Amazonian Cosmos*: Hugh-Jones, *From the Milk River*.

13. Janet M. Chernela, "Managing Rivers of Hunger: The Tukano of Brazil," in Darrell A. Posey and W. Balee, eds., *Resource Management in Amazonia: Indigenous and Folk Strategies* (New York: The New York Botanical Garden, 1989), p. 242.

14. Reichel-Dolmatoff, *Amazonian Cosmos*; Hugh-Jones, *From the Milk River*.

15. Hugh-Jones, *From the Milk River*, p. 259, provides a detailed drawing.

16. Reichel-Dolmatoff, *Amazonian Cosmos*.

17. Geraldo Reichel-Dolmatoff, "Cosmology as Ecological Analysis: A View from the Rain Forest," *Man* 12 (new series, 1976) 2: 307–318.

18. See Harold Morowitz, "Biology as Cosmological Science," *Main Currents in Modern Thought* 28 (1972): 151–157.

19. Reichel-Dolmatoff, "Cosmology as Ecological Analysis," pp. 310, 312.

20. Garrett Hardin, "Tragedy of the Commons," *Science* 162 (1968): 1243–1248.

21. Hugh-Jones, *From the Milk River*, p. 125.

22. Reichel-Dolmatoff, "Cosmology as Ecological Analysis."

23. Reichel-Dolmatoff, "Cosmology as Ecological Analysis," p. 313.

24. Geraldo Reichel-Dolmatoff, "Tapir Avoidance in the Colombian Northwest Amazon," in Gary Urton, ed., *Animal Myths and Metaphors in South America* (Salt Lake City: University of Utah Press, 1985), p. 135.

25. Reichel-Dolmatoff, "Cosmology as Ecological Analysis," p. 312.

26. Reichel-Dolmatoff, "Cosmology as Ecological Analysis."

27. Ibid.

28. Hugh-Jones, *From the Milk River*.

29. Reichel-Dolmatoff, "Tapir Avoidance," p. 110.

30. Hugh-Jones, *From the Milk River*; and Reichel-Dolmatoff, "Cosmology as Ecological Analysis."

31. Ibid., p. 315.

32. Reichel-Dolmatoff, "Tapir Avoidance," p. 119.

33. Hugh-Jones, *From the Milk River*, p. 61.

34. Reichel-Dolmatoff, "Tapir Avoidance," pp. 119–120, 123.

35. Reichel-Dolmatoff, "Cosmology as Ecological Analysis," p. 316.

36. Ibid., p. 318.

37. Ibid., p. 308.

38. Ibid., p. 318.

39. See Daniel Botkin, *Discordant Harmonies: A New Ecology for the Twenty-first Century* (New York: Oxford University Press, 1990). See also William K. Stevens, "New Eye on Nature: The Real Constant Is Eternal Turmoil," *New York Times* (July 31, 1990): section B, 5–6; and Donald Worster, "The Ecology of Order and Chaos," *Environmental Review* 14 (1990): 1–18.

40. Turner, "Kinship, Household, and Community among the Kayapo." Turner, "Role of Indigenous Peoples," reports that the present Kayapo population is around twenty-five hundred and that the largest community consists of about eight hundred inhabitants.

41. Turner, "Kinship, Household, and Community among the Kayapo."

42. See, for instance, J. H. Steward, "American Culture in the Light of South America," *Southwestern Journal of Anthropology* 3 (Summer 1947): 85–107 and J. H. Steward and L. Faron, *Native Peoples of South America* (New York: McGraw-Hill, 1959).

43. See Paul Shepard, *The Tender Carnivore and the Sacred Game* (New York: Charles Scribner's Sons, 1973).

44. Terrence S. Turner, "The Gê and Bororo Societies as Dialectical Systems," in Maybury-Lewis, ed., *Dialectical Societies*, p. 176.

45. Turner, "Role of Indigenous Peoples."

46. Turner, "Gê and Bororo Societies," p. 149.

47. Darrell A. Posey, "Kayapo Indian Natural-Resource Management," in J. D. Sloan and C. P. Padoch, eds., *People of the Tropical Rain Forest* (Berkeley, Los Angeles, London: University of California Press, 1988).

48. Turner, "Role of Indigenous Peoples," p. 543.

49. William K. Stevens, "Research in 'Virgin' Amazon Uncovers Complex Farming," *New York Times* (April 3, 1990), section B: 5, 7.

50. Jane L. Collins, "Small Holder Settlement of Tropical South America," *Human Organization* 45 (1986): 1–10.

51. Stevens, "Research in 'Virgin' Amazon."

52. Posey, "Kayapo Indian Natural-Resource Management," and Susanna B. Hecht and Darrell A. Posey, "Preliminary Results on Soil Management Techniques of the Kayapo Indians," in Posey and Balee, eds., *Resource Management in Amazonia*, pp. 174–188.

53. Susanna B. Hecht and Alexander Cockburn, *The Fate of the Forest: Developers, Destroyers, and Defenders of the Amazon* (New York: Verso, 1989).

54. Anthony B. Anderson and Darrell A. Posey, "Management of a Tropical Scrub Savannah by the Gorotire Kayapo of Brazil," in Posey and Balee, eds., *Resource Management in Amazonia*, pp. 159–173.

55. Posey, "Kayapo Indian Natural-Resource Management," p. 90. Posey's claims about the *apêtê* have been roundly and severely criticized by Eugene Parker, "Forest Islands and Kayapo Resource Management in Amazonia: A Reappraisal of the Apêtê," *American Anthropologist* 94 (1992): 406–428. Darrell A. Posey, "Reply to Parker," *American Anthropologist* 94 (1992): 441–443, defends his account.

56. Hecht and Cockburn, *Fate of the Forest*, pp. 38–39.

57. Ibid.

58. "Interview with Ailton Krenak," Appendix A, in Hecht and Cockburn, *Fate of the Forest*, p. 211.

59. See Johannes Wilbert, ed., *Folk Literature of the Gê Indians*, 2 vols. (Los Angeles: U.C.L.A. Latin American Studies, 1978, 1984).

60. Hecht and Cockburn, *Fate of the Forest*.

61. George Peter Murdock, "South American Culture Areas," in Lyons, ed., *Native South Americans*, pp. 22–43.

62. Johannes Wilbert, "Introduction," in Wilbert, ed., *Folk Literature of the Gê Indians*, vol. 1: 1–26. Hugh-Jones, in *From the Milk River*, distinguishes five such layers in Tukano cosmology.

63. See Alfonso Ortiz, *Tewa World: Space, Time, Being, and Becoming in a Pueblo Society* (Chicago: University of Chicago Press, 1969).

64. Wilbert, "Introduction."

65. See Curt Nimuendaju, *The Apinaye*, R. H. Lowie and J. M. Cooper, trans. (Anthropological Series, no. 8, Washington, D.C.: Catholic University Press, 1939), and Adolf E. Jensen, *Myth and Cult Among Primitive Peoples*, M. T. Choldin and W. Weissleder (Chicago: University of Chicago Press, 1963).

66. Wilbert, "Introduction."

67. Ibid. Terrence S. Turner, "Animal Symbolism, Totemism, and the Structure of Myth," in Gary Urton, ed., *Animal Myths and Metaphors in South America* (Salt Lake City: University of Utah Press, 1985), pp. 49–106, presents a very different Kayapo myth of the domestication of fire. However, in it (p. 55) Turner lists similar prefire foods: "rotten wood, fungi, caterpillars, honey, and palmito (heart of palm)." Otherwise the story is quite divergent.

68. Narratives 76–78 in Wilbert, ed., *Folk Literature of the Gê*, pp. 217–224.

69. Turner, "Animal Symbolism, Totemism, and the Structure of Myth."

70. Jon Christopher Crocker, *Vital Souls: Bororo Cosmology, Natural Symbolism, and Shamanism* (Tucson: University of Arizona Press, 1985), p. 54.

71. Ibid., p. 37.

72. Reichel-Dolmatoff, "Cosmology as Ecological Analysis," p. 312; also see Reichel-Dolmatoff, *Amazonian Cosmos*.

73. Crocker, *Vital Souls*, pp. 122, 163.

74. Ibid., p. 171.

75. Ibid., p. 143.

76. Ibid., p. 164.

77. Turner, "Role of Indigenous Peoples," pp. 531–532.

78. Ibid., p. 536.

79. Hecht and Cockburn, *Fate of the Forest*, p. 182.

80. "Interview with Ailton Krenak," in Hecht and Cockburn, *Fate of the Forest*, p. 213.

8.   AFRICAN BIOCOMMUNITARIANISM AND AUSTRALIAN DREAMTIME

1. Brian J. Huntly, "Conserving and Monitoring Biotic Diversity: Some African Examples," in E. O. Wilson, ed., *Biodiversity* (Washington, D.C.: National Academy Press, 1988), pp. 248–260.

2. Geoffrey Parrinder, *African Traditional Religion* (New York: Harper & Row, 1976), p. 32.

3. J. S. Mbiti, *Introduction to African Religion* (London: Heinemann, 1975), p. 40.

4. Noel Q. King, *African Cosmos: An Introduction to Religion in Africa* (Belmont, Calif.: Wadsworth, 1986), p. 4.

5. Mbiti, *Introduction to African Religion*, pp. 37–39.

6. Mary Douglas, "The Lele of Kasai," in Daryll Forde, ed., *African Worlds: Studies in the Cosmological Ideas and Social Values of African Peoples* (London: Oxford University Press, 1954), p. 9.

7. Benjamin C. Ray, *African Religions: Symbol, Ritual, and Community* (Englewood Cliffs, N.J.: Prentice-Hall, 1976).

8. Ibid.

9. E. Thomas Lawson, *Religions of Africa: Traditions in Transformation* (San Francisco: Harper & Row, 1984), pp. 5–6.

10. King, *African Cosmos*; Lawson, *Religions of Africa*.

11. Lawson, *Religions of Africa*, p. 57.

12. Ibid., p. 58.

13. Parrinder, *African Traditional Religion*, p. 39.

14. King, *African Cosmos*, p. 9.

15. See C. G. Seligman, *Races of Africa* (London: Oxford University Press, 1930).

16. J. B. Danqua, *Akan Doctrine of God* (London: Frank Cass, 1968); E. B. Idowu, *Olodumaré: God in Yoruba Belief* (London: SCM Press, 1973); J. S. Mbiti, *African Religions and Philosophy* (New York: Anchor Books, 1970).

17. For an exposition and discussion of the speculations of de Brosses,

Comte, and Tylor, see E. E. Evans-Pritchard, *Theories of Primitive Religion* (Oxford: The Clarendon Press, 1965).

18. Lawson, *Religions of Africa*, p. 61.

19. King, *African Cosmos*, pp. 13, 15.

20. Mbiti, *African Religions*, pp. 11–12.

21. Ibid., p. 102.

22. King, *African Cosmos*.

23. Lawson, *Religions of Africa*, p. 63.

24. Mbiti, *African Religions*, p. 141.

25. Ray, *African Religions*, p. 132.

26. Ibid., p. 134.

27. Ibid., p. 132.

28. Ibid.

29. Richard B. Lee, *The Dobe !Kung* (New York: Holt, Rinehart & Winston, 1984).

30. Richard Katz, "Education for Transcendence: !Kia-Healing with the Kalahari !Kung," in Richard B. Lee and Irven DeVore, eds., *Kalahari Hunter-Gatherers: Studies of the !Kung San and Their Neighbors* (Cambridge: Harvard University Press, 1976), pp. 281–301.

31. Lee, *The Dobe !Kung*, p. 49.

32. Laurens Van der Post, *The Lost World of the Kalahari* (New York: William Morrow, 1958), p. 253.

33. Ibid., pp. 106–107.

34. Megan Biesele, "Aspects of !Kung Folklore," in Lee and DeVore, eds., *Kalahari Hunter-Gatherers*, pp. 310, 308.

35. The quoted phrase is from Van der Post, *Lost World of the Kalahari*, p. 26.

36. Nicholas Blurton Jones and Melvin J. Conner, "!Kung Knowledge of Animal Behavior (or: The Proper Study of Mankind Is Animals)," in Lee and DeVore, eds., *Kalahari Hunter-Gatherers*, pp. 325–348.

37. Van der Post, *Lost World of the Kalahari*, p. 15.

38. Ibid.

39. See Paul S. Martin, "The Discovery of America," *Science* 179: 969–974.

40. Lee, *The Dobe !Kung*, p. 109.

41. Elizabeth Marshall Thomas, "Reflections: The Old Way," *The New Yorker* (October 15, 1990), p. 80.

42. Thomas, "Reflections."

43. Ibid., pp. 87, 94.

44. Ibid., p. 96.

45. Lee, *The Dobe !Kung*.

46. Van der Post, *Lost World of the Kalahari*, p. 204.

47. See Richard B. Lee and Irven DeVore, eds., *Man the Hunter* (Chicago: Aldine, 1966).

48. A. P. Elkin, *The Australian Aborigines* (New York: Doubleday, 1964), p. 12.

49. Elkin, *Australian Aborigines*, p. 252.

50. David H. Bennett, *Inter-species Ethics: Australian Perspectives, A Cross-cultural Study of Attitudes Towards Non-human Animal Species* (Canberra: Preprint Series in Environmental Philosophy #14, Department of Philosophy, Australian National University, 1986), p. 5.

51. See W. E. H. Stanner, *The White Man Got No Dreaming: Essays 1938–1973* (Canberra: Australian National University Press, 1979), pp. 23–40.

52. Ibid.

53. Elkin, *Australian Aborigines*, p. 206.

54. Gary Snyder, *The Practice of the Wild* (San Francisco: North Point Press, 1990), p. 84.

55. Nancy D. Munn, "The Transformation of Subjects into Objects in Walbiri and Pitjantjara Myth," in M. Charlesworth, H. Morphy, D. Bell, and K. Maddock, eds., *Religion in Aboriginal Australia: An Anthology* (St. Lucia: University of Queensland Press, 1984), p. 61.

56. Annette Hamilton, "Culture Conflict and Resource Management in Central Australia," in Paul A. Olson, ed., *The Struggle for the Land: Indigenous Insight and Industrial Empire in the Semiarid World* (Lincoln: University of Nebraska Press, 1990).

57. R. M. Berndt, "Traditional Morality as Expressed through the Medium of an Australian Aboriginal Religion," in Charlesworth et al., eds., *Religion in Aboriginal Australia*, p. 176.

58. See Munn, "The Transformation of Subjects into Objects," pp. 57–82, for a very thorough account of this process and its social and psychological implications.

59. R. M. Berndt, "A Profile of Good and Bad in Australian Aboriginal Religion," *Australian and New Zealand Theological Review* 12: 19.

60. Bennett, *Inter-species Ethics*, p. 103.

61. Elkin, *Australian Aborigines*, p. 200.

62. Elkin, *Australian Aborigines*.

63. Bennett, *Inter-species Ethics*, and Elkin, *Australian Aborigines*.

64. Elkin, *Australian Aborigines*, p. 200.

65. Bennett, *Inter-species Ethics*, p. 108.

66. Elkin, *Australian Aborigines*, pp. 153–154.

67. Snyder, *Practice*, p. 84.

68. Ibid., pp. 82–83.

69. Hamilton, "Culture Conflict," pp. 212–213.

70. Deborah Bird Rose, "Exploring an Aboriginal Land Ethic," *Meanjin* 47 (1988): 379.

71. See, for example, Daniel A. Guthrie, "Primitive Man's Relationship to Nature," *BioScience* 21 (1971): 721–723; and W. H. Hutchinson,

"The Remaking of the Amerind," *Westways* 64 (October 1972): 18–21, 94.

72. Frank G. Speck, "Aboriginal Conservators," *Bird-Lore* 40 (July 1938): 258–261; and "Savage Savers," *Frontiers* 4 (1939): 23–27 (in which the quoted phrase may be found).

73. A. Irving Hallowell, "Ojibwa Ontology, Behavior, World View," in Stanley Diamond, ed., *Culture in History: Essays in Honor of Paul Radin* (New York: Columbia University Press, 1960), pp. 19–52.

74. Elkin, *Australian Aborigines*, pp. 140, 206.

75. Ibid., p. 141. See Paul W. Taylor, *Respect for Nature: A Theory of Environmental Ethics* (Princeton: Princeton University Press, 1986).

76. Ibid., p. 208.

77. Berndt, "Traditional Morality," pp. 176–177.

78. Hamilton, "Culture Conflict," p. 221.

79. See Rhys Jones, "Fire-stick Farming," *Australian Natural History* 16 (1969): 224–228; and D. R. Horton, "The Burning Question: Aborigines, Fire, and Australian Ecosystems," *Mankind* 13 (1982): 237–251.

80. Bennett, "Inter-species Ethics," p. 137.

81. Ibid., p. 130.

82. T. G. H. Strehlow, "Culture, Social Structure, and Environment in Aboriginal Central Australia," in R. M. Berndt and C. H. Berndt, eds., *Aboriginal Man in Australia* (Sydney: Angus & Robertson, 1965), p. 144.

83. A. E. Newsome, "The Eco-mythology of the Red Kangaroo in Central Australia," *Mankind* 12 (1980): 327.

84. Newsome, "Eco-mythology," p. 333.

85. Bennett, "Inter-species Ethics," p. 133.

86. Ibid., pp. 142–143.

87. Rose, "Exploring an Aboriginal Land Ethic."

88. Holmes Rolston III, *Environmental Ethics: Duties to and Values in the Natural World* (Philadelphia: Temple University Press, 1988), pp. 349–352.

89. Bennett, "Inter-species Ethics," p. 157.

90. Snyder, *Practice*, pp. 27, 39.

91. Val Plumwood, "Plato and the Bush: Philosophy and Environment in Australia," *Meanjin* 49 (1990): 531.

9. A POSTMODERN EVOLUTIONARY-ECOLOGICAL ENVIRONMENTAL ETHIC

1. Jim Cheney, "Postmodern Environmental Ethics: Ethics as Bioregional Narrative," *Environmental Ethics* 11 (1989): 117–134.

2. Jim Cheney, "The Neo-stoicism of Radical Environmentalism," *Environmental Ethics* 11 (1989): 302.

3. The quoted phrase is from Karen J. Warren and Jim Cheney, "Ecosystem Ecology and Metaphysical Ecology," *Environmental Ethics* 15 (1993): 116.

4. Karen J. Warren, "The Power and the Promise of Ecological Feminism," *Environmental Ethics* 12 (1990): 125–146.

5. Val Plumwood, "Plato and the Bush," *Meanjin* 49 (1990): 533.

6. Fritjof Capra, *The Tao of Physics: An Exploration of the Parallels Between Modern Physics and Eastern Mysticism* (Boulder: Shambhala, 1975).

7. Deborah Bird Rose, "Exploring an Aboriginal Land Ethic," *Meanjin* 47 (1988): 378.

8. Gerald James Larson, " 'Conceptual Resources' in South Asia for 'Environmental Ethics,' " in J. Baird Callicott and Roger T. Ames, eds., *Nature in Asian Traditions of Thought: Essays in Environmental Philosophy* (Albany: State University of New York Press, 1989), pp. 267–277.

9. Rose, "Exploring an Aboriginal Land Ethic," p. 378.

10. In, for example, Aldo Leopold, "The Conservation Ethic," *Journal of Forestry* 31 (1933): 634–643.

11. See John Honner, *The Description of Nature: Niels Bohr and the Philosophy of Quantum Physics* (New York: Oxford University Press, 1987).

12. Aldo Leopold, *A Sand County Almanac* (New York: Oxford University Press, 1949), p. 109.

13. Charles Darwin, *The Descent of Man and Selection in Relation to Sex*, 2d ed. (New York: J. A. Hill, 1904), p. 107.

14. Ibid., p. 118.

15. Ibid., p. 124.

16. Ibid.

17. Mary Midgley, *Animals and Why They Matter* (Athens: University of Georgia Press, 1983).

18. Leopold, *Sand County*, pp. 202–203.

19. Ibid., p. 204.

20. Ibid., pp. 224–225.

21. Ibid., p. 203.

22. Ibid.

23. Paul Shepard, "Ecology and Man: A Viewpoint," in Paul Shepard and Daniel McKinley, eds., *The Subversive Science: Essays Toward an Ecology of Man* (Boston: Houghton Mifflin, 1969), p. 3.

24. Gary Snyder, "Song of the Taste," in Gary Snyder, *Regarding Wave* (New York: New Directions, 1967), p. 17.

25. Arne Naess, "The Shallow and the Deep, Long-Range Ecology Movement: A Summary," *Inquiry* 16 (1973): 16.

26. John Seed, "Anthropocentrism," Appendix E in Bill Devall and

George Sessions, *Deep Ecology: Living As If Nature Mattered* (Salt Lake City: Peregrine Smith Books, 1985), p. 243.

10. TRADITIONAL ENVIRONMENTAL ETHICS IN ACTION

1. Wallace Stegner, "The Legacy of Aldo Leopold," in J. Baird Callicott, ed., *Companion to A Sand County Almanac: Interpretive and Critical Essays* (Madison: University of Wisconsin Press, 1987).

2. Lynn White, Jr., "The Historical Roots of Our Ecologic Crisis," *Science* 155 (1967): 1203–1207.

3. The Heartland Regional Catholic Bishops Conference, *Strangers and Guests: Toward Community in the Heartland* (Des Moines: Heartland Project, 1980), p. 13.

4. The Eleventh Convention of the American Lutheran Church, *The Land: God's Giving, Our Caring* (Minneapolis: Augsburg Publishing House, 1982), p. 3.

5. Wendell Berry, *The Unsettling of America: Culture and Agriculture* (San Francisco: Sierra Club Books, 1977).

6. Anonymous, "LSP: A Decade of Work for Cultural Change," *The Land Stewardship Letter* 10/4 (Autumn 1992), p. 4.

7. Anonymous, " 'Planting in the Dust' Opens in Minnesota," *The Land Stewardship Letter* 2/3 (Fall 1984), p. 1.

8. "LSP: A Decade of Work," p. 4.

9. Ibid., p. 5.

10. Cornelia Butler Flora, "Evaluation of the Stewardship Farming Program" (unpublished report).

11. Anonymous, "Spirituality Inspires Farm Stewardship," *The Land Stewardship Letter* 9/4 (Autumn 1991), p. 6.

12. Ibid.

13. Ron Kroese, ed., *Excellence in Agriculture: Interviews with Ten Minnesota Stewardship Farmers* (Minneapolis: The Land Stewardship Project, 1988), p. 49.

14. Ibid., pp. 13–14.

15. "LSP: A Decade of Work."

16. Ibid.

17. Ibid.

18. Anonymous, "Constituents Envision LSP's Work for the Future," *The Land Stewardship Letter* 10/4 (Autumn 1992), pp. 5, 7.

19. Wes Jackson, *Altars of Unhewn Stone: Science and the Earth* (San Francisco: North Point Press, 1987).

20. Vandana Shiva and Jayanata Bandyopadhyay, "The Evolution, Structure, and Development of the Chipko Movement," *Mountain Research and Development* 6 (1986): 133–142.

21. Ramachandra Guha, *The Unquiet Woods: Ecological Change and*

Peasant Resistance in the Himalaya (Berkeley, Los Angeles, Oxford: University of California Press, 1990).

22. Jayanata Bandyopadhyay and Vandana Shiva, "Chipko: Rekindling India's Forest Culture," *The Ecologist* 17 (1987): 26–27.

23. Gerald D. Berreman, "Chipko: A Movement to Save the Himalayan Environment and People," in Carla Borden, ed., *Contemporary Indian Tradition* (Washington, D.C.: Smithsonian Institution Press, 1989), p. 240.

24. Guha, *Unquiet Woods*.

25. Mark Shepard, "Chipko: North India's Tree Huggers," *Coevolution Quarterly* (Fall 1981), p. 65.

26. Bandyopadhyay and Shiva, "Chipko."

27. Ibid.

28. Guha, *Unquiet Woods*.

29. Ibid.

30. Bandyopadhyay and Shiva, "Chipko," p. 29.

31. Ibid.

32. Guha, *Unquiet Woods*; Bandyopadhyay and Shiva, "Chipko."

33. O. P. Dwivedi, "*Satyagraha* for Conservation: Awakening the Spirit of Hinduism," in J. Ronald Engel and Joan Gibb Engel, *Ethics of Environment and Development: Global Challenge and International Response* (Tucson: University of Arizona Press, 1990), p. 209.

34. Guha, *Unquiet Woods*; Shepard, "Chipko."

35. Berreman, "Chipko," p. 239.

36. Shepard, "Chipko," p. 68.

37. Guha, *Unquiet Woods*, p. 162; Bandyopadhyay and Shiva, "Chipko," p. 30.

38. Sankar Sen Gupta, "Introduction by the Editor," in Sankar Sen Gupta, ed., *Tree Symbol Worship in India: A New Survey of a Pattern of Folk Religion* (Calcutta: Indian Publications, 1965), p. xx.

39. O. P. Dwivedi, "*Satyagraha* for Conservation," p. 206.

40. Bandyopadhyay and Shiva, "Chipko," p. 30.

41. Guha, *Unquiet Woods*, p. 170.

42. Ibid.

43. Bandyopadhyay and Shiva, "Chipko," p. 28.

44. Vandana Shiva, *Staying Alive: Women, Ecology, and Development* (London: Zed Books, 1989), p. 70.

45. Ibid.

46. Bandyopadhyay and Shiva, "Chipko," p. 28.

47. Quoted by Mahadev Desai, *The Gita According to Gandhi* (Ahmedabad: Navajivan Publishing House, 1946), pp. 128–129.

48. Shiva, *Staying Alive*, p. 38.

49. Dwivedi, "*Satyagraha* for Conservation," p. 205.

50. The term "maldevelopment" is borrowed from Vandana Shiva, *Staying Alive*.

51. Guha, *Unquiet Woods.*

52. Berreman, "Chipko," p. 248.

53. Ravi Sharma, "Assessing the Development Costs in India," *Environment* 29/3 (April 1987): 6–11, 34–38.

54. Quoted by Berreman, "Chipko," p. 248. Berreman cites Sunderlal Bahuguna, "What Man Does to Mountain, and to Man," *Future* (1983, first quarter), p. 7.

55. Bandyopadhyay and Shiva, "Chipko," p. 33. See Arne Naess, "The Shallow and the Deep, Long-Range Ecology Movement: A Summary," *Inquiry* 16 (1973): 95–100, and Bill Devall, "The Deep Ecology Movement," *Natural Resources Journal* (1980): 299–322.

56. Bandyopadhyay and Shiva, "Chipko," p. 33.

57. Ibid.

58. Shiva, *Staying Alive*, p. 70.

59. Guha, *Unquiet Woods*, p. 175.

60. Berreman, "Chipko," p. 252.

61. See Carolyn Merchant, *Ecological Revolutions: Nature, Gender, and Science in New England* (Chapel Hill: University of North Carolina Press, 1989).

62. Guha, *Unquiet Woods*, p. 164.

63. Ibid., p. 175.

64. Dwivedi, "*Satyagraha* for Conservation," p. 209.

65. Shiva, *Staying Alive*, p. 19.

66. Catherine Ingram, *In the Footsteps of Gandhi: Conversations with Spiritual Social Activists* (Berkeley: Parallax Press, 1990).

67. A. T. Ariyaratne, "Introduction," in Joanna Macy, *Dharma and Development: Religion as Resource in the Sarvodaya Self-Help Movement*, 2d ed. (West Hartford: Kumarian Press, 1985), p. 15.

68. Macy, *Dharma and Development*, p. 37.

69. Ingram, *In the Footsteps of Gandhi*, p. 135.

70. Macy, *Dharma and Development*, p. 27.

71. Macy, *Dharma and Development.*

72. Ingram, *In the Footsteps of Gandhi*, pp. 129–130.

73. Ingram, *In the Footsteps of Gandhi.*

74. Macy, *Dharma and Development.*

75. Ibid., p. 33.

76. Ingram, *In the Footsteps of Gandhi*, p. 136.

77. Ibid., p. 139.

78. Ibid.

79. Leslie E. Sponsel and Poranee Natadecha, "Buddhism, Ecology, and Forests," *The New Road* 21 (December 1991): 4.

80. Leslie E. Sponsel and Poranee Natadecha, "Buddhism, Ecology, and Forests in Thailand: Past, Present, and Future," in John Dargavel, Kay Dixon, and Noel Semple, eds., *Changing Tropical Forests: Historical Per-*

spectives on Today's Challenges in Asia, Australia, and Oceania (Canberra: Centre for Resource and Environmental Studies, 1988): 305–325.

81. Philip Hurst, *Rainforest Politics: Ecological Destruction in South-East Asia* (London: Zed Books, 1990).

82. Macy, *Dharma and Development*, p. 22.

83. Carla Deicke, "The Moral Philosophy of Forest Conservation Monks in Thailand," unpublished paper, p. 2.

84. Ibid.

85. Ibid.

86. Ibid., p. 7.

87. Ibid.

88. Ibid.

Index

263

Einstein, Albert, 192, 199
Eisler, Riane, 37, 238n31, 243n21
Eliade, Mircea, 239n7
Elkin, A. P., 173, 174, 176–180, 255n48
Elton, Charles, 129, 203–204
Embedded individuality, 167
Embedded self-interest, 208–209
Embree, Ainslee T., 239n2
Emerson, Ralph Waldo, 11, 53
Empedocles, 194, 195, 237n10
Endangered Species Act, xii, 10
Enlightened self-interest, 82–83, 208–209
Enlightenment
  possibility of, 95
  Zen, 99–100
Environment
  concern for, xiii
  degradation of, 7–8, 33
  as extension of the self, 50–51, 82, 208–209
  Islamic prohibition of, 33
  Japan's relationship to, 102–108
  management of, 79
  moral sensitivity to, 3
Environmental aesthetic, 101–102
Environmental attitudes
  African, 164
  Buddhist, 57–65
  Confucian, 75–85
  Gaian, 36–43
  Greco-Roman, 24–30
  Hindu, 44–53
  Islamic, 30–36
  Jainist, 53–57
  Judeo-Christian, 14–24
  South Asian, 44–66
  Taoist, 67–75
  Western European, 14–43
Environmental crisis, xii
"Environmental Decade," xii, 48

Environmental ethics, 1–3
  African, 156, 158–159, 167, 170
  Australian, 179–184
  Buddhist contribution to, 65
  Chinese, 85–86
  comparative, 11–13
  constructing, xiv
  ecofeminist approach to, 38
  familial, 122–123
  Far Western, 109–132
  and Greek philosophy, 26–30
  Hindu, 48–49, 50
  Hua-yen Buddhism and, 91–92
  Jain-based, 53–57
  local roots of, 183
  modern and postmodern, 7–11
  natural history of, 199–205
  network of, 234
  Ojibwa, 127
  Polynesian, 115–116
  postmodern evolutionary-ecological, 185–210
  traditional, 211–234, 7–11
  uniting, 186–187
  utilitarian, 9–10
Environmental Ethics, xv
Environmental legislation, xii
Environmental Protection Agency, xii
Erdoes, Richard, 248n29
Essences, theory of, 83
Esu, 163
Ethical limitations, 2
Ethical obligations, reciprocity of, 22
Ethics, 1–3. *See also* Environmental ethics
  Darwinian view of, 200
  extension to environment, 206
  practicality of, 3–7
  Western approaches to, 92
Etosha National Park, 171
Eurynome, 36